Concept Map

TOOLKIT

MOST POWERFUL RESOURCE FOR MASTERING CONCEPTS

Biology

A Visual Approach for
Enhanced Learning

Author
Dr. Parul Goel,
Kashvi & Rakhi Bisht

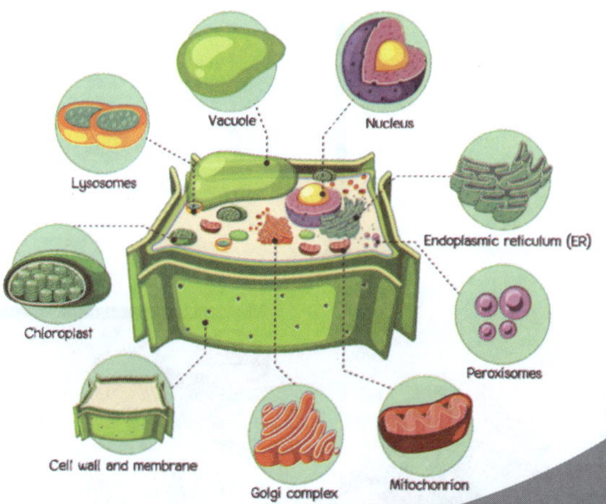

ARIHANT PRAKASHAN (Series), MEERUT

卐 Administrative & Production Offices

Regd. Office

'Ramchhaya' 4577/15, Agarwal Road, Darya Ganj, New Delhi -110002
Tele: 011- 47630600, 43518550

卐 Head Office

Kalindi, TP Nagar, Meerut (UP) - 250002
Tel: 0121-7156203, 7156204

卐 Sales & Support Offices

Agra, Ahmedabad, Bengaluru, Bareilly, Chennai, Delhi, Guwahati, Hyderabad, Jaipur, Jhansi, Kolkata, Lucknow, Nagpur & Pune.

卐 **PRICE** ₹399.00

卐 **PO No.** : TXT-59-T069370-2-26

Published by Arihant Publications (India) Ltd.

For further information about the books published by Arihant, log on to www.arihantbooks.com or e-mail at info@arihantbooks.com

Follow us on   

PRODUCTION TEAM

Project Head	*Inner Designer*	*Map Disigners*
Neha Singh	Ankit Tyagi	Brahampal Singh, Deepak Bisht, Arjun Verma
Cover Designer	*Proof Readers*	
Rakesh Rawat	Prashant	

Contents

SUN

Chapter 01 The Living World

CELLULAR ORGANISATION

- Composition and arrangement of cells in body.
- Macromolecules → Cells → Tissues → Organ → Organ system
- Defining feature of all life forms.

GROWTH

- Irreversible increase in mass.
- Not a **defining** property.
- Living organism grows by formation of cells.
- Non-living thing grows by accretion, e.g. mountains.

CONSCIOUSNESS

- Awareness of surroundings and response to external stimuli.
- E.g. moth movement towards light.
- Defining characteristic.

ADAPTATION

- Mechanism to survive, thrive and reproduce.
- E.g., Hibernation or aestivation in frogs, snakes.
- A defining character.

Characteristics

SENESCENCE & DEATH

- Inevitable in all organisms.
- A defining characteristic.

HOMEOSTASIS

- Maintenance of a suitable and constant environment internally.
- A defining feature.

REPRODUCTION

- Not a defining character. as, many organisms are incapable of reproducing, e.g., mules, infertile human couple, etc.

METABOLISM

- Sum total of all chemical reactions.
- A defining characteristic.
- Two types: **Anabolism** (formation of complex substance) and **Catabolism** (breakdown of complex substances).

LIVING BEINGS

Biodiversity

- Degree of variability among living organisms.
- Differs in morphology, size, colour, anatomy, habits and habitats.

Systematics

- Study of diversity of organisms, focusing both on their comparative relationships as well as evolutionary relationships.
- Classify plants, animals and other organisms into categories.

Characterisation

- Identifying and describing features or traits of a biological entity.
- Provides insights of physiological, biochemical and ecological characteristics.

Identification

- Assigning a pre-existing taxon to an organism based on its characteristics.
- Identified easily by selecting and eliminating similarities.

Nomenclature

- Providing proper scientific name to an organism for easy recognition and differentiation.

Classification

- Grouping of organisms into categories.
- Based on observable but fundamental characters.
- Hierarchy is maintained for these categories.

Nomenclature

Binomial Nomenclature (C. Linnaeus, 1753)

Mangifera indica L.

Generic name — Specific epithet — Scientist name

Vernacular (common) Name

Name given to organism in a particular language and region, e.g. Mango→Aam.

Rules of Nomenclature

- Biological names are generally in Latin and written in Italics.
- Generic name (genus) begins with capital letter.
- Specific epithet (species) begins with small letter.
- Name of author (abbreviated form) written after specific epithet.
- Scientific name should be underlined (when hand written) or Italicised (when printed).

Scientific Name

Based on agreed principles and criteria for their acceptability all over the worlds.

Trinomial Nomenclature

Name of sub-species or varieties are incorporated, e.g., *Brassica oleracea botrytis*.

Various Codes

ICZN

International Code of Zoological Nomenclature

ICBN

International Code of Botanical Nomenclature

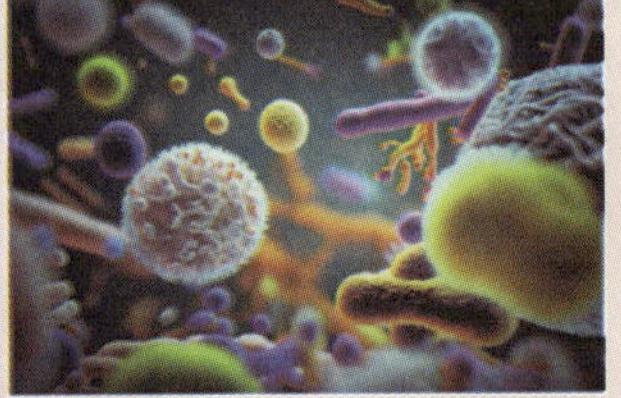

ICNCP

International Code of Nomenclature for Cultivated Plants

ICVN

International Code of viral Nomenclature

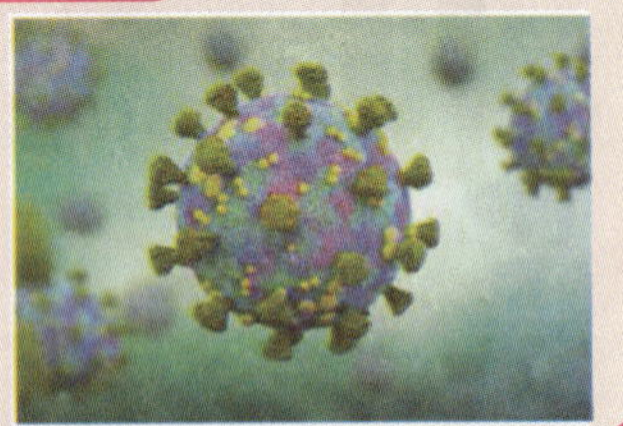

ICNB

International Code of Nomenclature of Bacteria.

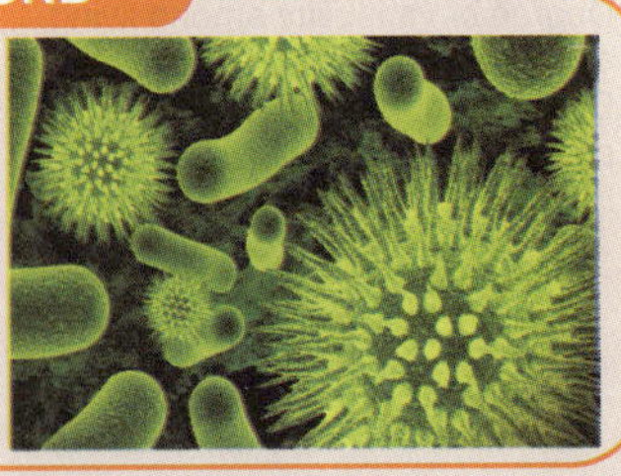

NEET POWER TIPS

- Human is the only organism who is aware of himself (self-consciousness); brain dead person is considered non-living.
- Isolated metabolic reaction can takes place outside the cell (*in vitro*).
- **Rules of priority** Oldest name given to organism is the correct scientific name (published on 1st may, 1753).
- Latin is a dead language, it's constant and reliable and does not change over time.

Taxonomy

Branches of Taxonomy

Various branches of taxonomy are as follows

Taxonomic Fields	Basic
Alpha (α) taxonomy	Morphological characters of organisms
Beta (β) taxonomy	Anatomical characters along with physiological and genetic traits
Gamma (γ) taxonomy	Phylogenetic relationships
Chemotaxonomy	Presence or absence of chemicals in cells or tissues.
Cytotaxonomy	Cellular studies (Chromosomal structure, number and behaviour).
Karyotaxonomy	Nuclear and chromosomal studies
Experimental taxonomy	Experimental determination of genetic inter-relationships
New systematics/ Neotaxonomy (omega taxonomy)	Cytological, morphological, genetical, anatomical, paleontological and physiological characters

TAXON

- Unit of classification.
- Represents any level of grouping of organisms.
- Belongs to any ranking where as category belongs to one particular ranking.

Taxonomic Categories

[Carolus Linnaeus (1751)]

- **Kingdom** Animalia
- **Phylum** Chordata
- **Class** Mammalia
- **Order** Carnivora
- **Family** Felidae
- **Genus** *Panthera*
- **Species** *tigris*

Decrease similarity (towards Kingdom) ↔ Increase similarity (towards Species)

NEET POWER TIPS

- Principles and procedures of identification, nomenclature and classification of organisms is called taxonomy.
- The term taxonomy coined by **AP de Candolle**, **1813**.

Types of Species

- **Morphospecies** divided on the basis of morphological characters only.
- **Taxonomic species** having definite binomial name.
- **Sibling species** morphologically similar species which do not interbreed.
- **Polytypic species** having two or more subspecies.
- **Allochronic** belonging to different time period.

Categories and Corresponding Suffix

Plants and Animals

Category		Suffix
Division	–	phyta
Class	–	phyceae or -opsida or ae
Order	–	ales
Family	–	aceae (plants), idae (animals)

Organism with Taxonomic Categories

	Man	Housefly	Mango	Wheat
Scientific Names	*Homo sapiens*	*Musca domestica*	*Mangifera indica*	*Triticum aestivum*
Species	*sapiens*	*domestica*	*indica*	*aestivum*
Genus	*Homo*	*Musca*	*Mangifera*	*Triticum*
Family	Hominidae	Muscidae	Anacardiaceae	Poaceae
Order	Primata	Diptera	Sapindales	Poales
Class	Mammalia	Insecta	Dicotylendonae	Monocotyledonae
Phylum/Division	Chordata	Arthropoda	Angiospermae	Angiospermae
Kingdom	Animalia	Animalia	Plantae	Plantae

Chapter 02

Biological Classification

1 System of Classification: Aristotle

Organisms

Plants
- Simple morphological features
- Herbs
- Shrubs
- Trees

Animals
- Presence or absence of red blood
- Anaima (animals without red blood)
- Enaima (animals with red blood)

NEET POWER TIPS

Drawbacks of two kingdom: Place unrelated organisms together, e.g.,
- Prokaryotes along with eukaryotes
- Unicellular and multicellular
- Heterotrophs and autotrophs
- Some organism shared characteristics of both plants and animals. e.g. *Chlamydomonas, Euglena.*
- **Drawback of five kingdom:** No place for viruses, viroids and lichens.

Classification

2 Two Kingdom Classification: Linnaeus (1753)

Kingdoms
- Plantae (Having cell wall)
- Animalia (Lack cell wall)

3 Three kingdom Classification: Haeckel (1866)

- Proposed Protista (either common or unique to animal and plants).

Kingdoms
- **Protista** Unicellular algae, fungi and bacteria
- **Plantae** Multicellular plants
- **Animalia** Multicellular animals

4 Four Kingdom Classification: Copeland (1956)

Kingdoms
- **Monera** Prokaryotic organisms
- **Protista** True nucleate unicellular organism
- **Plantae** Photosynthetic and multicellular organism
- **Animalia** Non-photosynthetic and multicellular organism

Five Kingdom Classification: RH Whittaker (1969)

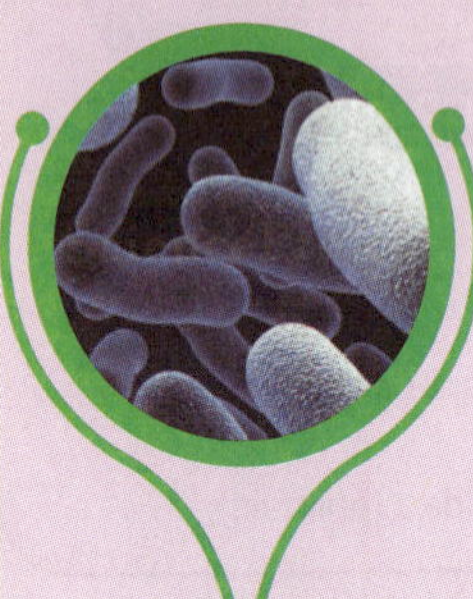

Monera
- **Cell type** Prokaryotic
- **Cell wall** Non-cellulosic (polysaccharide+amino acid)
- **Nuclear membrane** Absent
- **Body organisation** Cellular
- **Mode of nutrition** Autotrophic (chemosynthetic and photosynthetic) and heterotropic (saprophytic/parasitic)

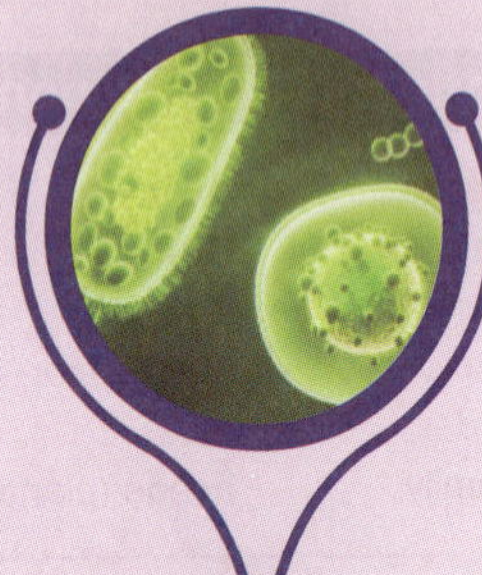

Protista
- **Cell type** Eukaryotic
- **Cell wall** Present in some
- **Nuclear membrane** Present
- **Body organisation** Cellular
- **Mode of nutrition** Autotrophic (photosynthetic) and heterotropic

Fungi
- **Cell type** Eukaryotic
- **Cell wall** Present (without cellulose) with chitin
- **Nuclear membrane** Present
- **Body organisation** Multicellular/loose tissue
- **Mode of nutrition** Heterotrophic (saprophytic/parasitic)

Plantae
- **Cell type** Eukaryotic
- **Cell wall** Present (cellulosic)
- **Nuclear membrane** Present
- **Body organisation** Tissue/organ
- **Mode of nutrition** Autotrophic (photosynthetic)

Animalia
- **Cell type** Eukaryotic
- **Cell wall** Absent
- **Nuclear membrane** Present
- **Body organisation** Tissue/organ/organ system
- **Mode of nutrition** Heterotrophic (holozoic/saprophytic, etc.)

Criteria for Classification

1. Complexity of cell structure (prokaryotic or eukaryotic)
2. Complexity of body structure (unicellular or multicellular)
3. Mode of nutrition (autotrophic or heterotrophic)
4. Reproduction
5. Phylogenetic relationship

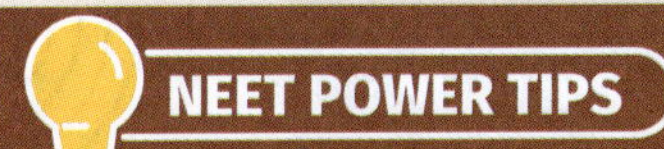

- Monera is diverse group of primitive organism.
- **Cosmopolition**, e.g., oceans, acidic and alkaline environment, hot springs or glaciers, etc.
- **Size**- 0.1-1.5 μm (diameter) and 2-10 μm (length).
- Mostly heterotrophic, some are autotrophic.

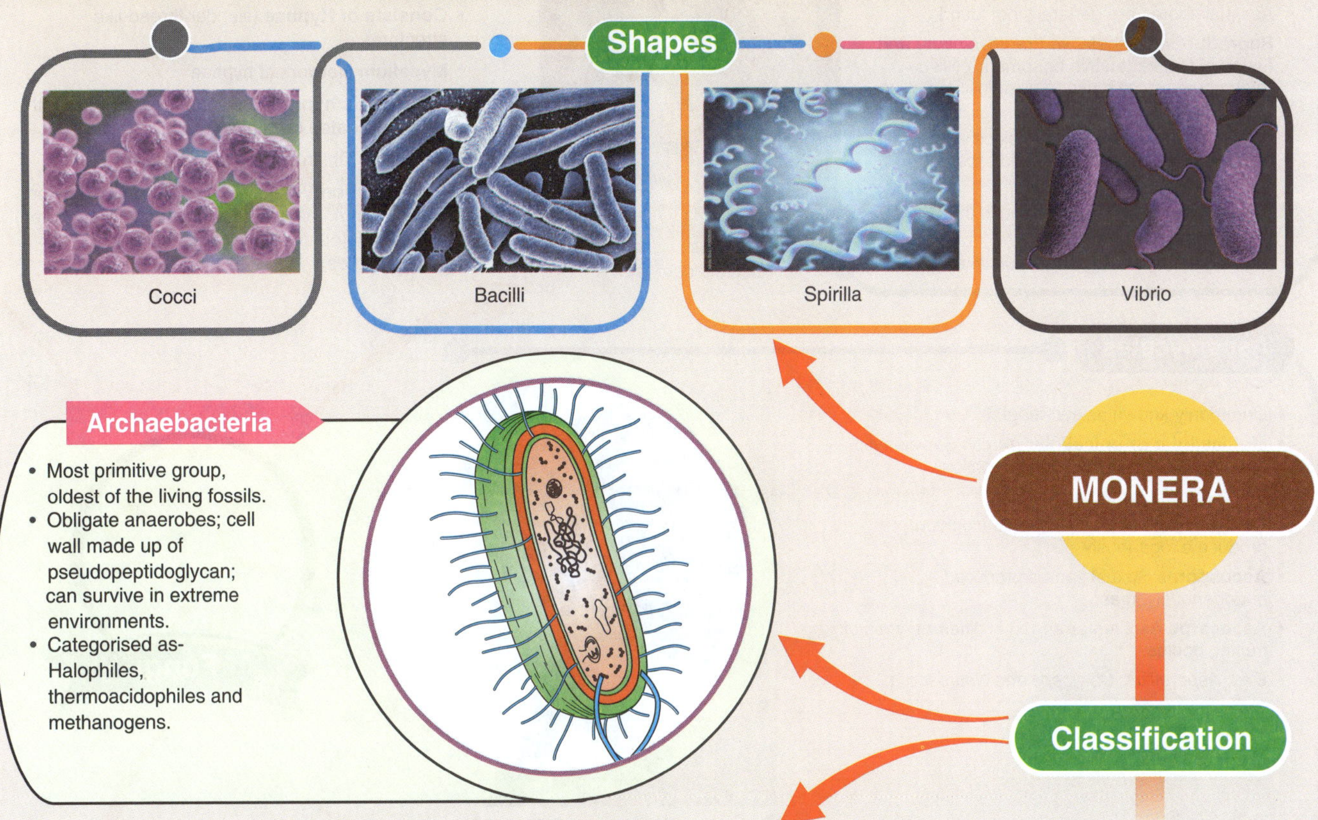

Archaebacteria

- Most primitive group, oldest of the living fossils.
- Obligate anaerobes; cell wall made up of pseudopeptidoglycan; can survive in extreme environments.
- Categorised as- Halophiles, thermoacidophiles and methanogens.

Eubacteria

- Large and diverse group of true bacteria.
- Peptidoglycan present in cell wall; lack membrane-bound cell organelles.
- Mode of nutrition
  - → **Autotrophic** Photoautotrophic, chemoautotrophic
  - → **Heterotrophic** Parasitic, saprophytic, symbiotic.

Cyanobacteria

- Predominantly freshwater forms, but few are marine.
- Photosynthetic autotrophs.
- **Photosynthetic Pigments-** Chlorophyll-*a*, carotenoids, *c*-phycocyanin and *c*-phycoerythrin
- Completely lack flagella;
- **Reproduction** Asexually by fission, etc., absence of sexual reproduction.

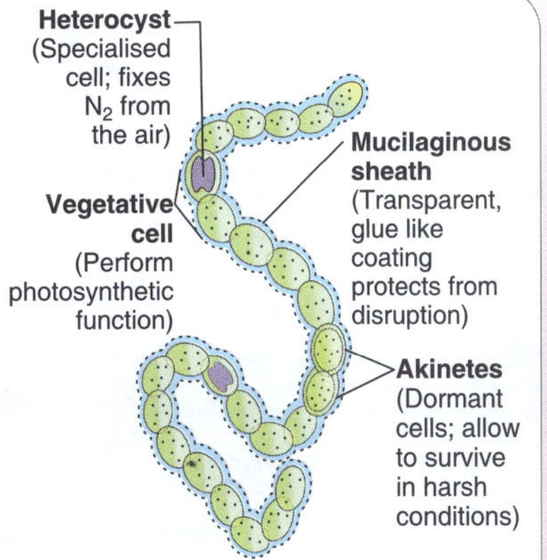

Mycoplasma/PPLO (Pleuro Pneumonia- Like Organisms)

- Smallest living cell; lack cell wall and are non-motile.
- Exhibit pleomorphism, can survive without O_2.

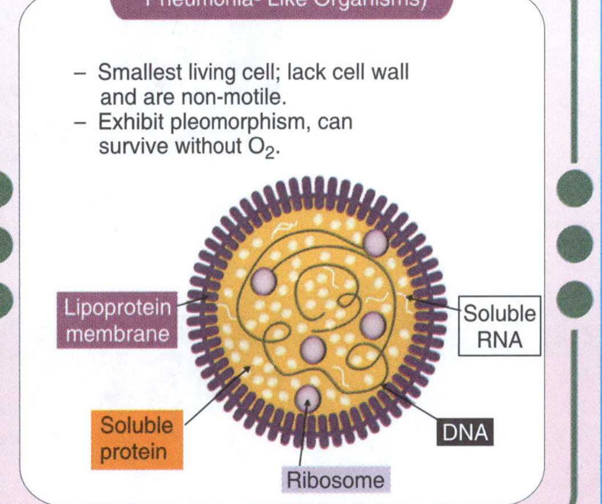

Basidiomycetes

- Commonly known forms- Mushrooms, bracket fungi or puffballs.
- Grow in soil, logs, tree stumps and as parasities (rusts and smuts).
- **Mycelium** Branched and septate
- Asexual spores are generally not found.
- **Reproduction** Vegetative (fragmentation) and fusion of two vegetative or somatic cells (plasmogamy); give rise to dikaryotic structure and ultimately to basidium.
- Karyogamy and meiosis take place in basidium, give rise to four basidiospores (exogenously)
- **Basidiocarps** Basidia arranged in fruiting bodies.
- E.g., *Agaricus*, *Ustilago* and *Puccinia*.

Puccinia coronata

NEET POWER TIPS

- Fungi Eukaryotic, achorophyllous, non-photosynthetic and heterotrophic organism.
- Filamentous, except yeast (unicellular)
- **Consists of Hyphae** (slender thread-like structure)
- **Mycelium** Network of hyphae
- **Coenocytic hyphae** Continuous tubes filled with multi- nucleated cytoplasm.
- **Cell walls** Chitin and polysaccharides
- **Reproduction** Vegetative (fragmentation, fission and budding), asexual (conidia or sporangiopores) and sexual (oospores, ascospores and basidiospores).

Ascomycetes

- Commonly known as sac-fungi.
- **Multicellular or unicellular** (rarely) Saprophytic, decomposers, parasitic or coprophilous.
- **Mycelium** Branched and septate
- **Conidiophores** Asexual spores (conidia) produce exogenously.
- **Ascospores** Sexual spores produced endogenously in asci.
- **Ascocarps** Asci are arranged in different types of fruiting bodies.
- E.g., *Aspergillus*, *Claviceps* and *Neurospora*.

Aspergillus niger

Phycomycetes

- Found in aquatic habitats and moist and damp places or as obligate parasites.
- **Mycelium** Aseptate and coenocytic.
- **Asexual reproduction** Endogenously produced in sporangium, zoospores or aplanospores.
- **Gametes** Isogamous, anisogamous or oogamous.
- E.g., *Mucor*, *Rhizopus* and *Albugo*.

Rhizopus nigricans

Deuteromycetes

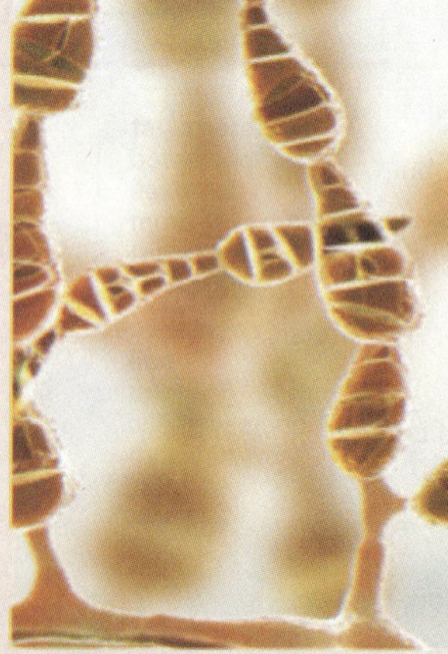

Alternaria alternata

- Commonly known as imperfect fungi.
- Saprophytes or parasities, decomposers (mostly)
- **Reproduce** Only asexual spores conidia.
- **Mycelium** Septate and branched.
- E.g., *Alternaria*, *Colletotrichum* and *Trichoderma*

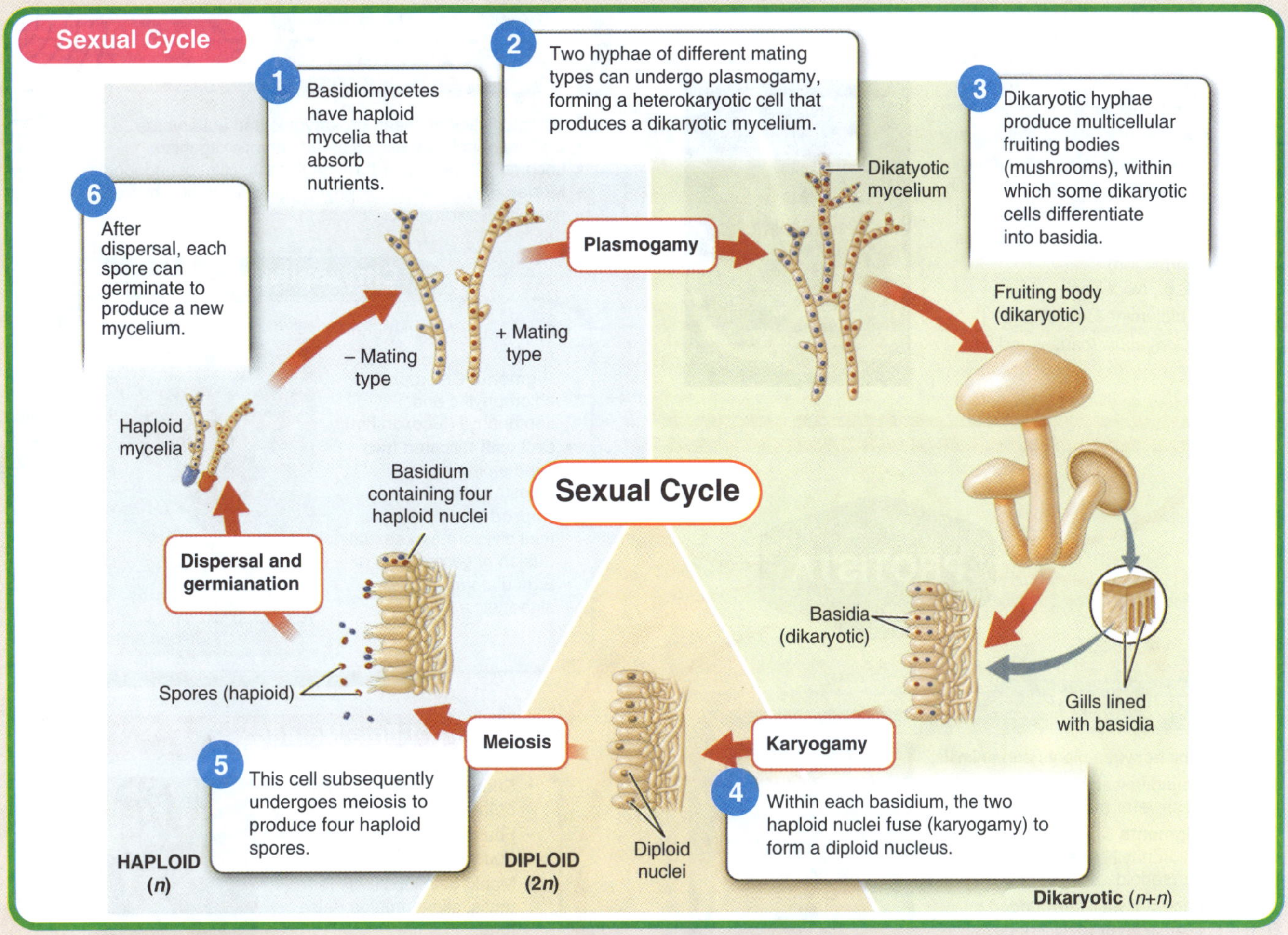

Sexual Cycle

1 Basidiomycetes have haploid mycelia that absorb nutrients.

2 Two hyphae of different mating types can undergo plasmogamy, forming a heterokaryotic cell that produces a dikaryotic mycelium.

3 Dikaryotic hyphae produce multicellular fruiting bodies (mushrooms), within which some dikaryotic cells differentiate into basidia.

4 Within each basidium, the two haploid nuclei fuse (karyogamy) to form a diploid nucleus.

5 This cell subsequently undergoes meiosis to produce four haploid spores.

6 After dispersal, each spore can germinate to produce a new mycelium.

Dikatyotic mycelium

– Mating type

+ Mating type

Plasmogamy

Fruiting body (dikaryotic)

Haploid mycelia

Basidium containing four haploid nuclei

Sexual Cycle

Dispersal and germination

Basidia (dikaryotic)

Gills lined with basidia

Spores (hapioid)

Meiosis

Karyogamy

Diploid nuclei

HAPLOID (n)

DIPLOID ($2n$)

Dikaryotic ($n+n$)

Higher kingdoms

Plantae
Chlorophyll-containing organisms; mainly autotrophic, some heterotrophic

Animalia
Heterotrophic eukaryotic organisms; multicellular, lacks cell wall.

Acellular Organisms

Virus

- Recognised by DJ Ivanowsky, demonstrated by MW Beijerinek.
- Non-cellular organisms, inert crystalline structure (outside the living cell)
- Connecting link between living and non-living.
- Consists of nucleic acids either RNA (single or double-stranded) or DNA (single or double-stranded), envelope, capsid and enzymes.
- **Diseases caused** Mumps, small pox, herpes, Influenza, etc.

Omicron

Viroids (TO Diener, 1971)

- Infectious agent smaller than viruses
- Free RNA (low molecular weight) devoid of protein coat
- Causes potato spindle tuber disease

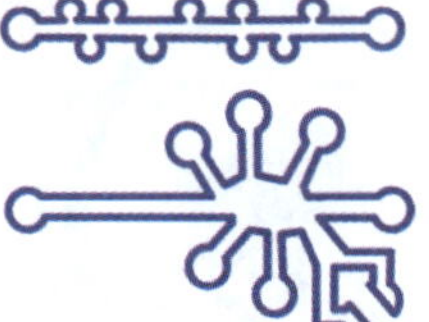

Prions

- Abnormally folded proteins, similar in size to viruses.
- **Diseases** Bovine Spongiform Encephalopathy (BSE) or mad cow disease in cattle.
- Analogous variant of BSE in humans Cr-Jacob Disease (CJD).

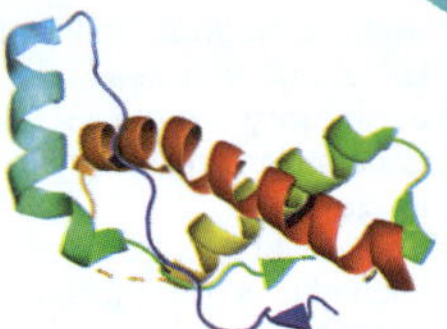

Human prion protein

Lichens

- Symbiotic association between algae and fungi.
- Algal component-Phycobiont (autotrophic) and fungal component-Mycobiont (heterotrophic)
- Good pollution indicators.

PROTISTA

Dinoflagellates

- Two flagella; marine (mostly) and freshwater (some)
- **Pigments** Chlorophyll-*a*, chlorophyll-*c* and xanthophyll
- **Cell wall** Cellulose and pectin
- **Reproduction** Asexual (cell division) and sexual (gamete formation)
- E.g., *Noctiluca* (bioluminescence) and *Gonyaulax* (causes red tide)

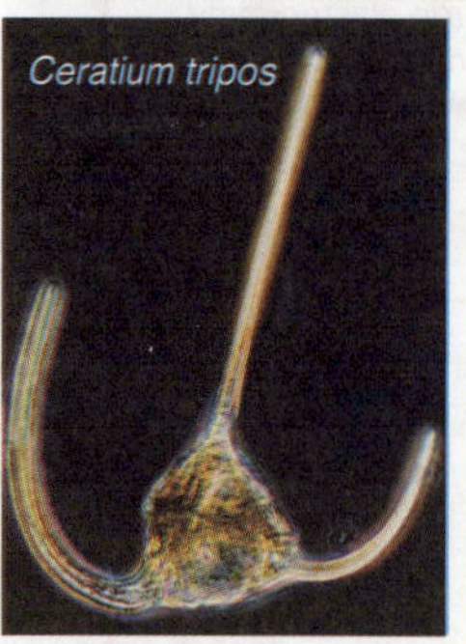
Ceratium tripos

NEET POWER TIPS

- Protista is link between prokaryotes and eukaryotes
- Solitary or colonial unicellular eukaryotic organism.
- Locomotion can occur through flagella, cilia, pseudopodia.
- **Modes of Nutrition** Holophytic, holozoic, saprophytic, parasitic, mixotrophic.

Chrysophyta

- Freshwater (mostly) and marine.
- **Pigments** Chlorophyll-*a*, chlorophyll-c and xanthophyll (fucoxanthin)
- **Cell wall** Silicated (two overlapping halves); indestructible.
- **Reproduction** Asexual (cell division) and sexual (fusion of gamete)
- E.g., diatoms, golden algae, etc.

Golden algae

Euglenophyta

- Link between plants and animals.
- Found in water or damp soil; freshwater (mostly)
- **Pigments** Chlorophyll-*a*, chlorophyll-*b*, xanthophyll and carotenoids.
- Lack cell wall; surrounded by flexible layer (pellicle); possess two flagella (one is functional and other is non-functional)
- **Reproduction** Asexually (binary fission) and sexually not known.
- E.g., *Euglena*

Euglena

Slime Moulds

- Share characteristics with both animal and fungi.
- Found in terrestrial and aquatic habitats; saprophytic.
- Mould develops a slimy mass, slime moulds (false fungi).
- **Type** Cellular (without cell wall) and acellular (multinucleate)
- **Plasmodial stage** Feeding stage of a slime mould (appears as giant *Amoeba* with multiple nuclei).

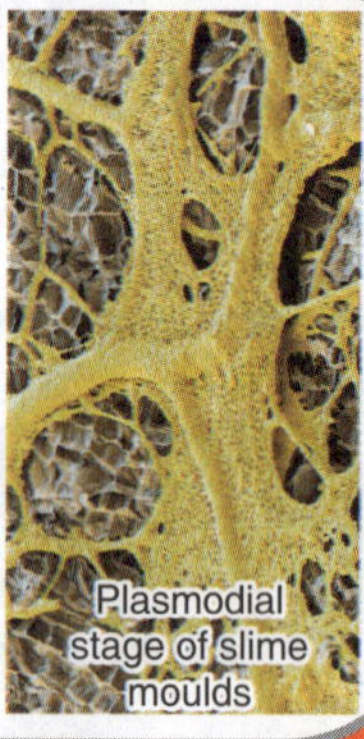
Plasmodial stage of slime moulds

Protozoa

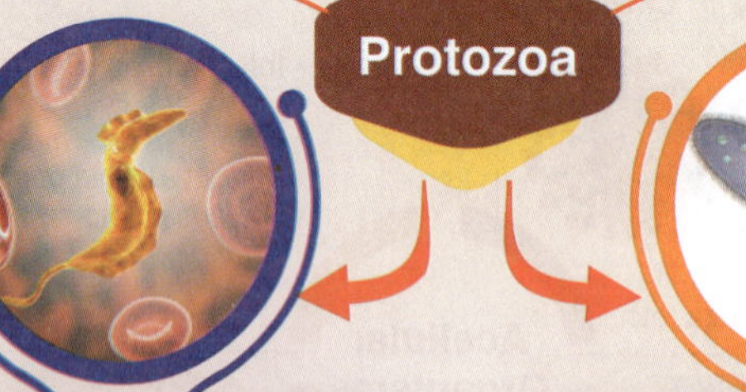

Amoeboid Protozoans

- **Habit and habitat** Freshwater, sea water or moist soil; mostly free living.
- **Locomotory structures** Pseudopodia (false feet)-help in movement and capturing of prey.
- **Special features** Marine protozoans possess silica shells
- **Examples and diseases** *Entamoeba*-dysentery

Flagellated Protozoans

- **Habit and habitat** Free living (aquatic) or parasitic
- **Locomotory structures** Flagella
- **Special features** Rare sexual reproduction with diverse type of associations-commensalism symbiont, parasitic.
- **Examples and diseases** *Trypanosoma*-sleeping sickness.

Cillated Protozoans

- **Habit and habitat** Freshwater or marine, few parasites
- **Locomotory structures** Cilia-help in locomotion and in engulfing food particle
- **Special features** Possess definite region of ingestion (gullet) and egestion.
- **Example** *Paramoecium*

Sporozoans

- **Habit and habitat** All endoparasites
- **Locomotory structures** None
- **Special features** Infectious spore-like stage present in life cycle
- **Examples and diseases** *Plasmodium malariae* are most notorious.

Chapter 03 Plant Kingdom

Classification

Plants

- No differentiation of plant body
  - Thallophytes 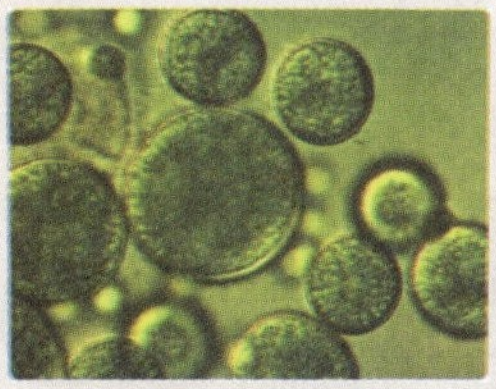
    - E.g., *Algae*
- Differentiated plant body
  - Without specialised vascular tissue
    - Bryophytes 
      - E.g., *Funaria*
  - With vascular tissue (Tracheophytes)
    - Produce seeds (Phanerogams)
      - Bears naked seeds
        - Gymnosperms 
          - e.g., *Cycas*
      - Bears seeds inside fruits
        - Seeds with one cotyledon (Monocot)
        - Seeds with two cotyledons (Dicots)
    - Do not produce seeds (cryptogams)
      - Pteridophytes
        - e.g., *Equisetum*

Different Systems of Classification

1 Artificial System (Linnaeus)

- Based mainly on vegetative characters or on the androecium structure.

2 Natural System (Bentham and Hooker)

- Based on natural affinities among the organisms and involves external as well as internal features.

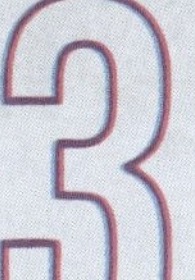

3 Phylogenetic System (Engler and Prantl)

- Based on evolutionary relationships among various organisms.

NEET POWER TIPS

Mnemonic to memorise the examples of various algae classes

Chlorophyceae

Unique	Students	Visualise	Complex	Concepts
↓	↓	↓	↓	↓
Ulothrix	*Spirogyra*	*Volvox*	*Chlorella*	*Chlamydomonas*

Phaeophycea

Everyone	Deserves	Sweet	Fresh	Lemonade
↓	↓	↓	↓	↓
Ectocarpus	*Dictyota*	*Sargassum*	*Fucus*	*Laminaria*

Rhodophyceae

Genius	Guys	Possess	Pure	Passion
↓	↓	↓	↓	
Gracilaria	*Gelidium*	*Porphyra*	*Polysiphonia*	

Algae

- Simplest plants with thallus-like body and no vascular tissues.
- Mostly aquatic, but also found in variety of other habitats like moist stones, soils and wood.
- May be **unicellular** (e.g., *Chlorella*), **filamentous** (e.g., *Ulothrix and Spirogyra*), **colonial** (e.g., *Volvox*) and with massive body (e.g., kelps)
- Also occurs in associations
  - with fungi (e.g., lichen)
  - with animals (e.g., sloth bear)

Reproduction in Algae

- **Vegetative** By fragmentation
- **Asexual** By flagellated zoospore
- **Sexual**
  - **Isogamy**
    - Motile gametes e.g., *Ulothrix*

    - Non-motile gametes e.g., *Spirogyra*

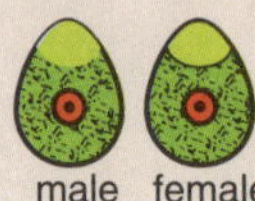

  - **Anisogamy** e.g., *Fucus*

  - **Oogamy** e.g., Human sperm and ova

female male

Major Classes

Chlorophyceae (Green algae)

- Unicellular, collonial or filamentous body.
- **Habitat** Freshwater, brackish water, salt water
- **Pigments** Chlorophyll-*a*, *b*
- Stores food in pyrenoids (protein beside starch) and oil droplets.
- **Cell wall** Cellulose (inner layer) + Pectose (outer layer)
- **Flagella** 2-8, equal, apical
- **Reproduction**
  - **Vegetative** By fragmentation or spores
  - **Asexual** Flagellated zoospores
  - **Sexual** Isogamous, anisogamous, oogamous.
- **Example** *Clamydomonas*, *Volvox*, *Spirogyra*

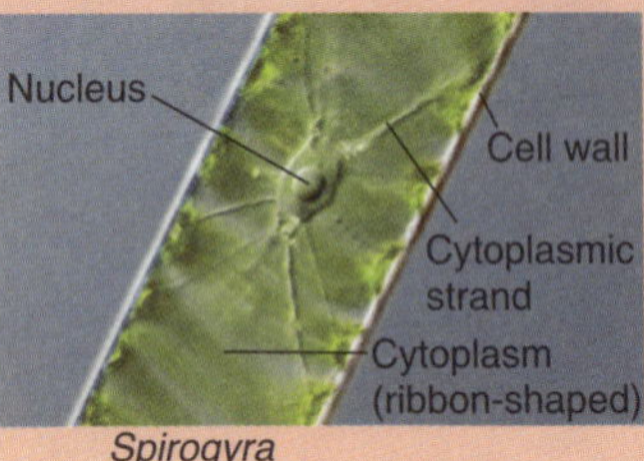

Spirogyra

Rhodophyceae (Red algae)

- Multicellular, complex plant body
- **Habitat** Freshwater (some), brackish water,salt water (most)
- **Pigments** Chlorophyll- *a*, *d*, phycoerythrin
- Food is stored as floridean starch
- **Flagella** absent
- **Reproduction**
  - **Vegetative** By fragmentation
  - **Asexual** Non-motile spores
  - **Sexual** Oogamous
- **Examples** *Polysiphonia*, *Porphyra*,

Gracilaria

Phaeophyceae (Brown algae)

- Simple branched, or Profusely branched, filamentous.
- **Habitat** Freshwater (rare), brackish water, salt water
- **Pigments** Chlorphyll-*a*,*c*, fucoxanthin
- Food stored in the form of laminarin or mannitol
- **Cell wall** cellulosic, covered by algin.
- **Flagella 2**, unequal, lateral.
- **Reproduction**
  - **Vegetative** By fragmentation
  - **Asexual** Biflagellated zoospores
  - **Sexual** Isogamous, anisogamous or oogamous
- **Examples** *Ectocarpus*, *Sargassum*

Fucus

Importance of Algae

- CO_2 fixation
- Increasing dissolved O_2
- Primary producers in aquatic food chains
- As food (*Laminaria*, *Porphyra*, *Sargassum*)
- Hydrocolloids
  - Algin
  - Carrageen
- As food supplement in space for traveller, e.g., *Chlorella*, *Spirulina*
- Agar (*Gelidium*, *Gracilaria*)
- Algal blooms

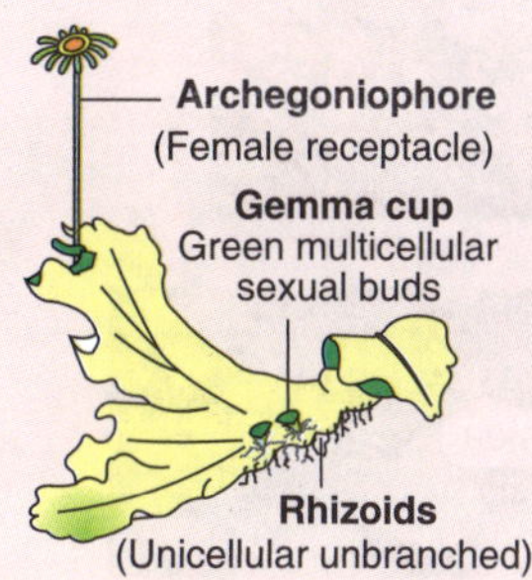

Marchantia-Female thallus

Liverworts (Hepaticopsida)

- The plant body is thalloid gametophyte that is dorsiventral
- **Vegetative reproduction** by fragmentation
- **Asexual reproduction** by gemmae
- **Sexual reproduction** sex organs placed on same (homothallic) or different thalli (heterothallic)
- **Sporophyte** (Foot, seta and capsule) ⟶ Spores $\xrightarrow{\text{germinate}}$ Free-living gametophytes
- E.g., *Marchantia*

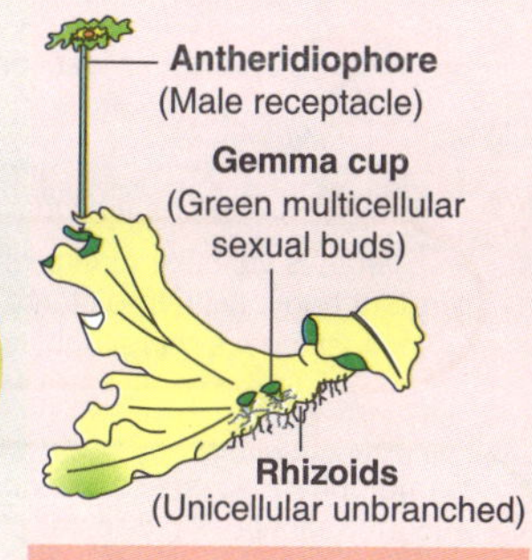

Male thallus

BRYOPHYTES

- Plants with thalloid body lacking true roots, stems and leaves, attached to substrate by rhizoids.
- **Main plant body** Haploid gametophyte (producing gametes)
- **Sex organs** Multicellular and jacketed; male-antheridium (producing biflagellated antherozoids) female-archegonium (flask-shaped, producing a single egg)
- Antherozoids (n) released in water gets in contact with Egg (n) $\xrightarrow{\text{Fertilisation}}$ Zygote ($2n$) → Sporophyte ($2n$) $\xrightarrow{\text{Meiosis}}$ Spores (n) $\xrightarrow{\text{Germination}}$ Gametophyte (n)
- **Two main classes: Liverworts and mosses**

Importance of Bryophytes

- Prevents soil erosion
- As pioneer species in xerarch succession
- Used as fuel, e.g., Peat of *Sphagnum*
- As packing material for trans-shipment of living material
- Food for herbaceous animals.

Sphagnum

Mosses (Bryopsida)

- Two stages of gametophyte
  1. **Protonema** Develops directly from spore; green, creeping and frequently filamentous.
  2. **Leafy stage** Upright, slender axes bearing spirally arranged leaves; bears rhizoids; possesses sex organs at apex
- **Vegetative reproduction** By fragmentation and budding in secondary protonema.
- **Sporophyte** more elaborate than liverworts
- Have elaborate mechanism of spore dispersal.
- E.g. *Funaria*, *Polytrichum* and *Sphagnum*, etc.

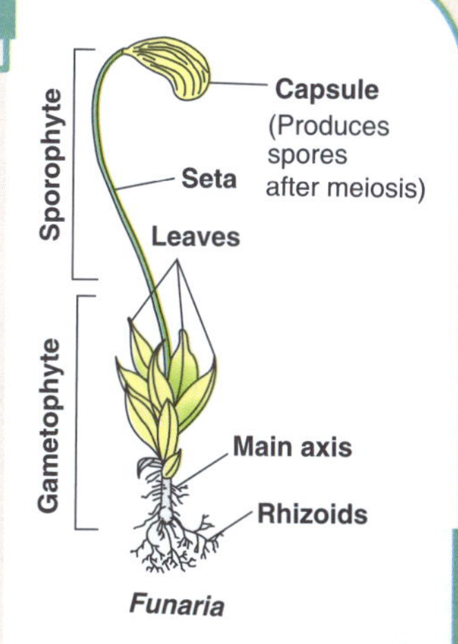

Funaria

NEET POWER TIPS

- Bryophytes are non-vascular plants, also known as amphibian of plant kingdom.
- They have haplontic life cycle with dominant gametophyte phase.
- In bryophytes, the simplest sporophyte occurs in *Riccia*.
- These have no specialised vascular tissues, but have conducting tissues called hydroids and leptoids.
- Leafy stage develops directly from secondary protonema as lateral bud.

Pteridophytes

1 **Habitat** - Most common in cool, damp, shady places,

2 Seedless vascular plants with sporophytes as main plant body, (with true stems, roots and leaves) and inconspicuous gametophyte.

3 Gametophyte possesses sex organs, antheridia (♂) and archegonia (♀); transfer of antherozodia to archegonia requires water.

4 **Homosporous genera**- Majority of pteridophytes; **Heterosporous genera**- *Selaginella* and *Salvinia*

5 Strobili or cones formed in *Selaginella* and *Equisetum*

6 Sporophyte → Sporophylls → Sporangia $\xrightarrow{\text{Meiosis}}$ Spores $\xrightarrow{\text{Germination}}$ Prothallus (gametophytes) $\xrightarrow{\text{Fusion}}$ Zygote ($2n$) → Sporophyte

Major Classes

- Psilopsida — *Psilotum*
- Lycopsida — *Selaginella*
- Sphenopsida — *Epuisetum*
- Pteropsida — *Dryopteris*

Importance of Pteridophytes

- First terrestrial plants with vascular tissues.
- N_2-fixation (e.g., *Azolla*)
- Ornamental use
- Medicinal purpose (e.g., *Equisetum*)
- Soil binders
- Food (e.g., *Marsilea*)

Gymnosperms

1 Group of seed-bearing plants

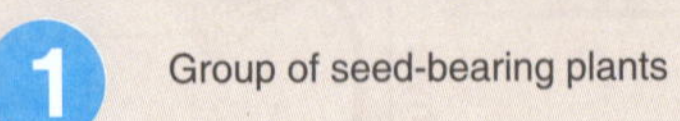

2 Vascular tissues contain xylem and phloem generally without vessels (exception- *Gnetum, Ephedra* and *Welwitschia*).

3 Spores produced within sporangia [megasporangia (♀) and microsporangia (♂)]

4 Microsporangiate/Male strobili → Microsporophylls → Microsporangia → Microspores

5 Megasporangiate/Female strobili → Megasporophylls → Megasporangia → Megaspores

6 Female gametophyte is multicellular, while male gametophyte is highly reduced; they do not have free living existence, instead gametophytes are contained with the sporangia on sporophyte.

7 Tallest living tree species known- *Sequoia* (giant redwood)

Cycas

- **Dioecious**; root form mycorrhizal association
- Unbranched with dimorphic leaves

Pinus

- **Monoecious**, roots associates with cyanobacteria
- Branched with dimorphic leaves

Importance of Gymnosperms

- Food
- Paper
- Medicines (e.g., *Ephedra*)
- Timber (soft wood)
- Ornamental use
- Evolutionary significance (*Ginkgo*-fossil plant)

Chapter **04**

Animal Kingdom

Basis of Clasification

Level of Organisation

Cellular level-Loosely arranged cells form aggregates.
Tissue level-Similar cells work together to perform a function.
Organ level-Tissues are grouped together to form organ.
Organ system level-Group of organs function together.

Body Plan

Cell aggregate type Cluster of cells with no coordination
Blind sac: Single cavity with one opening.
Tube-within-a tube Two tubes (one is formed by body wall and other is formed within it by digestive tract)

- **Protostomic-** Mouth develops first and anus later, e.g., Annelida, Arthropoda, Mollusca.
- **Deuterostomic-** Anus develops first and mouth later, e.g., Echinodermata, Hemichordata, Chordata.

Segmentation

Metamerism Both external and internal segmentation.
Pseudometamerism External segmentation only

Fate of Germ layers

- **Ectoderm** Epidermis of skin, nervous system, eyes, etc
- **Mesoderm** Blood, heart, bones, muscle, etc.
- **Endoderm** Epithelium of digestive tube, liver, pancreas, etc.

Body Symmetry

Asymmetrical
- Cannot be divided in two equal halves

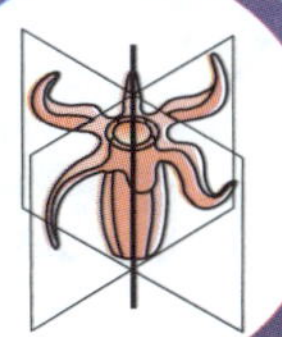

Radial symmetry
Can divide into equal halves by any plane passing through central axis.

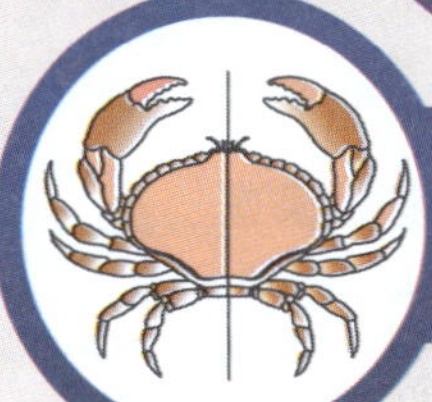

Bilateral symmetry
- Can divide into two equal halves by a single plane.

Germ layers

Diploblastic
- Develop from two embryonic layers, ectoderm and endoderm
- Mesoglea is present

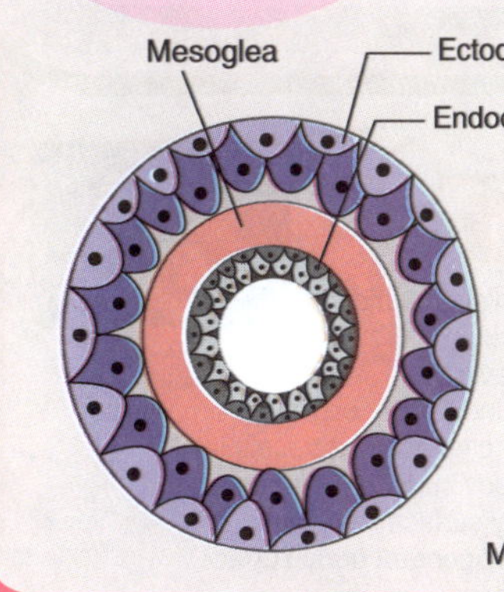

Triploblastic
- Develop from three embryonic layers, ectoderm, mesoderm and endoderm.
- Mesoglea is absent

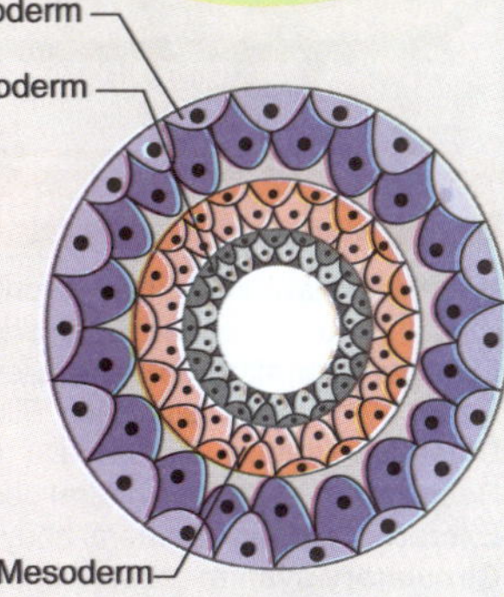

Coelom

Acoelomate
Body cavity absent

Ectoderm
Mesoderm
Endoderm

Coelomate
True body cavity present; **schizocoelom** (splitting of mesoderm), and **enterocoelom** (embryonic gut pouches).

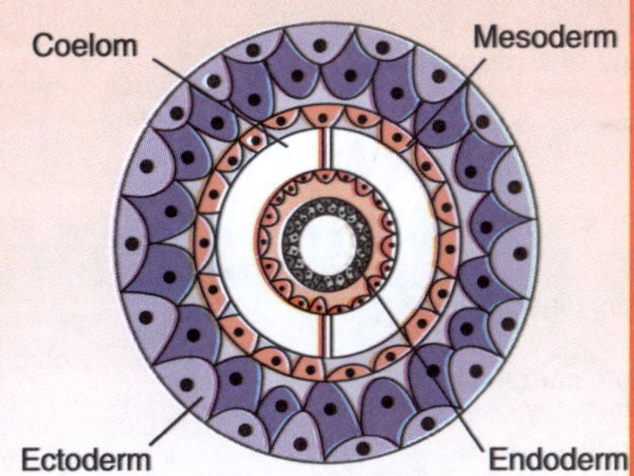

Pseudocoelomate
Mesoderm present in scattered pouches,

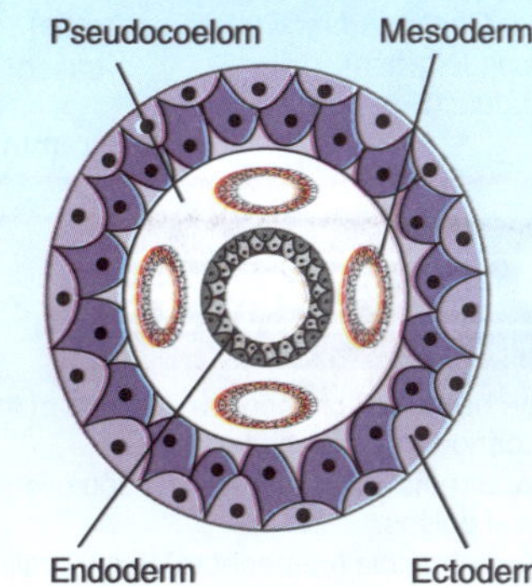

Porifera

- **Habit and Habitat**- Single, colonial, sedentory, aquatic, mostly marine, fresh water (*Spongilla*)
- **Level of Organisation**- Cellular
- Asymmetrical, Diploblastic, Acoelomate Organisms
- **Digestive system**- Absent, Intracellular digestion.
- **Respiratory system**- Absent or by general body surface (diffusion)
- **Excretion**- By general body surface (Ammonia, Ammonotelic)
- **Circulatory system**- Absent or general body surface
- **Nervous system and sense organ**- Absent
- **Reproduction**- Both sexual and asexual (budding and gemmules)
- **Fertilisation**- Internal
- **Development**- Indirect e.g., Amphiblastula larvae (*Sycon*) or parenchymula (*Leucosolenia*)
- **Examples**- *Euspongia, Spongilla, Sycon* (Scypha), *Euplectella*.

Unique Features

- Water canal system divided into three types: ascon, sycon and leucon.
- **Water current** Ostia → Spongocoel (lined with choanocytes) → Osculum

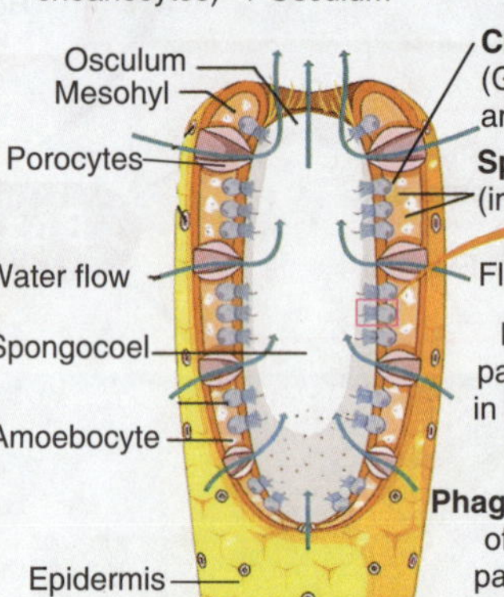

Lower Invertebrates

Cnidaria/Coelenterata

- **Habit and Habitat**- Solitary/colonial, aquatic mostly marine, fresh water (*Hydra*)
- **Level of Organisation**- Tissue level
- Radial symmetry, Diploblastic, Blind sac, Acoelomate organisms
- **Digestive system**- Extracellular followed by intracellular
- **Respiratory system**- General body surface (diffusion)
- **Excretory system**- General body surface (diffusion)
- **Circulatory system**- Absent or by general body surface
- **Nervous system and sense organ**- Apolar neuron (primitive form)
- **Reproduction**- Both sexual and asexual
- **Fertilisation**- External
- **Development**- Indirect (planula larva) or direct
- **Examples** *Physalia* (Portuguese man of war), *Hydra, Obelia, Adamsia* (Sea anemone), *Aurelia* (Jelly fish), *Pennatula* (Sea-pen), etc.

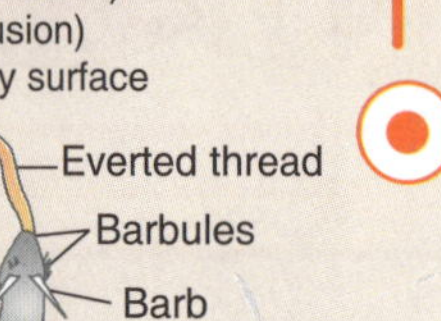

Diagrammatic view of Cnidoblast

Unique Features

- **Cnidoblast/stinging cell**- Anchorage, defense and capturing prey
- Nematocyst consisting of poisonous fluid (hypnotoxin)
- Alternation of generation/**metagenesis**.

Polyp
- Sedentary
- Cylindrical
- Asexual form
- No statocyst

Medusa
- Free swimming
- Umbrella-like
- Sexual form
- Statocyst present (balance and locomotion)

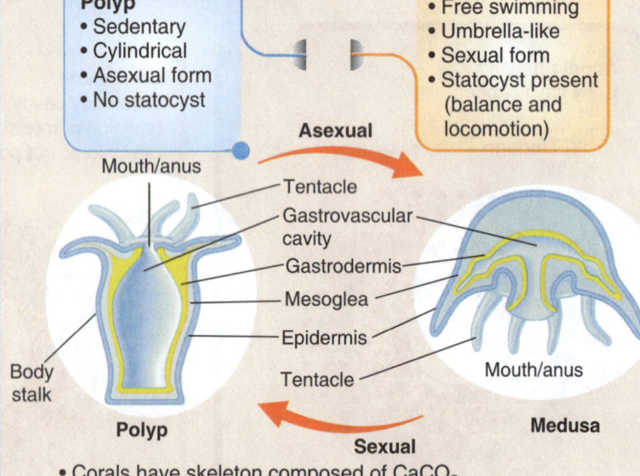

- Corals have skeleton composed of $CaCO_3$
- Shows polymorphism (different forms)

NEET POWER TIPS

- The body wall of sponges consists of three layers pinacoderm, choanoderm and mesenchyme.
- Coral reefs mainly formed by secretion of calcium carbonate by coral polyps.
- *Pleurobrachia* (ctenophora) is also called sea gooseberry.
- *Taenia solium* absorbs food directly from the body surface.

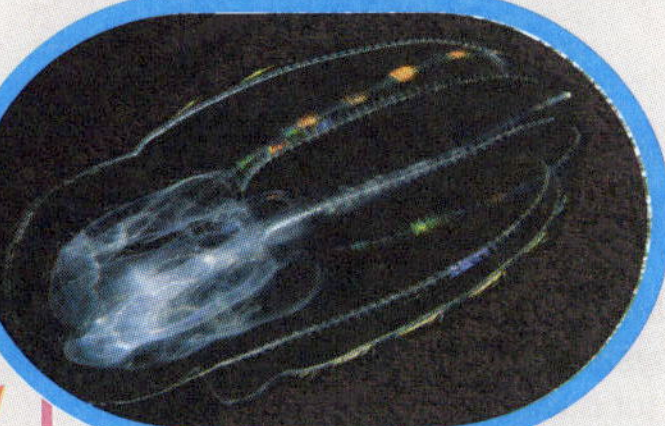

Ctenophora

(Sea walnuts/Comb jellies)

- **Habit and Habitat-** Solitary and pelagic, exclusively marine.
- **Level of Organisation-** Tissue
- Radial Symmetry ; diploblastic, blind sac, acoelomate organisms
- **Digestive system-** Complete, extracellular followed by intracellular
- **Respiratory system-** General body system (diffusion)
- **Excretory system-** General body system (diffusion)
- **Circulatory system-** General body system (diffusion)
- **Nervous system and sense organ-** Apolar neuron, statocyst present.
- **Reproduction-** Only sexually (Hermaphrodite organisms)
- **Fertilisation-** External
- **Development-** Indirect (e.g., Cydippid larva)
- **Examples-** *Pleurobrachia, Ctenoplana*

Unique Features

- Shows **bioluminescence**.
- **Colloblasts-**Present in epidermis of tentacles, help in food capture.
- **Comb plates-** Comb-like eight ciliary plates, help in swimming.

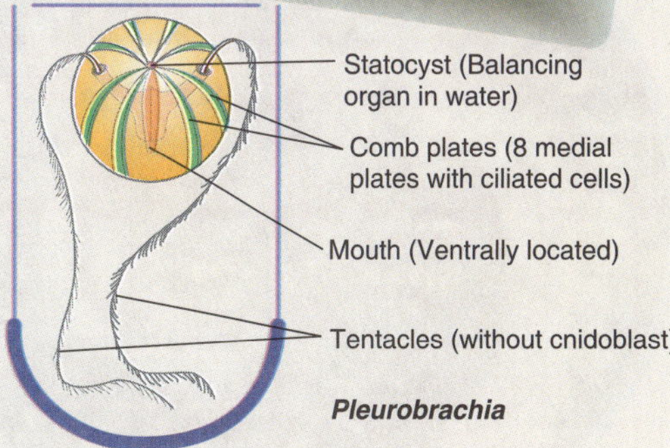

Pleurobrachia

Platyhelminthes

- **Habit and Habitat-** Endoparasite, aquatic (mainly) and terrestrial, free-living
- **Level of Organisation-** Organ level
- Bilateral symmetry (dorso-ventrally flattened); triploblastic, blind sac, acoelomate organisms.
- **Digestive system** Complete, both intracellular and extracellular
- **Respiratory system-** Absent or general body surface
- **Excretory system-** Flame cells/protonephridia/ solenocytes help in excretion and osmoregulation.
- **Circulatory system-** Absent
- **Nervous system and sense organ-** Nerve cells (two longitudinal nerve cords) and ganglia
- **Reproduction-** Both sexual and asexual (regeneration, fragmentation)
- **Fertilisation-** Internal
- **Development-** Indirect
- **Example-** *Planaria*, *Fasciola* (Liver fluke)

Unique Features

- Hooks (adhesion) and suckers in parasitic forms (endoparasite and ectoparosite)
- Exhibits pseudometamerisms (extermal segments).

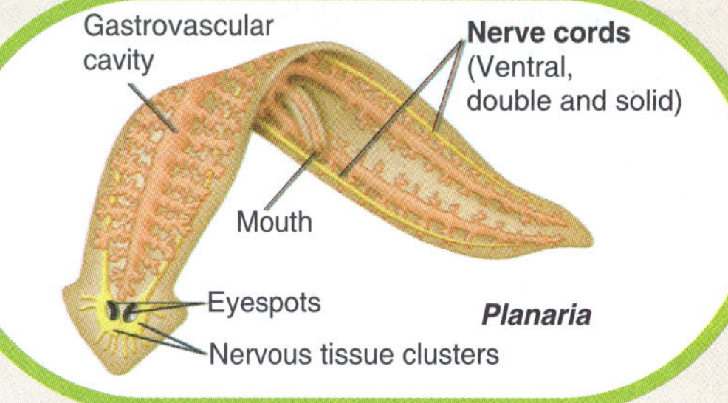

Planaria

Aschelminthes

- **Habit and Habitat-** Parasites on both animals and plants, aquatic and terrestrial
- **Level of Organisation-** Organ system
- Bilateral symmetry; Triploblastic, tube within tube; pseudocoelmate organism.
- **Digestive system-** Complete with muscular pharynx
- **Respiratory system-** Absent or general body surface (diffusion)
- **Excretory system-** Protonephridia (Ammonia)
- **Circulatory system-** Absent, coelomic fluid
- **Nervous system and sense organ-** Nerve ring and nerve cord
- **Reproduction-** Only sexual (show sexual dimorphism)
- **Fertilisation-** Internal
- **Development-** Either direct or indirect e.g., Filariform larva (Hookworm), rhabditiform larva (*Ascaris*)
- **Examples-** *Ascaris* (Round worm), *Wuchereria* (Filarial worm), *Ancylostoma* (Hookworm), etc.

Unique Features

- Renette cells from excretory tube; remove body waste through excretory pore.
- Body cavity partially enclosed by mesodermal tissue; round, tapering at ends

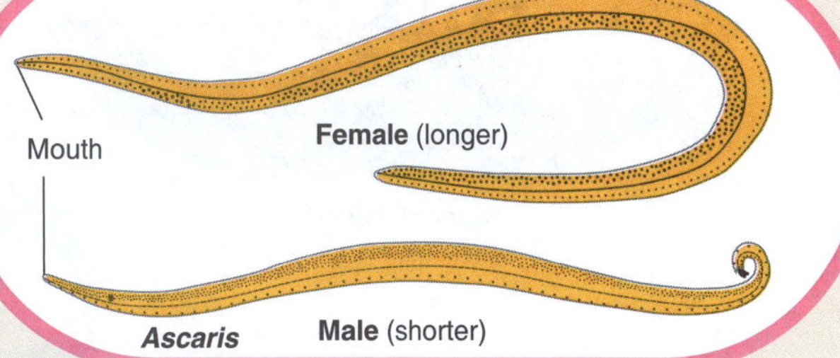

Ascaris

Unique Features

- Possess longitudinal and circular muscle help in locomotion.
- Locomotory organ: Setae (chitinous structure; earthworm) or parapodia (*Nereis*).

Nereis pelagica

Annelids

- **Habit and Habitat:** Parasitic or free living, terrestrial, aquatic.
- **Level of Organisation:** Organ system
- Bilateral symmetry; triploblastic, tube within tube; schizocoelomate; metamerically (true) segmentation
- **Digestive system:** Complete, extracellular
- **Respiratory system:** Branchial (aquatic) and cutaneous (terrestrial)
- **Circulatory system:** Closed (earthworm) and open (leeches); haemoglobin or erythrocruorin present
- **Excretory system:** Nephridia (osmoregulation and excretion)
- **Nervous system and sense organ:** Nerve ring; paired ganglia double, solid ventral nerve cord
- **Reproduction:** Both unisexual (*Nereis*) and bisexual (leech)
- **Fertilisation:** External (Earthworm)
- **Development:** Both direct and indirect (Trochophore larvae)
- **Example:** *Nereis, Hirudinaria, Pheretima*, etc.

NEET POWER TIPS

- *Peripatus* is a walking worm, connecting link between phyla Annelida and Arthropoda.
- *Hirudinaria granulosa* (cattle leech) saliva contain an anti-coagulant (hirudin) prevents blood clotting.
- *Neopilina* is connecting link between Annelida and Mollusca
- Mantle is thin, fleshy fold of dorsal body wall, covers visceral mass.
- Mantle cavity (feather like gills), a space between mantle and hump.

Higher Invertebrates

Arthropoda

- **Habit and Habitat:** Cosmopolitan (gregarious, colonial, solitary, parasitic)
- **Level of Organisation:** Organ system
- Bilateral symmetry; triploblastic, tube within tube; schizocoelom; segmentation present
- **Digestive system:** Complete, extracellular
- **Respiratory system:** Gills or book gills (aquatic) and tracheae or book lungs (terrestrial)
- **Circulatory system:** Open type
- **Excretory system:** Green gland (crustacean), Malpighian tubules (insect) and Coxal gland (spider and scorpion)
- **Nervous system:** Nerve ring and ventral nerve cord
- **Reproduction:** Sexual dimorphism present
- **Fertilisation:** Internal (mostly oviparous)
- **Development:** Direct or indirect
- **Examples:** *Apis, Bombyx, Limulus, Locusta, Anopheles*, etc.

Monarch butterfly

Unique Features

- Largest phylum, jointed appendages, externally segmentation (Head, Thorax and Abdomen).
- Body covered with exoskeleton (chitinous cuticle).
- Chephalothorax (fused head and thorax)-*Limulus*.
- **Sensory organs** Antennae, compound eyes and statocysts.
- **Metamorphosis**
  - Complete: Eggs→Larva→Pupa→Adult
  - Incomplete: Eggs→Nymph→Adult

Mollusca

- **Habit and Habitat:** Terrestrial, aquatic (mostly marine)
- **Level of Organisation:** Organ system
- Bilateral symmetry; triploblastic; tube within tube and schizocoelomate
- **Digestive system:** Complete, extracellular
- **Respiratory system:** Gills (ctenidia), mantle and pulmonary sac
- **Circulatory system:** Open type
- **Excretory system:** Ctenidia, organ of Bojanus, Keber's organs
- **Nervous system and sense organ:** Tentacles, ganglia, statocyst, etc
- **Reproduction:** Both unisexual and bisexual (mostly)
- **Fertilisation:** Both internal and external
- **Development:** Both direct and indirect
- **Examples:** *Octopus, Dentalium, Pila,* etc.

Unique Features

- Second largest phylum, unsegmented (head, muscular foot and visceral hump).
- Shell made up of calcium carbonate.
- Mouth contains a radula for feeding (file like rasping organ)
- Shows cephalisation and have both CNS and PNS.

Octopus (Devil fish)

Echinodermata

- **Habit and Habitat:** Exclusively marine, live on ocean hoor.
- **Level of Organisation:** Organ system
- Bilateral symmetry (larvae) and radial (adults); triploblastic and tube within tube; enterocoelomate
- **Digestive system:** Complete, extracellular
- **Respiratory, circulatory and excretory system:** Water vascular system
- **Nervous system and sense organ:** Nerve ring and radial nerve cords, chemoreceptors.
- **Reproduction:** Unisexual
- **Fertilisation:** External
- **Development:** Indirect (metamorphosis)
- **Examples:** *Antendon, Asterias, Echinus, Ophiura,* etc.

Unique Features

- Bear spines and calcareous plates.
- **Water vascular system:** Water enters through madreporite (sieve plate) → Stone canal → Ring canal → Radial canal → Ampullae (tube feet)
- **Tube feet:** Locomotion, exchange of gases and capturing of prey.
- They have the ability to regenerate.

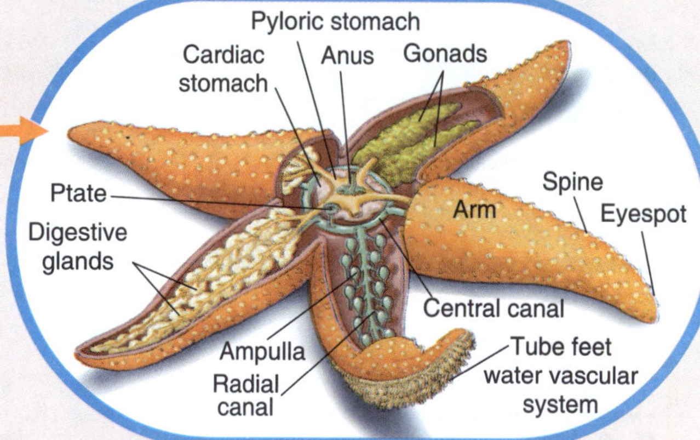

Asterias rubens

Hemichordata

- **Habit and Habitat:** Exclusively marine
- **Level of Organisation:** Organ system
- Bilateral symmetry; triploblastic; tube within tube and enterocoelomate
- **Digestive system:** Complete, extracellular
- **Respiratory system:** Bearing gill slits
- **Circulatory system:** Open type
- **Excretory system:** Proboscis gland
- **Nervous system and sense organ:** Hollow nerve cord
- **Reproduction:** Unisexual
- **Fertilisation:** External
- **Development:** Indirect (Tornaria larvae)
- **Examples:** *Balanoglossus, Saccoglossus,* etc.

Unique Features

- Worm-like body divisible in proboscis (stomochord present), collar and trunk.
- Acorn worm lives in burrow (soft sand or mud).

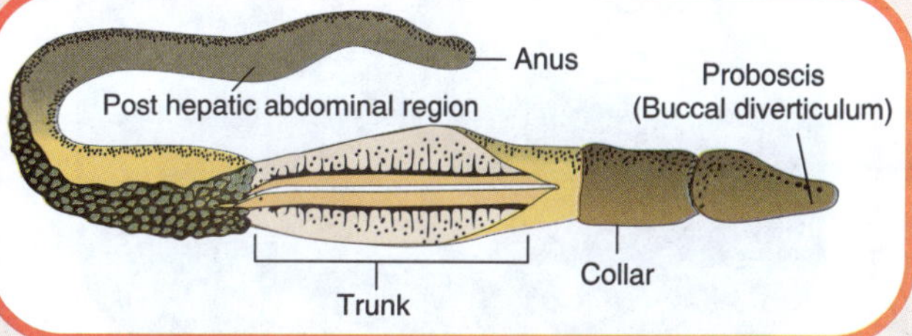

Notochord

- Rod-shaped structure, derived from mesoderm, formed dorsally between nerve cord and gut.
- Acts as a primary axial skeleton.
- **Chordates**-Animals with notochord
- **Non-Chordates**- Animals without notochord.

Chordata Characteristics

- Presence of notochord, dorsal hollow nerve cord and paired pharyngeal gill slits.
- Bilaterally symmetrical, triploblastic, coelomate with organ system level.
- Possess a post anal tail and closed circulatory system (Heart present ventrally).

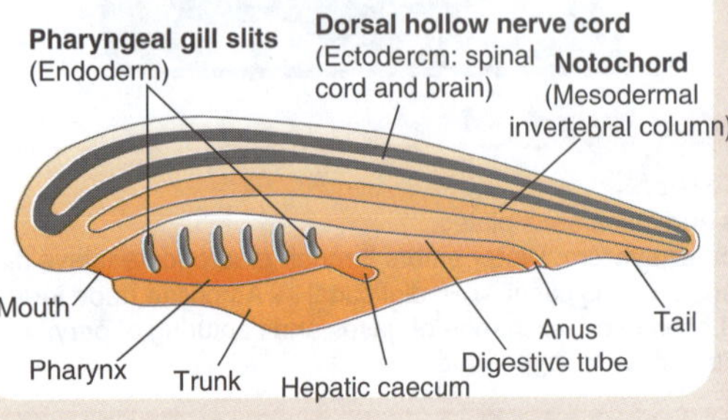

Chordata

- Acraniata (without cranium) — Subphylum
  - Uro chordata (Tail): Notochord present only in tail of larva e.g., *Ascidia*
  - Cephalo-chordata (Head): Notochord persistent throughout life; from head to tail e.g., Amphioxus
- Craniata (with cranium) — Subphylum (Vertebrata)
  - Agnatha (Jawless): Cyclo stomata (Circular mouth) e.g., *Lamprey*
  - Gnathostomata (With jaws) — (Super-class)
    - Pisces (Bear fins)
      - Chond richthyes (Cartilage)
      - Osteic hthyes (Bony)
    - Tetrapoda (Bear Limbs)
      - Amphibia
      - Reptilia
      - Aves
      - Mammalia

Agnatha

- Lack jaws and paired appendages.
- Have persistent notochord.
- Vertebral column is not fully developed.

Cyclostomata

- Mostly ectoparasite on same fishes.
- Cartilaginous cranium and vertebral column, closed circulation, heart in 2-chambered.
- 6-15 pair of gill slits, unpaired fins, devoid of scales, about 10 pairs of cranial nerves.
- **Anadramous** Marine but migrate for spawning to fresh water.
- e.g., *Petromyzon* and *Myxine*.

Lamprey

Differences between Urochordate and Cephalochordate

Features	Urochordate	Cephalochordate
Body	Protected by Tunic (Tunicate)	Transparent, slender, smooth (Lancelets)
Respiration	Pharyngeal gill slits	Gills/General body surface
Excretion	Neural glands	Solenocytes
Reproduction	Hermaphrodite	Unisexual
Development	Retrogressive metamorphosis (Indirect) e.g., *Ascidia*	Progressive metamorphosis (Indirect) e.g., *Branchiostoma*

Pisces

Chondrichthyes	Parameters Features	Osteichthyes
Ventral side	Mouth	Terminal side
Absent	Operculum	Present
Absent (Constant swim)	Air bladder	Present (regulates buoyancy)
Placoid scales (Modify to form teeth)	Scales	Cycloid/Ctenoid scales
Internal (Pelvic fin bear claspers in males)	Fertilisation	External
Pristis (Sawfish), *Scoliodon* (Dog fish), *Trygon* (Sting ray); *Carcharodon* (Great white shark), *Torpedo* (have electric organs), etc.	**Examples**	*Hippocampus* (Sea horse), *Catla, Labeo* (Rohu), *Exocoetus* (Flying fish)

Stingray (possess poison sting)

Hippocampus

Class-Amphibians

- Aquatic as well as terrestrial habitats.
- Moist skin (mucus gland) with no scales.
- Tympanum represents ear, eyes have eyelids.
- **Cloaca**- Common chamber where alimentary canal, urinary and reproductive tracts open.
- Respiration by gills, lungs and skin
- Mesonephric kidney; larva (aquatic, ammonotelic) and adult (terrestrial, ureoteltic)
- 3-chambered heart; cold-blooded; separate sexes; fertilisation external.
- Oviparous, indirect development (tadpole larva).
- **Example**- *Hyla* (Tree frog), Bufo (Toad), *Salamandra*, Ichythyophis (Limbless amphibian)

Hyla

Gnathostomata

- True jaws and paired appendages.
- Vertebral column replaces embryonic notochord.
- It consists of two super classes **Pisces** and **Tetrapoda**

Tetrapoda

Chelone

Class-Reptilia

- 3-chambered heart except crocodile (4-chambered); cold blooded vertebrates
- Dry, scaly (epidermal), cornified skin
- **Digestion** Complete, extracellular
- Eyes, tympanum and middle ear
- Unisexual, internal fertilisation
- Direct developments (Oviparous and ovoviviparous)
- **Examples** *Hemidactylus* (Wall lizard), *Chameleon* (Tree lizard), *Naja* (Cobra), *Vipera*, *Chelone*, *Testudo*.

Pavo

Class-Aves

- Dry, feathers, uropygial gland/oil gland
- Forelimbs are modified into wings, penumatic bones (hollow bones).
- **Digestive system** Crop + Gizzard→ Cloaca; mouth modified into beak (no teeth)
- **Respiration** Lungs, air sacs, syrinx (Voice box); unisexual (Internal, oviparous); direct development
- **Example** *Aptenodytes* (Penguin), *Neophron*, *Pavo* (Peacock).

Oryctolagus

Class-Mammalia

- Warm blooded, hairy and have mammary gland.
- Complete, alimentary canal, cloaca absent (except *Prototherians*)
- 4-chambered heart (Enucleated RBCs) ; metanephric kidney (Uriotelic)
- **Nervous system** Corpus callosum, brain + spinal cord, 12 pairs of cranial nerves.
- **Examples** *Pteropus* (Flying fox), Lions, Tiger, *Balaenoptera*, *Delphinus*, *Rattus rattus*, *Equus*, (Horse), etc.

Chapter **05**

Morphology of Flowering Plants

Stem

Modification of stems

Underground (For food storage)

- **Rhizome** (e.g. Ginger)
- **Corm** (e.g. *Crocus*, *Colocasia*) 
- **Tuber** (e.g. Potato) 
- **Bulb** (e.g. Onion) 

Sub-aerial (For vegetative reproduction)

- Crown, Stolon, Daughter plant — **Stolon** (e.g., Mint, Mentha) 
- Leaves, Roots, Offset — **Offset** (e.g. *Eichhornia*, *Pistia*)
- **Sucker** (e.g. *Chrysanthemum*, Banana, Pineapple) 
- **Runner** (e.g. *Cyanodon, dactylon, Oxalis,* grass and strawberry) 

Aerial (For support, protection and photosynthesis)

- **Tendril for support** (e.g. cucumber)
- **Thorns for protection** (e.g. *Citrus*) 
- **Phylloclade for photosynthesis** (e.g. *Opuntia*) 

NEET POWER TIPS

- Stems develops from plumule of the embryo of germinating seed.
- It bears terminal or axillary bud.

Root, Stem, Leaf and Inflorescence

Parts of Plant

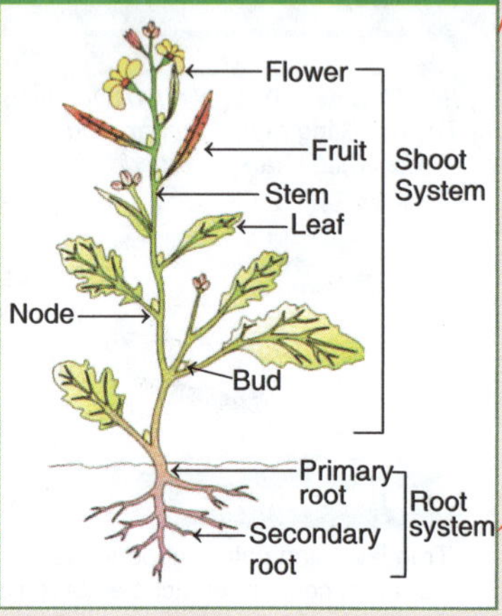

Flower, Fruit, Stem, Leaf, Node, Bud — Shoot System

Primary root, Secondary root — Root system

Roots

Types

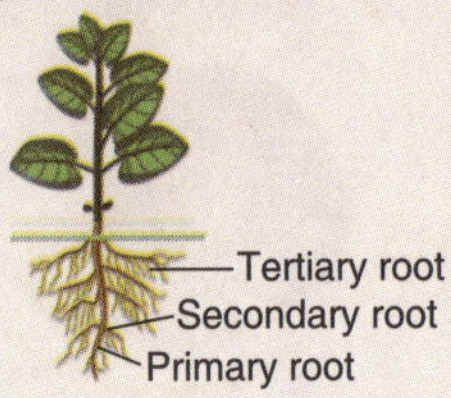

Tertiary root, Secondary root, Primary root

Tap root (e.g. Dicots)

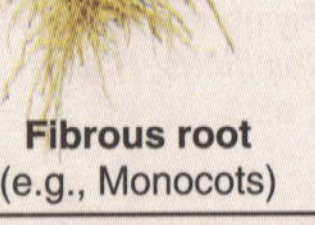

Fibrous root (e.g., Monocots)

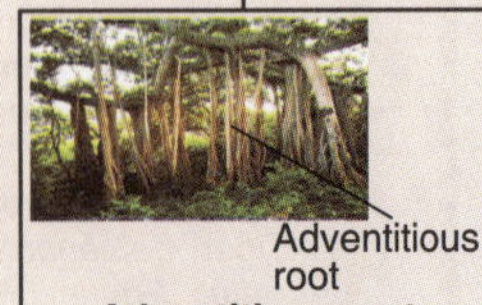

Adventitious root (e.g., Monstera)

Regions

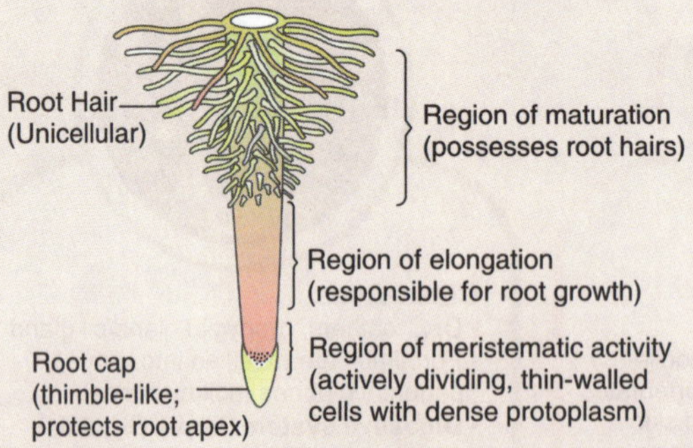

- Root Hair (Unicellular) — Region of maturation (possesses root hairs)
- Region of elongation (responsible for root growth)
- Root cap (thimble-like; protects root apex) — Region of meristematic activity (actively dividing, thin-walled cells with dense protoplasm)

Modifications

Storage

- E.g. tap roots of carrot and turnip; adventitious roots of sweet potato

Carrot

Support

- E.g. Prop root (Banyan tree) and stilt root (Maize,

Respiration

- E.g. Pneumatophores (breathing roots) found in *Rhizophora*

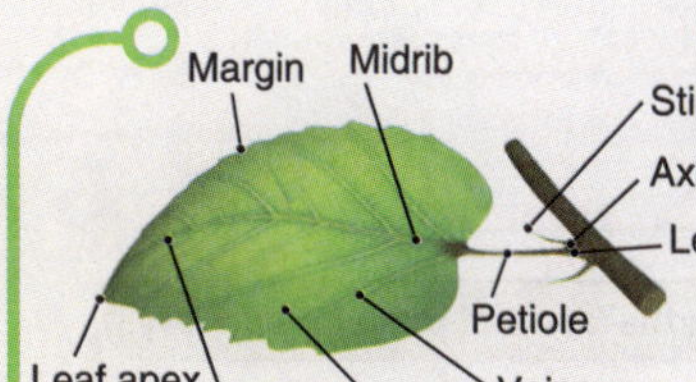

LEAF

Margin
Midrib
Stipule
Axillary bud
Leaf base
Petiole
Veins
Lamina (leaf blade)
Veinlets
Leaf apex

Venation

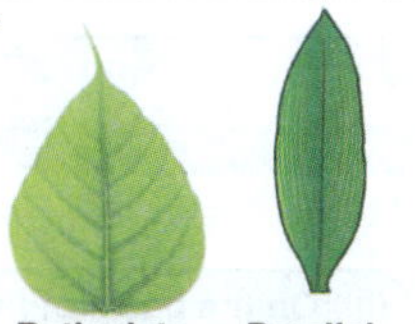

- **Reticulate** (Dicots)
- **Parallel** (Monocots)

Types

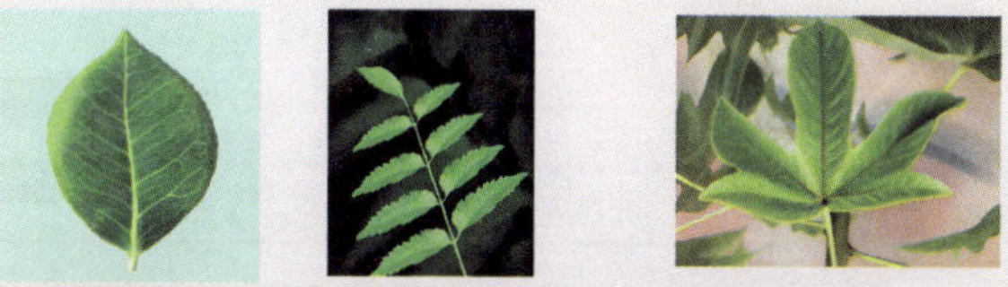

- **Simple** (e.g. Peepal tree)
- **Pinnately compound** (e.g. Neem)
- **Palmately compound** (e.g., Silk cotton)

MODIFICATIONS

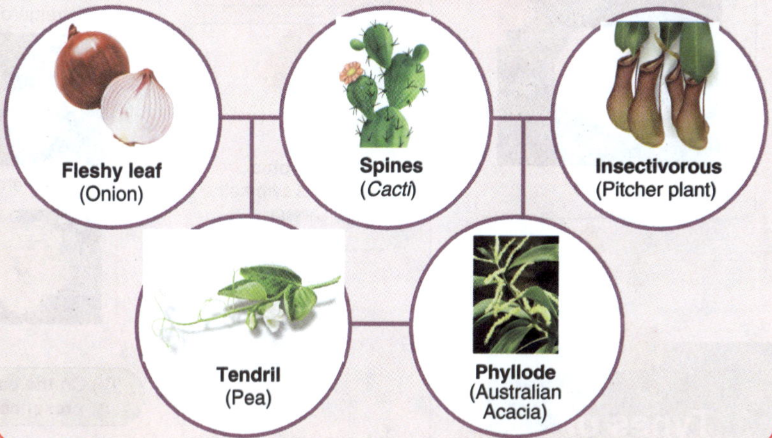

- **Fleshy leaf** (Onion)
- **Spines** (*Cacti*)
- **Insectivorous** (Pitcher plant)
- **Tendril** (Pea)
- **Phyllode** (Australian Acacia)

Phyllotaxy

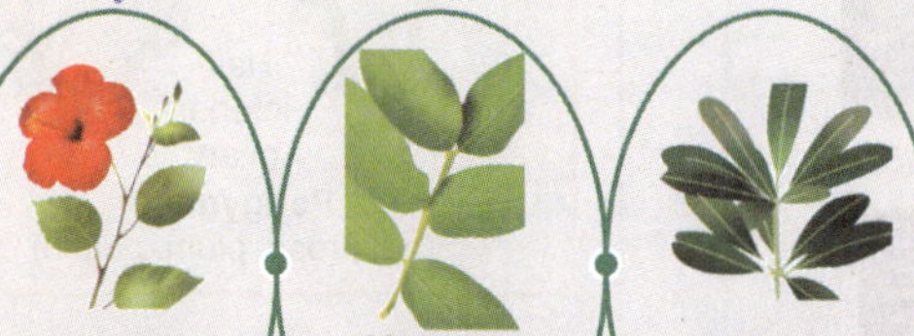

- **Opposite** (*Calotropis*, Guava)
- **Alternate** (China rose, mustard)
- **Whorled** (*Alstonia*)

NEET POWER TIPS

- Leaves are borne on stem at node and bears a bud on its axil which turns into branch.
- They originates from Shoot Apical Meristem (SAM)

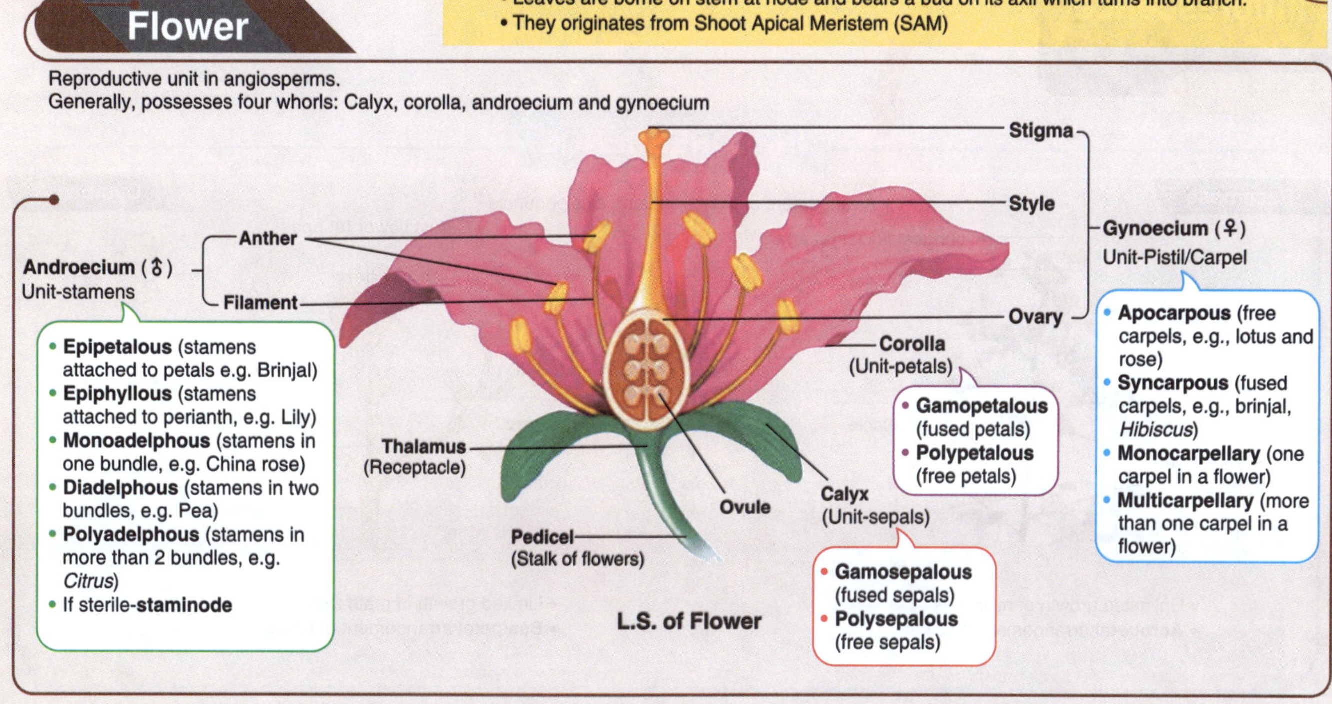

Types of Flowers and Inflorescence

Types of Flowers

(I) On the basis of presence or absence of bracts

- Bracteate (with bracts) 
  - Bract
- Ebracteate (without bracts)

(II) On the basis of symmetry

- **Actinomorphic** (Radial symmetry) e.g., mustard
- **Zygomorphic** (Bilateral symmetry) e.g., *Cassia* 
- **Asymmetric** e.g., Canna 

(III) On the basis of floral appendages

- Trimerous (3) 
- Tetramerous (4) 
- Pentamerous (5)

(IV) On the basis of presence of sex organs

- Unisexual (♂ or ♀ organs)
- Bisexual (♂ and ♀ organs)

(V) On the basis of position of ovary

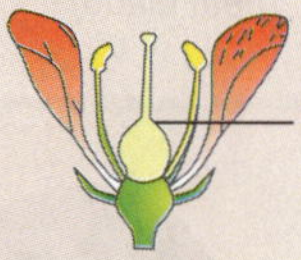

- **Hypogynous** (e.g., mustard, China rose and Brinjal) 
  - Superior ovary
- **Perigynous** (e.g., rose, plum, peach) 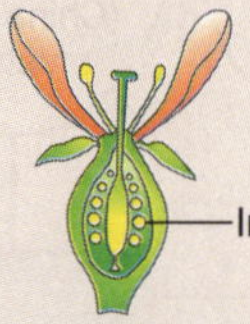
  - Half-inferior ovary
- **Epigynous** (e.g., guava, cucumber and the ray florets of sunflower)
  - Inferior ovary

INFLORESCENCE

- Arrangement of flower on floral axis peduncle

Racemose

- Unlimited growth of main axis
- **Acropetal** arrangement of flower

Cymose

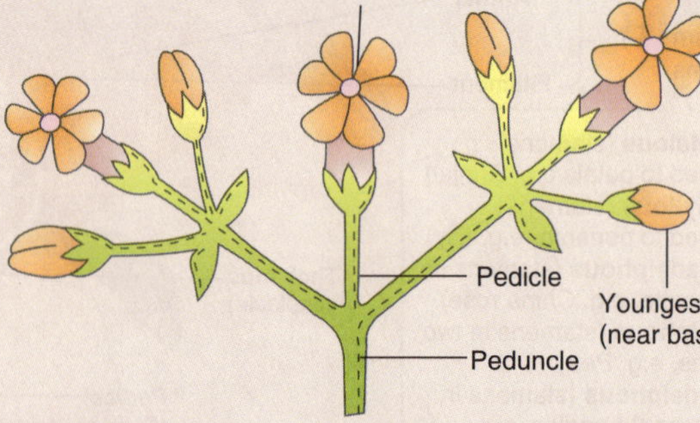

- Limited growth of main axis
- **Basipetal** arrangement of flower

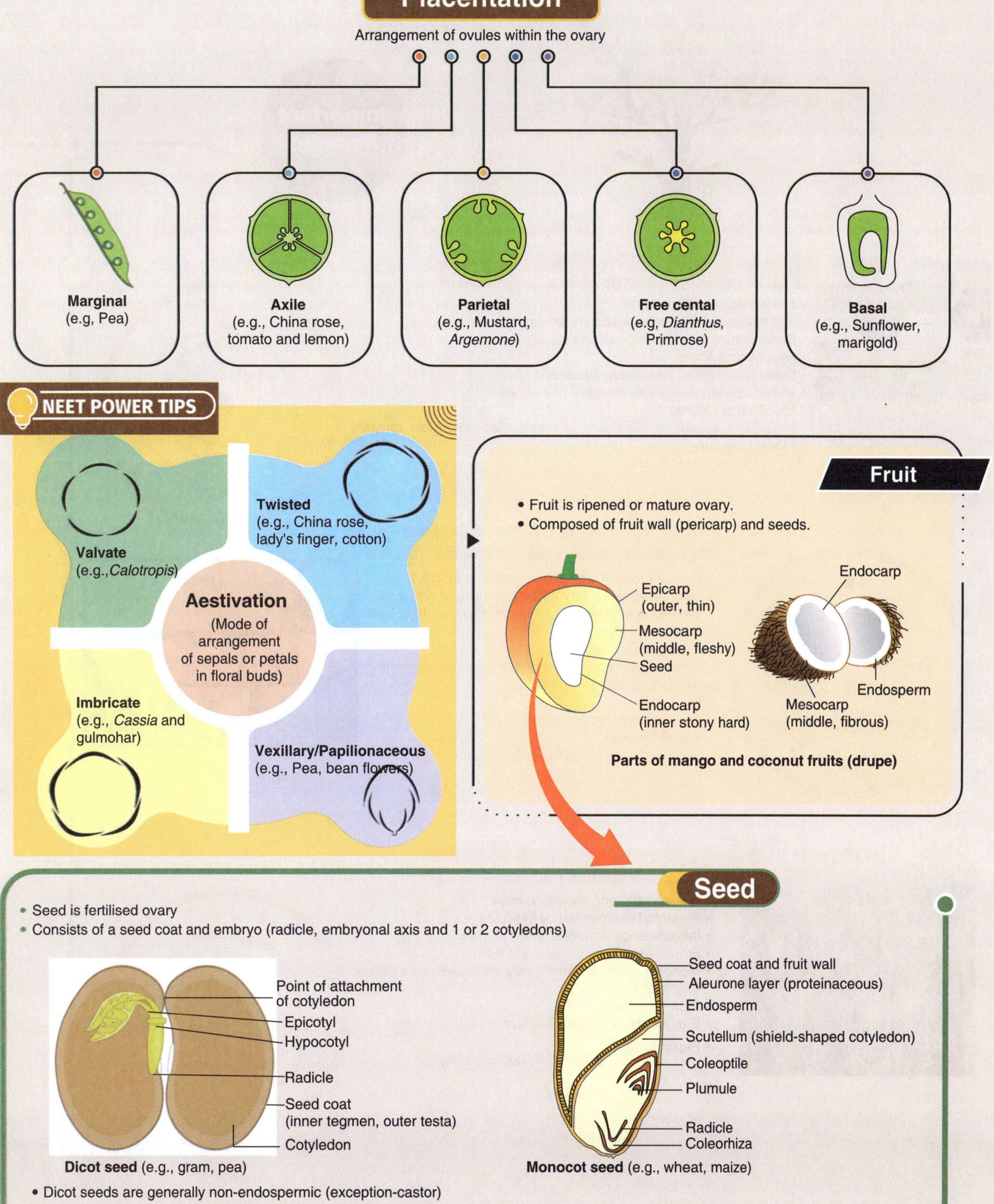

Placentation
Arrangement of ovules within the ovary
Marginal (e.g, Pea)
Axile (e.g., China rose, tomato and lemon)
Parietal (e.g., Mustard, Argemone)
Free cental (e.g Dianthus, Primrose)
Basal (e.g., Sunflower, marigold)
NEET POWER TIPS
Valvate (e.g., Calotropis)
Twisted (e.g., China rose, lady's finger, cotton)
Aestivation (Mode of arrangement of sepals or petals in floral buds)
Imbricate (e.g., Cassia and gulmohar)
Vexillary/Papilionaceous (e.g., Pea, bean flowers)
Fruit
• Fruit is ripened or mature ovary.
• Composed of fruit wall (pericarp) and seeds.
Epicarp (outer, thin)
Mesocarp (middle, fleshy)
Seed
Endocarp (inner stony hard)
Endocarp
Endosperm
Mesocarp (middle, fibrous)
Parts of mango and coconut fruits (drupe)
Seed
• Seed is fertilised ovary
• Consists of a seed coat and embryo (radicle, embryonal axis and 1 or 2 cotyledons)
Point of attachment of cotyledon
Epicotyl
Hypocotyl
Radicle
Seed coat (inner tegmen, outer testa)
Cotyledon
Dicot seed (e.g., gram, pea)
Seed coat and fruit wall
Aleurone layer (proteinaceous)
Endosperm
Scutellum (shield-shaped cotyledon)
Coleoptile
Plumule
Radicle
Coleorhiza
Monocot seed (e.g., wheat, maize)
• Dicot seeds are generally non-endospermic (exception-castor)
• Monocot seeds are generally endospermic (exception-orchid)

Leguminosae (Fabaceae)

- Leaves with pulvinate base
- Inflorescence-Racemose or solitary axillary
- Pentamerous flower with persistent calyx
- Hypogynous flower
- Diadelphous [(9)+1] condition of stamens
- Monocarpellary ovary with marginal placentation
- Fruit-Pod or legume
- E.g., Gram, soyabean, *Indigofera*, sunhemp, *Sesbania*, lupin, mulaithi
- **Floral formula**

  Br % ⚥ $K_{(5)}$ $C_{1+2+(2)}$ $A_{(9)+1}$ $\underline{G}_1$

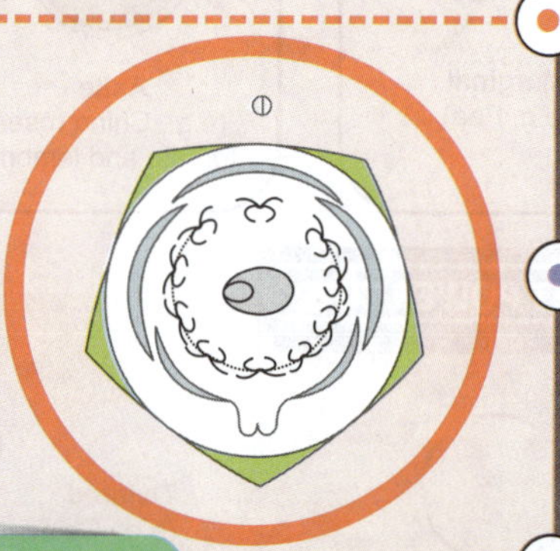

Malvaceae (Mallow family)

- Pentamerous flower with presence of epicalyx
- Inflorescence-Solitary axillary, cymose or racemose.
- Twisted aestivation of corolla; petals connate at base
- Persistent calyx
- Hypogynous flower
- Epipetalous, monoadelphous condition of stamens
- Axile Placentation
- Fruit-Capsule
- E.g., *Gossypium*, *Hibiscus*
- **Floral formula**:

  Br ⊕ ⚥ Epi_{3-8} K_5 $\overset{\frown}{C_5 A_{(\infty)}}$ $\underline{G}_{(\infty)}$

Gramineae (Poaceac)

- Leaves with long sheathing base
- Perianth-Represented by lodicules
- Inflorescence-Spikelets with 2 glumes
- Flower enclosed by palea and lemma
- Monocarpellary superior ovary with basal placentation; stigma-2, feathery
- Fruit-Caryopsis
- E.g., *Oryza*, *Triticum*, *Sorghum*
- **Floral formula**:

  Br %⊕ ⚥ P_2 (lodicules) A_3 G_1

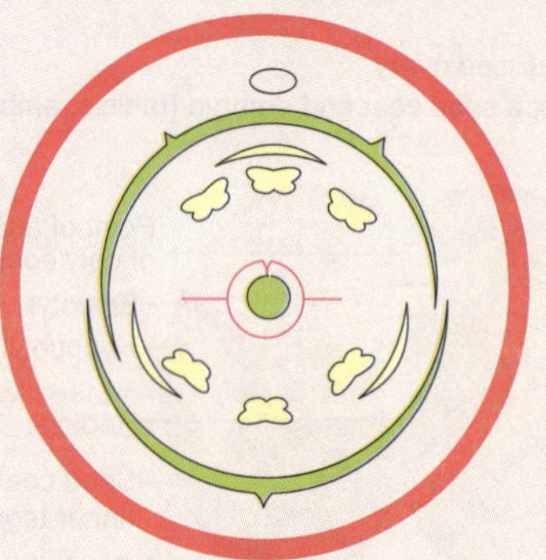

Cruciferae (Brassicaceae)

- Tetramerous flower with cruciform corolla
- Racemose inflorescence
- Hypogynous flower
- Tetradynamous (2+4) condition of stamens
- Bicarpellary ovary with parietal placentation
- Fruit-Siliqua/silicula
- E.g., *Brassica, Iberis*
- **Floral Formula:**

⊕ Ebr ⊕ ⚥ $K_{2+2}\ C_4\ A_{2+4}\ \underline{G}_{(2)}$

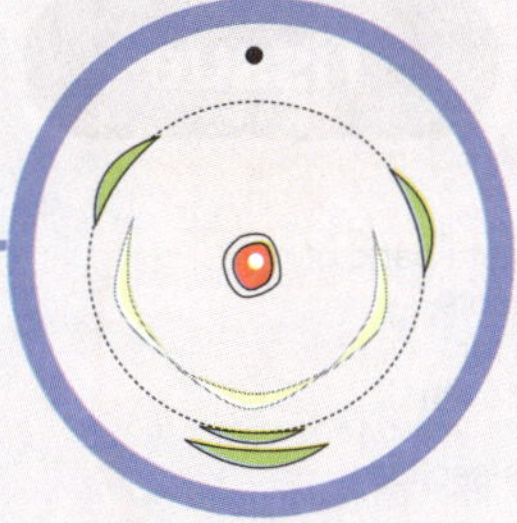

Compositae (Asteraceae)

- Pentamerous flower with calyx modified into pappus
- Inflorescence- Head/capitulum; having two types of flowers (peripheral ray florets and central disc florets)
- Flowers- Complete, bisexual or aclinomorphic (disc. flowers) or incomplete, unisexual or zygomorphic (ray florets)
- Epigynous flower
- Syngenesious, epipetalous condition of stamens
- Bicarpellary ovary with basal placentation; bifid stigma
- Fruit-Cypsella
- E.g., *Lactuca, Helianthus, Chrysanthemum, Eclipta*
- **Floral formula:**

Ray floret- Br⊕ or %, ⚥ K_5(pappus) $C_{(5)}\ A_0\ \overline{G}_{(2)}$

Disc floret- Br⊕ ⚥ K_5(pappus) $\overset{\frown}{C_{(5)}\ A_{(5)}}\ \overline{G}_{(2)}$

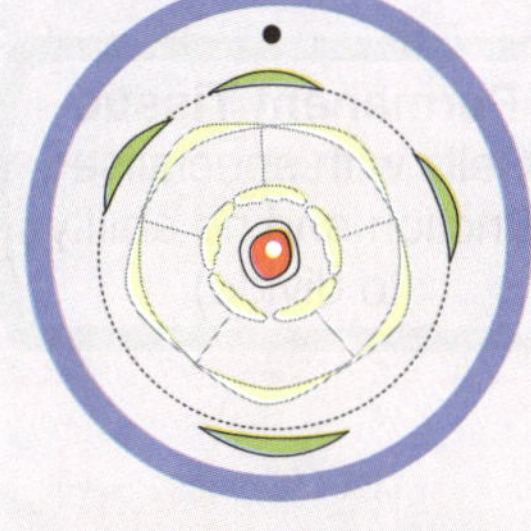

Solanaceae*

- Pentamerous flower with persistent calyx
- Corolla-Rotate or companulate
- Inflorescence-Solitary, axillary or cymose
- Epipetalous stamen
- Bicarpellary superior ovary with obliquely placed/swollen placenta
- Fruit-Berry/Capsule
- E.g., *Withania, Solanum, Nicotiana, Datura*
- **Floral Formula:**

⊕ ⚥ $K_{(5)}\ \overset{\frown}{C_{(5)}\ A_{(5)}}\ \underline{G}_{(2)}$

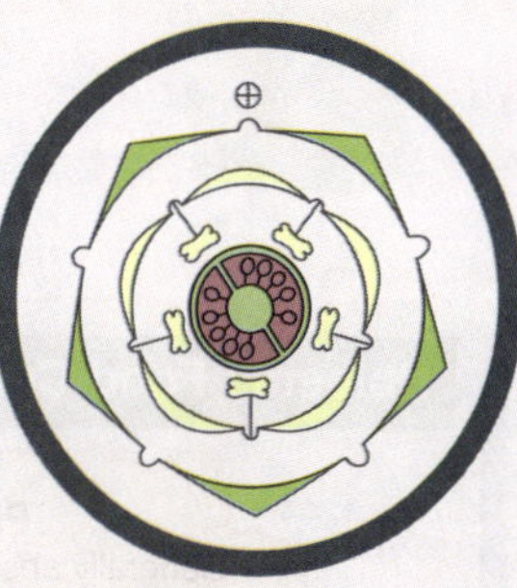

*Not included in NEET syllabus, but present in NCERT

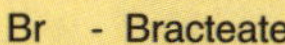

Br - Bracteate	K - Calyx	$\overline{G}$ - Inferior ovary
Ebr - Ebracteate	C - Corolla	1, 2, 3, 4, ... - Number of units
⊕ - Actinomorphic flower	P - Perianth	() - fused
% - Zygomorphic flower	A - Androecium	$\overset{\frown}{C\ A}$ - Epipetalous condition
⚥ - Bisexual flower	G - Gynoecium	$\overset{\frown}{P\ A}$ - Epiphyllous condition
♀ - Female flower	G– - Semi-inferior ovary	
♂ - Male flower	$\underline{G}$ - Superior ovary	

Chapter 06 Anatomy of Flowering Plants

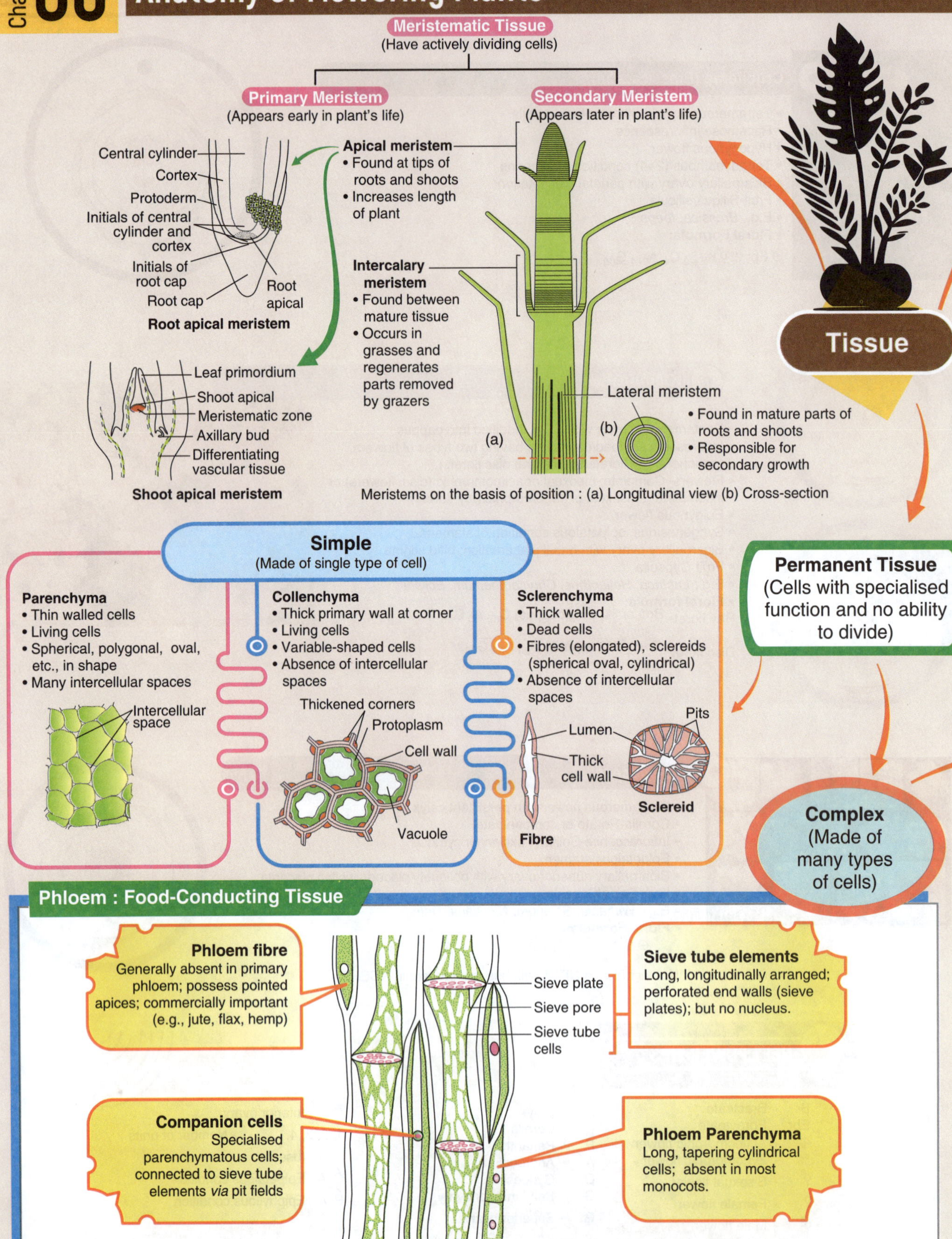

Tissue system

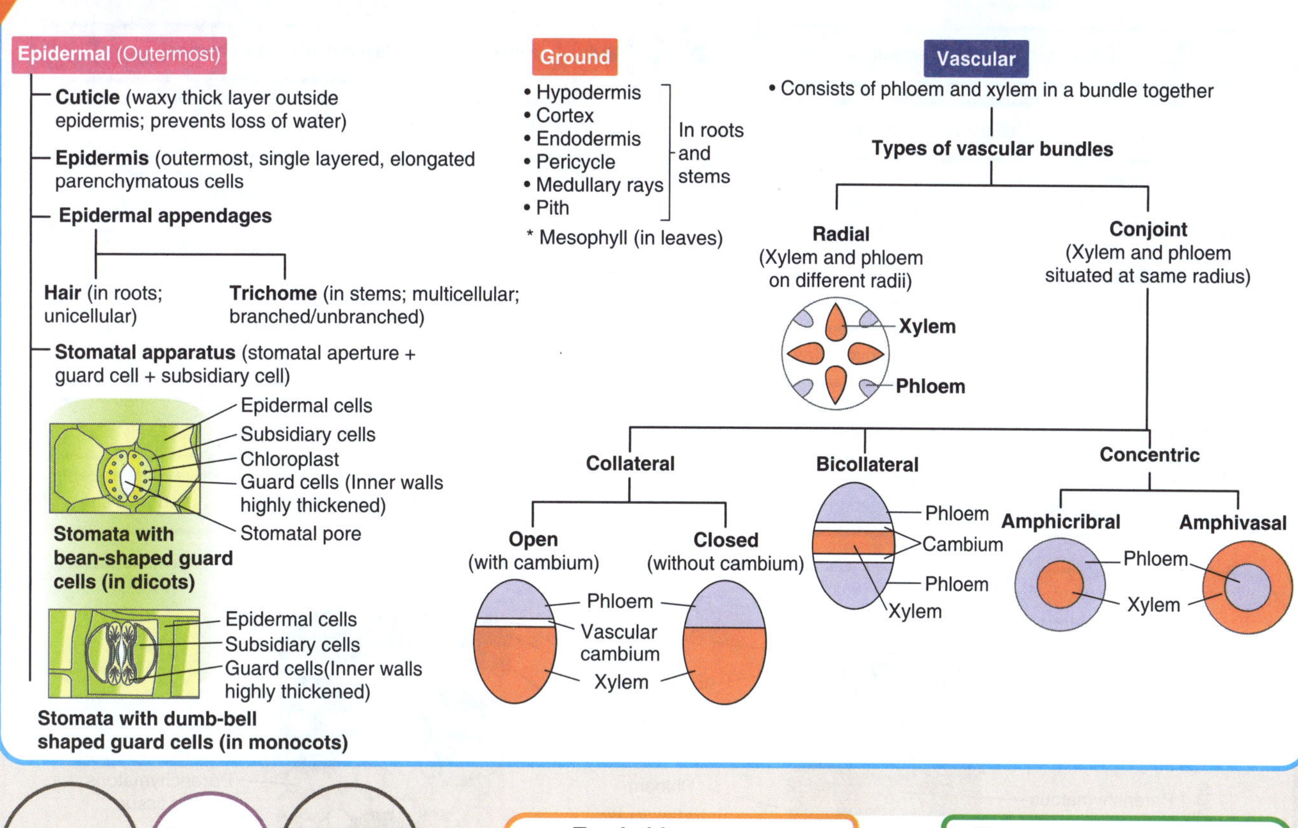

Xylem: Water-Conducting Tissue

Primary Xylem

- **Protoxylem** (First formed xylem)
- **Metaxylem** (Later formed xylem)

Arrangement of xylem

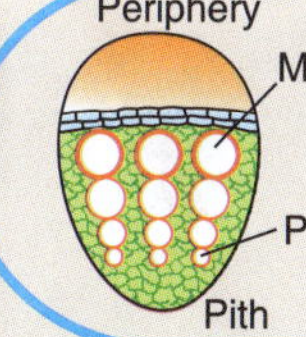

Endarch (centrifugal)
- Protoxylem towards centre, metaxylem towards periphery of organ
- Found in stem

Mesarch
- Direction of xylem differentiation is both centrifugal and centripetal
- Found in ferns

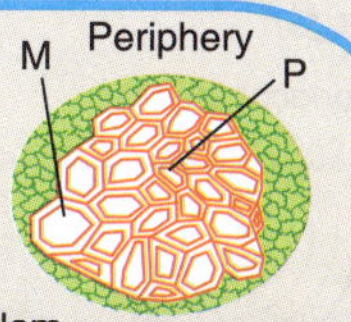

M-Metaxylem; P-Protoxylem

Periphery P M Pith

Exarch (centripetal)
- Protoxylem towards periphery and metaxylem towards centre
- Found in roots

Components

Tracheids
- Tube-like cells with thick and lignified walls and tapering ends; dead; without protoplasm.
- Most primitive component.

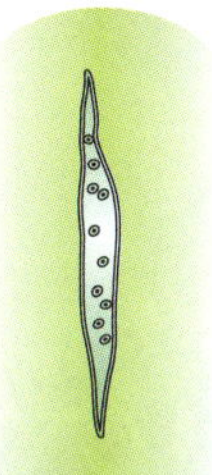

Vessels
- Long cylindrical structure with central cavity; no protoplasm
- Present in angiosperms

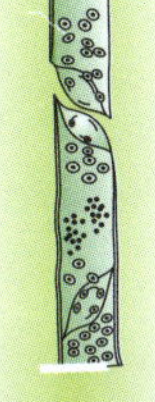

Xylem Parenchyma
- Living and thin-walled.
- Cellulosic cell wall
- Stores food in form of starch or fat

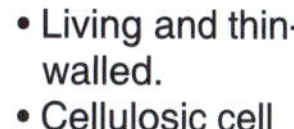

Xylem Fibres

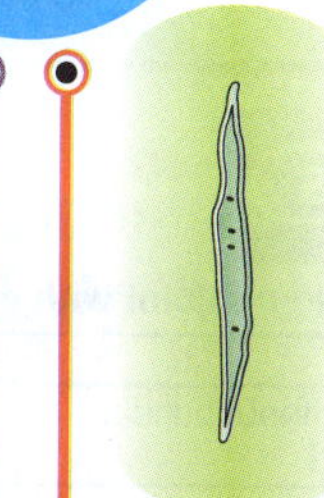

- Obliterated central lumen;
- septate or aseptate
- Highly thickened walls

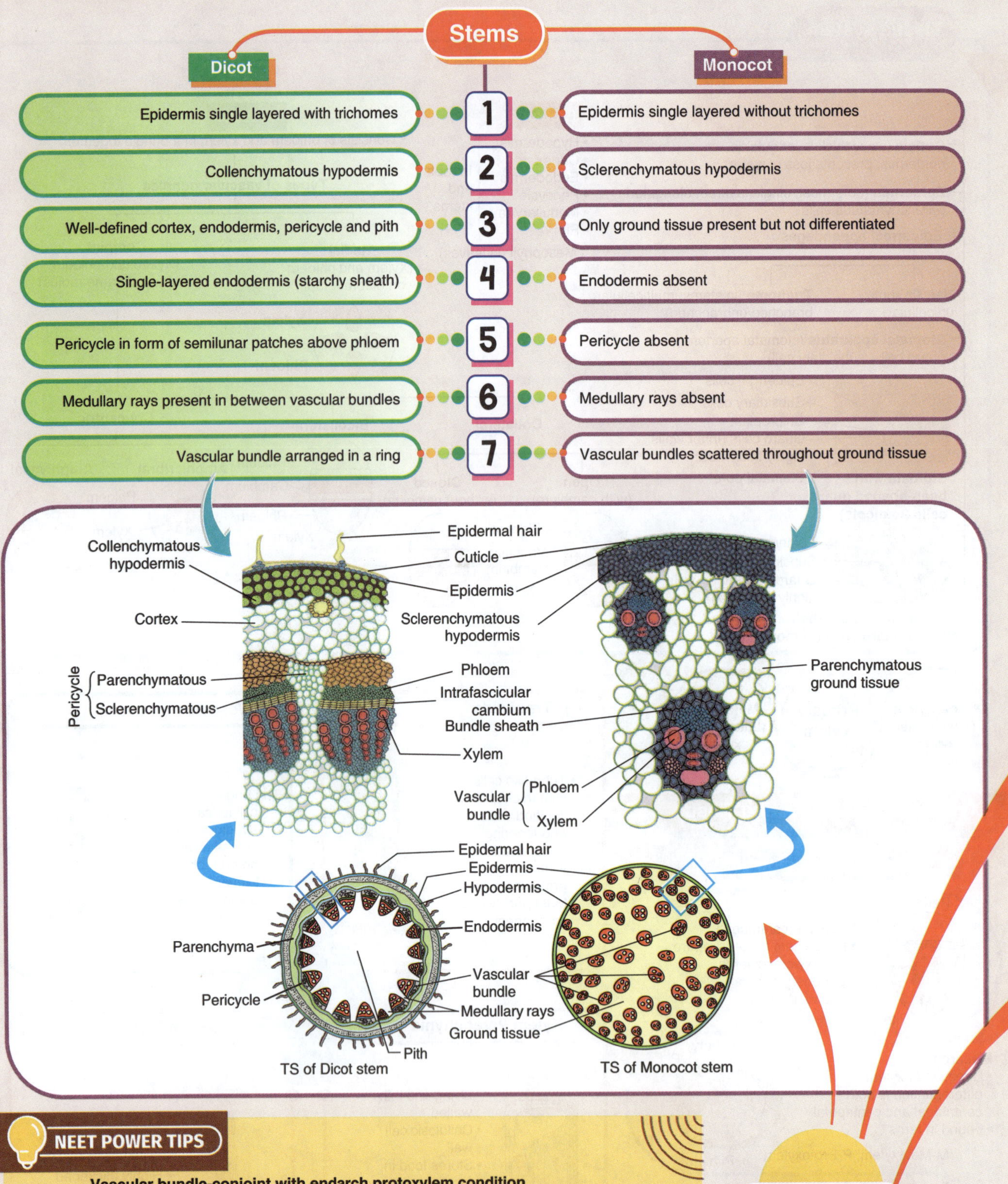

NEET POWER TIPS

Vascular bundle-conjoint with endarch protoxylem condition

Dicot stems	Monocot stems
Vascular bundles-open, without bundle sheath and wedge-shaped	Vascular bundles-closed with sclerenchymatous bundle sheath
Absence of lysigenous cavity	Presence of water-containing lysigenous cavity
Well-defined pith made of parenchymatous cells with large intercellular spaces	Absence of pith

Anatomy

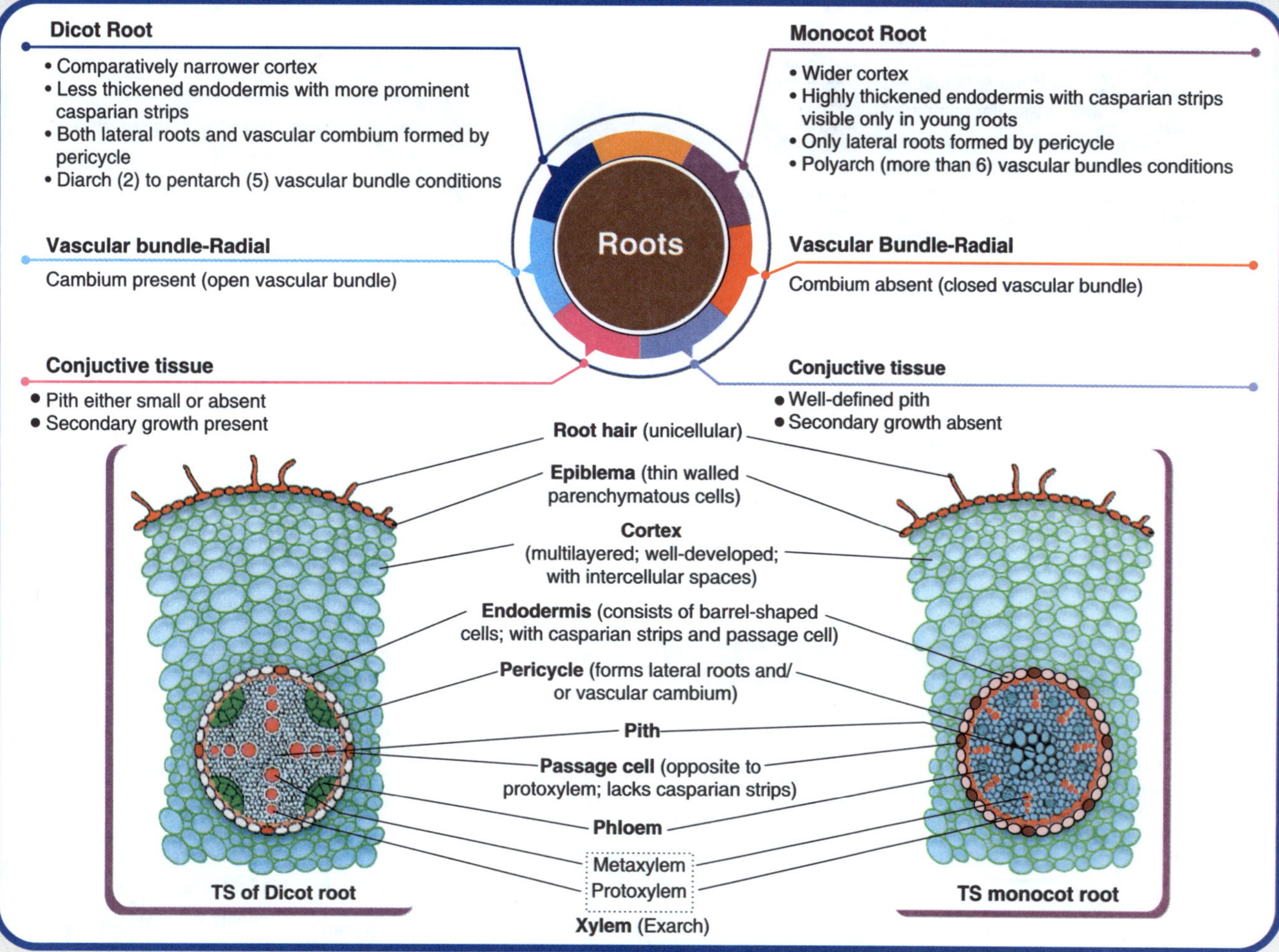

Leaf

Dorsiventral (Dicot)

- Stomata absent or less abundant on the upper side (adaxial)
- Differentiated mesophyll tissue with upper palisade parenchyma and lower spongy parenchyma
- Single-layered bundle sheath
- Veins (and thus, bundles) of different size (reticulate venation)
- Stomata with kidney-shaped guard cells
- Absence of bulliform cells

Bundle sheath
Xylem
Phloem
Adaxial (upper) **epidermis**
Palisade mesophyll (vertically elongated, closely placed cells)
Air cavity
Spongy mesophyll (almost spherical or irregular cells with intercellular spaces)
Sub-stomatal cavity
Stoma
Abaxial epidermis (lower)

TS of Dicot Leaf

Isobilateral (Monocot)

- Stomata equally distributed on both sides
- Undifferentiated mesophyll
- Single or double-layered bundle sheath
- Veins of same size, except in main vein
- Stomata with dumb-bell shaped guard cells
- Presence of bulliform cells (colourless cells helping to minimise water loss by leaf curling)

Adaxial (upper) **epidermis**
Xylem
Mesophyll
Sub-stomatal cavity
Abaxial (lower) **epidermis**
Phloem
Stoma

TS of Monocot Leaf

Formation of cambial ring

Steps 1

Epidermis
Cortex
Primary phloem
Vascular cambium
Primary xylem
Pith

Intrafascicular cambium cambium between vascular bundle

Intrafascicular cambium formed by meristematic activity of medullary rays

Activity of cambial ring

Steps 2

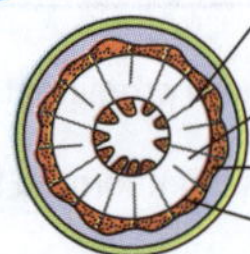

Formation of secondary phloem and secondary xylem by cambial cells.

Vascular Cambium

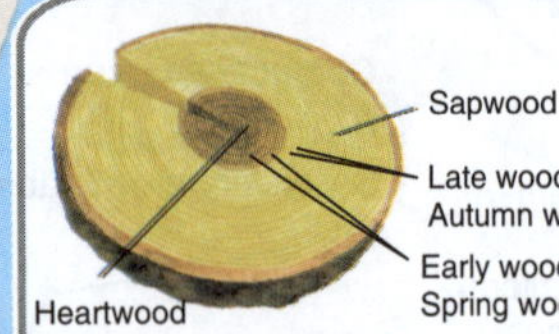

Section of Dicot stem showing different regions.

Spring wood (Early wood)	**Autumn wood** (Late wood)
• More active cambium • Produce more xylary elements • Vessels with wide cavities • Light in colour • Low density	• Less active cambium • Produce less xylary elements • Vessels with narrow cavities • Dark in colour • High density

Heart wood	Sapwood
• Central or innermost region of stem • Dark in colour • Durable and resistant to insects and microbial attack • Proxide mechanical support to stem	• Light in colour • Vulnerable to attack by insects and microbes • Involved in conduction of water and minerals

Development of cork cambium (Phellogen)

Steps 3

Production of cambium from cells of outer cortex.

Cork Cambium (Phellogen)
- Cork (phellem)- on outer side
- Secondary cortex (phelloderm)- on inner side

Phellogen + Phellem + Phelloderm → Periderm

- **Bark** (non-technical term): All tissues exterior to vascular cambium, i.e. periderm with secondary phloem
- **Lenticels**: Lens-shaped openings formed by ruptured epidermis; involved in gaseous exchange.

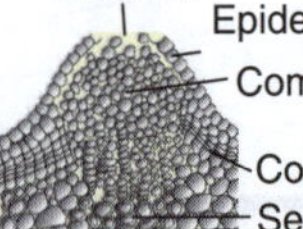

Phellem
Phellogen
Medullary rays
Secondary xylem
Secondary phloem
Cambium ring

Stem

Cork Cambium

Secondary Growth

Dicot Root

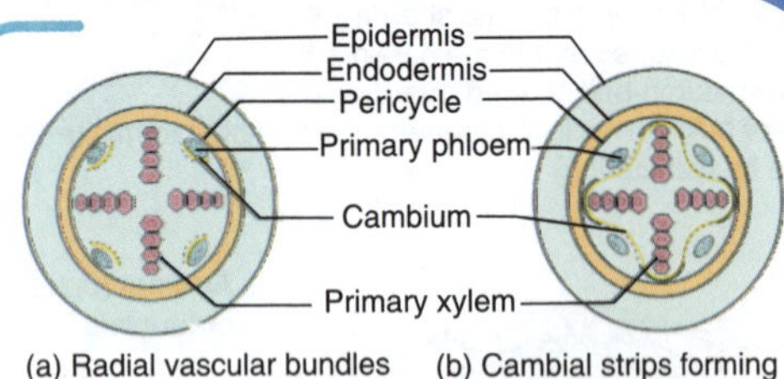

(a) Radial vascular bundles showing cambial groups below phloem

(b) Cambial strips forming opposite primary protoxylem.

Epidermis
Cortex
Endodermis
Pericycle
Primary phloem
Secondary phloem
Cambial ring
Primary xylem
Secondary xylem

(c) Formation of complete cambial ring,

(d) Activity of cambial ring to produce secondary vascular tissue,

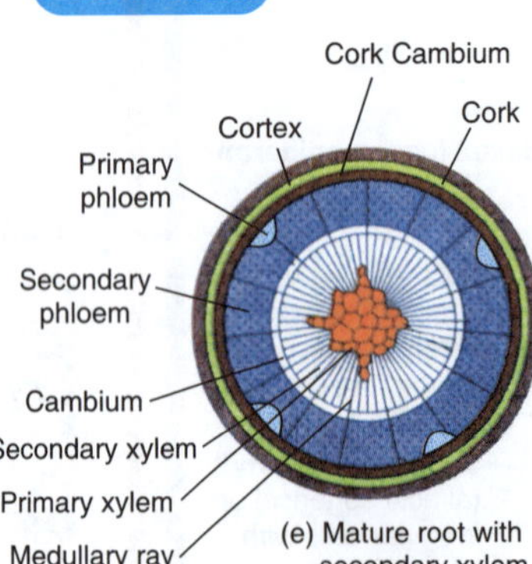

(e) Mature root with secondary xylem, secondary phloem and periderm.

NEET POWER TIPS

- Anomalous secondary growth found in monocots like *Dracaena*, *Yucca*, *Aloe*, *Agave*, etc.
- **Porous wood or hard wood**- found in dicots; possessing vessels
- **Non-porous wood or soft wood**- found in gymnosperms; lacks vessels
- Annual rings-formed by alternate concentric rings of spring wood and autumn wood; used for estimating age
- Annual rings- not found in coastal regions (as no seasonal variation); irregular or missing in desert; mostly seen in temperate region

Chapter 07

Structural Organisation in Animals

Simple squamous epithelium

- Single layer of flat thin cell.
- Pavement epithelium
- **Function** Exchange of gases, nutrient, filtration.
- **Location** Alveoli, blood capillaries, Bowman's capsule

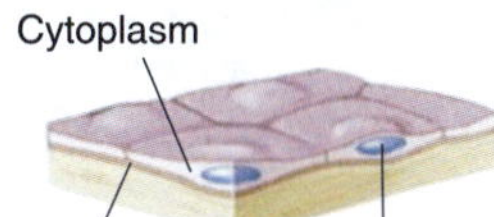

Cuboidal epithelium

- Germinal epithelium cube-shaped cells.
- **Function** Absorption and secretion
- **Location** Small bronchioles (ciliated cuboidal epithelium) and PCT (brush bordered epithelium).

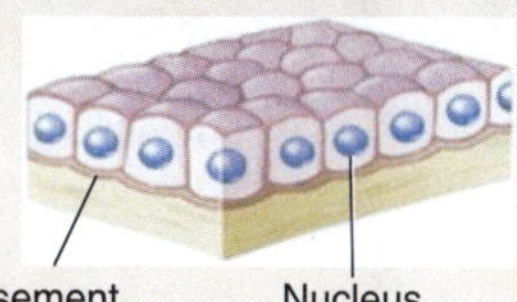

Columnar epithelium

- Lines most organs
- **Function**: Absorption and secretion
- **Location**: Fallopian tube, ependymal cells (ciliated columnar epithelium) and small intestine (brush bordered columnar epithelium)

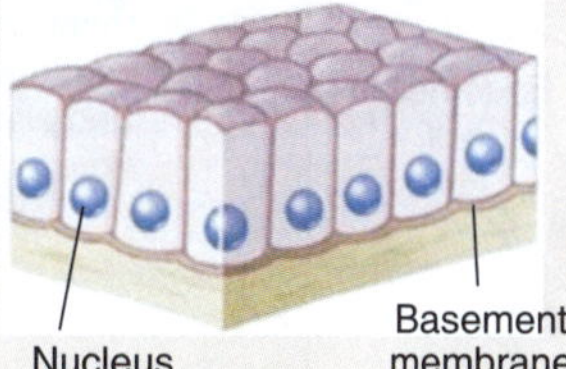

Pseudostratified epithelium

- Single layer of cells with nuclei (different levels)
- **Function** Protection, secretion, etc.
- **Location** Trachea (ciliated pseudostratified) and male urethra (non-ciliated smooth pseudostratified)

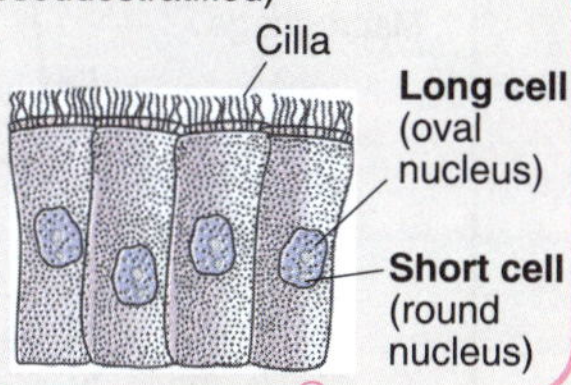

Simple Epithelial Tissue

Glandular epithelium

- Modified cuboidal and columnar cells
- **Function** Secretion
- **Types** - **Basis of number** Unicellular (Goblet cell) and multicellular (salivary gland)
  - **Bases of mode of secretion**: Exocrine (mammary gland), heterocrine (pancreas) and endocrine (hypothalamus)

Epithelial Tissue

Compound Epithelium

Stratified

Keratinised

- Layers of dead cells
- Forms epidermis of skin (land vertebrates)

Non-Keratinised

- Lacks keratin, protection against abrasion
- Lines the buccal cavity,pharynx, oesophagus, etc.

Transitional Epithelium

Keratinised

- Allows organs to expand and stretch
- Lines the urinary bladder, urethra and the ureters

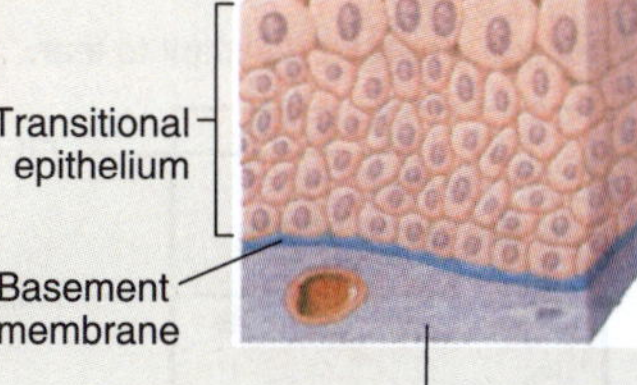

Cell Junction

Gap junction Allows for intercellular communication, e.g., heart, smooth muscle.

Tight junction prevents molecules from passing through intercellular space, e.g., GIT.

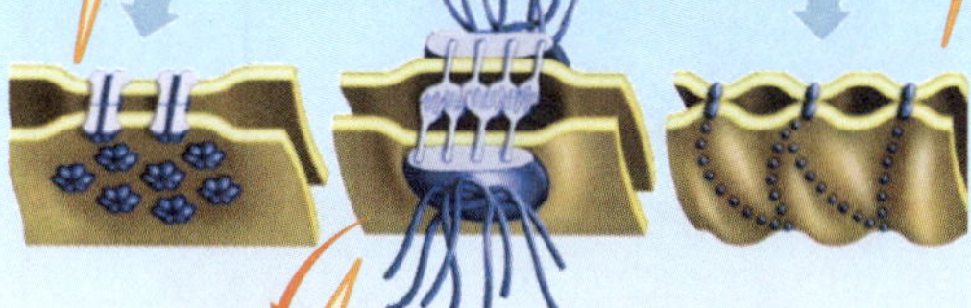

Anchoring junction i.e., desmosomes binds adjacent cell together, e.g., skin.

Connective Tissue (Mesodermal)

Components

Fibres
Collagenous Unbranched and inelastic white fibres
Elastic Branched and elastic yellow fibres

Matrix
Ground substances (Glycoprotein + Hyaluronic acid)

Cells
Fibroblasts, adipose cells, plasma cells, mast cells, macrophages, lymphocytes, etc.

Loose Connective Tissue

Areolar Connective Tissue

- Connects muscle and skin (integuments)
- **Function:** Provide strength, elasticity and support
- **Location:** Present beneath the skin (primarily).

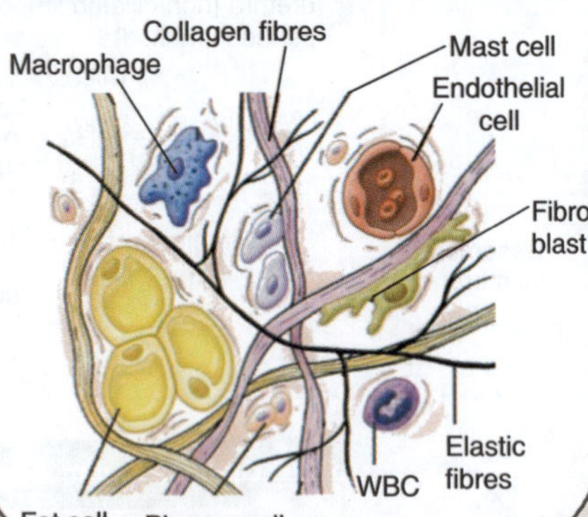

Adipose Connective tissue

- Prevents heat loss and absorbs shock
- **Function** Food reserve of fat depot for storage
- **Types** White fat (large adipose cells) and brown fat (small fat globules)
- **Location** Around heart, kidneys, eyeballs, blubber (whales), hump (camel), etc.

Adipocytes (white adipose cells)

Dense Connective Tissues

Dense regular

- **Two types** White fibrous connective tissue and yellow elastic connective tissue
- **Tendons** Connects skeletal muscle to bone
- **Ligaments** Joints a bone to another bone.
- **Location** Joints between skull, skin, larynx, trachea, etc.
- **Functions** Connects one tissue with another, give strength and elasticity.

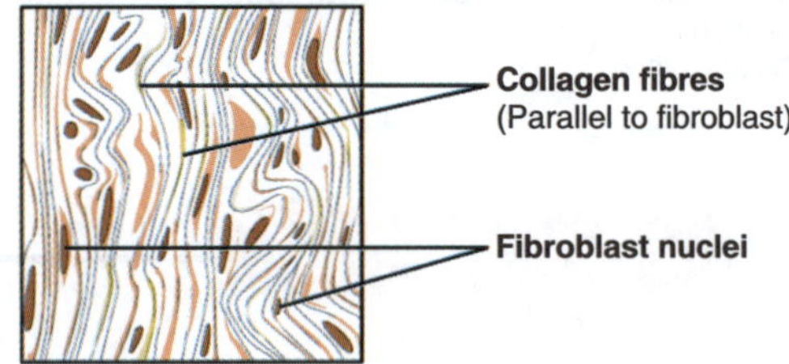

Dense irregular

- Fibroblasts and fibres are oriented differently
- **Location** Dermis of skin
- **Function** Produce strength, resistant to tear.

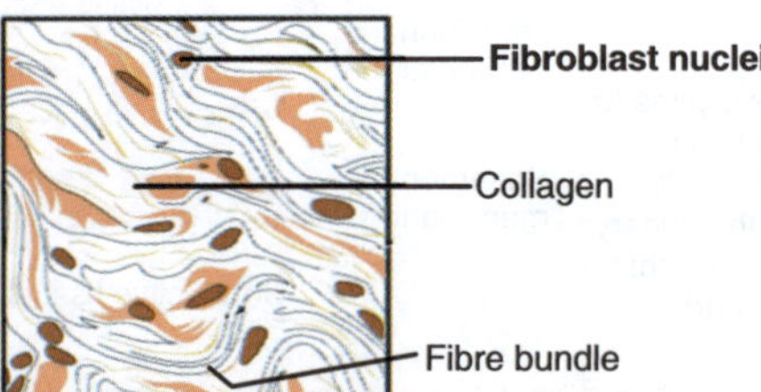

Neural Tissue

Ectodermal in origin, except microgliocytes (mesodermal)

Neurons
- Excitable
- Shows no division (no centriole)
- Consists of cyton, dendrites and axon

Neuroglial cells
- Supporting cell
- Show division
- **Types** Macroglia (astrocytes and oligodendrocytes) and microglia

Ependymal cells
- Lines cavities of brain and central canal of spinal cord
- Bears numerous microvilli and cilia

Neuro-secretory cells
- Secrete neuro-hormones

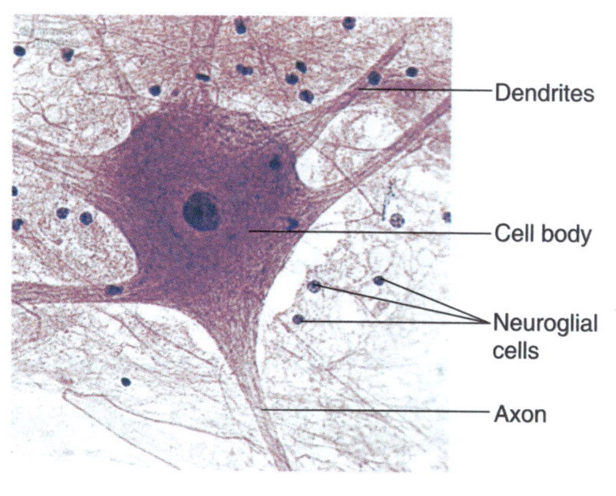

Specialised Connective Tissue

Cartilage

Chondrocyte (cartilage forming cell)
Matrix
Lacuna (fluid filled cavity)
Perichondrium (dense irregular connective tissue)

- Soft skeletal tissue
- **Types** Hyaline, fibrous and calcified

Bone

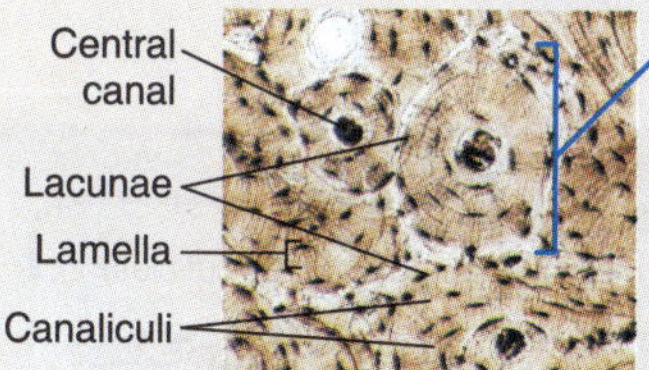

Osteon/Harvesian canal

- Hardest tissue
- Contains periosteum, matrix, endosteum and bone marrow.
- Forms skeletal framework

Blood

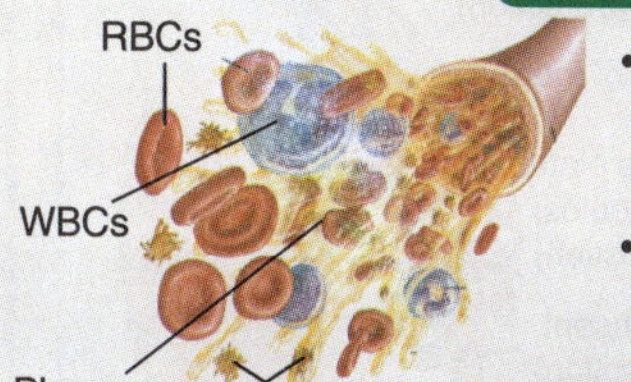

- Fluid connective tissue; composed of plasma, RBC's, WBC's and platelets.
- Transport nutrients and waste products

Lymph
- Extracellular fluid, flows in lymphatic vessels

Muscular Tissue (Mesodermal)

Smooth Muscle Tissue
- Uninucleate; involuntary
- Slow contraction
- Spindle-shaped and unstriped
- **Location** Oesophagus, urinary bladder, etc.

Cardiac Muscle Tissue
- Uninucleate; involuntary
- Rapid contraction
- Cylindrical and striped
- **Location** Walls of heart, pulmonary veins and superior vena cava.

Skeletal Muscle Tissue
- Multinucleate; voluntary
- Very rapid contraction
- Cylindrical and unstriped
- **Location** Limbs, body walls, etc.

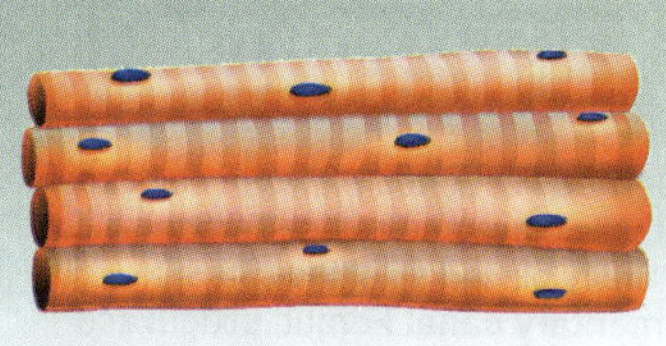

Mouth Region

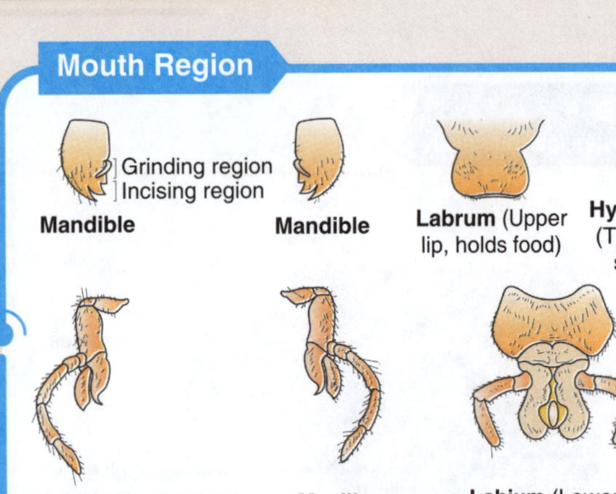

Head Region

Antenna (Olfaction and vibration)

Ocellus (Simple eye, perceives light)

Comound eye (2000 hexagonal-shaped ommatidia, mosaic vision)

Maxilla (a pair)

Mandible (a pair)

Labrum

Labium

Morphology

External Features

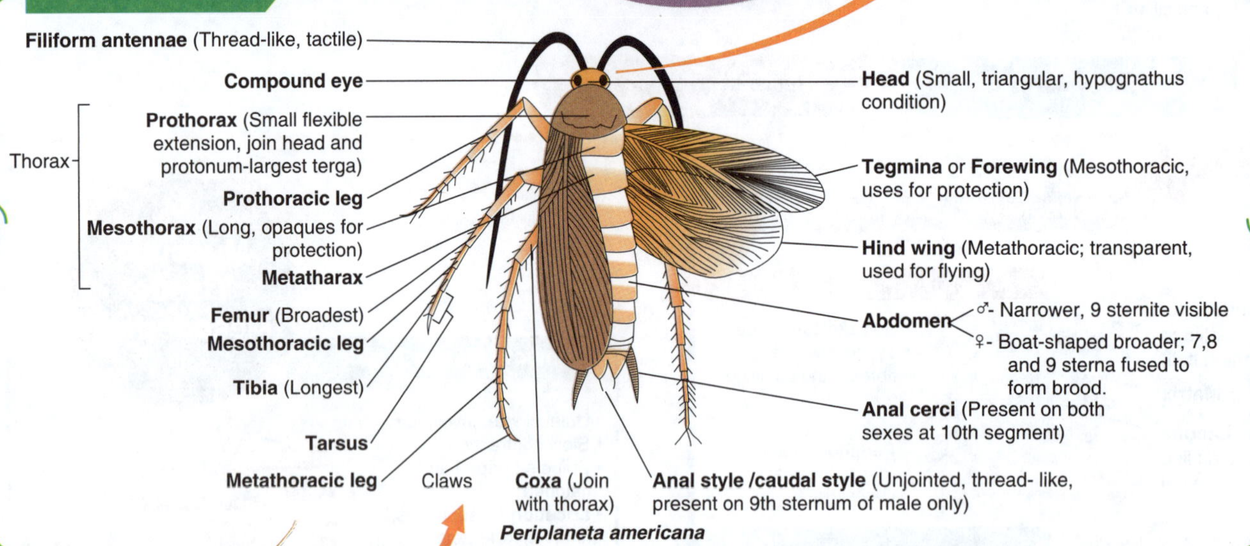

Periplaneta americana

Cockroach

Life Cycle

- Sperms transferred through spermatophores.
- Female produces 9-10 oothecae (encased fertilised 14-16 eggs)
- Nymph grows by 13 times of moulting.

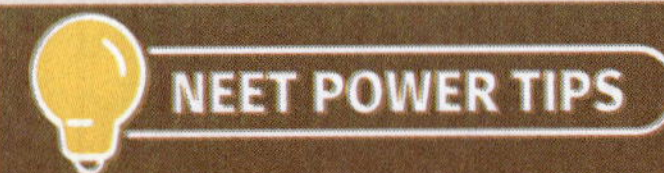

NEET POWER TIPS

- **Sclerites** Hardened plates in each segment
- Dorsally placed sclerites- Tergite
- Ventrally placed sclerites- Sternites

  (Held together by thin and flexible articular membrane-Arthrodial membrane.)
- **Alimentary canal** Forgut, midgut and hindgut.
- Auricular valves gaurd the ostia to prevent blood from flowing backward.

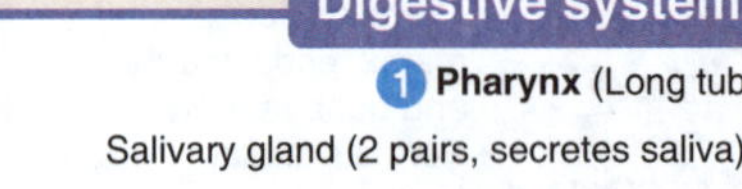

Digestive system

1. **Pharynx** (Long tubule, lined by cuticles)

Salivary gland (2 pairs, secretes saliva)

Salivary reservoir (1 pair, concentrate saliva)

2. **Oesophagus** (Passage for food and lined by cuticle for protection)
3. **Crop** (Storage and softning of food)
4. **Gizzard** (Grinding of food; 6 chitinous plate)
5. **Hepatic caeca** (6-8 blind tubules, produce enzyme for digestion)
6. **Mesenteron or midgut** (Cuticle absent, maximum digestion and absorption)
7. **Malpighian tubules** (100-150 yellow tubules, helps in excretion-uricotelic)
8. (Checks water loss, maximum absorption) Ileum, Colon, Rectum

Reproductive System

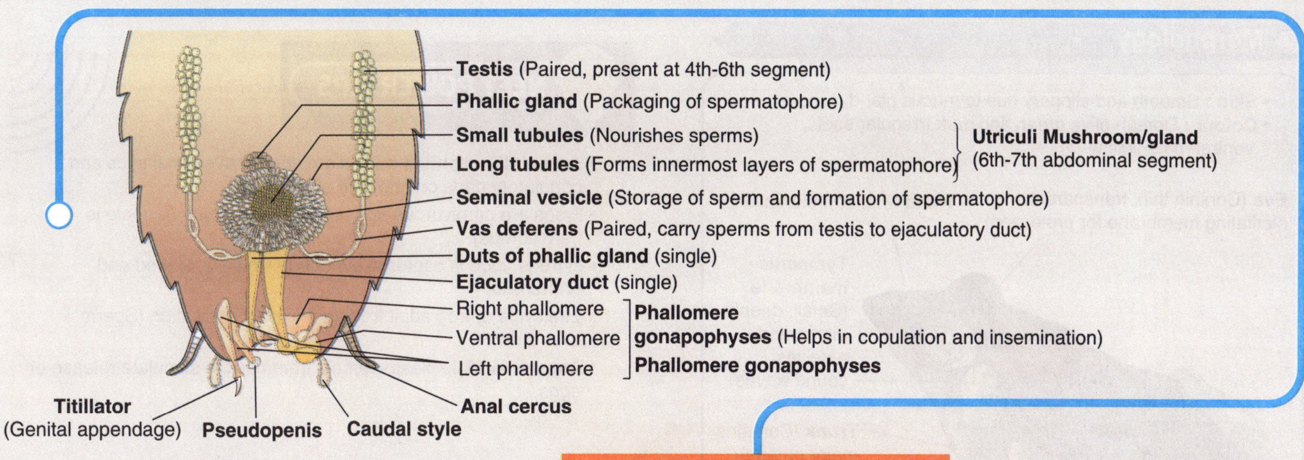

Male Reproductive System

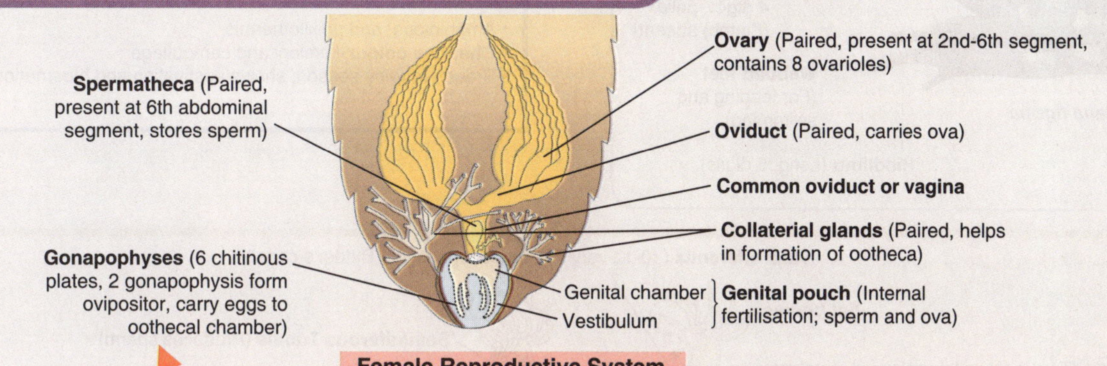

Female Reproductive System

Anatomy of Cockroach

Respiratory system

- **Spiracles** Opening of tracheal tubes, are 10 pairs (2 pair in thorax and 8 pair in abdomen).
- **Longitudinal tracheal trunks** Present all along the length of the body, connects with each other with the help of transverse tracheae and are in pair of three.

Nervous system

- **CNS** Brain, ventral nerve cord, etc.
- **PNS** Nerves originating from brain, sub-oesophageal ganglion, etc.
- **Sympathetic Nervous System** Frontal ganglion, occipital ganglion and Ingluvial ganglion

Excretory System

- **Uricotelic animal** Malpighian tubules (present at junction of midgut and hindgut), fat bodies and nephrocytes (excreta storage) and uricose gland (only in male)

Circulatory System

Blood from sinuses enter heart through ostia.

Anterior aorta

Alary muscles (12 pairs, fan-shaped)

Haemocoel (Contains haemolymph colourless plasma and haemocytes)

13 Chambers of heart (Dorsal side, neurogenic heart)

Morphology

- **Skin :** Smooth and slippery due to mucus gland
- **Colour :** Dorsal- olive green and dark irregular spots, ventral- pale yellow

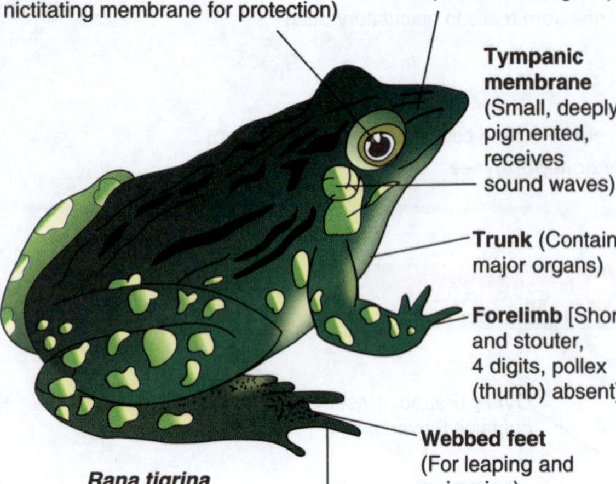

- **Sexual dimorphism** makes are small, have vocal sacs and copulatory pads on first digit of forelimb.
- Frogs are carnivorous and have short intestine (tadpole is herbivorous).
- In frogs, food is captured by tongue which is bilobed and prehensile.

Life cycle of frog adult frog amplexus* Fertilisation (Sperm + ova) tadpole metamorphosis → Adult

* **Amplexus** Male clasps female from back to stimulate release of eggs.

Frog

- Amphibious, and poikilothermic
- **Changes colour**-Mimicry and camouflage
- Breeds in rainy season; shows aestivation and hibernation.

Reproductive System

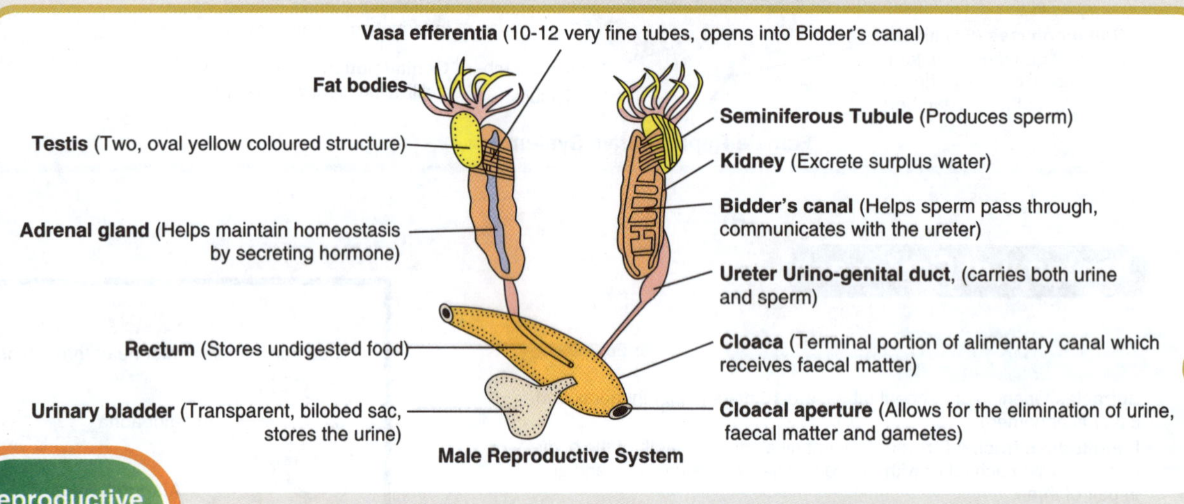

Male Reproductive System

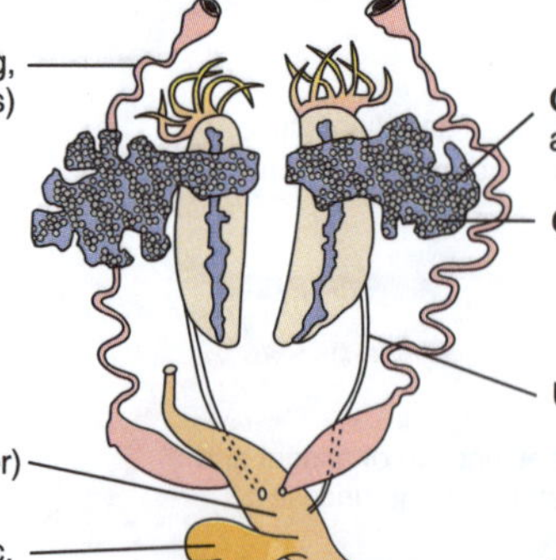

Female Reproductive System

Sense Organs

- **Touch** → Sensory papillae
- **Taste** → Taste bud
- **Smell** → Nasal epithelium
- **Vision** → Eyes (mono-locular vision)
- **Hearing** → Tympanum with internal ear (balancing)

Anatomy

Control and Coordination (Highly evolved)

- **Nervous system**: Central (brain and spinal cord), autonomic (sympathetic and parasympathetic) and peripheral (cranial nerves and spinal)
- **Endocrine glands** Pituitary, thyroid, thymus, parathyroid, adrenal, pineal body and gonads.

Respiratory system

- **Land** Buccal cavity, skin and lungs (pulmonary respiration)
- **Water** -Skin (cutaneous respiration)

Excretory system

- **Ureotelic Animal** Kidney filters blood and excretes waste.
- **Kidney** Compact, dark red bean-like, situated posteriorly, contains around 2000 nephrons/per kidney.

Circulatory system

- **Heart-** 3-chambered, triangular and muscular structure; myogenic (self contractile or auto-excitable)
- **Associated structures-** Sinus venosus and truncus arteriosus
- **Vascular system**
  - **Blood** : Heart, blood and blood vessels
  - **Lymphatic** : Lymph, lymph nodes, etc.
- **Special venous connection**
  - **Hepatic portal system** Liver and intestine
  - **Renal portal system** Kidney and lower body parts

Digestive system

Alimentary canal
Mouth→Buccal cavity and pharynx
↓
Oesophagus → Stomach
Cloaca←Rectum←Intestine

Digestive glands
Gastric glands (gastric juice and HCl)
- Liver- Bile (emulsify fat)
- Gall bladder (stores bile juice)
- Pancreas (pancreatic juice)

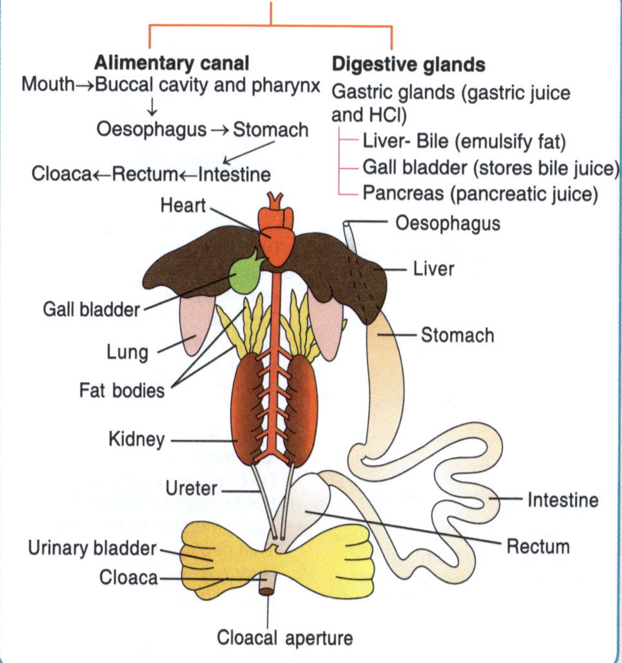

Heart of *Rana tigrina*

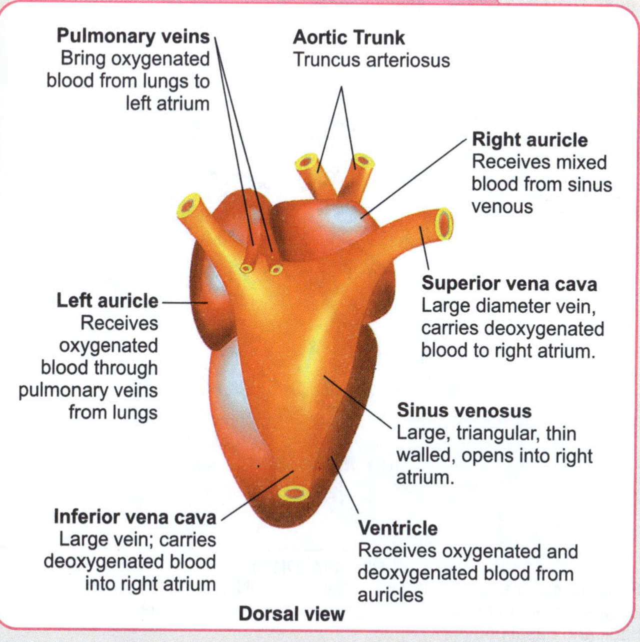

Dorsal view

Chapter 08 Cell : The Unit of Life

Historical Aspect

- **Robert Hooke (1665)** (Discovered cell in bottle cork)
- **Antonie van Leeuwenhoek (1667)** (First saw and described a live cell)
- **Robert Brown (1831)** (Discovered nucleus)

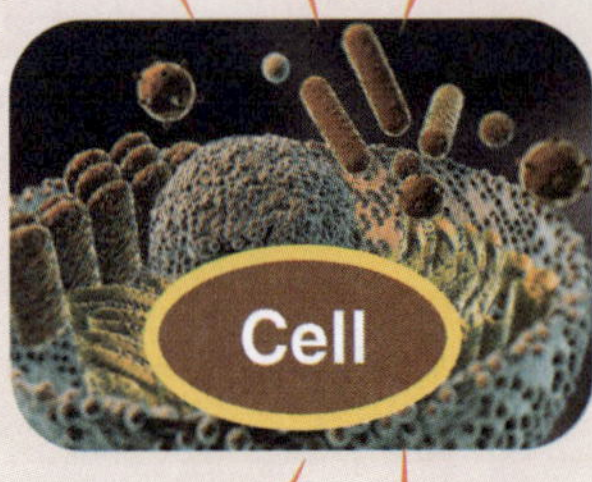

CELL THEORY

Classical Cell Theory
(Schleiden and Schwann, 1838-1839)

- All living organisms are composed of cells and products of cells
- Cell is the basic unit of structure, function and organisation in all organisms.

Addition of New Postulate

Modern Cell Theory
(R. Virchow, 1855)

- All cells, arise from pre-existing cells (*Omnis cellula-e-cellula*)

Shape

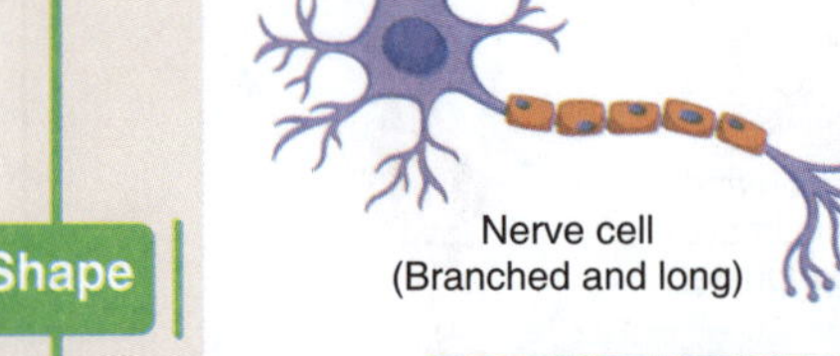
Nerve cell (Branched and long)

RBCs (Round and biconcave)

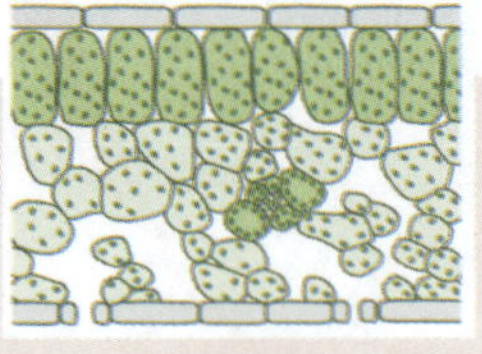
Mesophyll cells (Round and oval)

A tracheid (Elongated)

Size

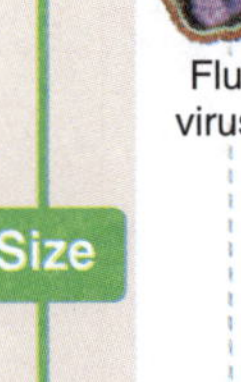

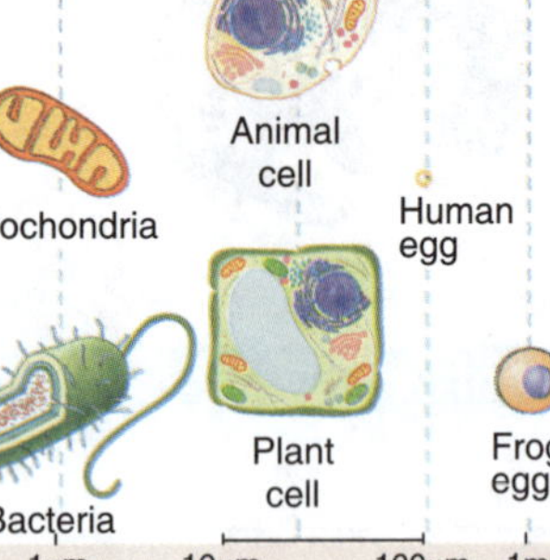

Prokaryotic Cell

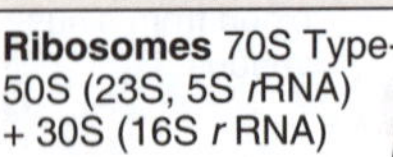

- **Chromosome** (Nucleoid region) naked circular DNA
- **Pili** Elongated tubular structures made of pilin.
- **Ribosomes** 70S Type-50S (23S, 5S *r*RNA) + 30S (16S *r* RNA)
- **Mesosome** Infolding of plasma membrane
- **Inclusion Bodies** Storage forms of reserve materials
- **Glycocalyx** Outermost layer of cell envelope
- **Cell Wall** Middle layer, prevent the bacterium from bursting
- **Plasma Membrane** Inner semi-permeable layer
- **Plasmid (DNA)** Small circular DNA
- **Flagellum** Consists of 3 parts-filament (longest), hook and basal body

NEET POWER TIPS

- Types of bacteria based on Gram staining

Gram-Positive

- Take up Gram stain
- Single-layered cell wall
- Outer membrane absent
- Thick peptidoglycan cell wall layer e.g., *Staphylococcus, S. epidermidis.*

Gram-Negative

- Do not take Gram stain
- Double layered cell wall
- Outer membrane present
- Thin peptidoglycan cell wall layer e.g., *Salmonella providencia.*

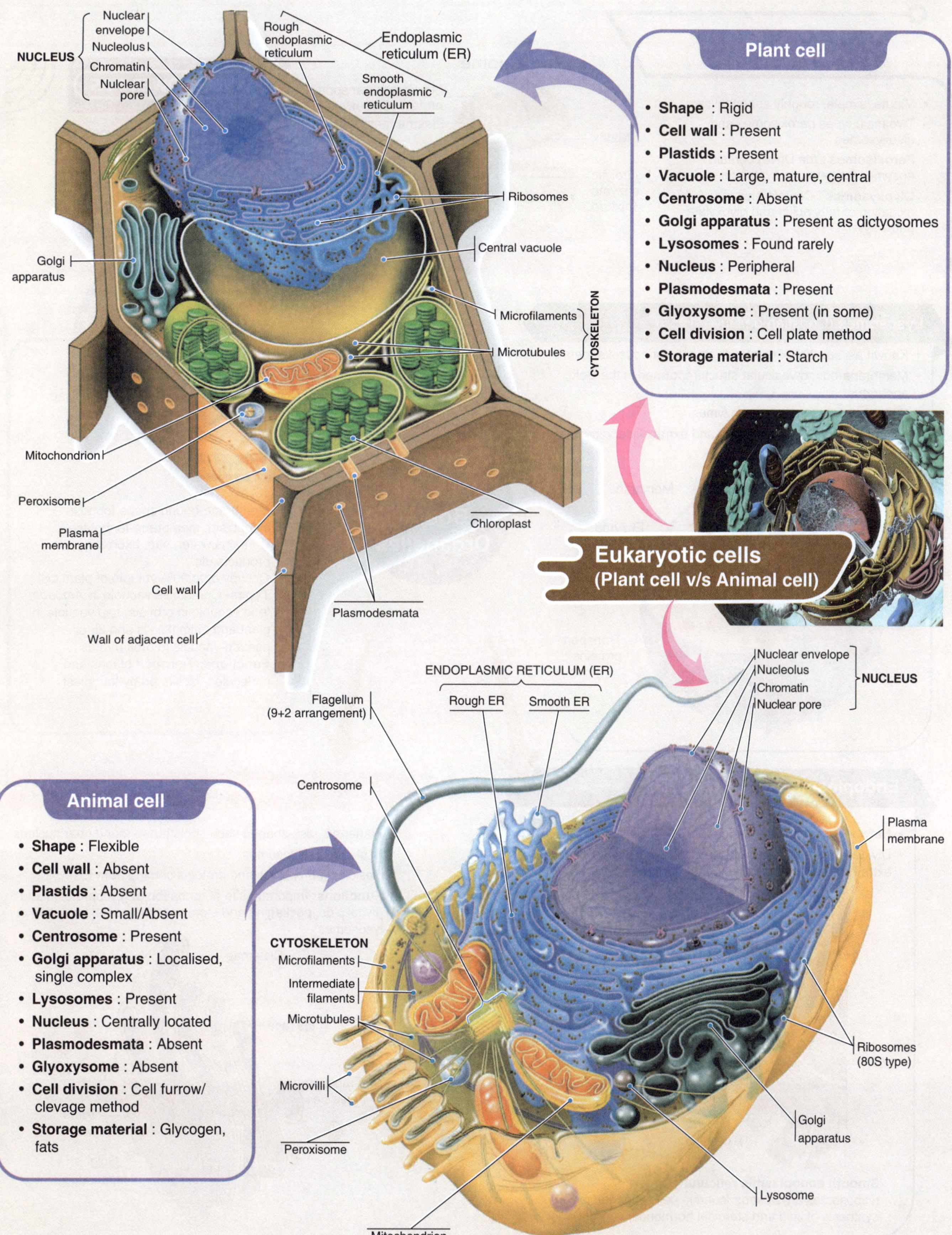
NUCLEUS
Nuclear envelope
Nucleolus
Chromatin
Nuclear pore
Rough endoplasmic reticulum
Endoplasmic reticulum (ER)
Smooth endoplasmic reticulum
Ribosomes
Golgi apparatus
Central vacuole
Microfilaments
Microtubules
CYTOSKELETON
Mitochondrion
Peroxisome
Plasma membrane
Cell wall
Wall of adjacent cell
Plasmodesmata
Chloroplast
Plant cell
• Shape : Rigid
• Cell wall : Present
• Plastids : Present
• Vacuole : Large, mature, central
• Centrosome : Absent
• Golgi apparatus : Present as dictyosomes
• Lysosomes : Found rarely
• Nucleus : Peripheral
• Plasmodesmata : Present
• Glyoxysome : Present (in some)
• Cell division : Cell plate method
• Storage material : Starch
Eukaryotic cells
(Plant cell v/s Animal cell)
ENDOPLASMIC RETICULUM (ER)
Rough ER
Smooth ER
Flagellum (9+2 arrangement)
Centrosome
Nuclear envelope
Nucleolus
Chromatin
Nuclear pore
NUCLEUS
Plasma membrane
Animal cell
• Shape : Flexible
• Cell wall : Absent
• Plastids : Absent
• Vacuole : Small/Absent
• Centrosome : Present
• Golgi apparatus : Localised, single complex
• Lysosomes : Present
• Nucleus : Centrally located
• Plasmodesmata : Absent
• Glyoxysome : Absent
• Cell division : Cell furrow/ clevage method
• Storage material : Glycogen, fats
CYTOSKELETON
Microfilaments
Intermediate filaments
Microtubules
Microvilli
Peroxisome
Mitochondrion
Ribosomes (80S type)
Golgi apparatus
Lysosome

Single Membrane Bound Organelles

Microbodies

- Minute, simple, roughly spherical sac
- Two main types peroxisomes and glyoxysomes
- **Peroxisomes** : (de Duve) contain enzymes for peroxide synthesis
- **Glyoxysomes** : Contain enzymes for β-oxidation of fatty acids and glyoxylate pathway.

Peroxisome

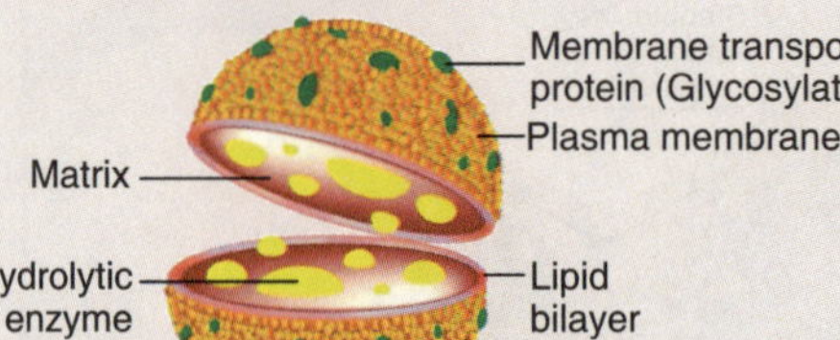

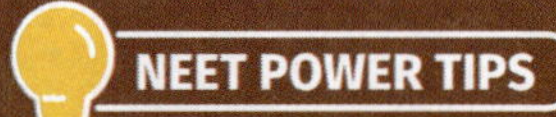

- Lysosomes help in secretion of thyroid hormones.
- Sperms lysins are lysosomal enzymes.

Lysosomes (Christian de Duve, 1955)

- Known as 'suicidal bags of cell' or 'cellular housekeepers'.
- Membrane-bound vesicular structure formed in the Golgi apparatus
- Rich in all types hydrolytic enzymes
- **Function:** Helps in intracellular and extracellular digestion.

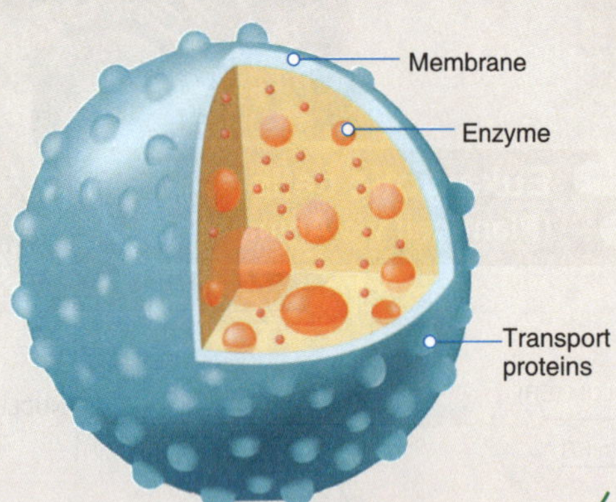

Vacuole

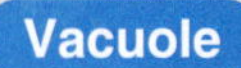

- Membrane-bound space found in cytoplasm; membrane-tonoplast
- Contains water, sap, excretory products etc.
- Occupy upto 90% volume of plant cell
- **Types-** Contractile vacuole in *Amoeba*, food vacuole in protists, sap vacuole in plant and animal cells and air or pseudo-vacuole in prokaryotes
- **Functions:** Transport of ions and molecules, facilitated by tonoplast

Endoplasmic Reticulum (ER)

- Network of tiny tubular structures
- Divides the intracellular space into luminal (inside ER) and extra luminal (cytoplasm) compartments

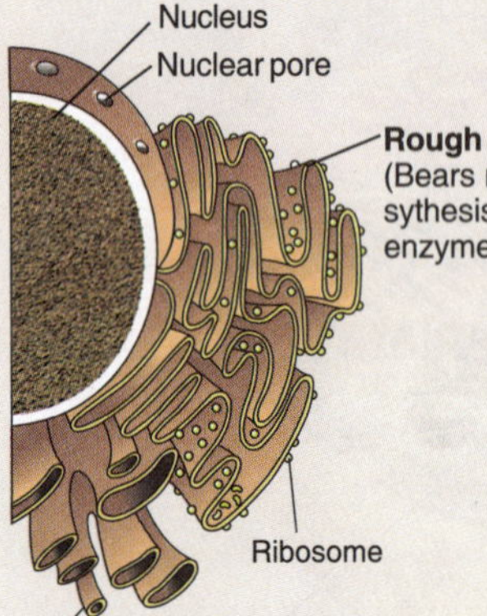

Golgi Apparatus (Camillo Golgi, 1898)

- Flattened, disc-shaped sacs or cisternae found near nucleus
- In plants- 'dictyosomes'
- Vesicles (carry lipids and proteins coming from ER).
- **Functions:** Important site of formation of glycoproteins and glycolipids, packaging and storage of materials, formation of lysosomes

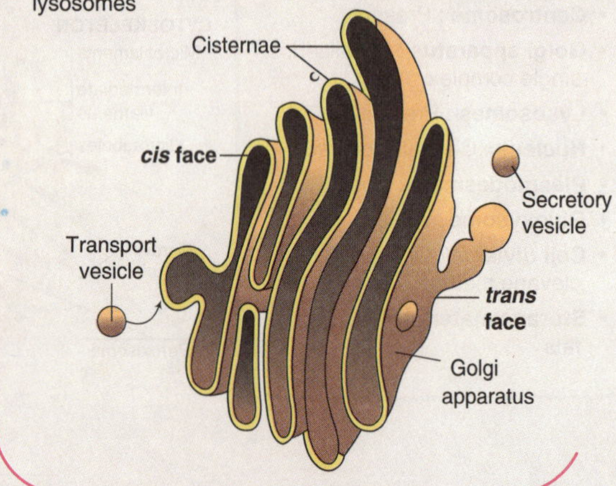

Mitochondria (Powerhouse of the Cell)

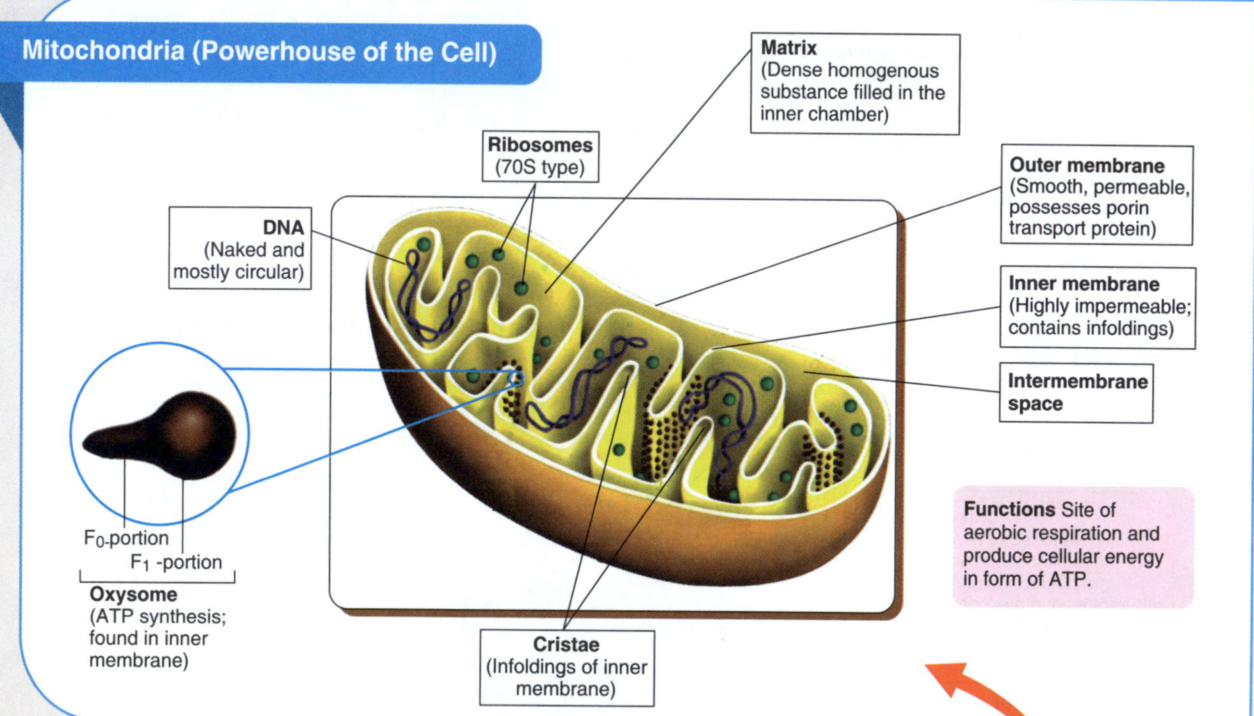

Functions Site of aerobic respiration and produce cellular energy in form of ATP.

Double Membrane Bound Organelles

Plastids

- Found in all plant cells and in euglenoids
- Based on the pigments, classified into 3 types:
  - **Chloroplast** (Contains chlorophyll and carotenoids)
  - **Chromoplast** (Contains fat soluble carotenoid pigments like carotene, xanthophyll, etc.)
  - **Leucoplast** (Colourless plastids with stored nutrients)
- **Chloroplasts** Mostly found in the mesophyll cells of leaves; semi-autonomous organelle
- **Function of chloroplast** Photosynthesis

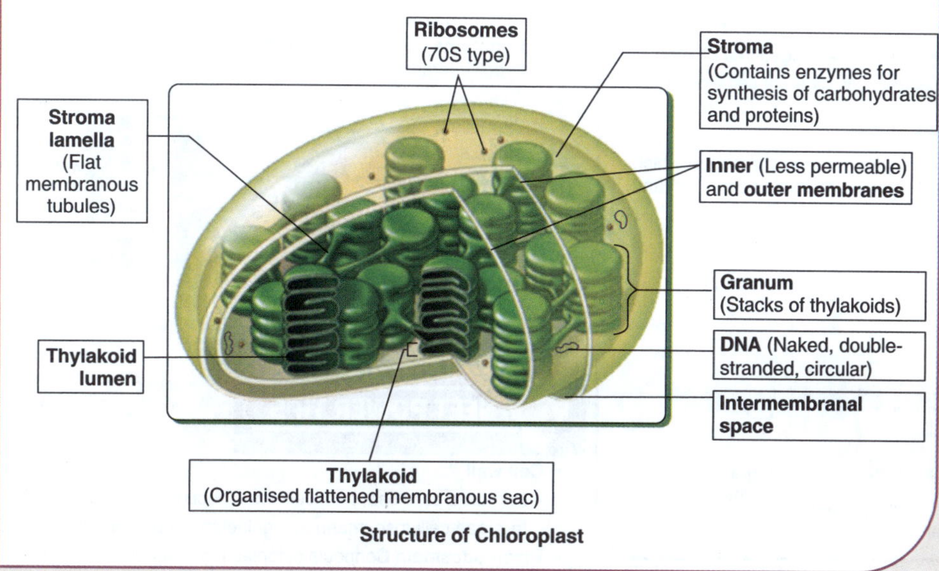

Structure of Chloroplast

NEET POWER TIPS

- Mitochondria divides by binary fission
- Both mitochondria and plastids are **semi-autonomous** as they contain their own DNA and can replicate independently.
- Leucoplasts are of three types
  - **Amyloplasts**-Store carbohydrates
  - **Elaioplasts**-Store oils and fats
  - **Aleuroplasts**-Store proteins

Chromosome

Satellite

Secondary constriction

One chromatid

Centromere (Primary constriction)

Spindle fibres

Kinetochore (Disc-shaped; connects chromosomes to microtubules)

Sister chromatids

Structure

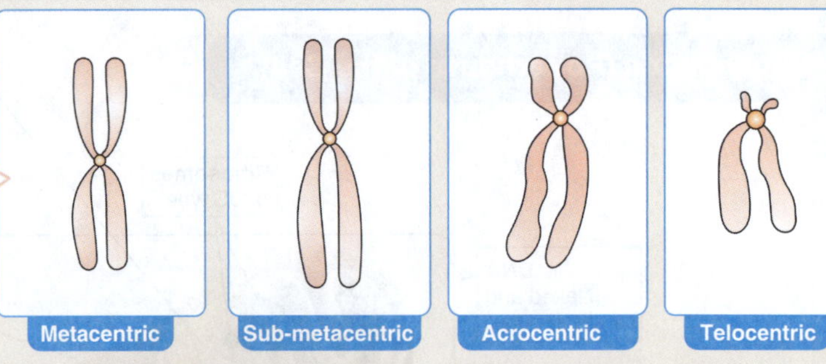

Types on the basis of centromere position

Nucleus (Robert Brown, 1831)

Perinuclear space (Space between two nuclear membranes)

Chromatin (Named by Flemming) Loose and indistinct network of nucleoprotein fibres, differentiated into euchromatin and hetero chromatin

Nucleolus (Pl. nucleoli) Spherical structure that houses the ribosomal machinery

Nucleoplasm Transparent, semifluid nuclear matrix

Nuclear Pores Control transport of molecules between cytoplasm and nucleus

Outer envelope (continuous with RER)

Inner envelope

Cisternae

- Controlling centre
- **Functions** Houses genetic materials, produces *m*RNA production of ribosomes (nucleolus)

Cell Coverings

Cell Membrane

- Composed of lipids and proteins, phospholipids arranged in a bilayer.
- Ratio of protein and lipids varies considerably in different cell types (e.g., RBCs-52% protein and 40% lipids).
- Widely accepted model - **Fluid Mosaic Model**.
- **Functions** Selectively permeable; helps in of molecules transport which occurs by-passive transport (diffusion, osmosis, facilitated diffusion) and active transport.

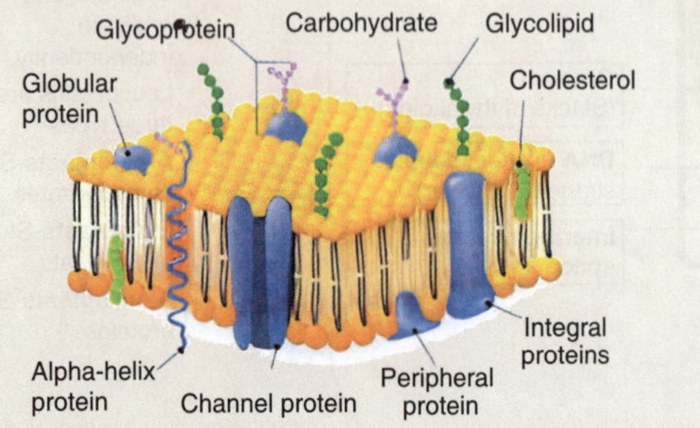

CELL WALL

- Non-living rigid structure; metabolically active and capable of growth.
- **Plasmodesmata** Connects cytoplasm of neighbouring cells.
- **Functions** Gives shape to cell, provides protection, help in cell to cell interaction.

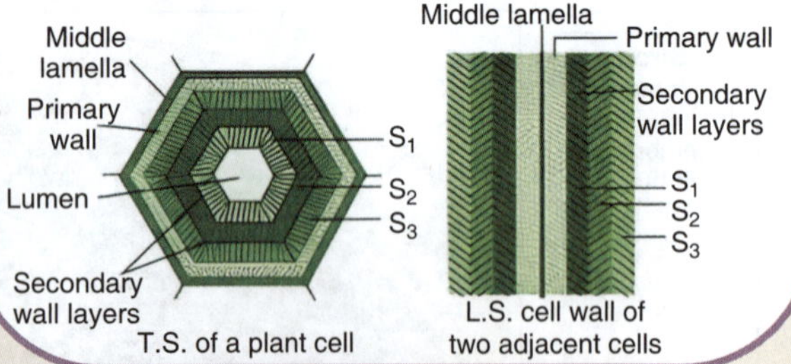

- **Cell wall**
  - **In plants** cellulose, hemicellulose, pectins, proteins
  - **In algae** cellulose, mannans, galactans and minerals like $CaCO_3$
- **Plasmodesmata** Connects cytoplasm of neighbouring cells.

Cytoskeleton

- Network of proteinaceous filaments

Microtubules
Unbranched; made up of α-tubulin, β-tubulin proteins

Intermediate filaments
Often form a network; made up of several proteins

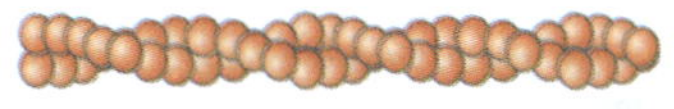

Microfilaments Unbranched; made up of actin proteins

- **Functions** Mechanical support, motility, maintenance of shape of the cell.

Cilia and Flagella

- Hair-like outgrowths of cell membrane
- Emerge from centriole like structure, basal bodies.
- Core-axoneme. 9+2 arrangement of microtubules.
- Cilia work like oars, smaller than flagella
- **Functions** Locomotion and movement

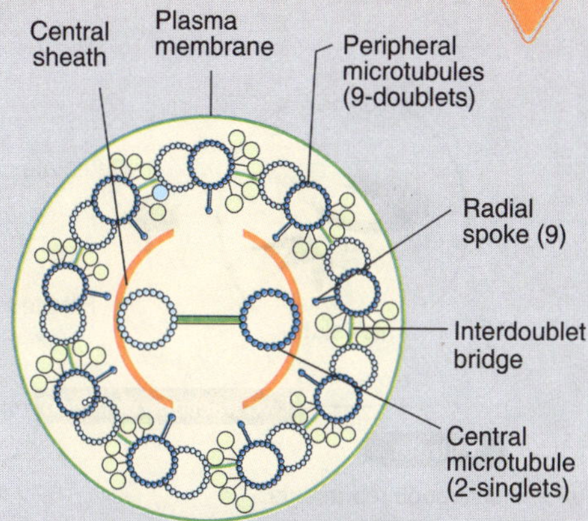

Diagrammatic representation of internal structure of cilia and flagella

Ribosomes (George Palade, 1953)

- Granular structures composed of RNA and proteins
- **Functions:** Site of protein synthesis (Protein factory) and of interaction between *t*RNA-amino acid complex and *m*RNA.

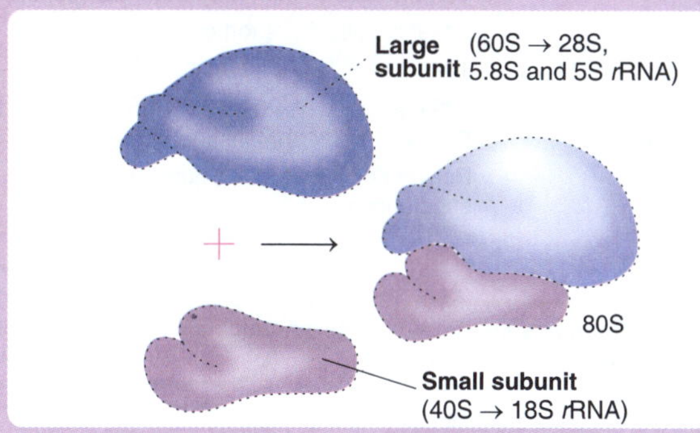

Non-Membrane Bound Organells

Centrosome and Centrioles

Cart-wheel structure
Massule or pericentriolar satellite
Connetive
Triplet fibril (peripheral tubulin proteins)
X
Y
A
B
C
Central rod (Hub)
9 radial spokes
Centrioles (lie perpendicular to each other)

9+0 structure of centriole

- 1 centrosome-2 cylindrical centrioles
- Surrounded by amorphous pericentriolar materials
- **Functions:** Form the basal body of cilia and flagella that give rise to spindle apparatus during cell division in animal cells

NEET POWER TIPS

Ribosomes

- S refers to Svedberg unit of sedimentation coefficient.
- Two spatially separated populations of ribosomes in cytosol are membane bound (RER) and free ribosomes.

Comparative account

Features	Prokaryotes	Eukaryotes
Size	Mostly 0.1 to 5 μm	Mostly 10-100 μm
Cell wall	Present in most (peptidoglycan), but not in all cells	Present in plant (cellulosic) and fungal cells (chitinous)
Nucleus	Absence of well-defined nucleus; nucleoid present	Presence of well-defined nucleus
Cellular Organelles	Not membrane-bound	Membrane-bound except ribosome, centrioles, etc.

Chapter 09 Biomolecules

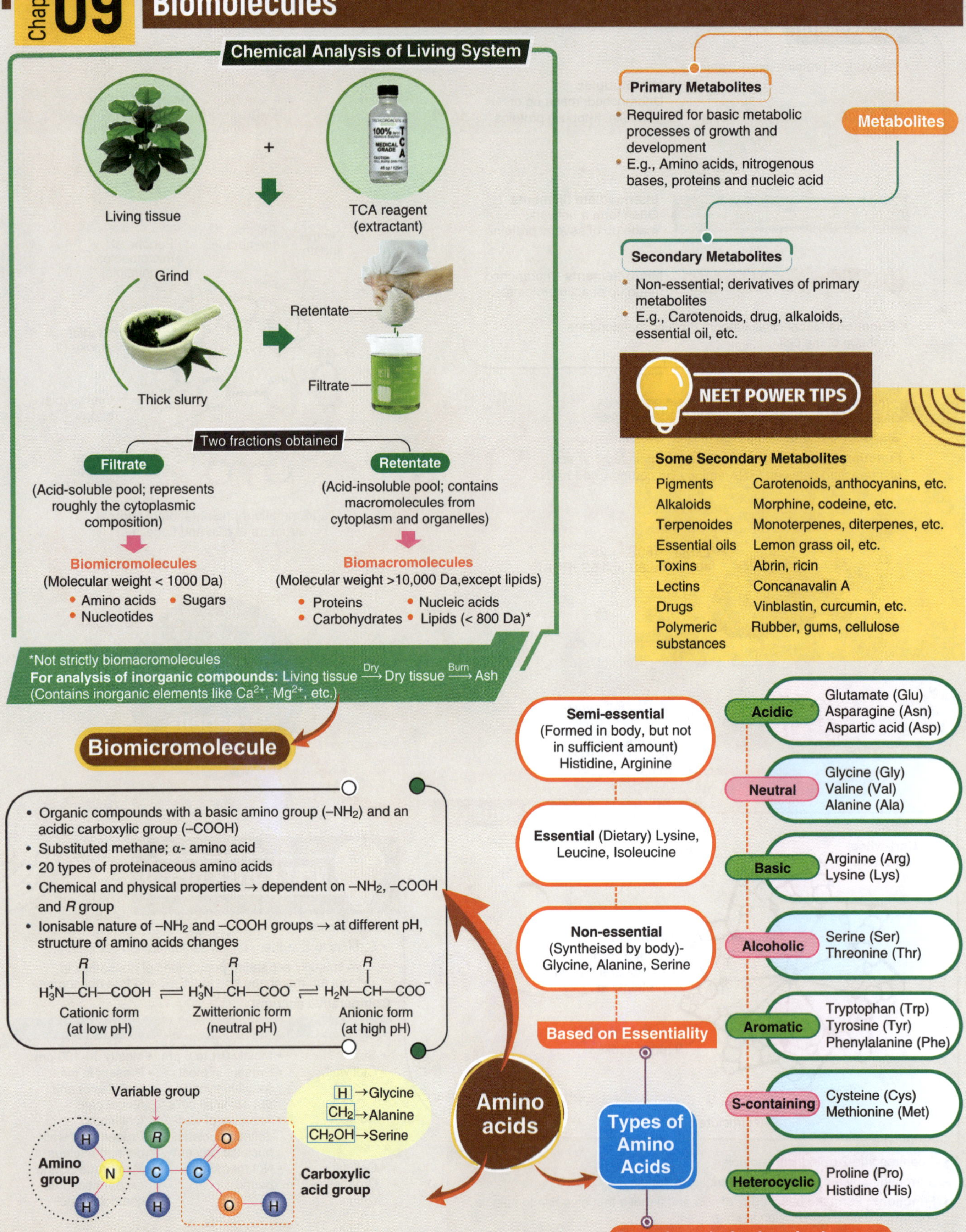

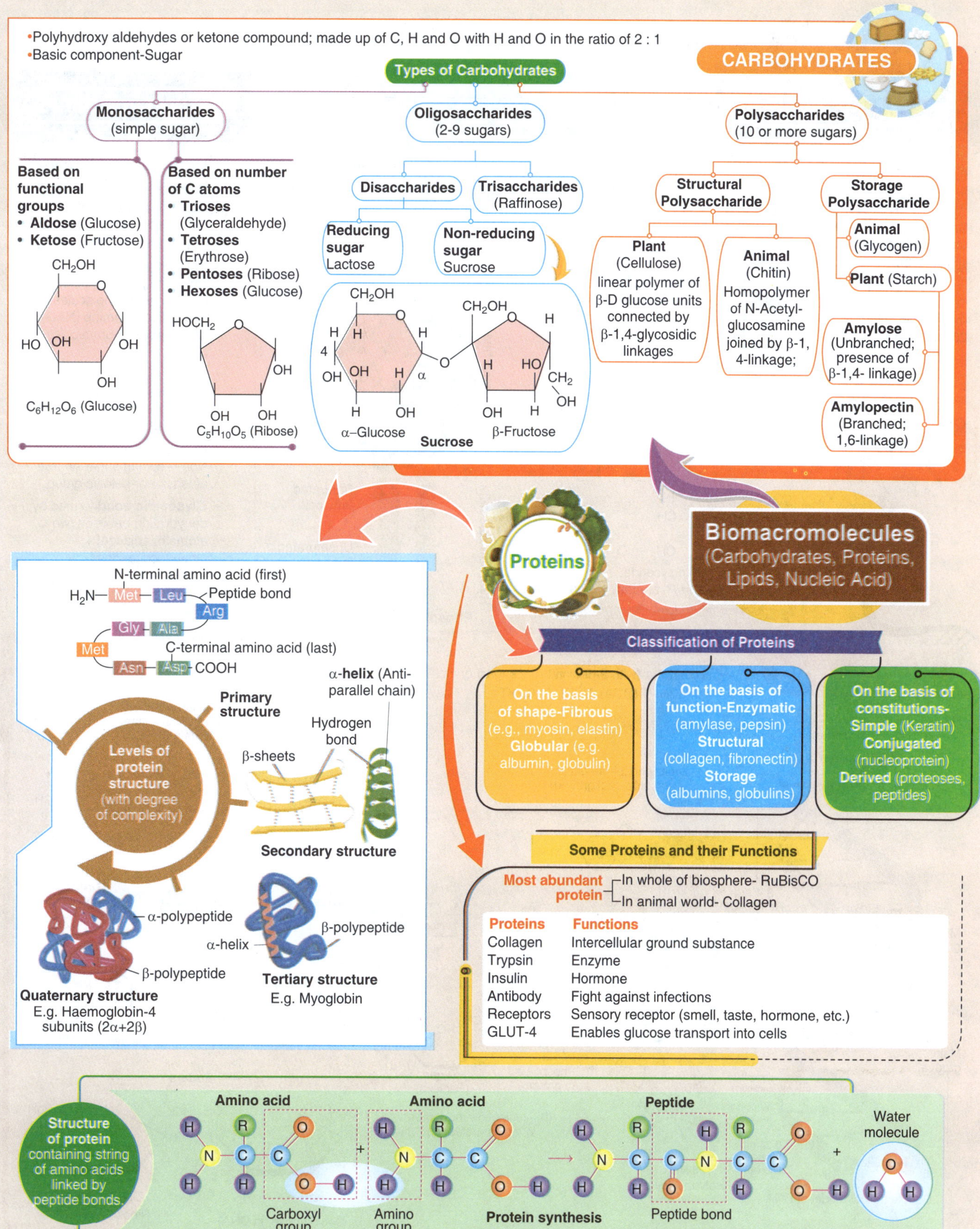

Proteins	Functions
Collagen	Intercellular ground substance
Trypsin	Enzyme
Insulin	Hormone
Antibody	Fight against infections
Receptors	Sensory receptor (smell, taste, hormone, etc.)
GLUT-4	Enables glucose transport into cells

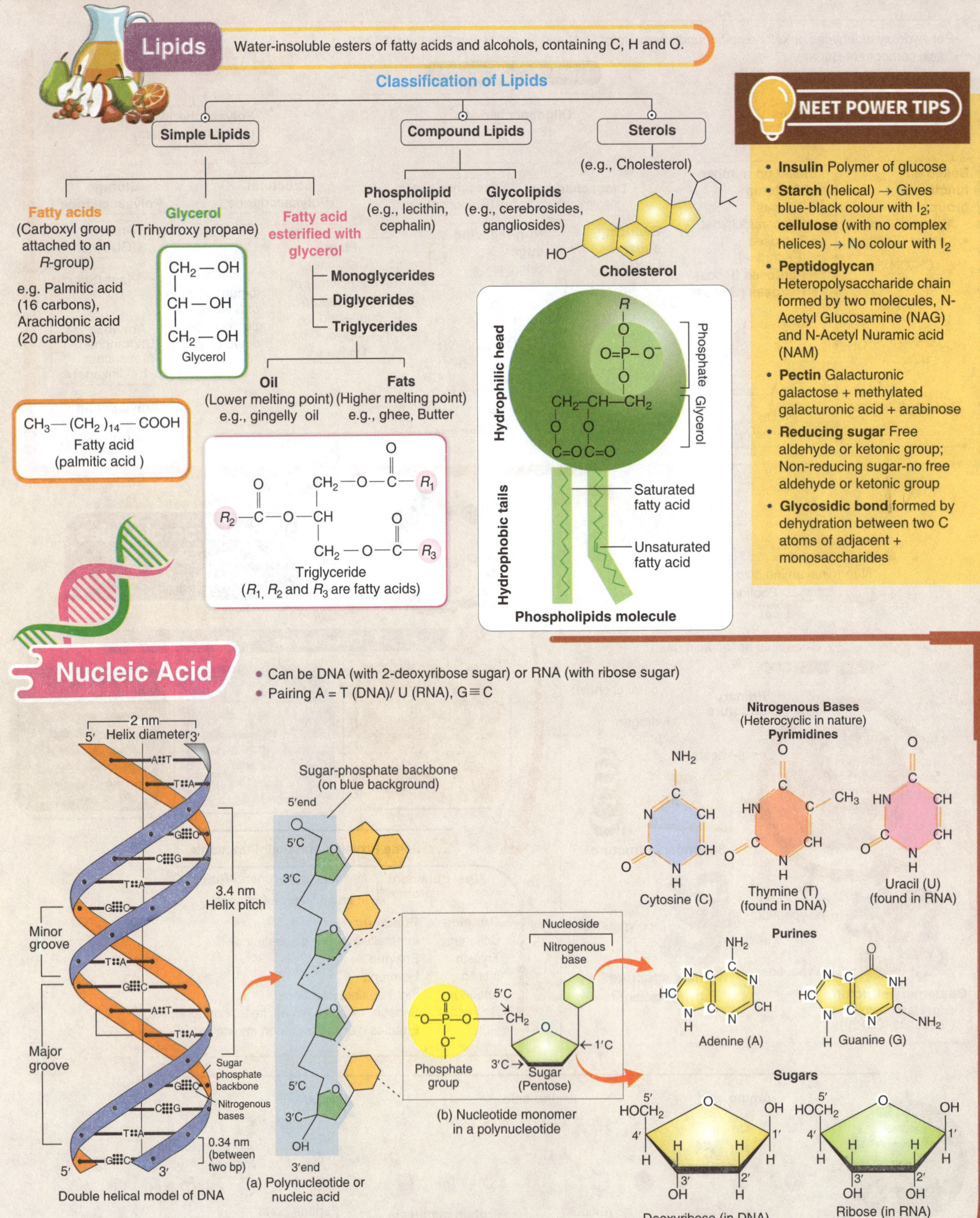
Lipids
Water-insoluble esters of fatty acids and alcohols, containing C, H and O.
Classification of Lipids
Simple Lipids
Compound Lipids
Sterols
(e.g., Cholesterol)
Fatty acids
(Carboxyl group attached to an R-group)
e.g. Palmitic acid (16 carbons), Arachidonic acid (20 carbons)
Glycerol
(Trihydroxy propane)
CH2 — OH
CH — OH
CH2 — OH
Glycerol
Fatty acid esterified with glycerol
Monoglycerides
Diglycerides
Triglycerides
Oil
(Lower melting point)
e.g., gingelly oil
Fats
(Higher melting point)
e.g., ghee, Butter
CH3—(CH2)14—COOH
Fatty acid
(palmitic acid)
Triglyceride
(R1, R2 and R3 are fatty acids)
Phospholipid
(e.g., lecithin, cephalin)
Glycolipids
(e.g., cerebrosides, gangliosides)
HO
Cholesterol
Hydrophilic head
Phosphate
Glycerol
Hydrophobic tails
Saturated fatty acid
Unsaturated fatty acid
Phospholipids molecule
NEET POWER TIPS
• Insulin Polymer of glucose
• Starch (helical) → Gives blue-black colour with I2; cellulose (with no complex helices) → No colour with I2
• Peptidoglycan Heteropolysaccharide chain formed by two molecules, N-Acetyl Glucosamine (NAG) and N-Acetyl Nuramic acid (NAM)
• Pectin Galacturonic galactose + methylated galacturonic acid + arabinose
• Reducing sugar Free aldehyde or ketonic group; Non-reducing sugar-no free aldehyde or ketonic group
• Glycosidic bond formed by dehydration between two C atoms of adjacent + monosaccharides
Nucleic Acid
• Can be DNA (with 2-deoxyribose sugar) or RNA (with ribose sugar)
• Pairing A = T (DNA)/ U (RNA), G≡C
2 nm
Helix diameter
3.4 nm
Helix pitch
Minor groove
Major groove
Sugar phosphate backbone
Nitrogenous bases
0.34 nm (between two bp)
Double helical model of DNA
Sugar-phosphate backbone (on blue background)
5′end
3′end
(a) Polynucleotide or nucleic acid
Nucleoside
Nitrogenous base
Phosphate group
Sugar (Pentose)
(b) Nucleotide monomer in a polynucleotide
Nitrogenous Bases
(Heterocyclic in nature)
Pyrimidines
Cytosine (C)
Thymine (T) (found in DNA)
Uracil (U) (found in RNA)
Purines
Adenine (A)
Guanine (G)
Sugars
Deoxyribose (in DNA)
Ribose (in RNA)
(c) Nucleoside components nitrogenous bases
Components of a nucleic acid

Types of Enzymes

Simple Enzymes E.g., Amylase, pepsin and trypsin

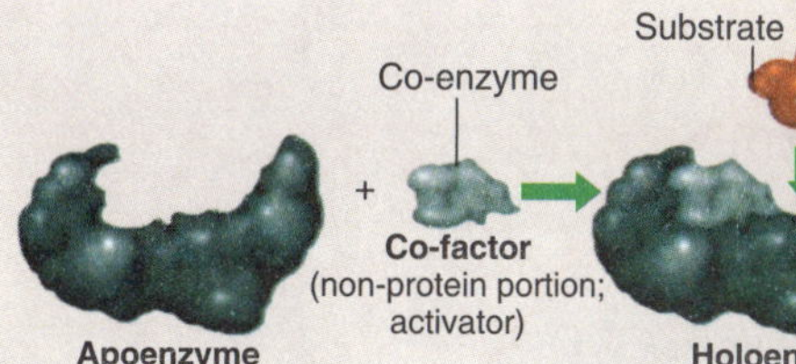

Sturucture of a Conjugated Enzyme

Conjugated Enzymes

- **Protein part** → Apoenzyme
- **Non-protein part** → Co-factor

Prosthetic groups
- Organic; tightly bound to apoenzyme
- E.g., Haem in peroxidase and catalase

Co-enzymes
- Organic; transient binding to apoenzyme
- E.g., Co-enzyme NAD and NADP (contains vitamin niacin)

Metal ions
- Inorganic; forms coordination bonds with side chains at active site and substrate
- E.g. Zn-enzyme carboxypeptidase

Enzyme Action

1. Entry of substrates into active site.
2. Substrates being held in the active site by weak interactions, such as H bonds and ionic bonds.
3. The active site lowers the activation energy and speeds up the reaction
4. Conversion of substrates to products.
5. Release of products
6. Active site becomes available for new substrate molecules.

Enzyme-substrate complex (E-S)

Enzyme product complex (E-P)

Products

Catalytic cycle of an enzyme

TRANSITION STATE

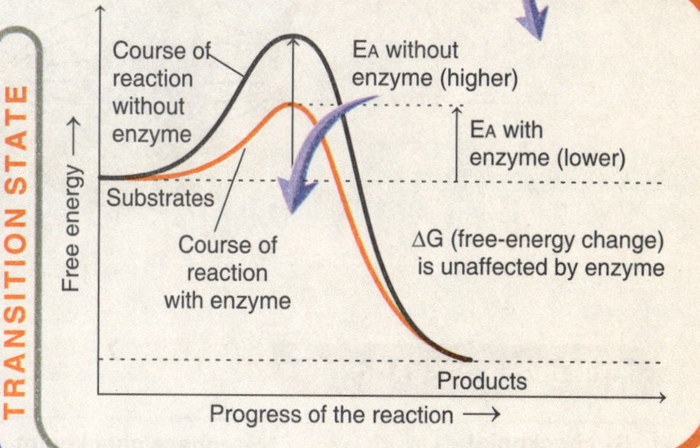

Type of Enzyme Inhibition

Competitive inhibition
Inhibitor mimics the substrate, competing for the active site; e.g inhibition of succinic dehydrogenase by malonate.

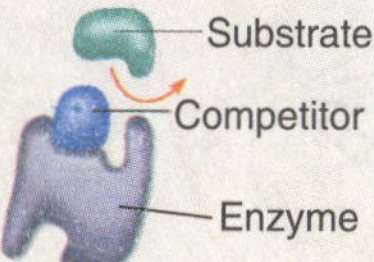

Non-competitive inhibition
Inhibitor binds to the enzyme away from the active site, altering the shape of the enzyme; e.g., binding of cyanide to cytochrome oxidiase

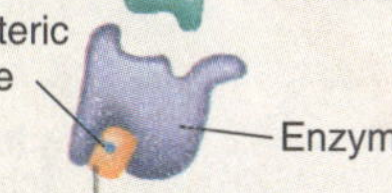

NEET POWER TIPS

- Enzymes are biocatalyst; influencing speed of biochemical reactions without taking part in it
- Almost all enzymes-proteinaceous in nature (exception-Ribozyme, i.e., a RNA molecule)

Classification of Enzymes

1. **Oxidoreductases /dehydrogenases**	S(reduced)+S′(oxidised) → S(oxidised) + S′(reduced)
2. **Transferases**	Transfer of group; S — G + S′ → S + S′ — G
3. **Hydrolases**	Catalyses hydrolysis of ester, ether, peptide, glycosidic, C-C, C-halide or P-N bonds
4. **Lyases**	Catalyses removal of groups from substrate X — C — C — Y → X — Y + C = C
5. **Isomerases**	Catalyses inter-conversion of optical, geometric or positional isomers
6. **Ligases**	Join two substrate molecule C—O, C—S, C—N, P—O, etc.

Factors Affecting Enzyme Activity

pH (Optimum pH; maximum activity)

Temperature (Optimum temperature; maximum activity)

Substrate concentration (Increase in [S] increases velocity of enzymes upto a limit)

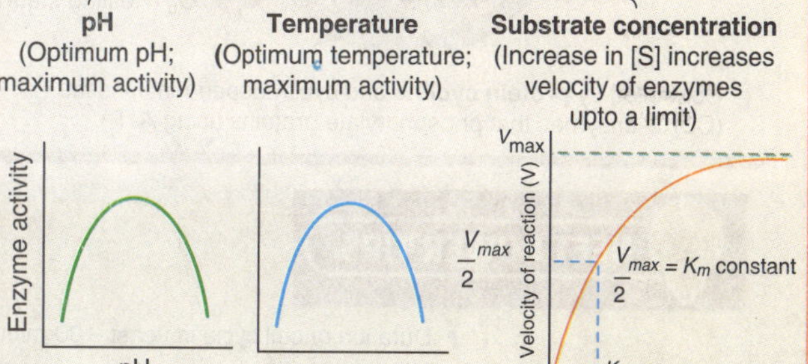

Chapter 10 Cell Cycle and Cell Division

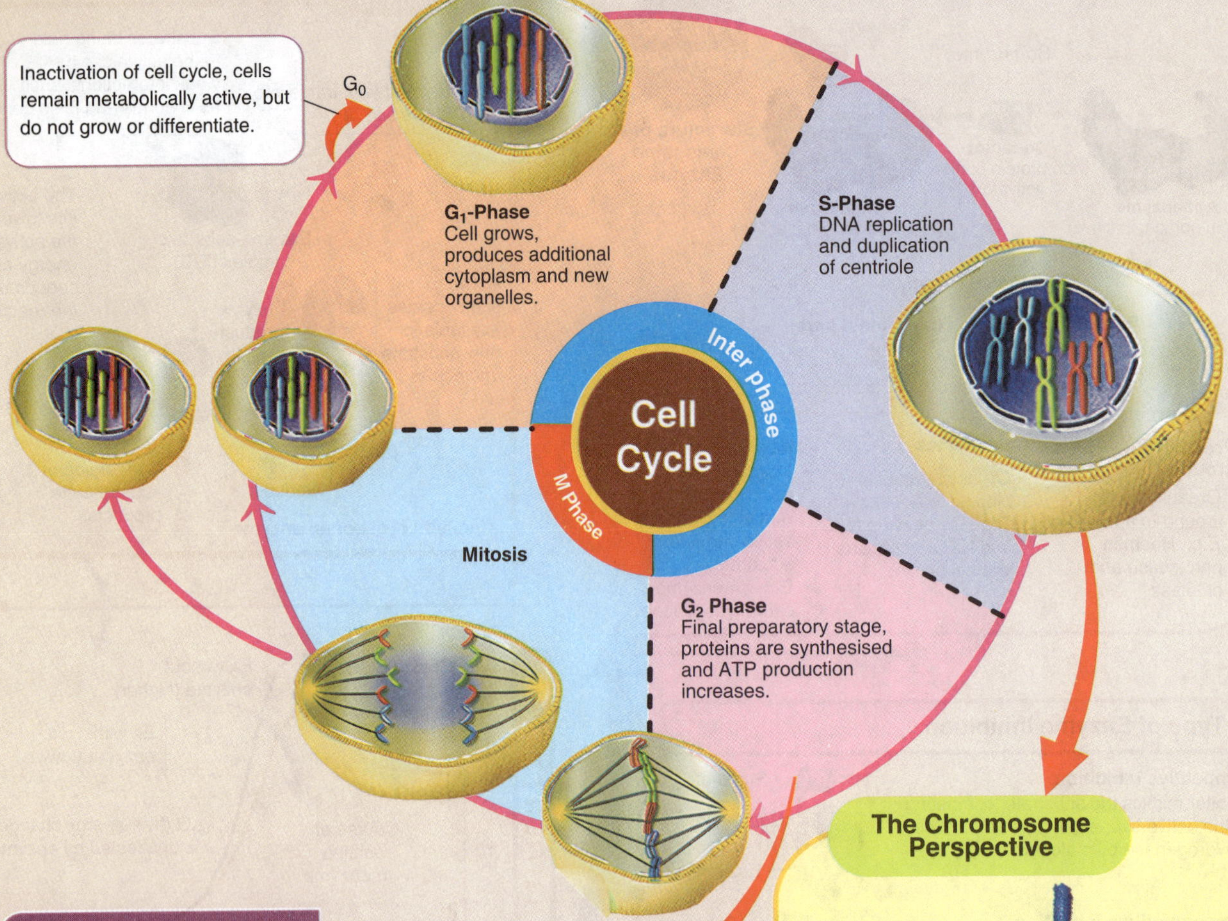

Inactivation of cell cycle, cells remain metabolically active, but do not grow or differentiate.

G_0

G_1-Phase
Cell grows, produces additional cytoplasm and new organelles.

S-Phase
DNA replication and duplication of centriole

Cell Cycle

Inter phase

M Phase

Mitosis

G_2 Phase
Final preparatory stage, proteins are synthesised and ATP production increases.

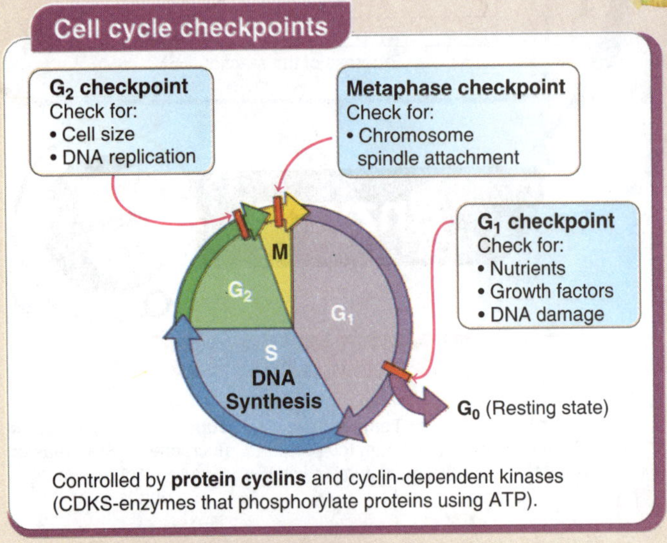

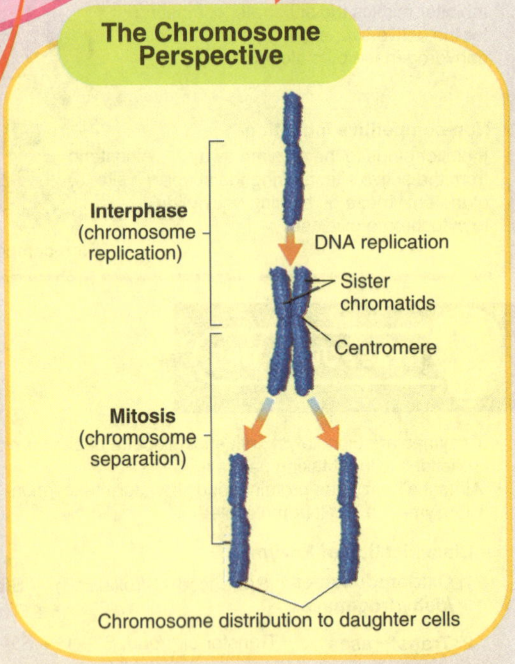

The Chromosome Perspective

Interphase (chromosome replication)

DNA replication

Sister chromatids

Centromere

Mitosis (chromosome separation)

Chromosome distribution to daughter cells

Cell cycle checkpoints

G_2 checkpoint
Check for:
- Cell size
- DNA replication

Metaphase checkpoint
Check for:
- Chromosome spindle attachment

G_1 checkpoint
Check for:
- Nutrients
- Growth factors
- DNA damage

M

G_2

G_1

S
DNA Synthesis

G_0 (Resting state)

Controlled by **protein cyclins** and cyclin-dependent kinases (CDKS-enzymes that phosphorylate proteins using ATP).

- Duration of cell cycle in yeast – 90 minutes
- Duration of cell cycle in eukaryotes – 24 hours. (Cell division phase –1 hour, interphase – 23 hours)
- Nerve cells and heart cells exit the cell cycle and enter into G_0-phase
- G_0 phase is called quiescent stage

Interphase
- Preparatory phase of the cell cycle.
- Cell makes a copy of the DNA and produces more organelles and cytoplasm.

Mitosis/Equational division
- The sister chromatids of each chromosome separate setting up the two identical nuclei of the daughter cells.

Cytokinesis

Early Prophase
- Condensation of chromosomal material
- Mitotic spindle starts to form.

Telophase
- Cell membrane completes constriction followed by cytokinesis.
- Nuclear membrane form around the separated chromosome.
- Golgi apparatus and endoplasmic reticulum reappears.

Late Prophase
- Asters reach the opposite poles.
- Nucleolus and nuclear membrane disintegrates.
- Golgi apparatus and endoplasmic reticulum disappaears.

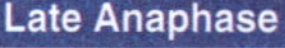

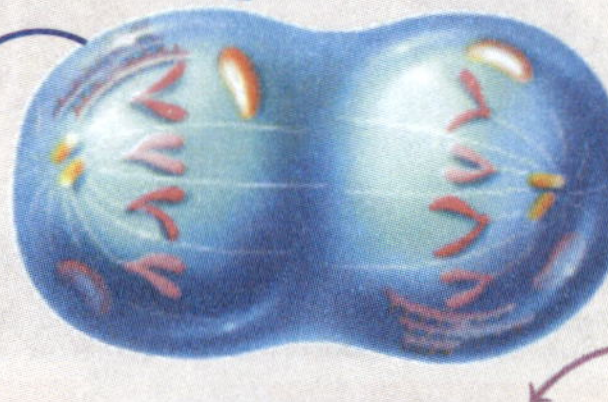

Late Anaphase
- Different shapes of chromosomes may be observed (V, J, L or I-Shaped) depending on position of kinetochore.

Metaphase
- Spindle fibres attach to kinetochores of chromosomes.
- Chromosomes move and get aligned along equatorial plate.

Early Anaphase
- Centromeres split, chromosomes move to opposite poles.

- Enzyme ribonuclease acts as poison at prophase; azide and cyanide also inhibit prophase.
- Colchicine (an alkaloid) disrupts the microtubule formation and arrests cell cycle at metaphase.
- **Amitosis** : Direct cell division, nucleus elongates and constricts in the middle to form two daughter nuclei followed by cytoplasm division, e.g. some protozoans.

Significance
- Restores surface/volume ratio of cells and nucleo-cytoplasmic index.
- Helps to maintain stability of chromosome number.
- Essential for growth, cell repair and development of a multicellular organism.
- Method of multiplication in unicellular organisms.

Stages of Prophase of Meiosis-I

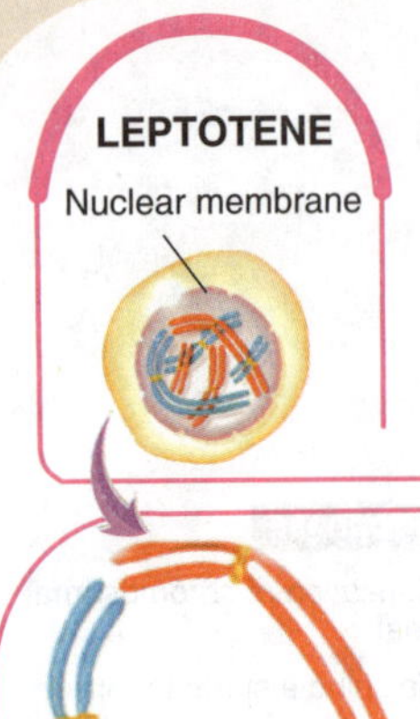

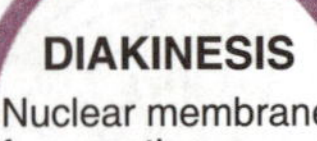
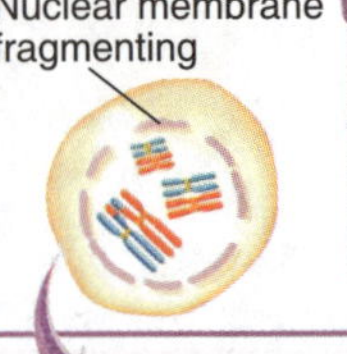
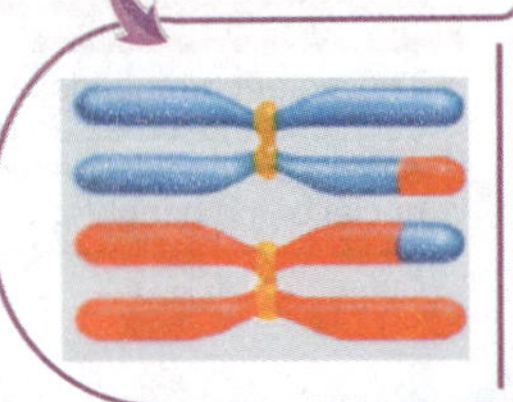

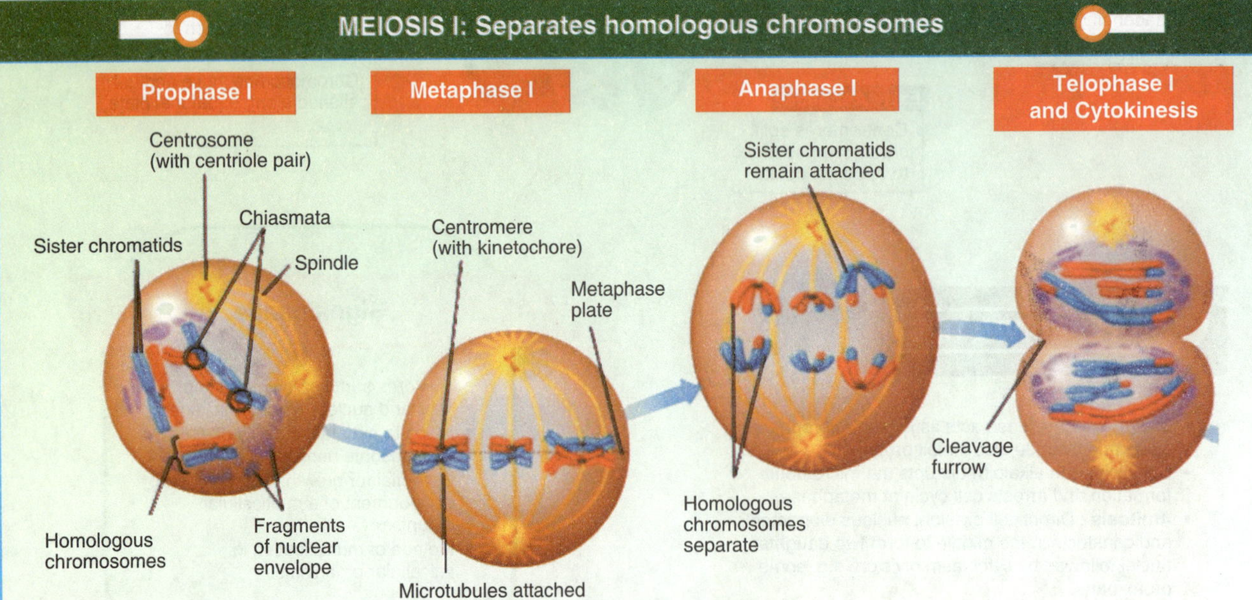

MEIOSIS II: Separation sister chromosomes

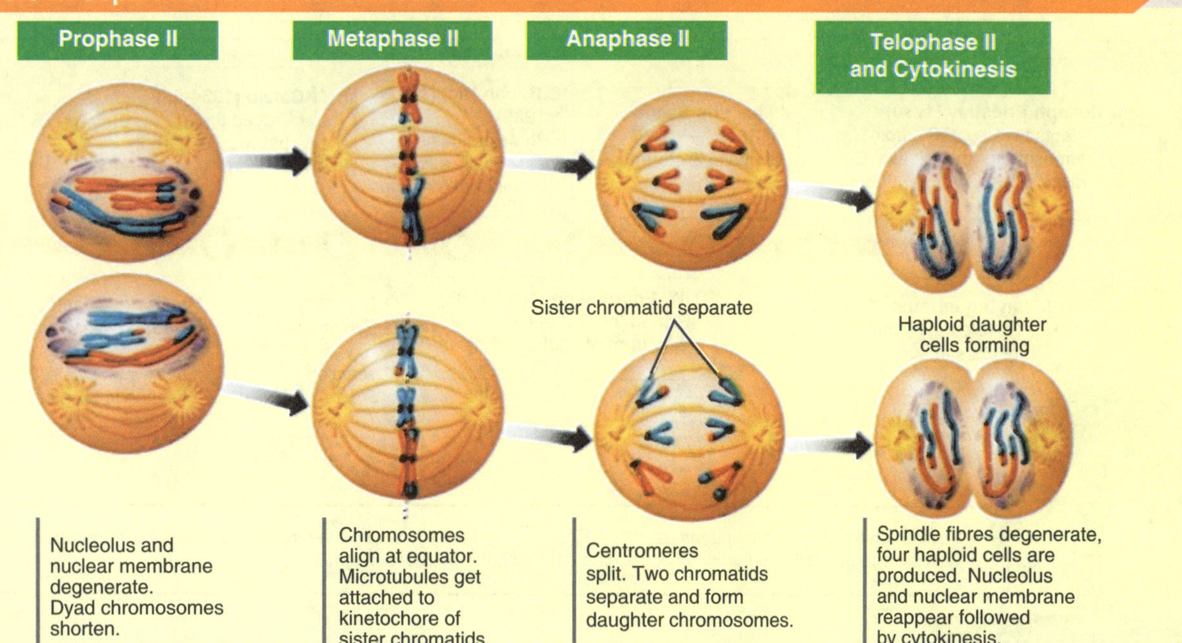

Significance

- Maintains fixed number of chromosomes in sexual reproduction.
- Crossing over introduces genetic variation and new traits.
- Involves independent assortment and reshuffling of paternal and maternal chromosome.

Cytokinesis

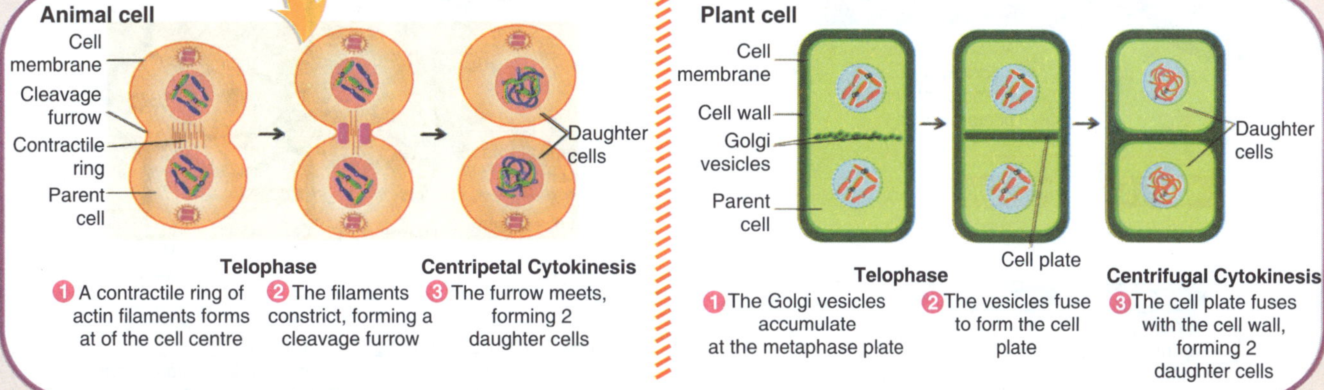

NEET POWER TIPS

In plant cells , Phagmoplast coordinates cytokinesis by transporting vesicles to form a new cell plates.

- **Comparative accounts of Mitosis and Meiosis**

Mitosis	Meiosis
Takes place in somatic cells.	Occurs in reproductive cells.
The cells undergoing mitosis may be haploid or diploid.	The cells undergoing meiosis are always diploid.
Single division, produces two cells.	Double division, forms four cells.
The number of chromosomes remains the same after mitosis.	The number of chromosomes is reduced to half after meiosis.
The daughter nuclei or cells formed are exactly similar to the parent one.	The daughter nuclei or cells formed after meiosis are not exactly similar to either parent.

- **Multinucleated cell** or **syncytium**: When cytokinesis fails, single cell ends up containing multiple nuclei, e.g., skeletal muscle cell.

Chapter **11**

Photosynthesis in Higher Plants

Historical Perspectives

Joseph Priestley (1770)
- Plants take up CO_2 from atmosphere and release O_2; discovered O_2.

Jan Ingenhousz (1730-99)
- O_2 release by the green parts of plant in sunlight.

Julius von Sachs (1854)
- Glucose is stored as starch

T.W. Engelmann (1843-1909)
- Plotted the first action spectrum of photosynthesis.

C.B. van Niel (1897-1985)
- Photosynthesis is essentially a light-dependent reaction.

Hill (1937)
- Evolution of oxygen in light reaction.

Calvin (1954-55)
- Traced the pathway of carbon fixation.

Hatch and Slack (1965)
- Discovered C_4-pathway of CO_2 fixation in C_4-plant.

Photosynthesis

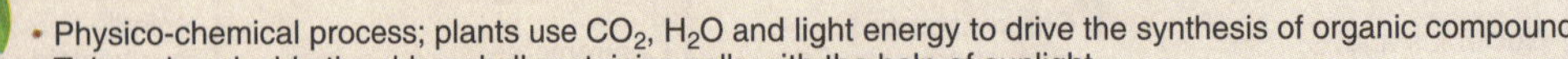

- Physico-chemical process; plants use CO_2, H_2O and light energy to drive the synthesis of organic compound.
- Takes place inside the chlorophyll containing cells with the help of sunlight.

Photosynthetic Pigment

01 Primary pigment (Chlorophyll- *a*)
- Most abundant/chief plant pigment
- Maximum absorption-Blue and red region

02 Accessory pigments
- Absorbs light and transfers to chlorophyll- *a*
- Protects chlorophyll- *a* from photo-oxidation

Chlorophyll- *b* (Yellow green)

Carotenoids
- Carotene (Yellow, red or orange)
- Xanthophylls (Yellow)

Site of Photosynthesis

- Chloroplasts are found in mesophyll cells of leaves.

Dark Reaction
- Biosynthetic phase or carbon reaction
- Light independent reaction
- Requires product of light reactions (ATP and NADPH) to synthesise sugars.

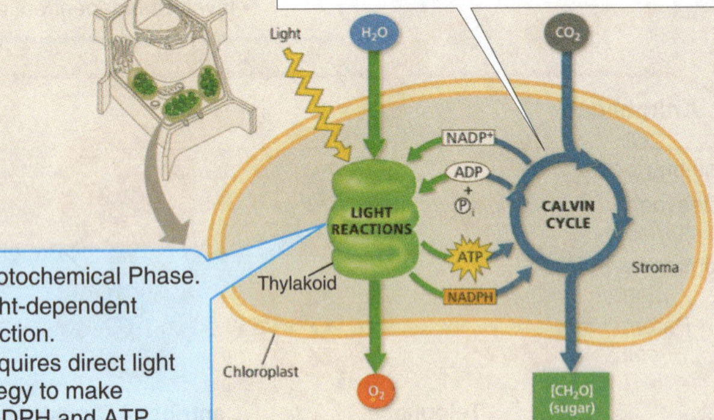

- Photochemical Phase.
- Light-dependent reaction.
- Requires direct light enegy to make NADPH and ATP.

- **Response of chlorophyll to light conditions**
  - **Weak light:** Chloroplast orient perpendicular to the incident light.
  - **Strong light:** Chloroplast orient parallel to the incident light.

Absorption v/s Action Spectrum

Absorption spectrum

Measurement of how much light is absorbed by a substance at different wavelength

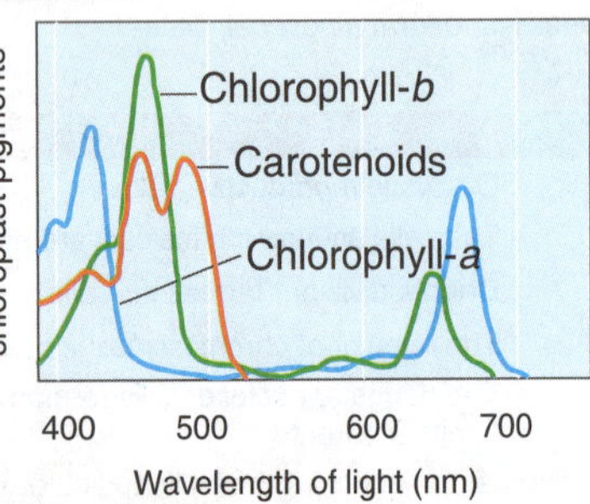

Action spectrum

Rate of photosynthesis (measured by O_2 release)

400 500 600 700

Wavelength of light (nm)

Rate of photosynthesis at different wavelengths of light.

Light Reaction

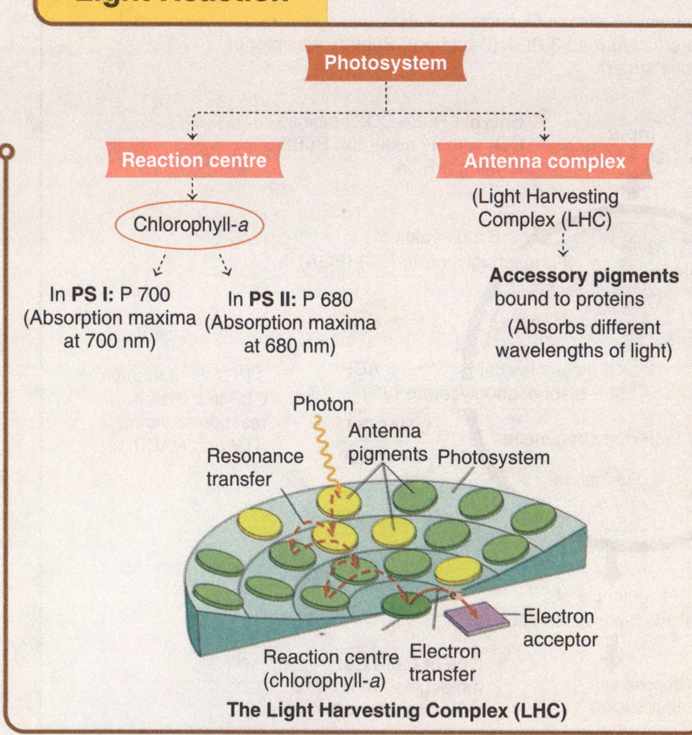

- **Light Reaction Steps:** Light absorption → water-splitting → Oxygen release → Electron transport → Formation of high- energy chemical intermediates, (ATP and NADPH)
- **Photosystems** (Chlorophyll-*a* with other pigments bound to proteins)- Present on the inner thylakoid membrane
- PSII is present in the inner part of grana thylakoids.
- PSI is located in the outer part of grana thylakoids as well as stroma thylakoids.
- **Chemiosmotic hypothesis** (Peter Mitchell, 1961)- Free energy of electron transport is conserved by the formation of a transmembrane proton gradient.

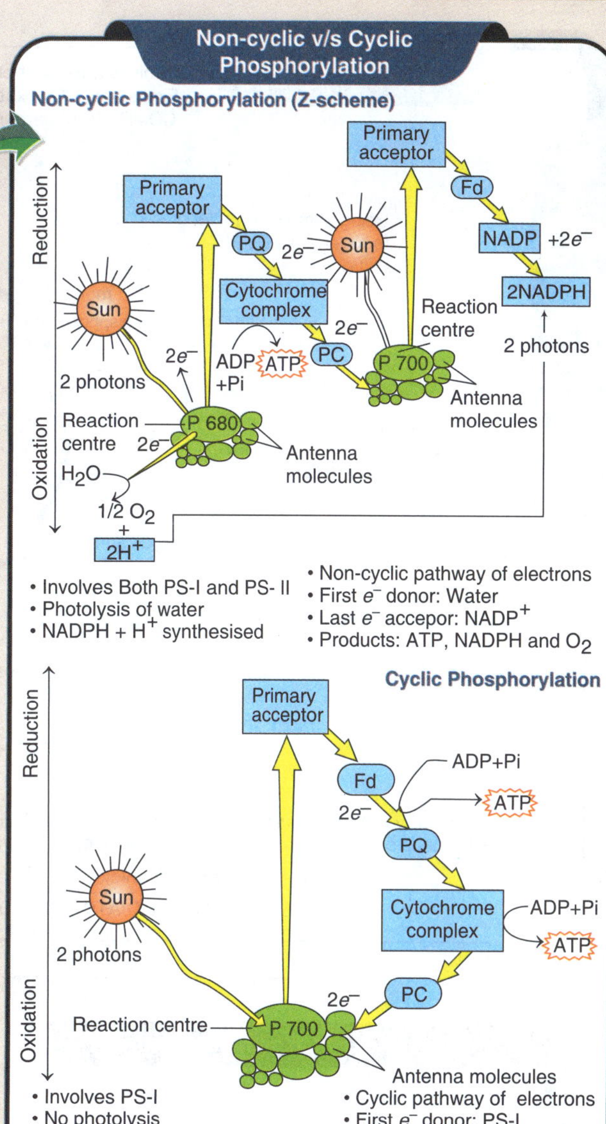

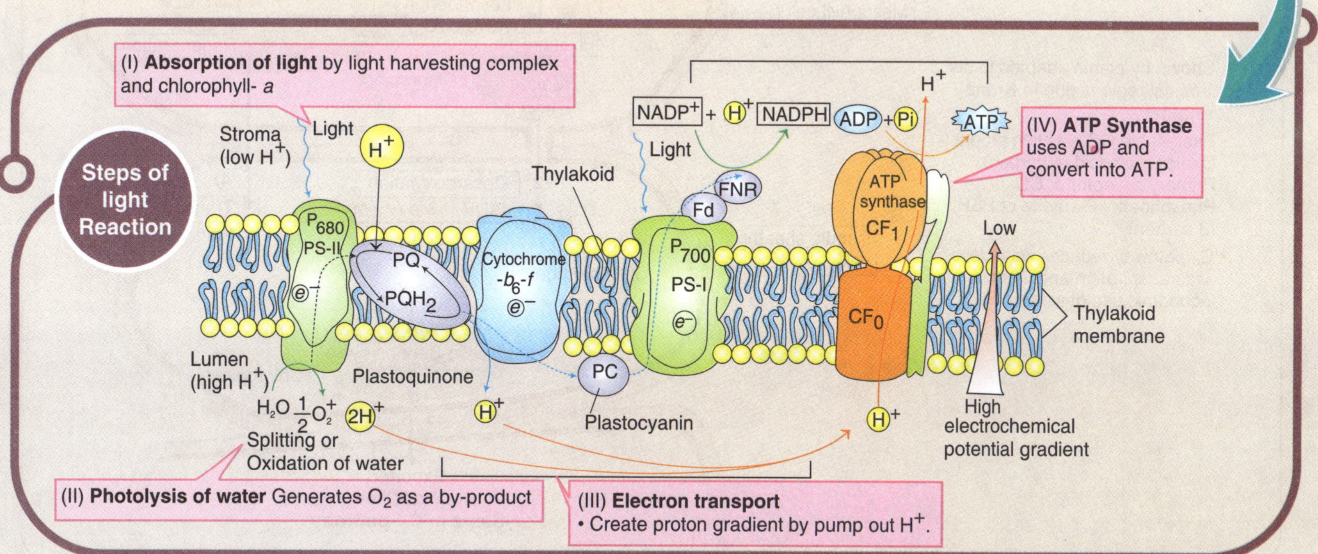

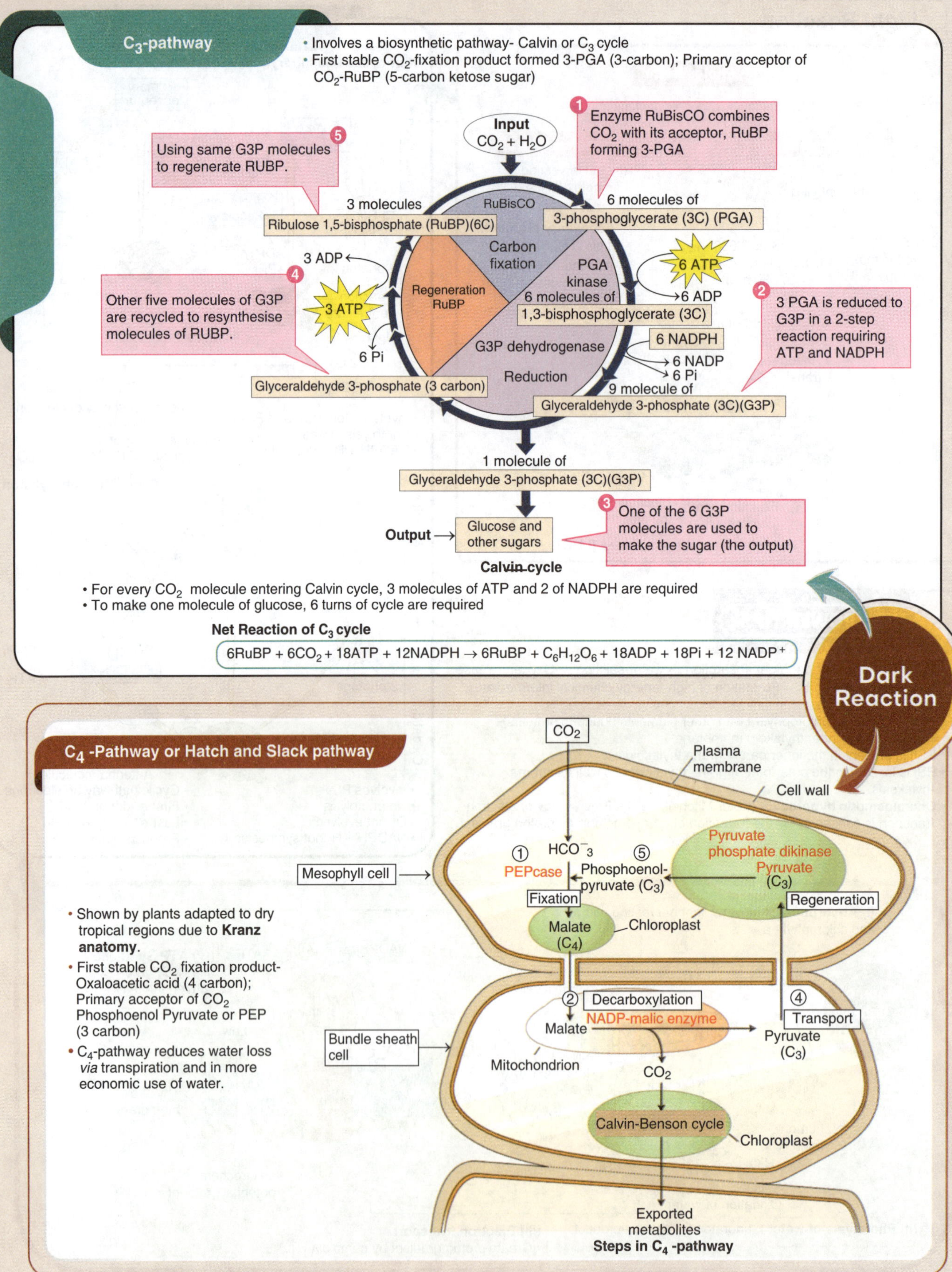
C_3-pathway
• Involves a biosynthetic pathway- Calvin or C_3 cycle
• First stable CO_2-fixation product formed 3-PGA (3-carbon); Primary acceptor of CO_2-RuBP (5-carbon ketose sugar)
Input
$CO_2 + H_2O$
1 Enzyme RuBisCO combines CO_2 with its acceptor, RuBP forming 3-PGA
5 Using same G3P molecules to regenerate RUBP.
3 molecules
Ribulose 1,5-bisphosphate (RuBP)(6C)
RuBisCO
6 molecules of
3-phosphoglycerate (3C) (PGA)
Carbon fixation
3 ADP
PGA kinase
6 ATP
6 ADP
4 Other five molecules of G3P are recycled to resynthesise molecules of RUBP.
3 ATP
Regeneration RuBP
6 molecules of
1,3-bisphosphoglycerate (3C)
2 3 PGA is reduced to G3P in a 2-step reaction requiring ATP and NADPH
6 NADPH
G3P dehydrogenase
6 Pi
6 NADP
6 Pi
Reduction
Glyceraldehyde 3-phosphate (3 carbon)
9 molecule of
Glyceraldehyde 3-phosphate (3C)(G3P)
1 molecule of
Glyceraldehyde 3-phosphate (3C)(G3P)
3 One of the 6 G3P molecules are used to make the sugar (the output)
Output
Glucose and other sugars
Calvin cycle
• For every CO_2 molecule entering Calvin cycle, 3 molecules of ATP and 2 of NADPH are required
• To make one molecule of glucose, 6 turns of cycle are required
Net Reaction of C_3 cycle
$6RuBP + 6CO_2 + 18ATP + 12NADPH \rightarrow 6RuBP + C_6H_{12}O_6 + 18ADP + 18Pi + 12\ NADP^+$
Dark Reaction
C_4 -Pathway or Hatch and Slack pathway
• Shown by plants adapted to dry tropical regions due to **Kranz anatomy**.
• First stable CO_2 fixation product- Oxaloacetic acid (4 carbon); Primary acceptor of CO_2 Phosphoenol Pyruvate or PEP (3 carbon)
• C_4-pathway reduces water loss *via* transpiration and in more economic use of water.
CO_2
Plasma membrane
Cell wall
Mesophyll cell
① HCO^-_3
PEPcase
⑤ Phosphoenol-pyruvate (C_3)
Pyruvate phosphate dikinase
Pyruvate (C_3)
Fixation
Regeneration
Malate (C_4)
Chloroplast
② Decarboxylation
NADP-malic enzyme
④ Transport
Malate
Pyruvate (C_3)
Bundle sheath cell
Mitochondrion
CO_2
Calvin-Benson cycle
Chloroplast
Exported metabolites
Steps in C_4 -pathway

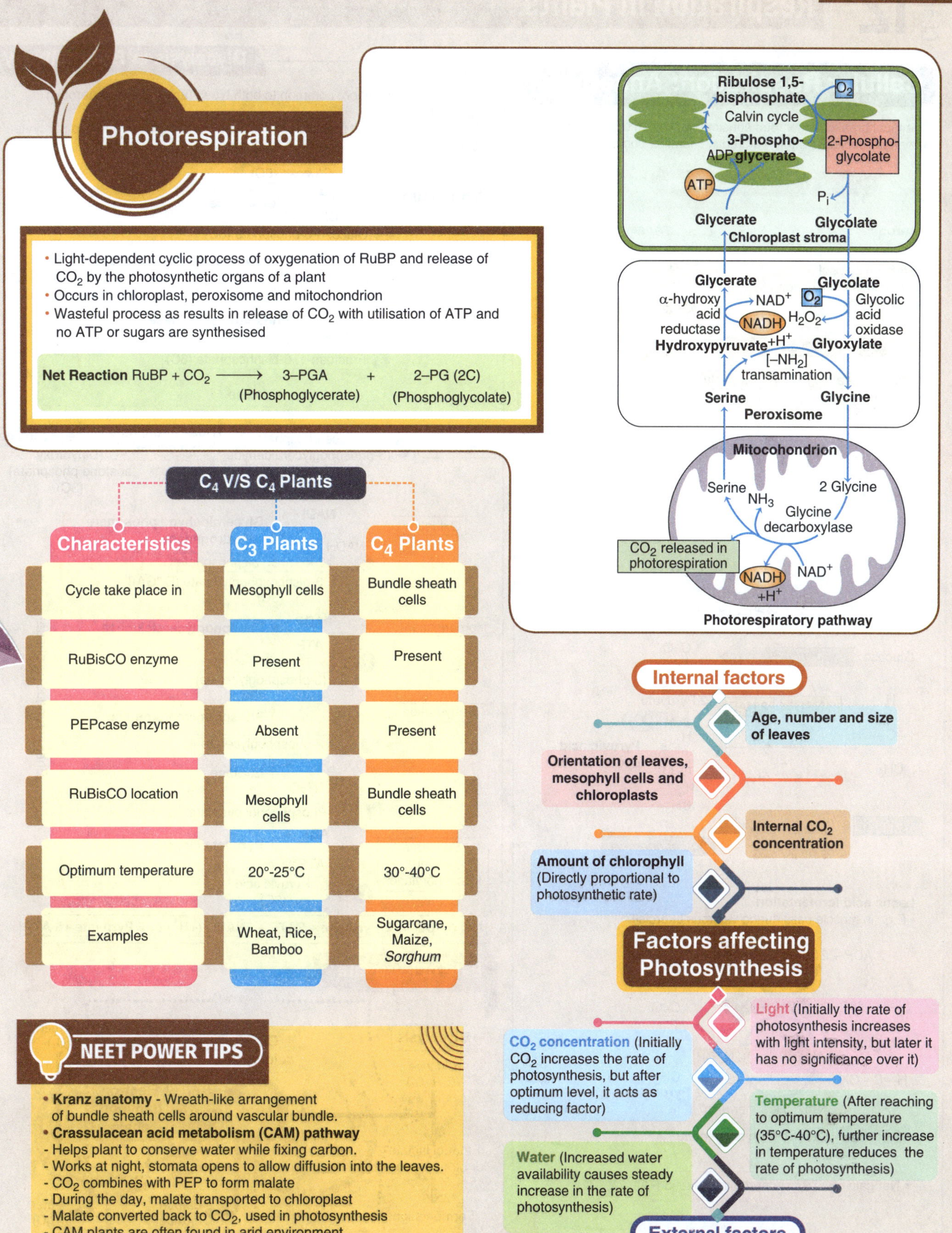

Photorespiration

- Light-dependent cyclic process of oxygenation of RuBP and release of CO_2 by the photosynthetic organs of a plant
- Occurs in chloroplast, peroxisome and mitochondrion
- Wasteful process as results in release of CO_2 with utilisation of ATP and no ATP or sugars are synthesised

Net Reaction RuBP + CO_2 $\longrightarrow$ 3–PGA (Phosphoglycerate) + 2–PG (2C) (Phosphoglycolate)

C_4 V/S C_4 Plants

Characteristics	C_3 Plants	C_4 Plants
Cycle take place in	Mesophyll cells	Bundle sheath cells
RuBisCO enzyme	Present	Present
PEPcase enzyme	Absent	Present
RuBisCO location	Mesophyll cells	Bundle sheath cells
Optimum temperature	20°-25°C	30°-40°C
Examples	Wheat, Rice, Bamboo	Sugarcane, Maize, *Sorghum*

NEET POWER TIPS

- **Kranz anatomy** - Wreath-like arrangement of bundle sheath cells around vascular bundle.
- **Crassulacean acid metabolism (CAM) pathway**
- Helps plant to conserve water while fixing carbon.
- Works at night, stomata opens to allow diffusion into the leaves.
- CO_2 combines with PEP to form malate
- During the day, malate transported to chloroplast
- Malate converted back to CO_2, used in photosynthesis
- CAM plants are often found in arid environment.

Chapter 12 Respiration in Plants

Cellular Respiration: Anaerobic

Chemical breakdown of food substrate mediated by several enzymes to release energy stored in chemical bonds

Types of Cellular Respiration

Aerobic
(in presence of O_2)
- Starts in cytosol and continues in mitochondria
- **Steps:**

Glycolysis → Pyruvate oxidation → Krebs' cycle → Terminal oxidation

Anaerobic
(in absence of O_2)
- Occurs in cytosol
- **Steps:**

Glycolysis → Fermentation

Fermentation

Alcohol fermentation

- Conversion of pyruvate to alcohol and organic acids in the absence of O_2.
- E.g. in yeast.

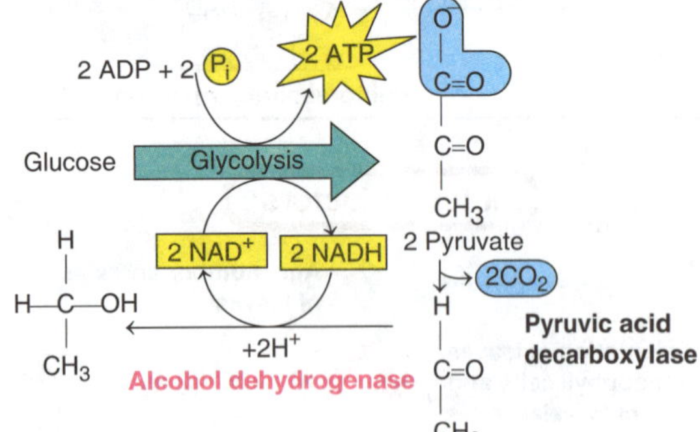

Lactic acid fermentation

- E.g., in muscle cells during vigorous exercise

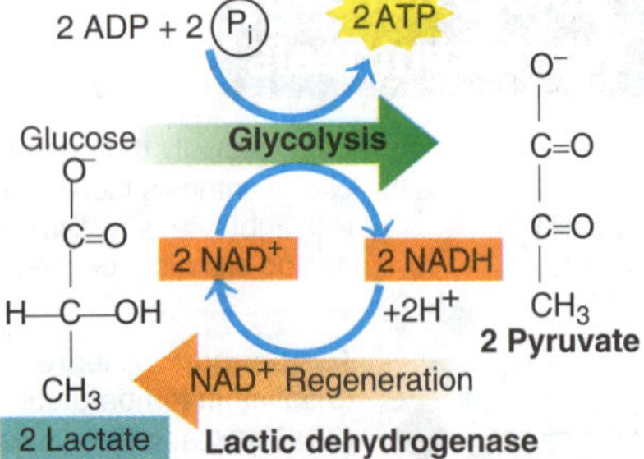

- Net gain of ATP in anaerobic respiration- Only 2 ATP

Glycolysis or EMP-pathway

- First step of respiration; common to both types (anaerobic and aerobic)
- **Site**: Cytosol
- Series of biochemical reactions in which glucose is broken down to pyruvate with release of usable energy in the form of ATP

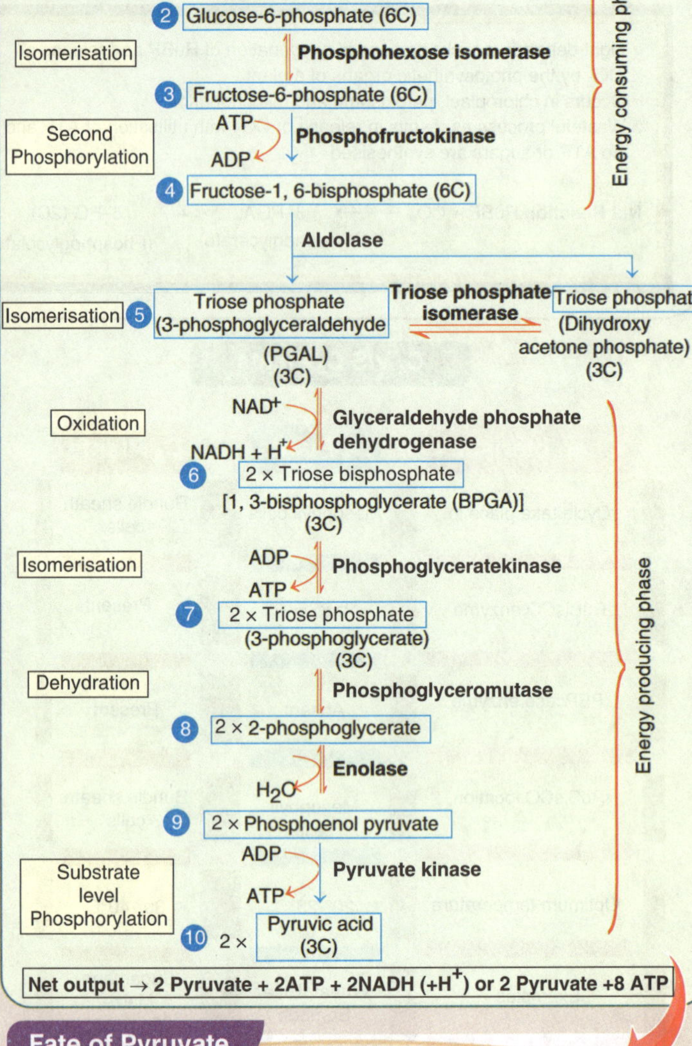

Fate of Pyruvate

Glycolysis

Glucose ($C_6H_{12}O_6$)

NADH

Citric acid cycle

Matrix

$FADH_2$

NADH

Electron transport chain

Oxygen (O_2)

Cristae

Ethanol lactate or other product

Fermentation

ATP

Carbon dioxide (CO_2)

ATP

Water (H_2O)

ATP

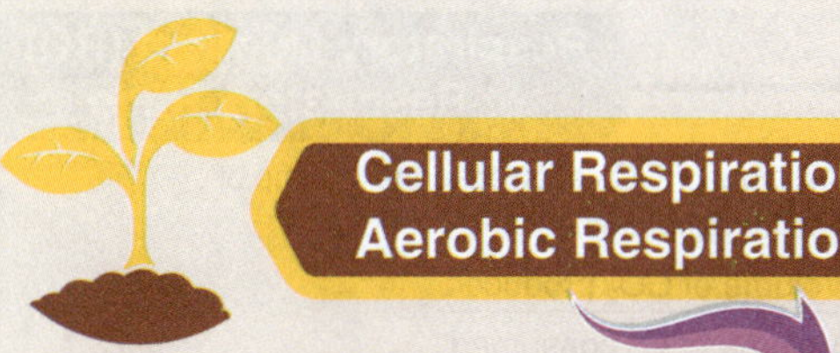

Pyruvate Oxidation/Oxidative Decarboxylation

- Involves conversion of glycolytic product, pyruvate into acetyl Co-A that enters the next step, i.e., Krebs' cycle
- Also called link reaction
- Includes participation of several coenzymes, including NAD^+ and Coenzyme A
- **Product-** 2 molecule of NADH (from 2 pyruvate molecules)

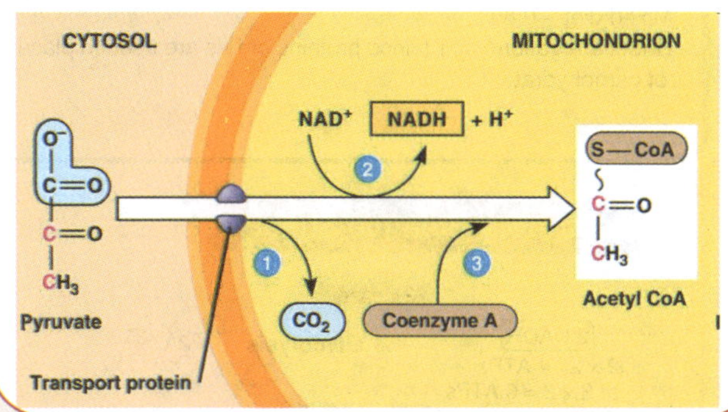

Krebs' TCA /Citric acid Cycle

- First elucidated by Hans Krebs'; occurs in mitochondrial matrix
- Amphibolic pathway (both catabolism and anabolism)

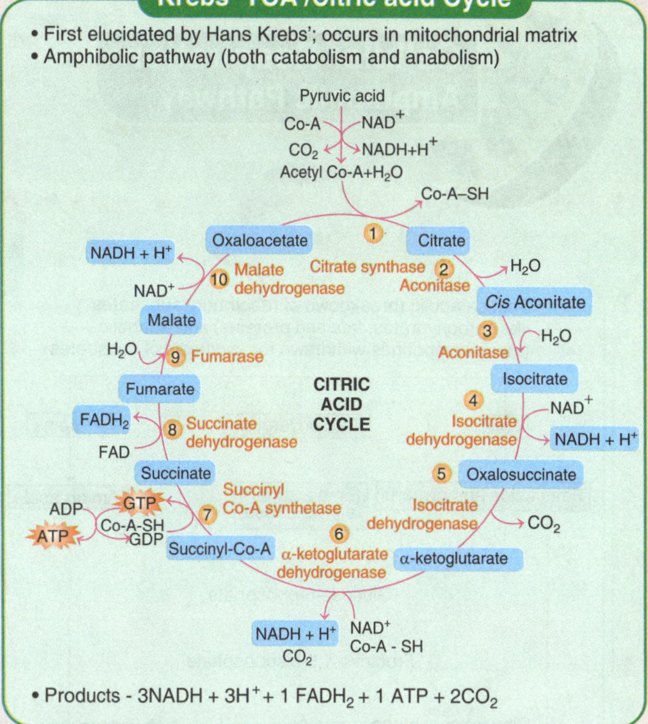

- Products - $3NADH + 3H^+ + 1\ FADH_2 + 1\ ATP + 2CO_2$

Electron Transport System (ETS) and Oxidative Phosphorylation

- **ETS**: Series of four protein complexes that couple redox reactions, creating an H^+ gradients across the membrane
- **Oxidative phosphorylation**: Use of protein gradient to make ATP by ATP synthase
- Results in formation of 32-34 ATP molecules

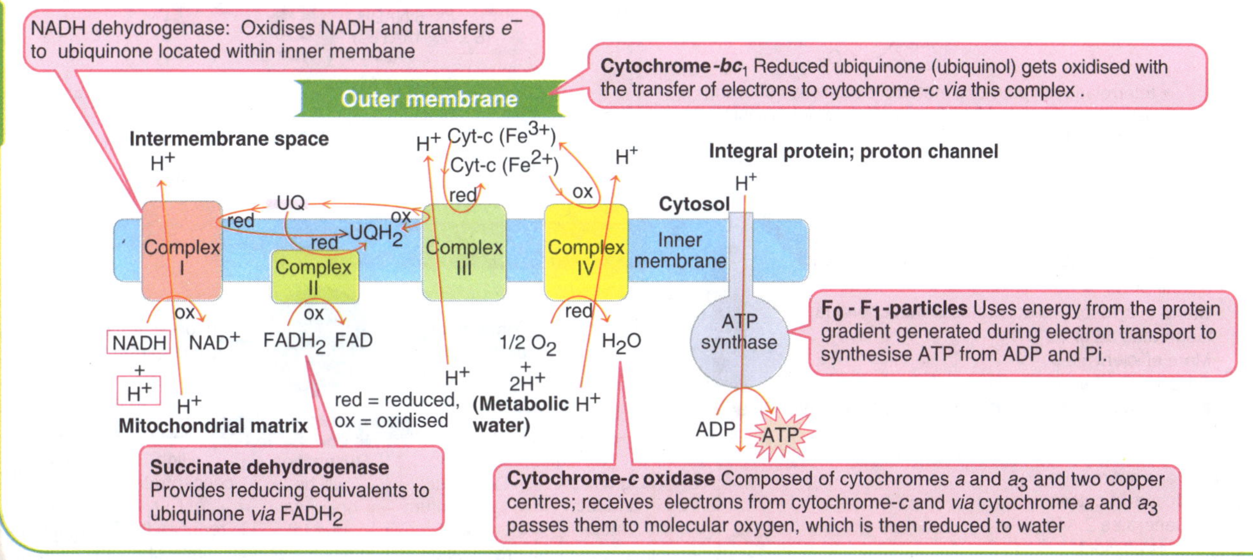

Flow of electrons in electron transport chain

NEET POWER TIPS

- **Aerobic Respiration** Complete breakdown of pyruvate into CO_2 and water with release of energy in the presence of oxygen.
- All enzymes of TCA located in the mitochondrial matrix itself except succinic dehydrogenase (i.e., present in inner mitochondrial membrane in eukaryotes).
- ETS occurs in the inner mitochondrial membrane.
- NADH synthesised during glycolysis and TCA cycle undergo oxidative phosphorylation.

Cellular Respiration: Amphibolic Pathway

- Both catabolic (breakdown of respiratory substrates like carbohydrates, fats and proteins) and anabolic (many compounds withdrawn for synthesis of substrates)

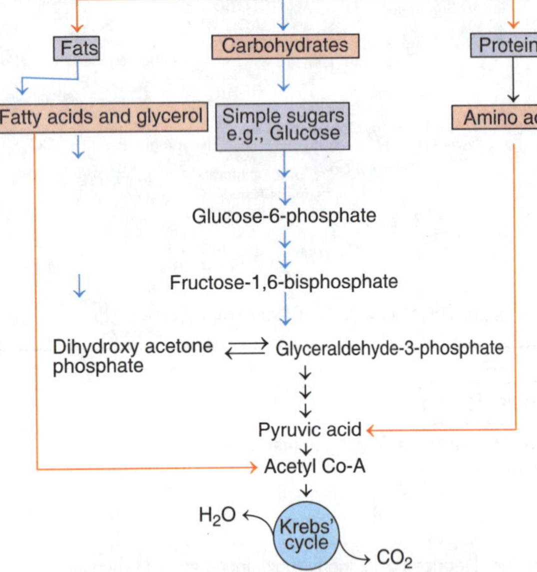

- Interrelationship among metabolic pathways showing respiration mediated breakdown of different organic molecules to CO_2 and H_2O

Respiratory Quotient (RQ) or Respiratory Ratio

- Ratio of the volume of CO_2 evolved to the volume of O_2 consumed in respiration

$$RQ = \frac{\text{Volume of } CO_2 \text{ produced}}{\text{Volume of } O_2 \text{ consumed}}$$

- Depends on type of respiratiory substrate used
- Can be less than one, zero, unity, more than one or infinity

RQ for different respiratory substrates

- Proteins = 0.9
- Fats = < 1 (e.g., tripalmitin = 0.7)
- Organic acids = > 1
- Carbohydrates = 1
- Anaerobic respiration = ∞ (since no O_2 is consumed)
- Mixed diet ~ 0.85
- Under starvation = < 1 (since proteins or fats are used in place of carbohydrates)

Respiratory Balance Sheet

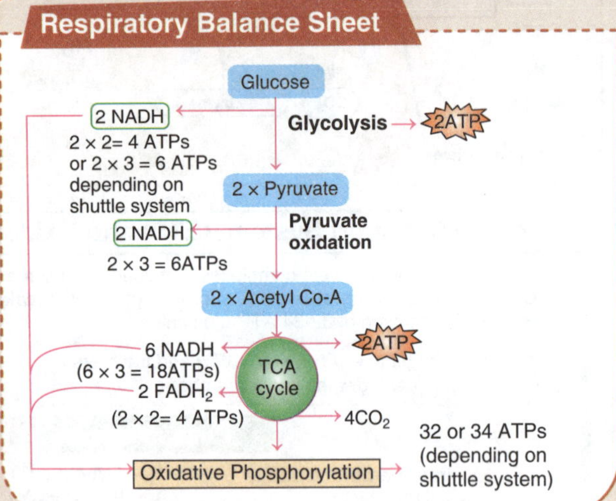

Aerobic v/s Anaerobic Respiration

AEROBIC

- Requires O_2
- Starts in cytosol and continues in mitochondria
- Generates 36 or 38 ATP
- More efficient
- Produces water
- Includes both substrate and oxidative phosphorylation

ANAEROBIC

- Does not require O_2
- Occurs in cytosol
- Generates 2 ATP only
- Less efficient
- Does not produce water
- Includes only substrate level phosphorylation

Factor Affecting Respiration

Internal factors

- Amount of protoplasm
- Concentration of respiratory

External Factor

- Light is an indirect factor
- Decrease temperature rate of respiration
- Respiration will be optimum due to presence of sufficient O_2.
- High concentration of CO_2 reduces the rate of respiration.
- Water stress can decrease respiration in plants.

NEET POWER TIPS

- **Respiratory substrates**: Compounds oxidised during respiration; usually carbohydrates used as substrate
- **Types of respiration based on respiratory substrate**
  - Protoplasmic (proteins)
  - Floating (carbohydrates and fats)
- **Respirometer**: Instrument to measure respiratory rate; most common-Ganong's respirometer
- **Shultle System** (mitochondria)- Chemical systems transports e^- across the mitochondrial membrane.

Chapter 13

Plant Growth and Development

Phases of Growth

Maturation phase (3)
Maximum size in terms of wall thickenings and protoplasmic modification

Elongation phase (2)
Cell enlargement, increased vacuole formation and new cell wall deposition

Formative/Meristematic phase (1)
Constant division of cells in shoots and roots; cells are rich in protoplasmand possess large nuclei

Plant Growth

Properties of Plant Growth

Indeterminate growth pattern
- Continuous growth throughout life
- Two types of growth based on origin and function:
  - Primary (elongation along their axis)
  - Secondary (increase in the girth of organs in dicot plants and gymnosperms)

Measurable
- At cellular level, measured as increase in amount of protoplasm
- Can also be measured in terms of increase in cell number, size, etc.

Quantitative comparison between growth of living systems can be made by

(I) **Absolute Growth Rate (AGR)**

AGR = Final growth – Initial growth

(II) **Relative Growth Rate (RGR)**

RGR = (Growth per unit time/Initial size) × 100

Example ▶

Leaf X

A[1] 10 cm^2

5 cm^2 A

$$AGR = 10cm^2 - 5cm^2 = 5cm^2$$

$$RGR = \frac{10cm^2 - 5cm^2}{5cm^2} \times 100$$

= **100%**

Leaf Y

B[1] 55 cm^2

50 cm^2 B

$$AGR = 55cm^2 - 50cm^2$$

$$= 5cm^2$$

$$RGR = \frac{55cm^2 - 50cm^2}{50cm^2} \times 100$$

= **10%**

Growth Rates

- Increase in growth per unit time
- May be arithmetic or geometrical growth

Arithmetic Growth

- Constant growth rate
- Following mitotic division, only one daughter cell continues to divide, while other differentiates and matures

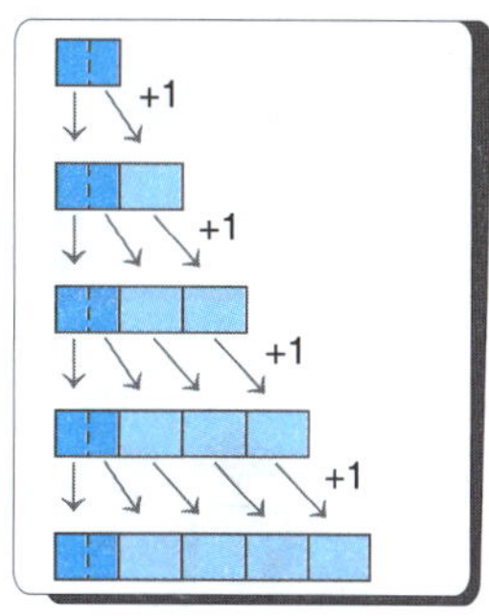

- Shown by elongating roots and shoots
- Mathematically, expressed as

$$L_t = L_o + rt$$

Where, L_t = Length at time t
L_o = Length at time zero
r = Growth rate

- Linear curve

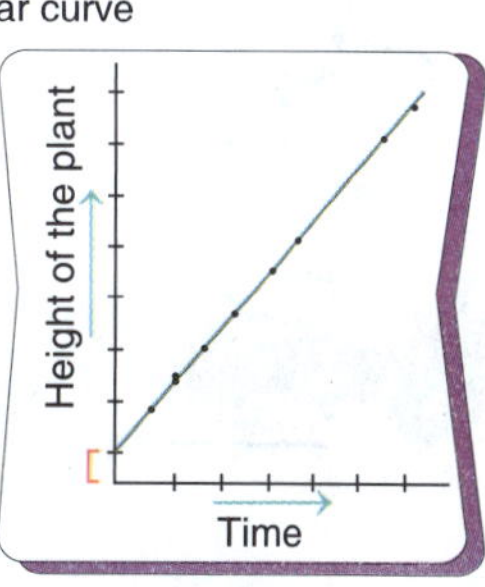

- **More idealistic growth**

Geometrical Growth

- Slow initial growth rate which increases rapidly thereafter
- Following mitotic divisions, both progeny cells retain the ability to divide

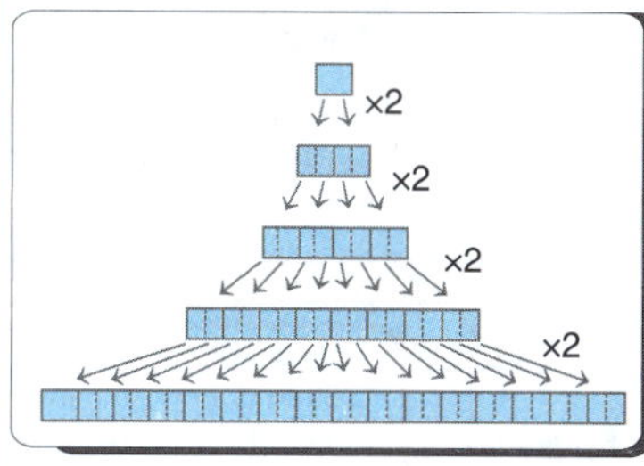

- Common in organisms growing in natural environment
- Mathematically, expressed as

$$W_1 = W_0 e^{rt}$$

Where, W_0 = Initial size
W_1 = Final size
r = Growth rate
t = Time of growth
e = Base of logarithms

- S-shaped or sigmoid curve

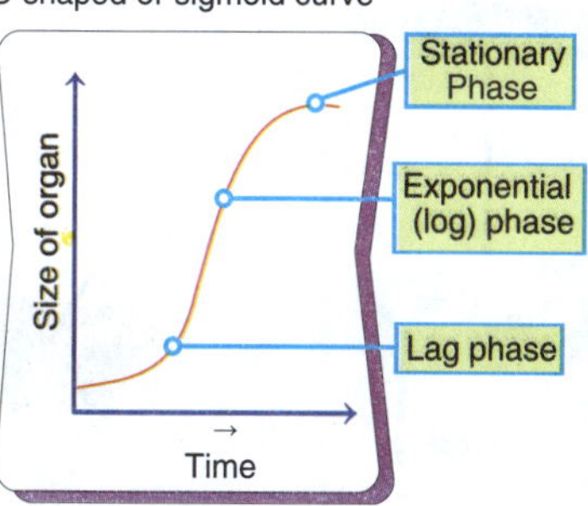

- **More realistic growth**

Differentiation, De-differentiation and Re-differentiation

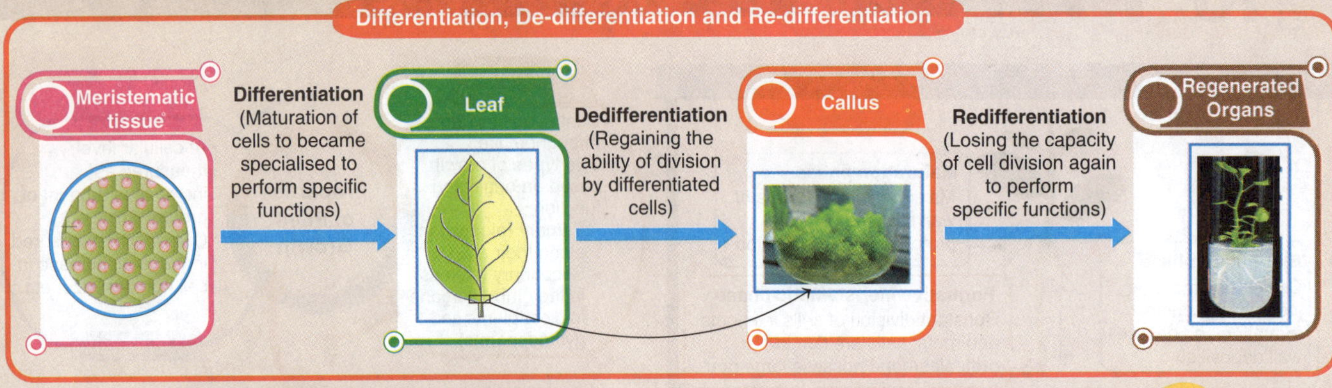

Plant Development

Sequence of development in higher plants

- Includes all the changes that an organism goes through during its life cycle from germination of the seed to senescence.

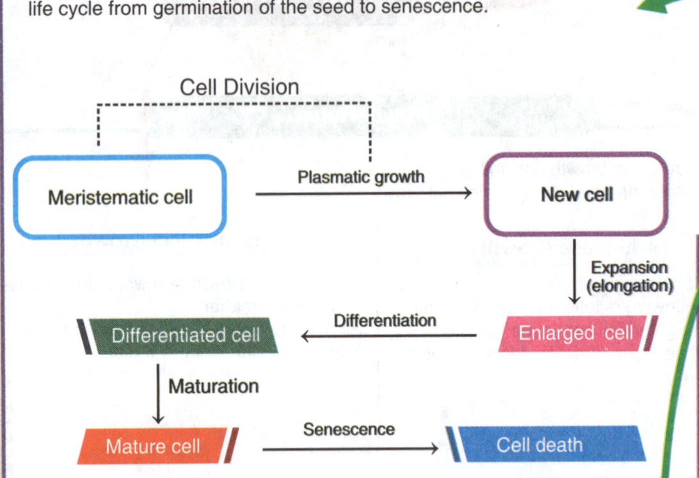

Plasticity

Ability of a plant to follow different pathways in response to environment or phases of life to form different structures.

Heterophylly

(Appearance of different forms of leaves on the same plant).

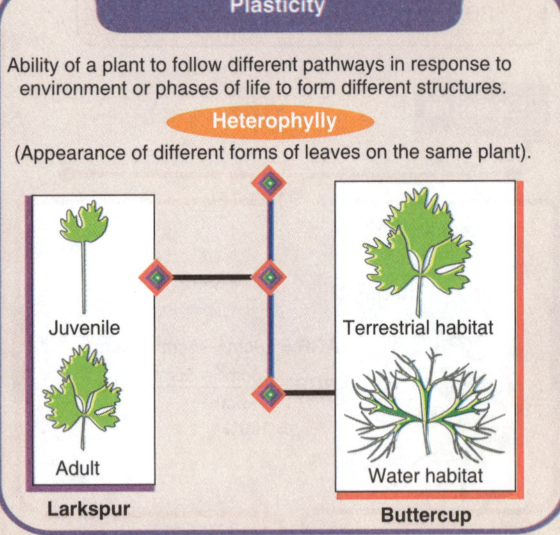

Seed Germination

Epigeal

Cotyledons emerge from the ground during germination due to elongation of hypocotyl, e.g., castor, bean

Hypogeal

Cotyledons stay below the ground; epicotyl elongates leading to emergence of cotyledonary leaves, e.g. maize, pea, gram

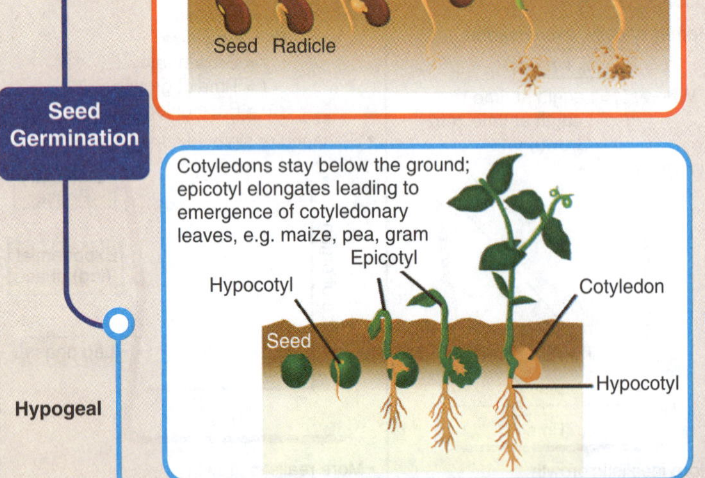

NEET POWER TIPS

- **Growth v/s Development**
  - **Growth**- An irreversible increase in the size of an organ or its parts or even of an individual cell
  - **Development**- Sum of two processes- growth and differentiation
- **Factors affecting Plant Growth**
  - **Nutrients** For synthesis of protoplasm as well as energy source
  - **Oxygen** Essential for metabolic activities
  - **Optimum temperature** Suitable for growth
  - **Environmental signals** Like light, and gravity
  - **Water** For maintenance of turgidity; providing medium for enzymatic action
  - **Other factors** Excess salt, mineral deficiency and other stress factors.
- **Factors affecting plant development**
  - **Extrinsic factors** Light, Temperature, Water, Oxygen,
  - **Intrinsic factors** Nutrients, Genetic factors, Growth regulators

Auxins

- **Discovery**: Charles Darwin and Francis Darwin (in coleoptile tip of canary grass; isolated by F.W. Went (from tips of coleoptile of oat seedlings)
- **Location**: Found in shoot apices, leaf primordium and developing seeds.
- **Bioassay**: Avena curvature test
- **Natural-**Indole- Acetic Acid (IAA), IBA, Phenyl Acetic Acid (PAA); **Synthetic**- 2, 4-D, Naphthalene Acetic acid (NAA)
- Weakly acidic growth hormone having an unsaturated ring structure
- **Polar movement** : Basipetal in stem, but acropetal in root

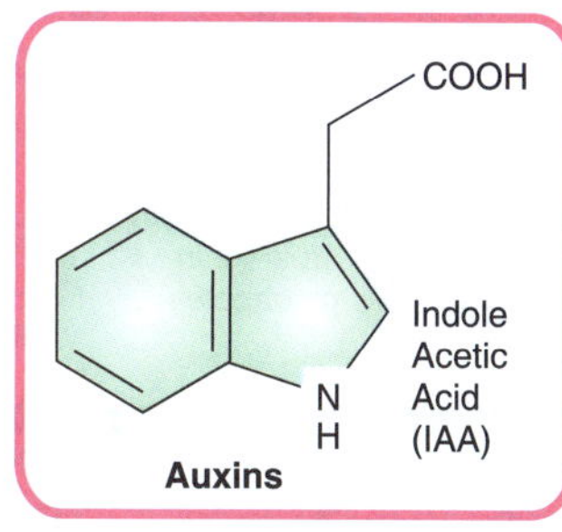

Auxins

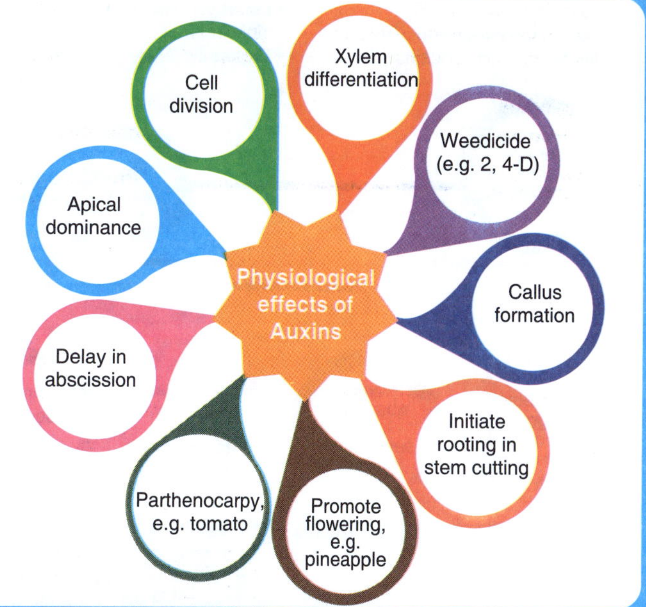

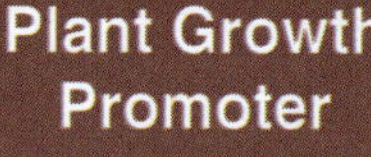

Gibberellins

- **Discovery** E. Kurosowa (Japan) in rice with 'Bakanae' or foolish seedling disease caused by *Gibberella fujikoroi*
- **Location** Embryos, roots and young leaves near the shoots
- **Bioassary** Barley endosperm test
- More than 100 gibberellins reported from fungi and higher plants, i.e. GA_1, GA_2, GA_3 (most studied) and so on.
- Weakly acidic hormone having gibbane ring structure.

O, OH, CH_2, CO, HO, CH_3, COOH

Gibberellin

Physiological effects of Gibberellins

- Improving shape of fruit (apple)
- Promotes bolting in plants with rosette habits
- Delay senescence
- Hastens maturity period
- Speed up malting process
- Increasing length of stem (sugarcane)

NEET POWER TIPS

Plant Growth Regulators

Growth Inhibitors (Involved in growth inhibiting activities like dormancy and abscission)

- Ethylene (Gaseous)
- Abscisic acid (ABA) (Derivatives of carotenoids)

Growth Promoters (Involved in growth promoting activities such as cell division, cell enlargement, flowering, fruiting and seed formation)

- Auxins (Indole compounds)
- Gibberellins (Terpenes)
- Cytokinins (Adenine derivatives)

Ethylene could fit either of the group, but is largely an inhibitor of growth activities.

Cytokinins

- Basic in nature (either amino purine or phenyl urea derivative)
- **Natural:** Zeatin; **Synthetic**: Kinetin
- **Discovery:** Skoog and Miller
- **Location:** Roots, endosperms of seeds, growing embryos, young fruits and developing shoot buds
- **Bioassay:** Tobacco pith culture, chlorophyll retention test

NH, OH, N, N, N, N, H

Zeatin

Cytokinins

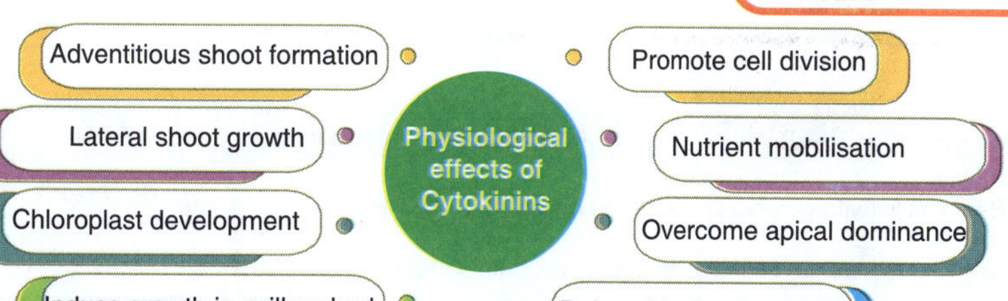

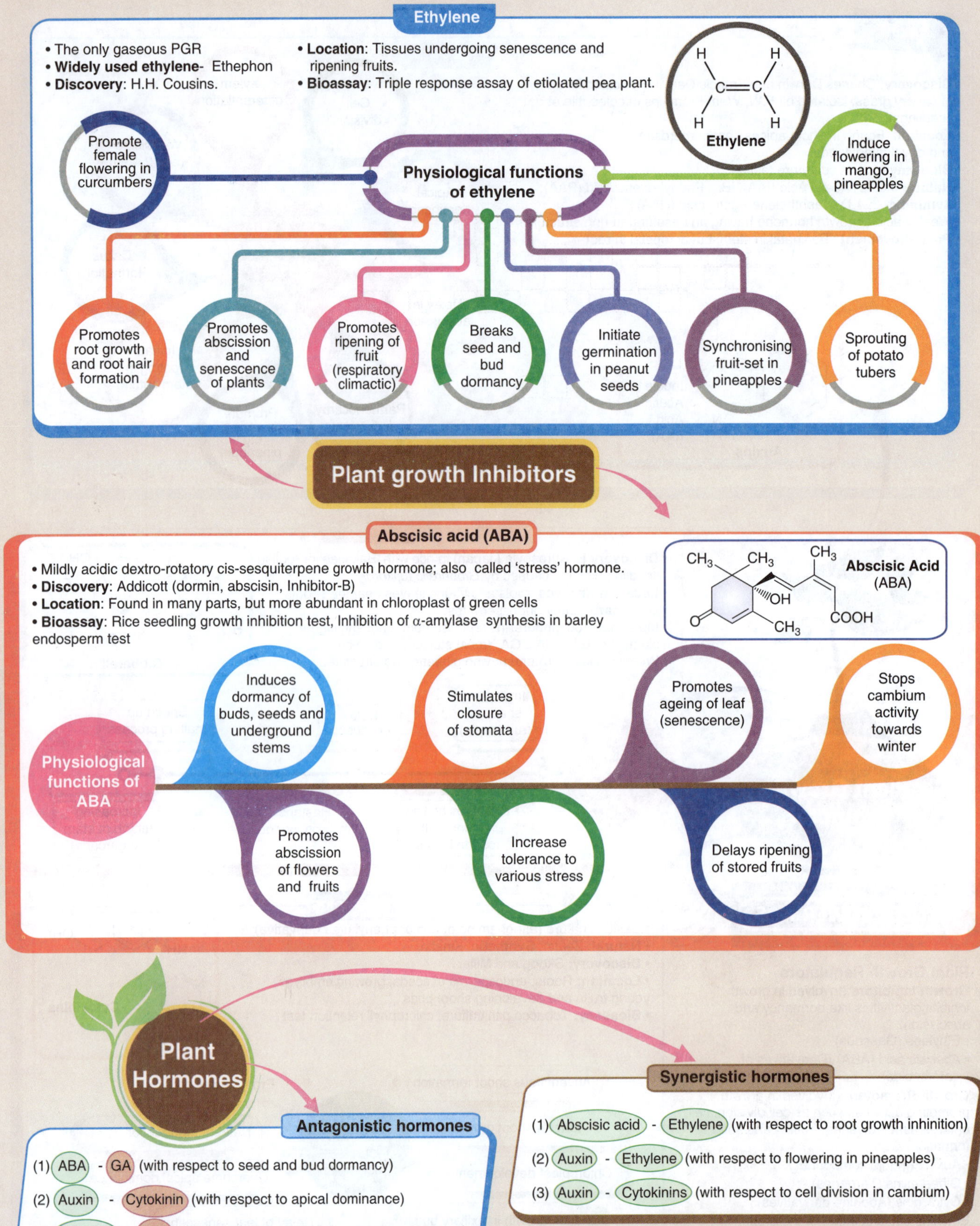
Ethylene
• The only gaseous PGR
• Widely used ethylene- Ethephon
• Discovery: H.H. Cousins.
• Location: Tissues undergoing senescence and ripening fruits.
• Bioassay: Triple response assay of etiolated pea plant.
Ethylene
Physiological functions of ethylene
Promote female flowering in curcumbers
Induce flowering in mango, pineapples
Promotes root growth and root hair formation
Promotes abscission and senescence of plants
Promotes ripening of fruit (respiratory climactic)
Breaks seed and bud dormancy
Initiate germination in peanut seeds
Synchronising fruit-set in pineapples
Sprouting of potato tubers
Plant growth Inhibitors
Abscisic acid (ABA)
• Mildly acidic dextro-rotatory cis-sesquiterpene growth hormone; also called 'stress' hormone.
• Discovery: Addicott (dormin, abscisin, Inhibitor-B)
• Location: Found in many parts, but more abundant in chloroplast of green cells
• Bioassay: Rice seedling growth inhibition test, Inhibition of α-amylase synthesis in barley endosperm test
Abscisic Acid (ABA)
Physiological functions of ABA
Induces dormancy of buds, seeds and underground stems
Stimulates closure of stomata
Promotes ageing of leaf (senescence)
Stops cambium activity towards winter
Promotes abscission of flowers and fruits
Increase tolerance to various stress
Delays ripening of stored fruits
Plant Hormones
Antagonistic hormones
(1) ABA - GA (with respect to seed and bud dormancy)
(2) Auxin - Cytokinin (with respect to apical dominance)
(3) Cytokinin - ABA (with respect to stomatal opening and closure)
Synergistic hormones
(1) Abscisic acid - Ethylene (with respect to root growth inhinition)
(2) Auxin - Ethylene (with respect to flowering in pineapples)
(3) Auxin - Cytokinins (with respect to cell division in cambium)

Chapter 14 Breathing and Exchange of Gases

Human Respiratory System

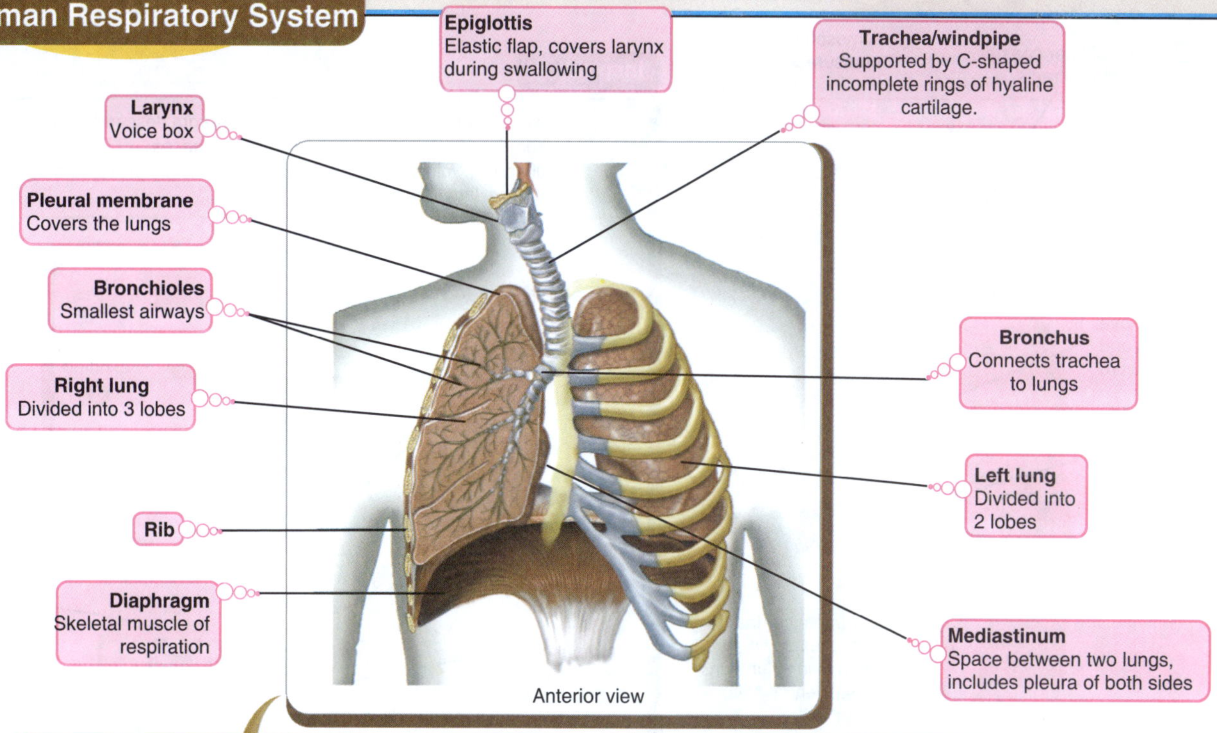

Epiglottis
Elastic flap, covers larynx during swallowing

Trachea/windpipe
Supported by C-shaped incomplete rings of hyaline cartilage.

Larynx
Voice box

Pleural membrane
Covers the lungs

Bronchioles
Smallest airways

Right lung
Divided into 3 lobes

Rib

Diaphragm
Skeletal muscle of respiration

Bronchus
Connects trachea to lungs

Left lung
Divided into 2 lobes

Mediastinum
Space between two lungs, includes pleura of both sides

Anterior view

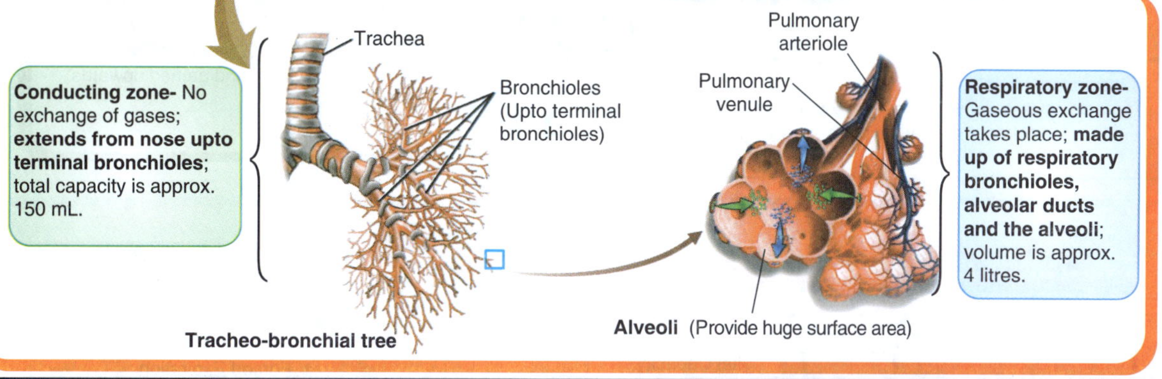

Conducting zone- No exchange of gases; **extends from nose upto terminal bronchioles**; total capacity is approx. 150 mL.

Trachea

Bronchioles (Upto terminal bronchioles)

Tracheo-bronchial tree

Pulmonary arteriole

Pulmonary venule

Alveoli (Provide huge surface area)

Respiratory zone- Gaseous exchange takes place; **made up of respiratory bronchioles, alveolar ducts and the alveoli**; volume is approx. 4 litres.

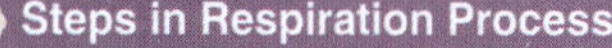

Steps in Respiration Process

Breathing (Inspiration + Expiration) → Diffusion of gases (CO_2 and O_2) across alveolar membrane → Transport of gases by the blood → Diffusion of gases between the blood and tissues → Cellular respiration

NEET POWER TIPS

- Breathing- Exchange of gases; extracellular process
- Respiration- Oxidation of glucose; intracellular process
- Humans- Aerobic respiration
  - Anaerobic respiration- RBCs and skeletal muscles (excess exercise)
- Respiratory pathway: External nares (passage way for air) → Nasal cavity (contain ciliated and goblet cells)→Internal nares→Nasopharynx→Laryngopharynx→Trachea→1° bronchi→2° bronchi→3° bronchi→Initial bronchioles→Terminal bronchioles → Duct of alveoli → Alveoli
- Alveoli composed of three cellular layers:
  - Type I pneumocytes
  - Type II pneumocytes (produce lecithin)
  - Capillary endotheloum
- Respiratory system composed of : Nasal passages, olfactory epithelium, conducting airway and respiratory portion of the lungs.

Mechanism of Breathing

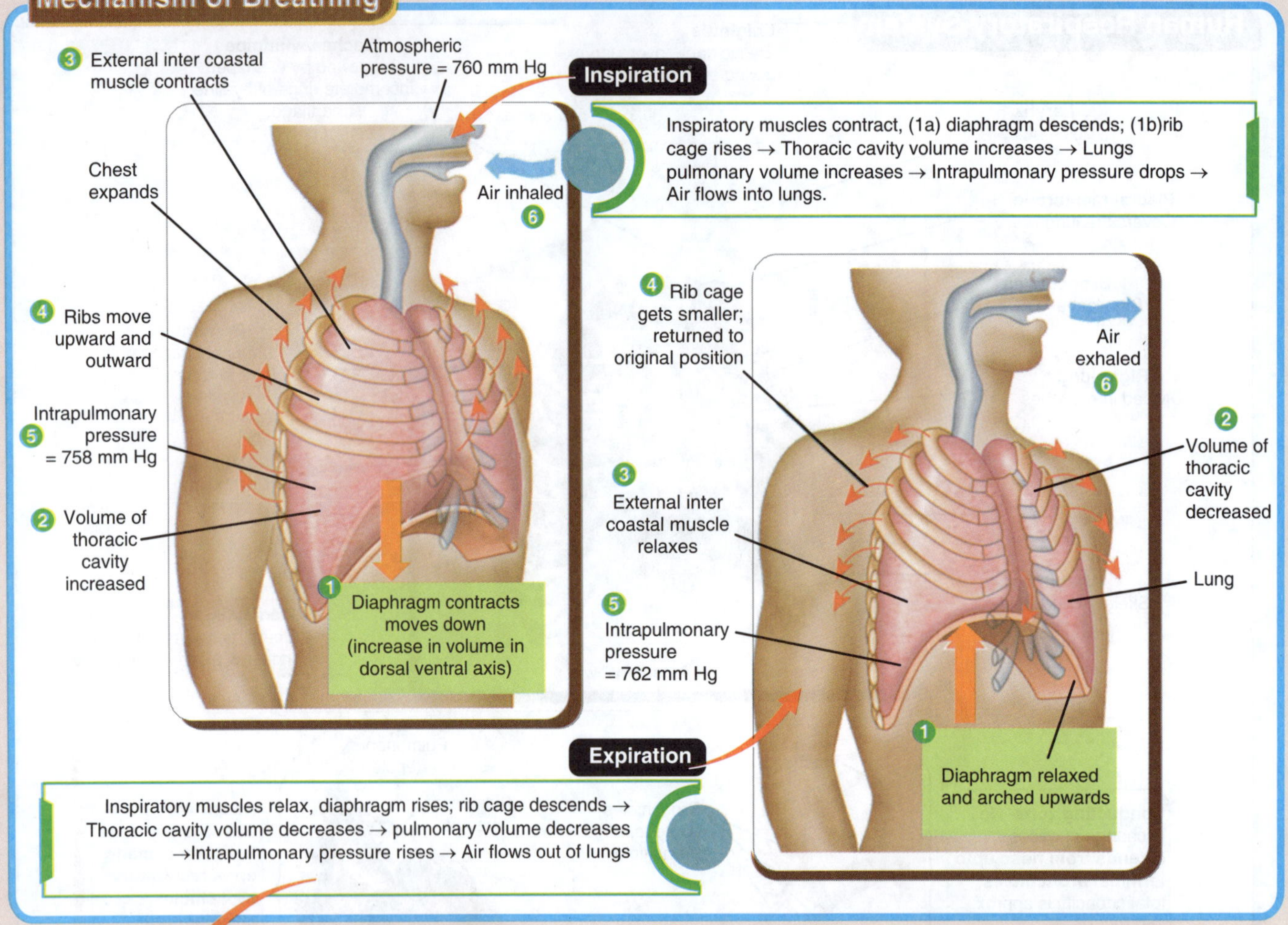

Inspiration

Inspiratory muscles contract, (1a) diaphragm descends; (1b)rib cage rises → Thoracic cavity volume increases → Lungs pulmonary volume increases → Intrapulmonary pressure drops → Air flows into lungs.

1. Diaphragm contracts moves down (increase in volume in dorsal ventral axis)
2. Volume of thoracic cavity increased
3. External inter coastal muscle contracts
4. Ribs move upward and outward
5. Intrapulmonary pressure = 758 mm Hg
6. Air inhaled

Atmospheric pressure = 760 mm Hg

Chest expands

Expiration

Inspiratory muscles relax, diaphragm rises; rib cage descends → Thoracic cavity volume decreases → pulmonary volume decreases →Intrapulmonary pressure rises → Air flows out of lungs

1. Diaphragm relaxed and arched upwards
2. Volume of thoracic cavity decreased
3. External inter coastal muscle relaxes
4. Rib cage gets smaller; returned to original position
5. Intrapulmonary pressure = 762 mm Hg
6. Air exhaled

Lung

Respiratory volumes and capacities

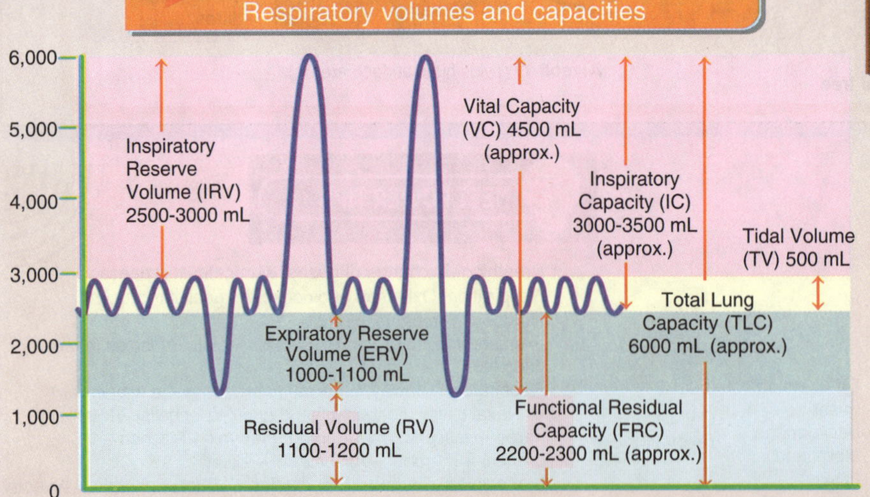

NEET POWER TIPS

- Forced Expiration
  - –Active process
  - –Abdominal internal intercostal muscle contracts.
- **Tidal volume** made up of two parts; dead space (150 mL) and alveolar volume (350 mL)
- **Residual volume** Amount of air left in lungs after forceful exhalation; prevents collapse of alveoli.
- Spirometer measures the volume of air in lungs; except residual volume, total lung capacity, functional residual capacity and dead space air.
- Birds have a unique way of breathing. They have stationary lungs that gets air pumped through it in one constant direction by a series of balloon - like air pocket.

Gaseous Exchange at Alveoli and Tissue Level

Route (1-6) of air with pressure changes in different parts of the body.

6 Exhaled air: pO_2 120, pCO_2 27

1 Atmospheric air: pO_2 159, pCO_2 0.3

2 Alveoli: pO_2 104, pCO_2 40

3 Oxygenated blood: pO_2 95, pCO_2 40

4 Tissues: pO_2 <40, pCO_2 <45

5 Deoxygenated blood: pO_2 40, pCO_2 45

Exhaled air, Inhaled air, Alveolar epithelial cells, Alveolar spaces, CO_2, O_2, Blood entering alveolar capillaries, Alveolar capillaries, Pulmonary arteries, Pulmonary veins, Systemic veins, Systemic arteries, Heart, Systemic capillaries, Body tissues

Differences in the partial pressures (in mm Hg) **are responsible for gaseous exchange (through diffusion)**

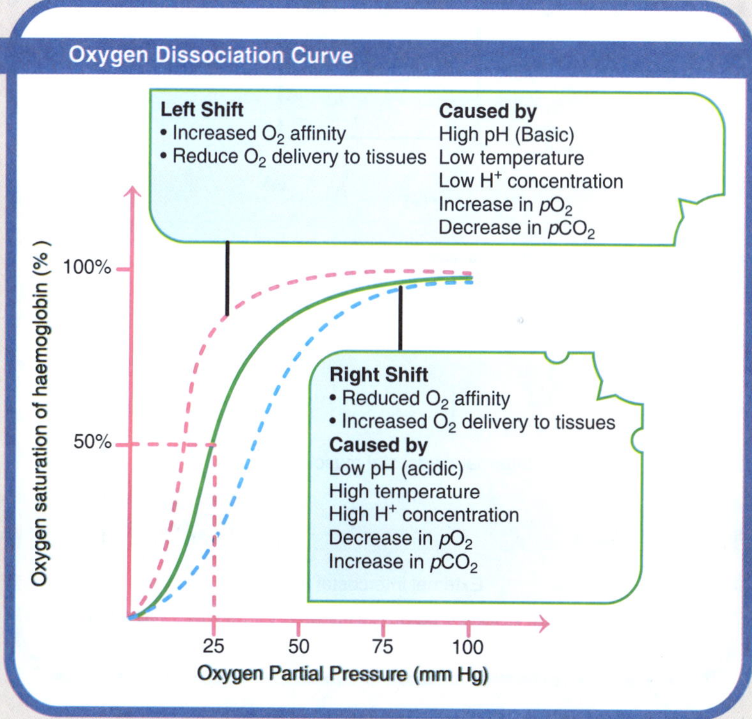

NEET POWER TIPS

Factors affecting alveolar- capillary gas exchange

- Surface area for diffusion (large surface-more gas exchange).
- Thickness of the alveolar membrane (thinner membrane- faster gas exchange).
- Partial pressure gradient (greater difference in partial pressure between air and blood- faster diffusion).
- Solubility for Hb with respect to O_2
  - CO_2 → 20–25 times more soluble
  - CO → 200–250 times more soluble
- **Haldane Effect** Binding of O_2 with haemoglobin leading to displacement of CO_2 from blood.
- **Bohr Effect** Increase in CO_2 concentration resulting in increased dissociation of oxyhaemoglobin.

Transport of Gases

Transport of Oxygen

- About 3% -Plasma (dissolved form)
- About 97% -Oxyhaemoglobin
  - Normal condition: 5 mL of O_2 transport to tissue by 100 mL of blood

$$Hb + O_2 \underset{tissue}{\overset{lungs}{\rightleftharpoons}} HbO_2$$

Transport of Carbon dioxide

- About 7%-Plasma (dissolved form)
- About 25% -Carbaminohaemoglobin

$$CO_2 + Hb \rightleftharpoons HbCO_2$$

- About 70% -Bicarbonate ion (HCO_3^-)

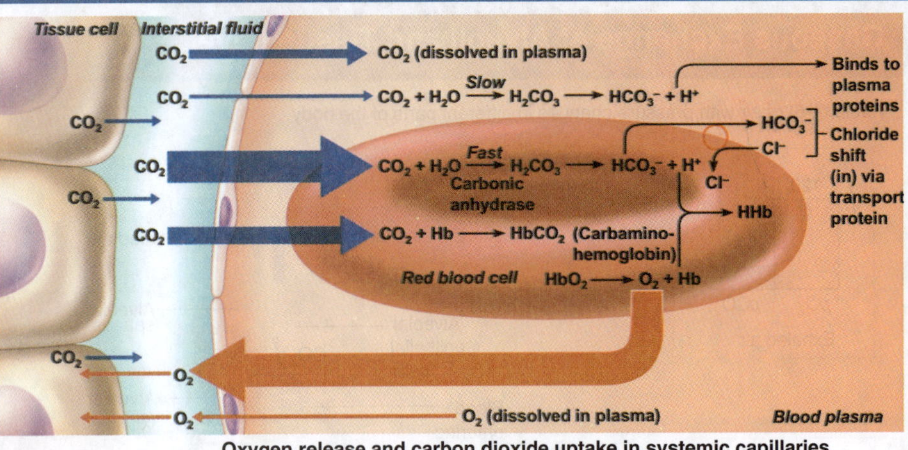

Oxygen release and carbon dioxide uptake in systemic capillaries

NEET POWER TIPS

- Most of the bicarbonate ions formed within RBCs diffuse into plasma to restore ionic balance, chloride ions diffuse from plasma to RBCs.

Hamburger's phenomena/chloride shift.

- Movement of chloride ions from RBCs to plasma Reverse Chloride shift
- Increase in H^+ and CO_2 levels activates chemoreceptors and leads to exhalation.
- If the CO_2 content of blood drops below a critical level, breathing stops.
- The level of CO_2 has more effect on breathing than the level of O_2.

Regulation of Respiration

Neural Regulation

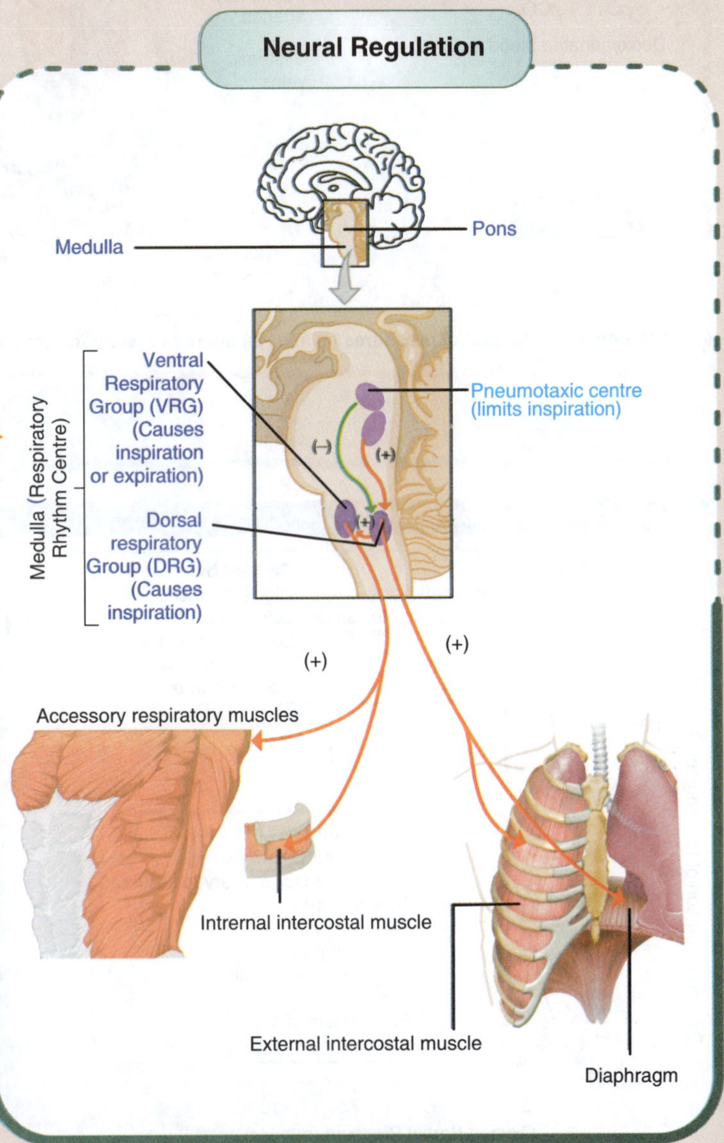

Chemical

Medulla (Central chemoreceptors; sensitive to H^+ levels and pCO_2)

Glossopharyngeal nerve

Vagus nerve

Carotid body

Aortic bodies

Peripheral chemoreceptors; sensitive to pO_2, pCO_2 and H^+ concentration

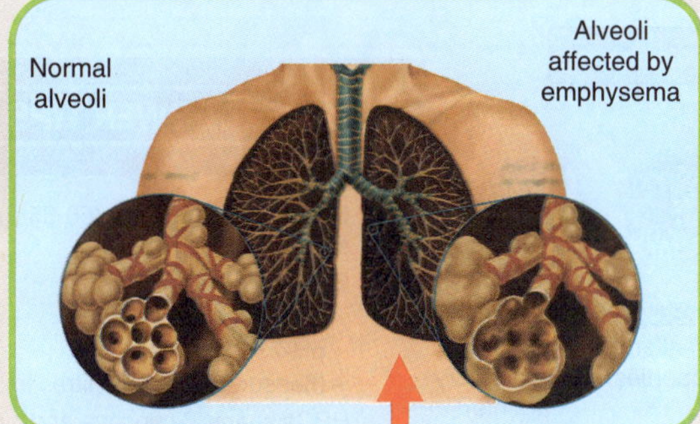

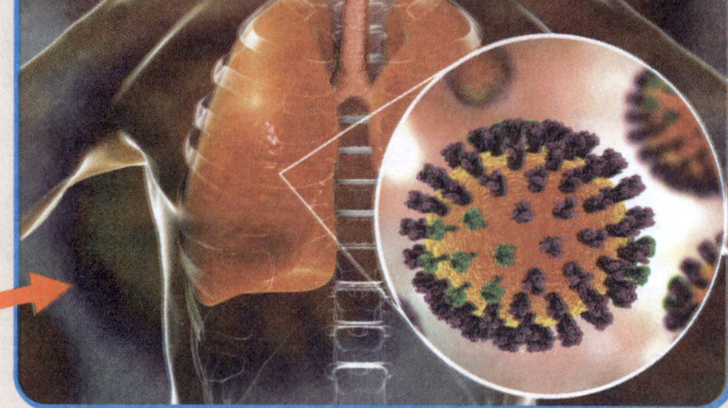

Disorders of Respiratory System

Emphysema- Reduction in alveolar ventilation; due to cigarette smoking

Severe Acute Respiratory Syndrome (SARS) A viral disease characterised by dry cough, headache, fever, hyoxia, etc.

Bronchitis- Inflammation of bronchi

Asthma- Difficulty in breathing due to an allergic reaction.

Occupational Respiratory Disorders- Proliferation of fibrous connective tissue of upper respiratory tract; causing inflammation

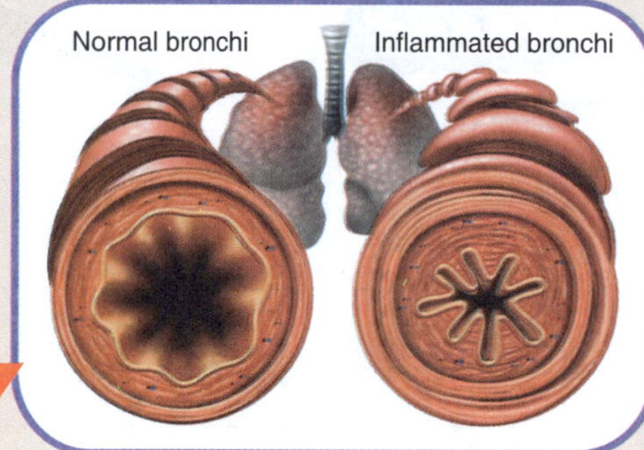

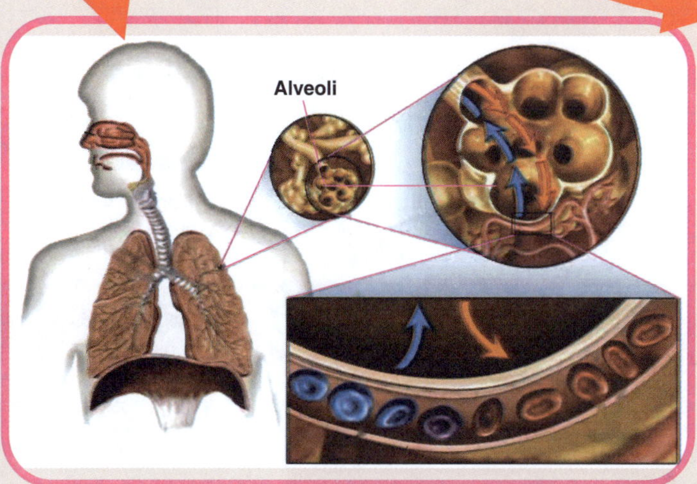

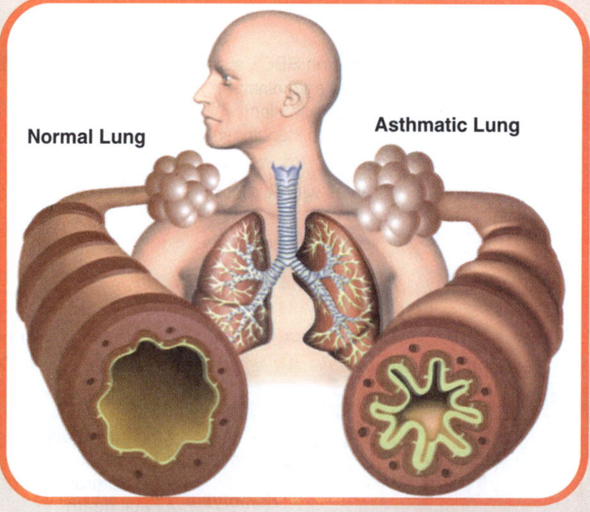

Chapter 15 Body Fluids and Circulation

Components of blood

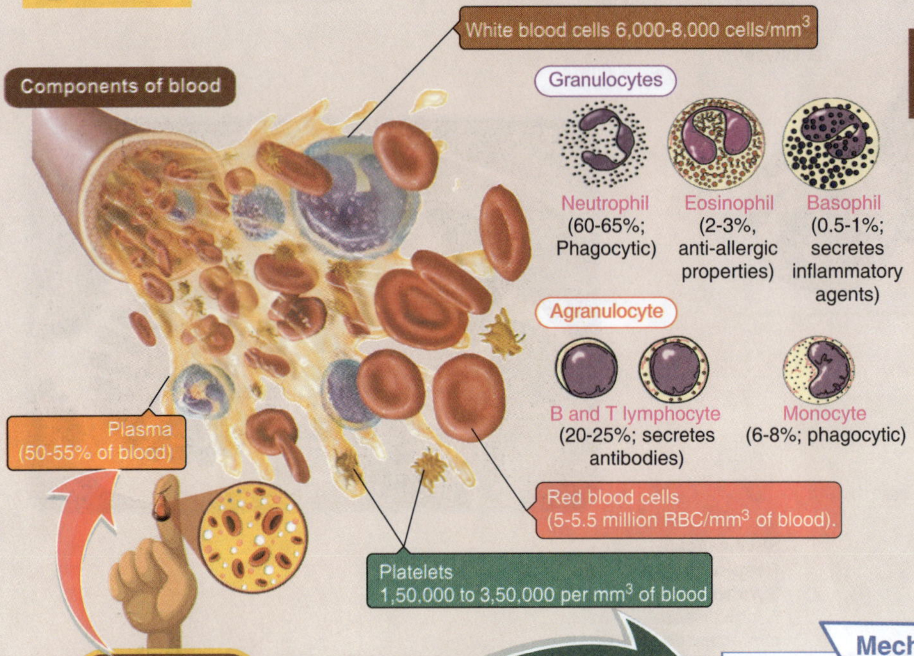

White blood cells 6,000-8,000 cells/mm³
Granulocytes
Neutrophil (60-65%; Phagocytic)
Eosinophil (2-3%, anti-allergic properties)
Basophil (0.5-1%; secretes inflammatory agents)
Agranulocyte
B and T lymphocyte (20-25%; secretes antibodies)
Monocyte (6-8%; phagocytic)
Red blood cells (5-5.5 million RBC/mm³ of blood).
Platelets 1,50,000 to 3,50,000 per mm³ of blood
Plasma (50-55% of blood)

NEET POWER TIPS

- Composed of plasma (50-55%) and formed elements (45%).
- **Blood**
  - Fluid connective tissue
  - pH-7.4 (alkaline)
  - Measures about 5.5 litres in human body.
- RBCs shape-Biconcave and circular; nucleus absent.
- RBCs of camels and Llamas are oval shaped and nucleated.
- Erythropoiesis occurs in liver and spleen in fetus and in red bone marrow after birth.

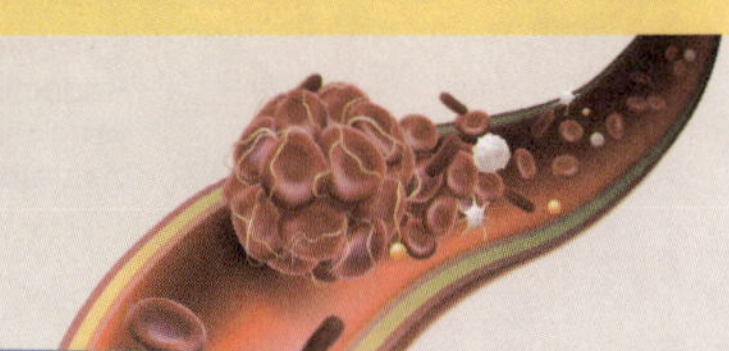

Blood

Blood Group **Karl Landsteiner**

Blood Groups	A	B	AB (Universal Recipient)	O (Universal donor)
Antigens on RBC's surface	A	B	AB	O
Antibodies in plasma	Anti-B	Anti-A	None	Anti-A and Anti-B

Rh Blood Group

- Rhesus antigen, present on RBC's surface.
- If present –Rh+ve (blood agglutinates)
- If absent –Rh–ve (no agglutination)
- *Erythroblastosis foetalis* Rh incompatibility in pregnancy

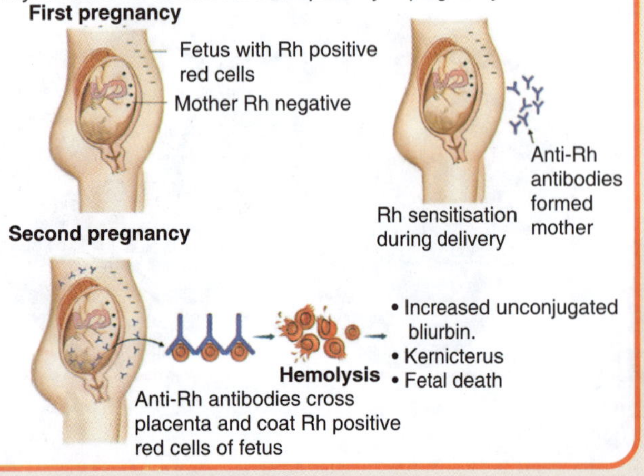

First pregnancy
Fetus with Rh positive red cells
Mother Rh negative
Anti-Rh antibodies formed mother
Rh sensitisation during delivery
Second pregnancy
Hemolysis
• Increased unconjugated bliurbin.
• Kernicterus
• Fetal death
Anti-Rh antibodies cross placenta and coat Rh positive red cells of fetus

Mechanism of Blood Clotting

Injured tissue → (Releases) → Thromboplastin → (Ca^{2+} proteins)

Blood platelets → (Disintegrate and release) → Platelet factor-3 → (Ca^{2+} proteins)

→ Prothrombinase → (Inactivates heparin and catalyses)

Prothrombin (Inactive plasma protein) → (Ca^{2+}) → Thrombin (Active protein catalyses)

Fibrinogen → Fibrin → (Traps blood corpuscles) → Clot

Red blood cell
Platelet
Damaged cells
Platelets
Fibrin (Thread of protein)
Clot (Fibrin + Blood cells)

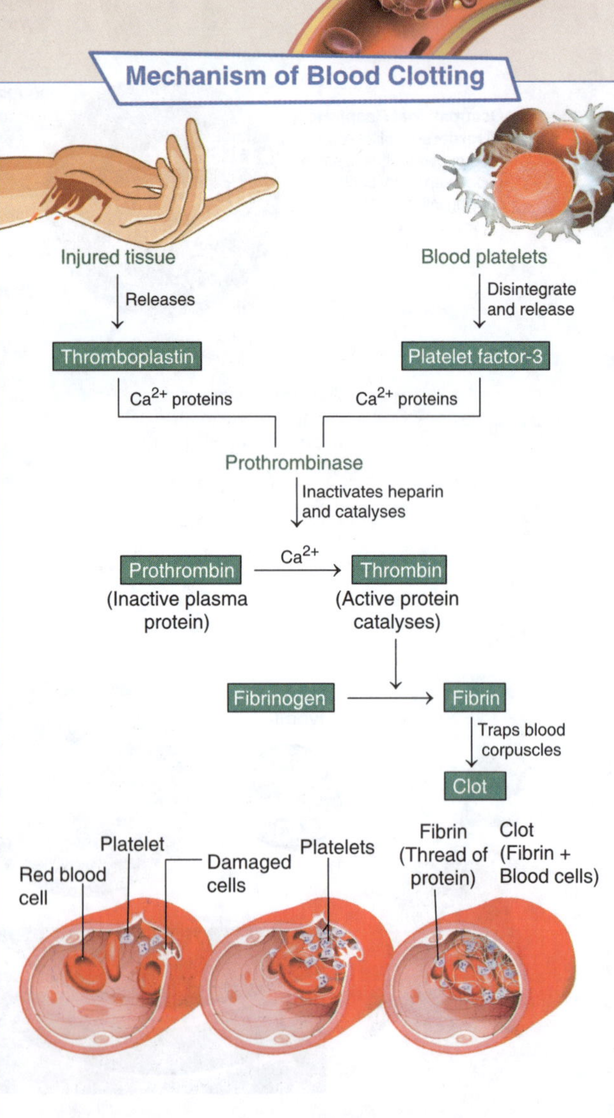

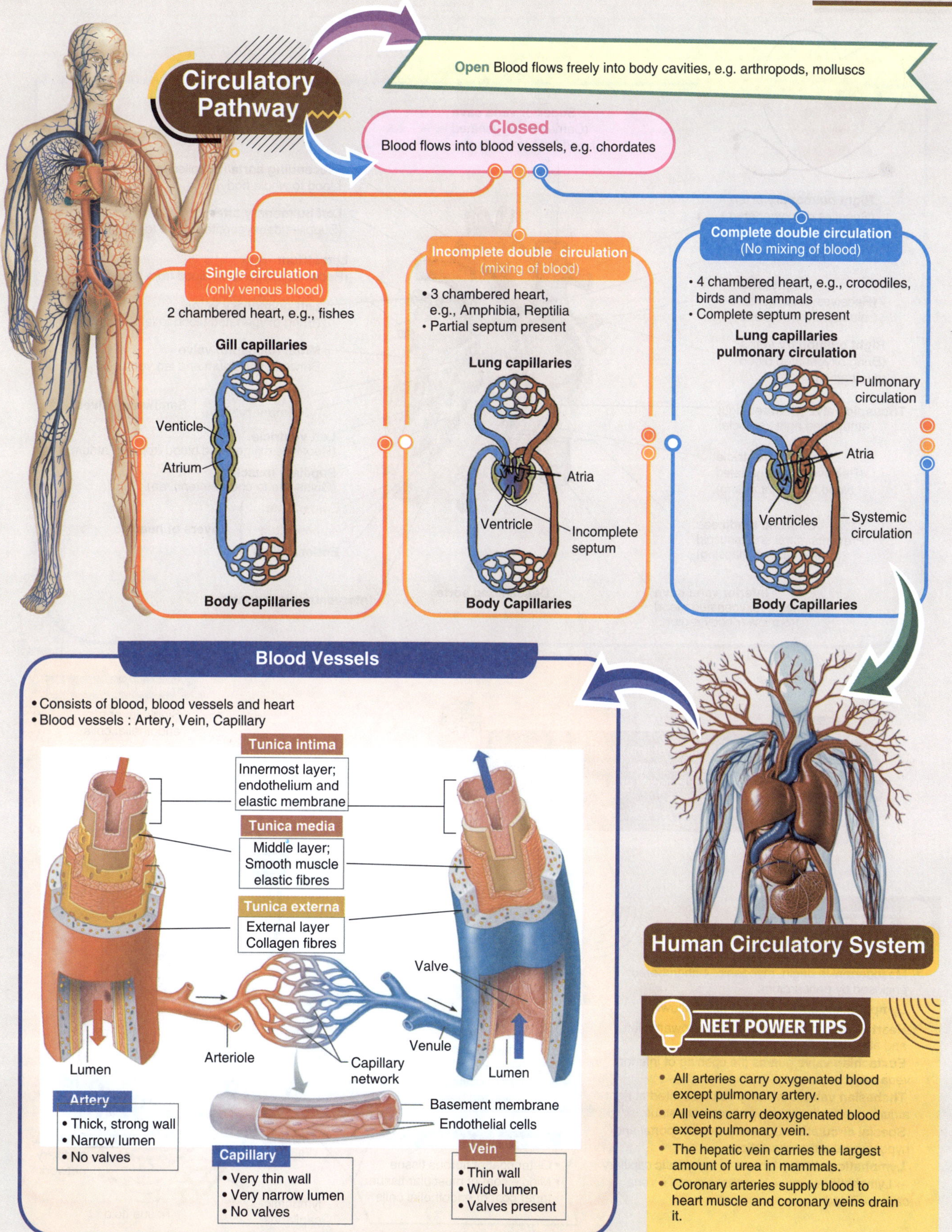
Circulatory Pathway
Open Blood flows freely into body cavities, e.g. arthropods, molluscs
Closed
Blood flows into blood vessels, e.g. chordates
Single circulation
(only venous blood)
2 chambered heart, e.g., fishes
Gill capillaries
Venticle
Atrium
Body Capillaries
Incomplete double circulation
(mixing of blood)
• 3 chambered heart, e.g., Amphibia, Reptilia
• Partial septum present
Lung capillaries
Atria
Ventricle
Incomplete septum
Body Capillaries
Complete double circulation
(No mixing of blood)
• 4 chambered heart, e.g., crocodiles, birds and mammals
• Complete septum present
Lung capillaries pulmonary circulation
Pulmonary circulation
Atria
Ventricles
Systemic circulation
Body Capillaries
Blood Vessels
• Consists of blood, blood vessels and heart
• Blood vessels : Artery, Vein, Capillary
Tunica intima
Innermost layer; endothelium and elastic membrane
Tunica media
Middle layer; Smooth muscle elastic fibres
Tunica externa
External layer Collagen fibres
Valve
Venule
Arteriole
Capillary network
Lumen
Lumen
Artery
• Thick, strong wall
• Narrow lumen
• No valves
Basement membrane
Endothelial cells
Capillary
• Very thin wall
• Very narrow lumen
• No valves
Vein
• Thin wall
• Wide lumen
• Valves present
Human Circulatory System
NEET POWER TIPS
• All arteries carry oxygenated blood except pulmonary artery.
• All veins carry deoxygenated blood except pulmonary vein.
• The hepatic vein carries the largest amount of urea in mammals.
• Coronary arteries supply blood to heart muscle and coronary veins drain it.

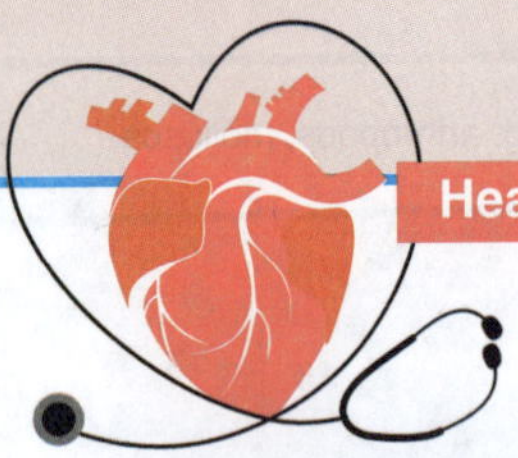

Heart

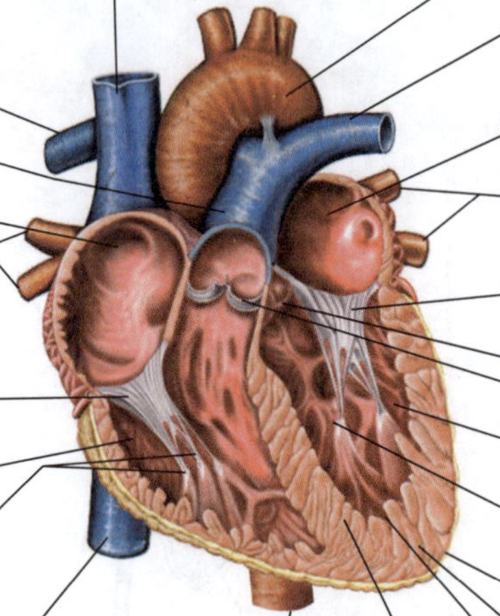

Superior vena cava (Carries deoxygenated blood from upper body.)
Right pulmonary artery (Supplies deoxygenated blood to the right lung)
Pulmonary trunk
Right atrium (Receives deoxygenated blood from whole body)
Right pulmonary veins (Bring oxygenated blood to left atrium)
Tricuspid valve (Between right atrium and right ventricle)
Right ventricle (Receives deoxygenated blood from right atrium)
Chordae tendineae (Prevents mitral and tricuspid valves from collapsing)
Inferior vena cava (Carries deoxygenated blood from lower body region.)
Descending aorta
Interventricular septum
Asecending aorta (Supplies oxygenated blood to whole body)
Left pulmonary artery (Supplies deoxygenated blood to the left lung)
Left atrium (Receives oxygenated blood from lungs)
Left pulmonary veins (Bring oxygenated blood to left atrium)
Mitral (bicuspid) valve Between left atrium and left ventricle)
Aortic valve
Pulmonary valve
Semilunar valves
Left ventricle (Receives oxygenated blood from left atrium)
Papillary muscle (Gives rise to chordae tendirae)
Epicardium
Myocardium
Endocardium
Layers of heart

Lymphatic System

Comprises of lymph, lymphatic capillaries lymphatic vessels lymphatic nodes and lymphatic ducts.

Lymphatic capillaries

Single layer of endothelial cells

Tissue fluid
Pulmonary capillary network
Blood flow
Systemic capillary network
lymph flow
lymphatic capilaries
Tissue fluid

Lymphatic nodes

- Small oval or bean-shaped.
- Lymphocytes are produced here.

Lymphatic vessels

- Outer coat of fibrous tissue
- Middle coat of muscular tissue
- Inner coat of endothelial cells

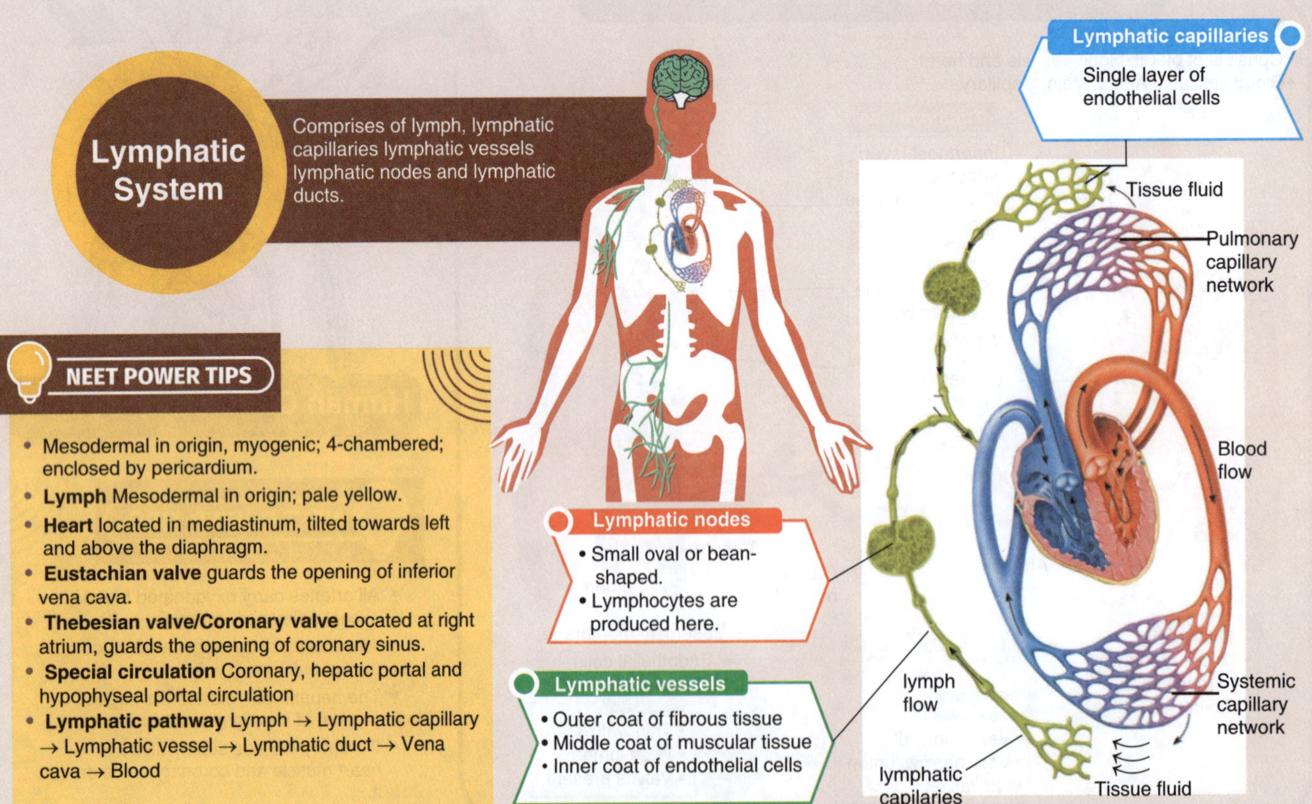

NEET POWER TIPS

- Mesodermal in origin, myogenic; 4-chambered; enclosed by pericardium.
- **Lymph** Mesodermal in origin; pale yellow.
- **Heart** located in mediastinum, tilted towards left and above the diaphragm.
- **Eustachian valve** guards the opening of inferior vena cava.
- **Thebesian valve/Coronary valve** Located at right atrium, guards the opening of coronary sinus.
- **Special circulation** Coronary, hepatic portal and hypophyseal portal circulation
- **Lymphatic pathway** Lymph → Lymphatic capillary → Lymphatic vessel → Lymphatic duct → Vena cava → Blood

Impulse Conducting System

1. **The Sino-Atrial** (SA) **node** (pacemaker) generates impulses, initiation rate is 70-80 beats/min.
2. The impulses pause (0.1 sec) at the **Atroventcirular** (AV) **node** (pacesetter) strengthes SA node signals and produces 40-45 depolarisation/min.
3. The atrioventricular bundle/bundle of His connects the atria to the ventricle; receives signals from A.V. node.
4. **The bundle branches** conduct the impulses through the interventricular septum.
5. **Purkinje fibres** stimulate the signal to both ventricles to contract.

Superior vena cava

Right atrium

NEET POWER TIPS

- **Types :** Neurogenic (nerve impulse) and myogenic (heart muscle)
- **Pulse:** Rhythmic contraction and relaxation in the aorta and its main arteries.
- **Heart murmur**- Irregular heart sound

Cardiac output = Stroke Volume (Blood pumped by ventricle/cardiac cycle) × Heart rate (Number of cardiac cycle/min).

= 70 mL × 72 ≅ 5L

Heartbeat

- Rhythmic contraction and relaxation of the heart.
- Includes one systole and one diastole
- Healthy heart beats 72 times/min.

Regulation of Cardiac Activity

- **Hormonal Regulation** : Adrenaline and nor-adrenaline secreted by medulla of adrenal gland accelerate heart beat.
- **Neural Regulation** : Cardiac centre lies in medulla, parasympathetic nerve fibres decrease heart beat and sympathetic nerve fibres increase heart beat.

Cardiac Cycle

Atrial systole (0.1 sec)

Blood flows into relaxed ventricles

Isovolumic/ isovolumetric contraction
Ventricles begin to contract (AV node), bicuspid 'LUB' closure of A.V valves and tricuspid valves close

Ventricular contraction

Ventricular ejection
Ventricular pressure rises,semilunar valves open

Ventricular systole (0.3 sec)

Isovolumic/ isovolumetric relaxation (ventricular diastole-early)

Ventricles relax , semilunar valves close 'DUB' closure of semilunar valve; blood flows into the relaxed atria.

Ventricular diastole-late

Tricuspid and bicuspid valves open

Ventricular diastole (0.4 sec)

Electrocardiogram

- Record of electric current produced by excitation of cardiac muscle.
- Use electrocardiograph machine.

	QRS Complex
Q wave	• Ventricular depolarisation
R wave	• Followed by ventricular contraction
S wave	

P-wave
- Depolarisation of atria
- Followed by atrial contraction

T-wave
- Repolarisation of ventricles
- Followed by ventricle relaxation
- End of ventricle systole

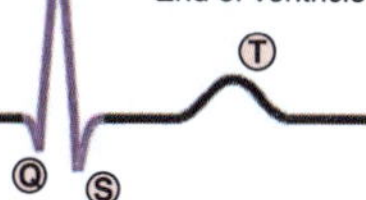

Disorders of circulatory system

Hypertension
High blood pressure, 140/90 mm Hg, can harm brain, kidney and heart

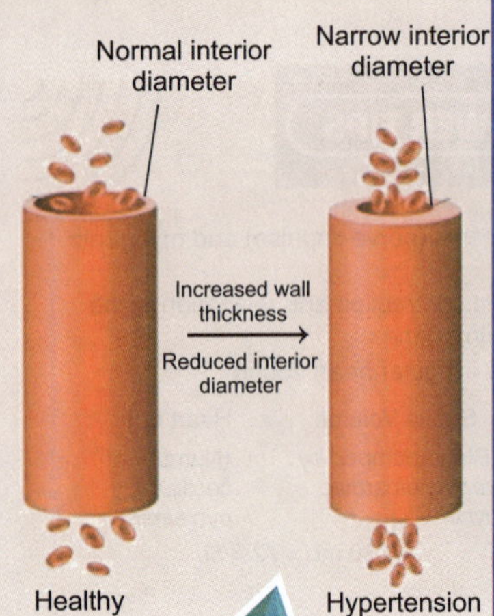

Atherosclerosis/Coronary Artery Disease (CAD)
Deposit of fat, cholesterol, calcium and fibrous tissues around blood vessel.

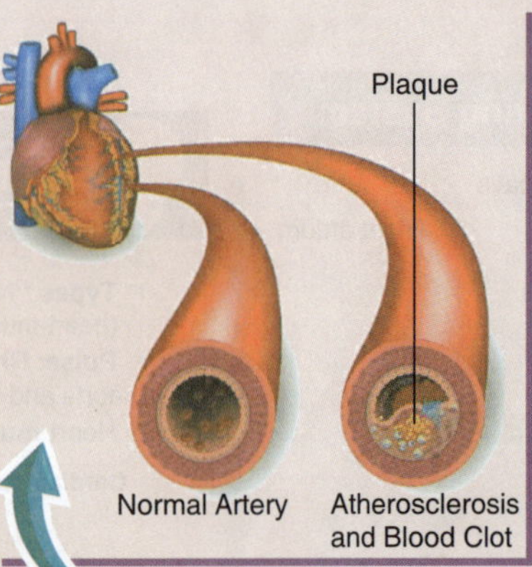

Heart Attack/ Myocardial Infarction
Sudden damage in heart muscle by an inadequate blood supply

Artery
Blood clot
Cholesterol
Dying muscle
Healthy muscle
Coronary arteries

Congenital Heart Disease
Defect of heart from birth

Normal anatomy

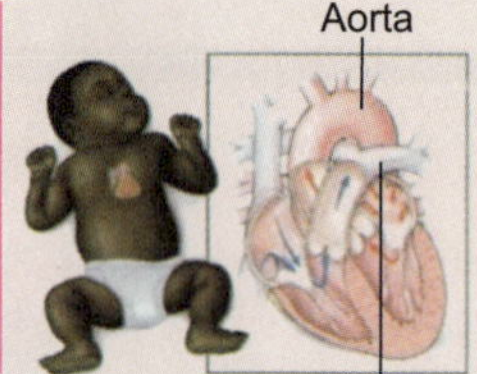

Examples of congenital heart issues

Aortic coarctation
Transposition of the great arteries
Atrial septal defect
Ventricular septal defect

Angina Pectoris
Chest pain due to inadequate oxygen reaching heart muscles; blockage in coronary artery

Tightness or pain in chest

Cardiac Arrest
Sudden unexpected loss of heart function, leads to death.

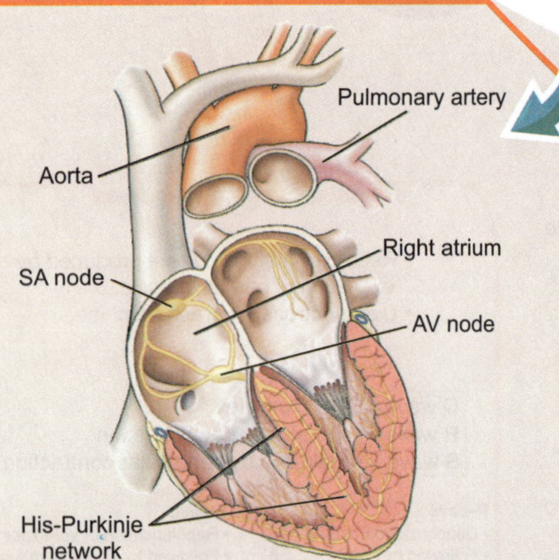

Heart Failure
Chronic condition, heart is not able to pump blood effectively

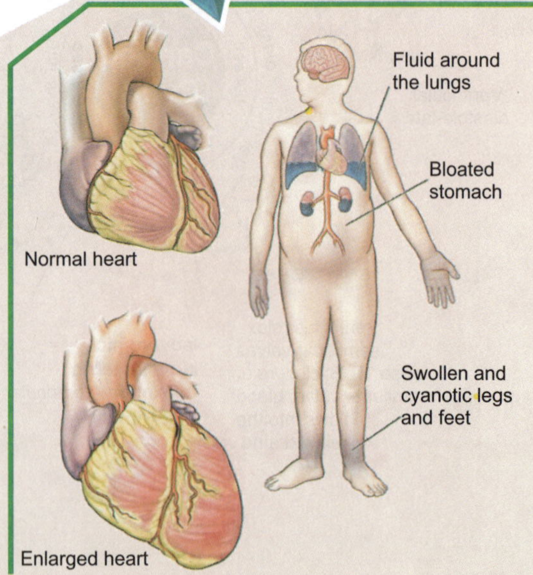

Chapter 16

Excretory Products and Their Elimination

Kidney

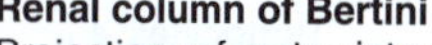

Renal Cortex
Outer dark region

Fibrous / Renal capsule
Thin, tough layer of collagen and elastin fibres

Major calyxes
Major calyces 2-3 open into renal pelvis

Renal artery
A large blood vessel, carries blood from the heart to the kidney

Renal vein
Drains blood from kidneys and ureter into the inferior vena cava

Renal pelvis
Proximal part of ureter; breaks into 2-3 branches towards kidney (major calyx)

Ureter
Opens into urinary bladder

Renal column of Bertini
Projections of cortex into medulla

Renal papilla
Opening of medullary pyramids in the lumen of minor calyx

Minor calyxes
Medullary pyramids are connected with minor calyces

Medullary pyramids
Medulla divided into a number of conical areas to form medullary pyramids

Arcuate vein
Carry blood from renal cortex to interlobar veins.

Arcuate artery
Arch-like shape, run between the cortex and medulla

Human Urinary System

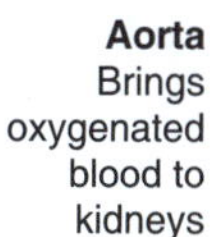

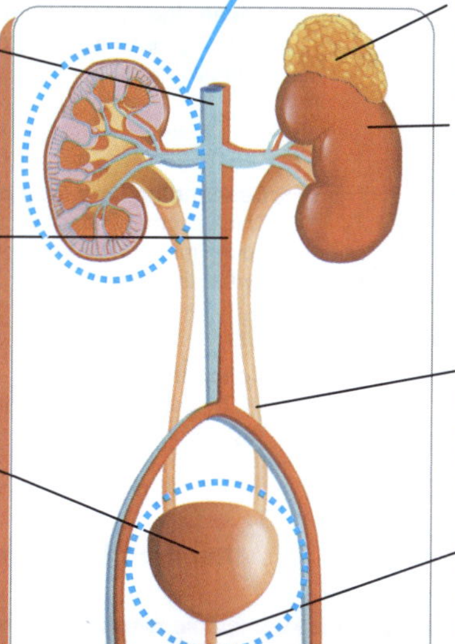

Aorta
Brings oxygenated blood to kidneys

Inferior vena cava
Carries deoxygenated blood from kidneys to the heart.

Urinary Bladder
Reservoir of urine in the pelvic cavity.

Adrenal gland
Produces hormones; divided into cortex and medulla

Kidney
Dark red, bean-shaped structure, metanephric; Located between T12 and L3

Ureter
Narrow, tubular structure opens into urinary bladder.

Urethra
Canal-like structure, opens to exterior by urethral orifice.

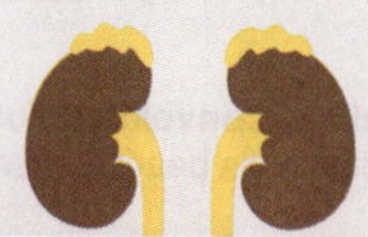

Human Excretory System

Types of Organisms based on Excretory Products

Ammonotelic- Excretes ammonia (aquatic animals), highly toxic, highly soluble in water e.g., protozoans, sponges, etc.
Ureotelic- Excretes urea (semi-aquatic animals), less toxic, less soluble in water, e.g., frogs, mammals, etc.
Uricotelic- Excretes uric acid (aminals living in dry condition), insoluble in water, e.g., snails, birds, etc.
Aminotelic- Excretes amino acids, e.g., molluscs and echinoderms
Guanotelism- Excretes guanine, e.g., spiders.

NEET POWER TIPS

Excretion Organs in Animals

Organs of Excretion	Animals	Organs of Excretion	Animals
Contractile vacuoles and plasma membrane	Protozoans	Malpighian tubules	Insects (Arthropoda)
General body surface	*Hydra* and sponges	Coxal glands	Spider (*Arachnida*, Phylum- Arthropoda)
Renette cells	Aschelminthes	Antennal glands or green glands	Prawn (Crustacea, Phylum- Arthropoda)
Flame cells (solenocytes and protonephridia)	Planarians (Platyhelminthes)	Keber's organ and organs of Bojanus	Molluscs
Nephridia and chloragogen cells	Earthworm (Annelida)	Kidneys	Vertebrates

Nephron

- Nephron is basic structural and functional unit of the kidney.
- Differentiated into-Renal corpuscle or Malpighian corpuscle and renal tubule.

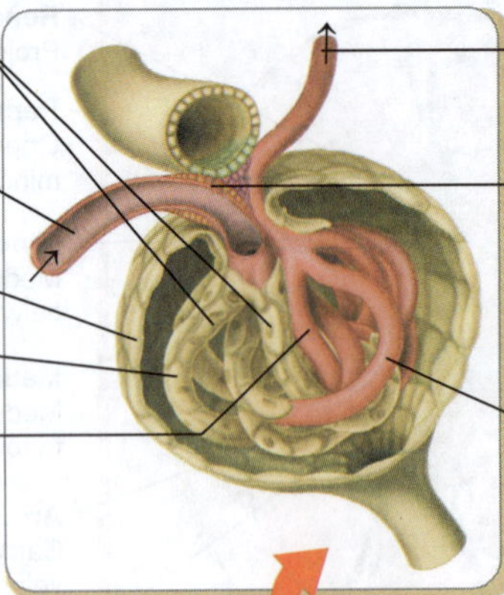

Podocytes
Highly specialised cell plays an active role in glomerular filtration

Afferent arteriole
Blood enters into glomerulus

Bowman's capsule
Double layered, cup-shaped structure
- Glomerular capsule parietal layer
- Glomerular capsule visceral layer

Glomerular capillary
Network of looped capillaries, filtres blood

Efferent arteriole
Blood leaves from glomerulus

Juxtaglomerular cells
Specialised smooth muscle, release hormone-enzyme renin

Glomerulus
Consists of a complex anastomosing plexus of vessel

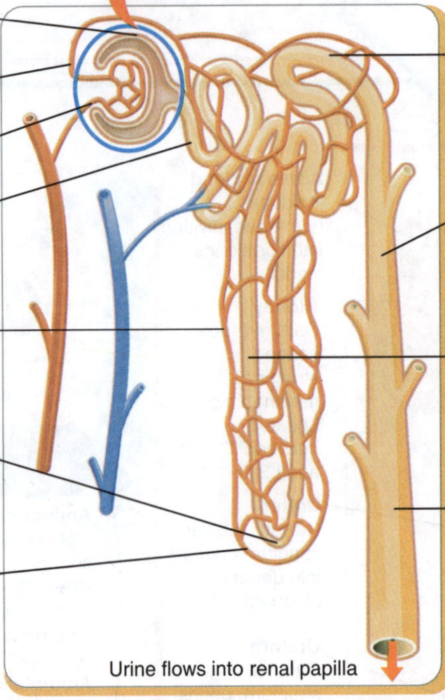

Glomerular capsule

Efferent arteriole

Afferent arteriole

Proximal Convoluted Tubule
Lined by cuboidal cells bearing microvilli

Vasa recta
Vessels network runs parallel to the Henle's loop

U-loop
Length of cells is minimised in this region

Peritubular capillary network
Allows reabsorption and secretion between blood and inner lumen of nephron

Distal Convoluted Tubule
Lined by cuboidal cells, small and irregularly spaced microvilli

Ascending limb of loop of Henle
Thin segment, linked by cuboidal epithelial cells.

Descending limb loop of Henle
Thick segment lined by cuboidal epithelium and thin segment lined by flat epithelial cells

Collecting Duct
DCT joins and unite to form larger ducts of Bellini

Urine flows into renal papilla

Nephron Structure

- **Urea Formation in Liver** (Krebs' Henseleit cycle)
  – Convert ammonia into urea.
  – **Pathway of urea**: Hepatic vein → Inferior vena cava → Right atrium → Right ventricle → Pulmonary artery → Lungs → Pulmonary vein → Left atrium → Left vein → Aorta → Renal artery → Kidney
- The amount of filtrate formed by kidney per minute is GFR; healthy individual-125 mL/min, i.e., 180L per day.

Steps of Urine Formation

1. **Glomerular filtration:** H_2O, nutrients and wastes are filtered from glomerular capillaries into Bowman's capsule.
2. **Tubular reabsorption:** In the proximal tubule, most water and nutrients are reabsorbed into the blood.
3. **Tubular secretion:** In the distal tubule, additional wastes are actively secreted into the tubule from the blood.
4. **Concentration:** Collecting duct creates concentrated urine more than the blood.

Types of Nephron

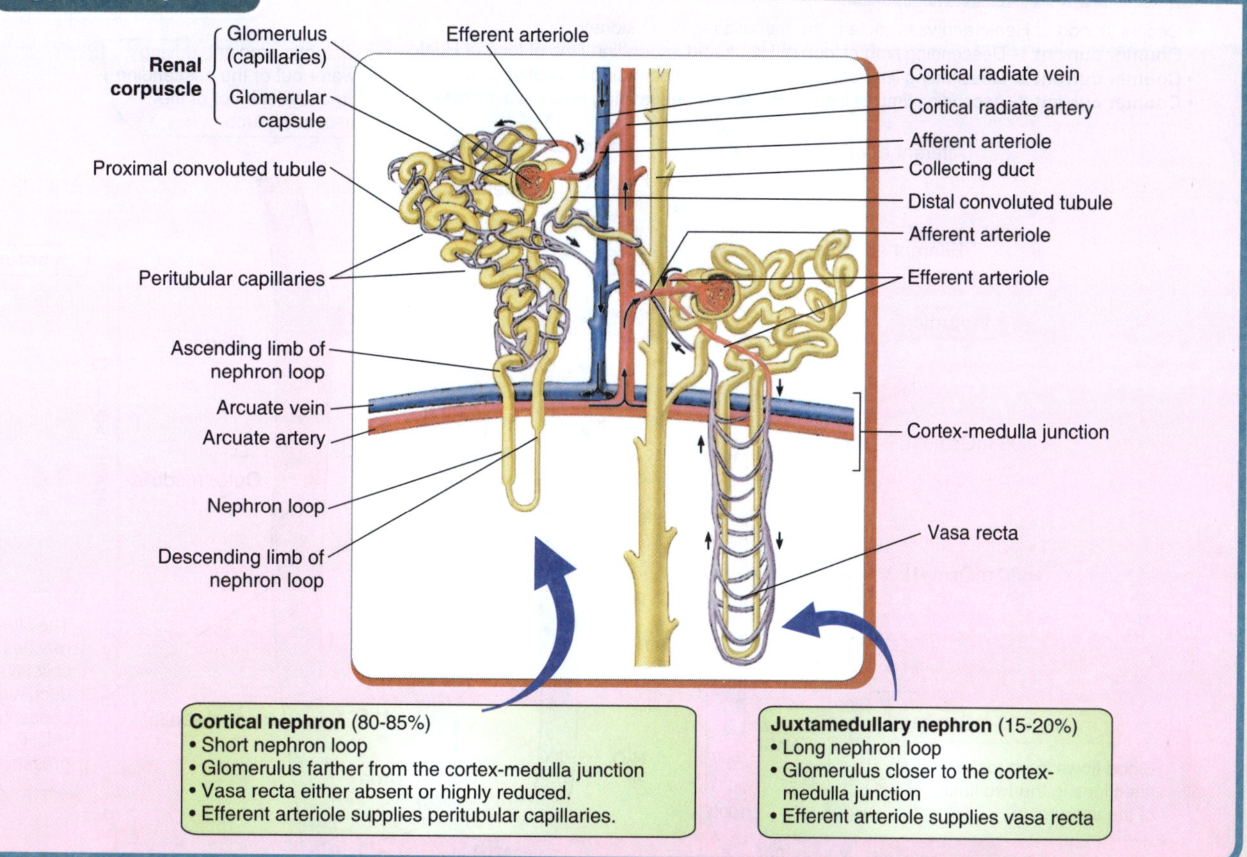

Cortical nephron (80-85%)
- Short nephron loop
- Glomerulus farther from the cortex-medulla junction
- Vasa recta either absent or highly reduced.
- Efferent arteriole supplies peritubular capillaries.

Juxtamedullary nephron (15-20%)
- Long nephron loop
- Glomerulus closer to the cortex-medulla junction
- Efferent arteriole supplies vasa recta

Function of Tubules

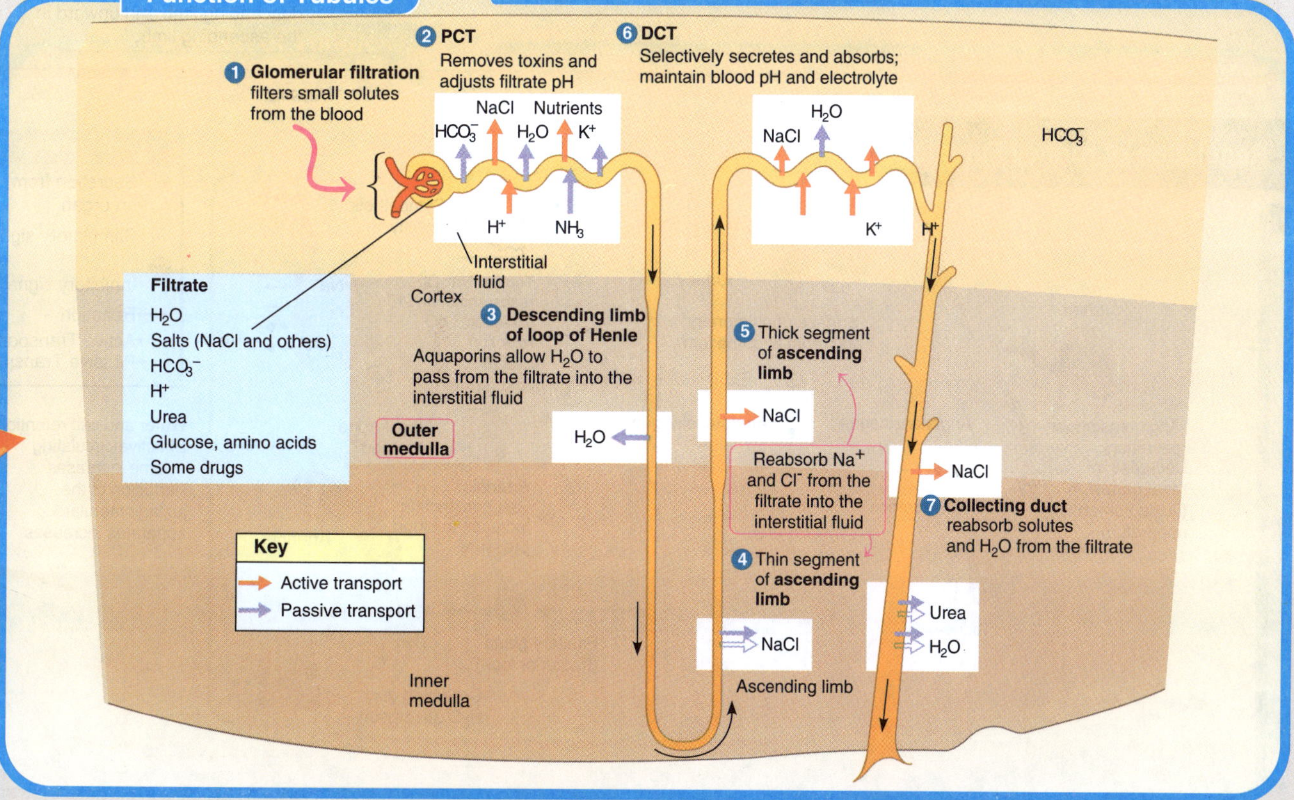

Counter Current Mechanism

- Occurs in loop of Henle and vasa recta in the medulla region of kidney.
- **Counter current 1**- Descending limb of loop of Henle and ascending limb of loop of Henle.
- **Counter current 2**- Descending limb of loop of Henle and ascending limb of vasa recta
- **Counter current 3**- Ascending limb of loop of Henle and descending limb of vasa recta

① Blood flows in opposite directions in the two limbs of the vasa recta.

② Osmotic gradient, driving water out of the descending limb and salt out of the ascending limb.

③ Filtrate flows downward in the descending limb and upward in the ascending limb.

④ The filtrate reaches the collecting duct, highly concentrated (ADH present.)

Afferent arteriole
Bowman's capsule
Glomerulus
Efferent arteriole
Isotonic
Hypotonic
Hypertonic
Cortex
Outer medulla
Inner medulla
Osmotic Gradient
300 mOsmo1L^{-1}
600 mOsmo1L^{-1}
900 mOsmo1L^{-1}
1200 mOsmo1L^{-1}
Vasa recta: 300, 400, 600, 800, 1000, 1200, 1000, 800, 600, 400, 300; NaCl; H_2O
Nephron: 300, 400, 600, 800, 1000, 1200, 900, 600, 400, 300, 200; NaCl; H_2O; Urea

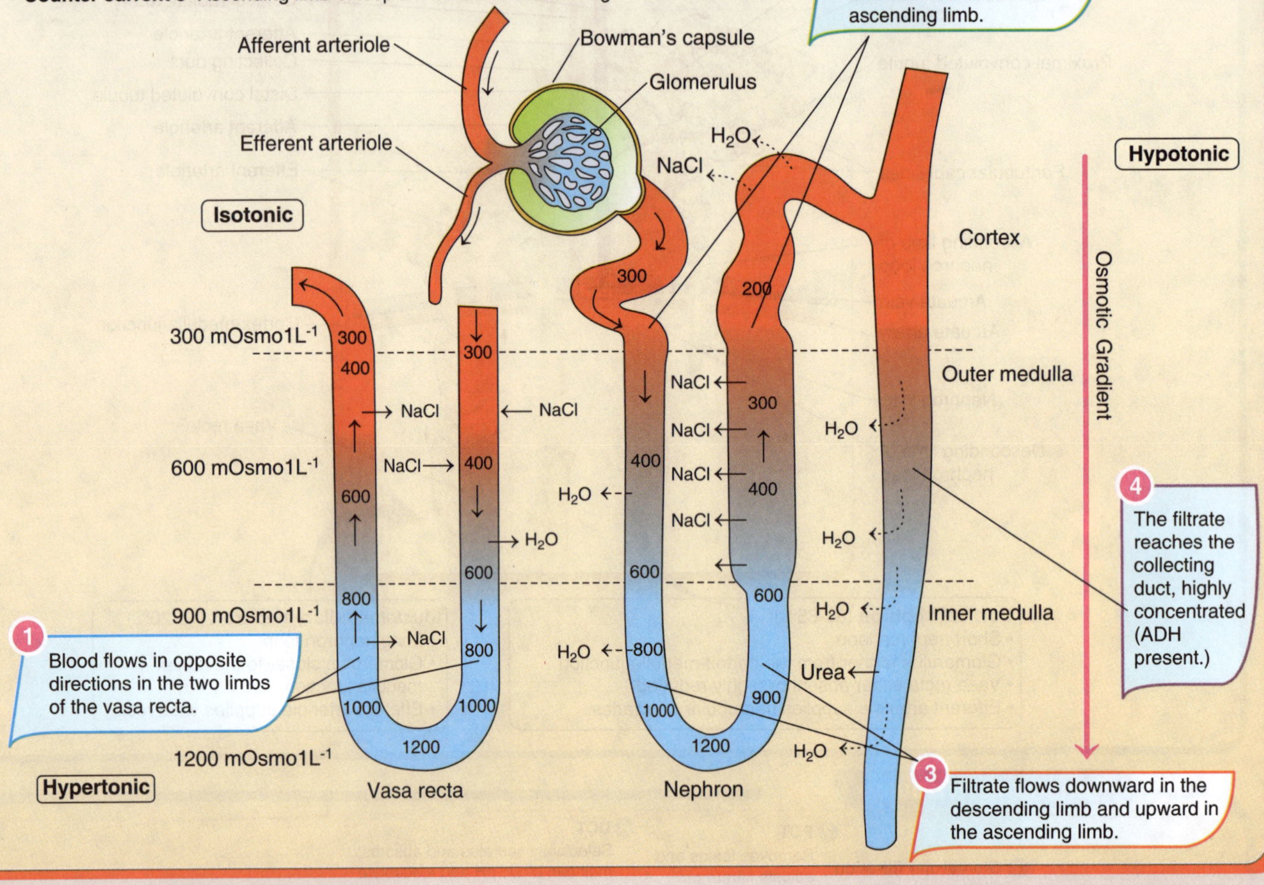

Regulation of Kidney Functions

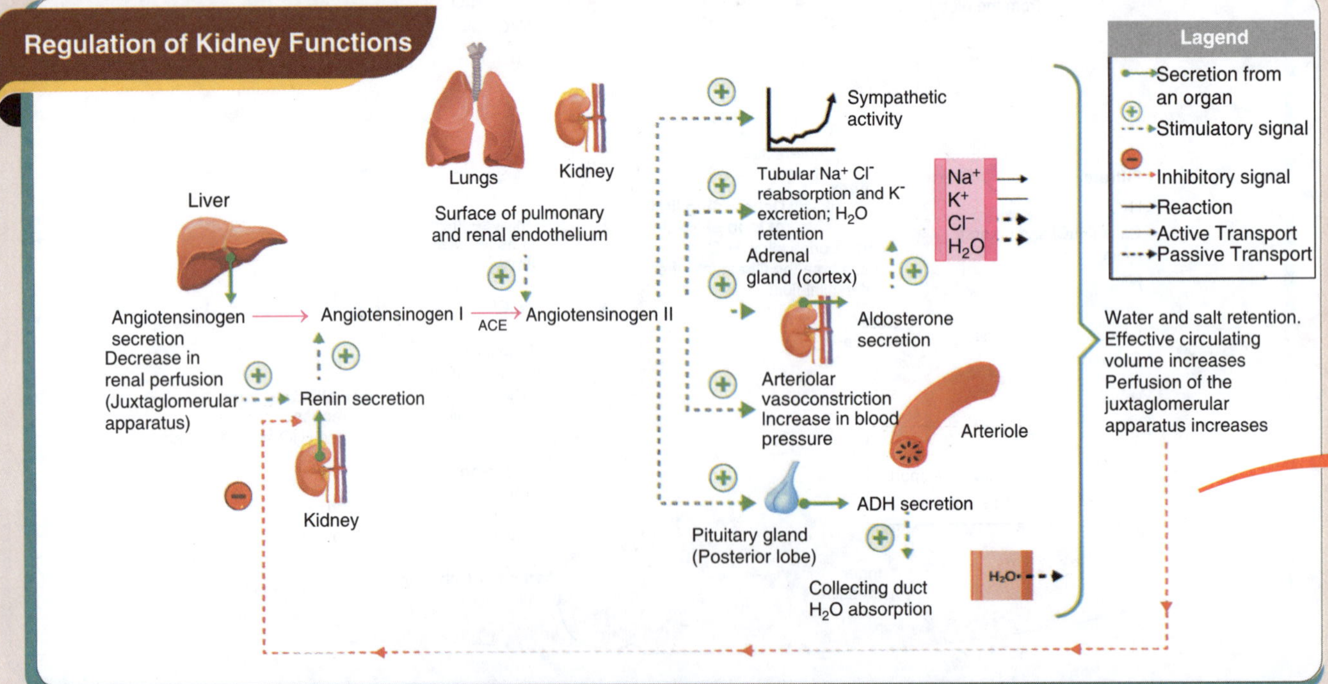

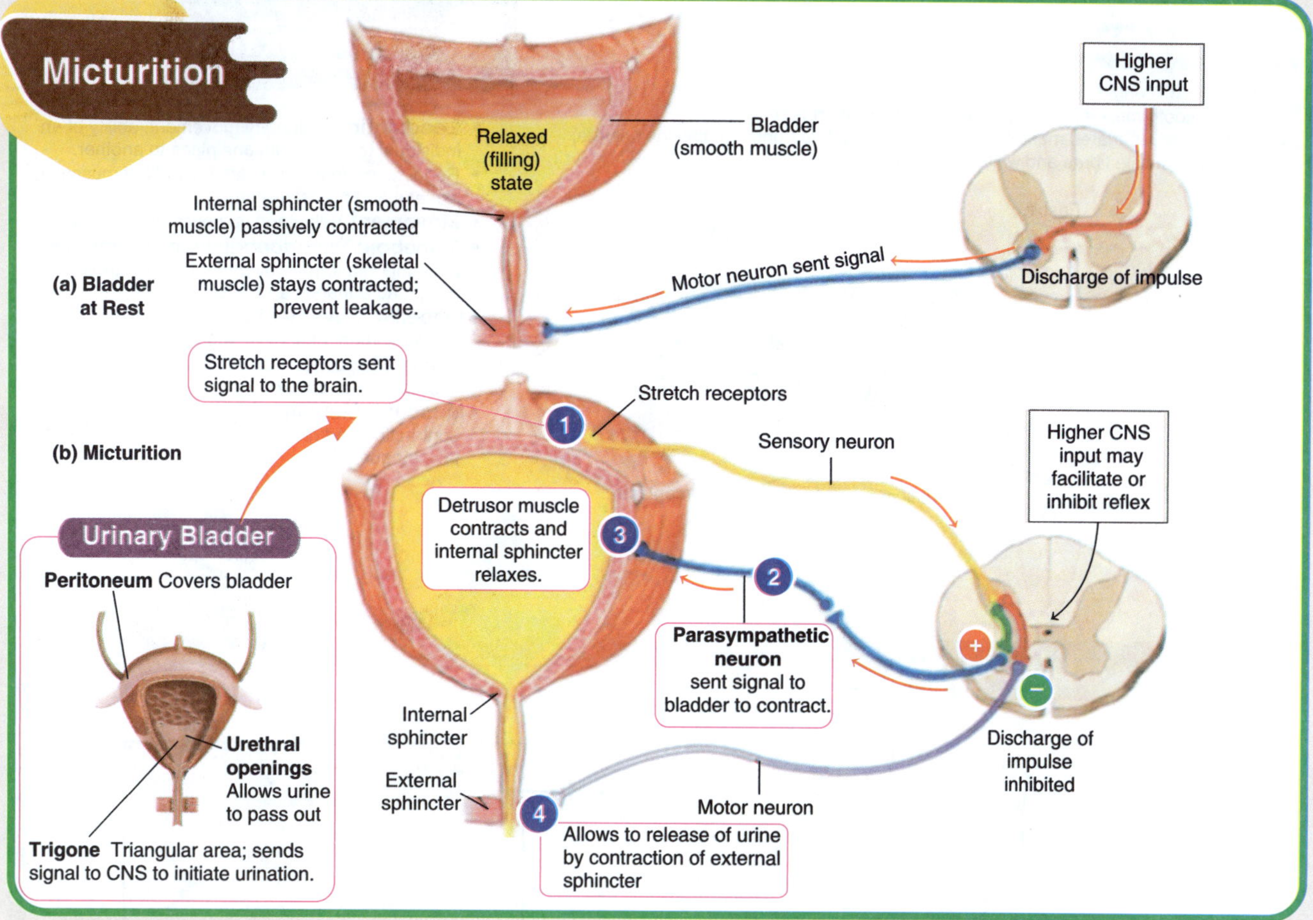

Disorders

- **Uremia**- Increase of pH in blood (high urea) due to kidney malfunction
- **Diabetes mellitus** Glycosuria (Glucose in urine) and ketonuria (Ketone in urine)
- **Glomerulonephritus**- Inflammation of kidney glomeruli.
- **Renal calculi**- Formation of crystalline salts (Calcium oxalate).
- **Diabetes Insipidus**- Caused by low ADH, results in diuresis.
- **Renal failure**- Inability of kidney to carry out secretory function.

Artificial Kidney/ Haemodialysis

Haemodialysis used in case of uremia patient.

Dialyser inflow pressure monitor

Venous pressure monitor

Heparin pump (to prevent clotting)

Dialyser (Filter)

Air trap and air detector

Air detector clamp

Filtered blood return to body

Arterial pressure monitor

Blood pump

Blood removed for dialysis

Other Excretory Organs

Lungs- Removal of CO_2 and H_2O
Liver- Secretes bilirubin, cholesterol, vitamins, etc.
Skin- Sweat and sebaceous gland
Saliva- Small amount of N_2 waste

Kidney Transplant

Done in case of total failure of kidney; if both kidney damaged, transplanted from healthy donor; recipient has to take immuno-suppressents throughout life.

Chapter 17 Locomotion and Movement

Skeletal Muscle

- Mesodermal in origin.
- Types; Smooth muscle, cardiac muscle and skeletal muscle
- Skeletal muscle/Striated muscle fibre- Muscles attach to bones; maintains posture; types- Red muscle fibres and white muscle fibres

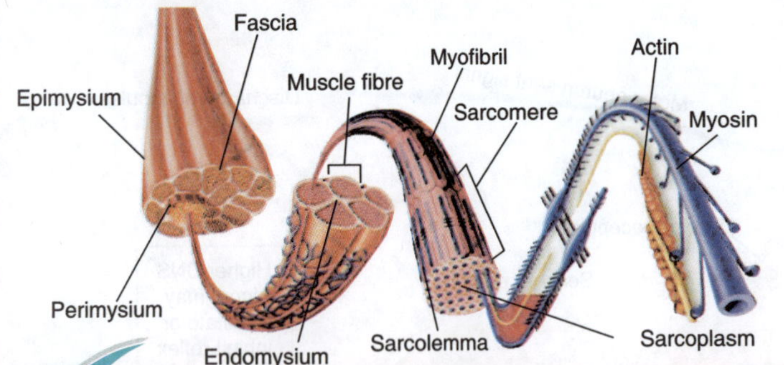

- **Locomotion** Voluntary movement; ability of an individual to move from one place to another.
- Requires perfect coordinated activity of muscular, skeletal and neural systems.
- **Movement** Voluntary; do not change location
- **Amoeboid/Pseudopodial Movement** Due to pseudopodia formed by protoplasmic streaming, E.g., macrophages and leucocytes etc.
- **Flagellar Movement** Due to propulsion, whip-like movement of flagella, e.g., human sperm.
- **Ciliary Movement** Due to cilia present in organs, e.g., respiratory tract, fallopian tube, etc.
- **Muscular Movement** Due to alternate contraction and relaxation of muscles E.g., limbs, jaw, tongue, etc.

Muscle

Structure of Skeletal Muscle

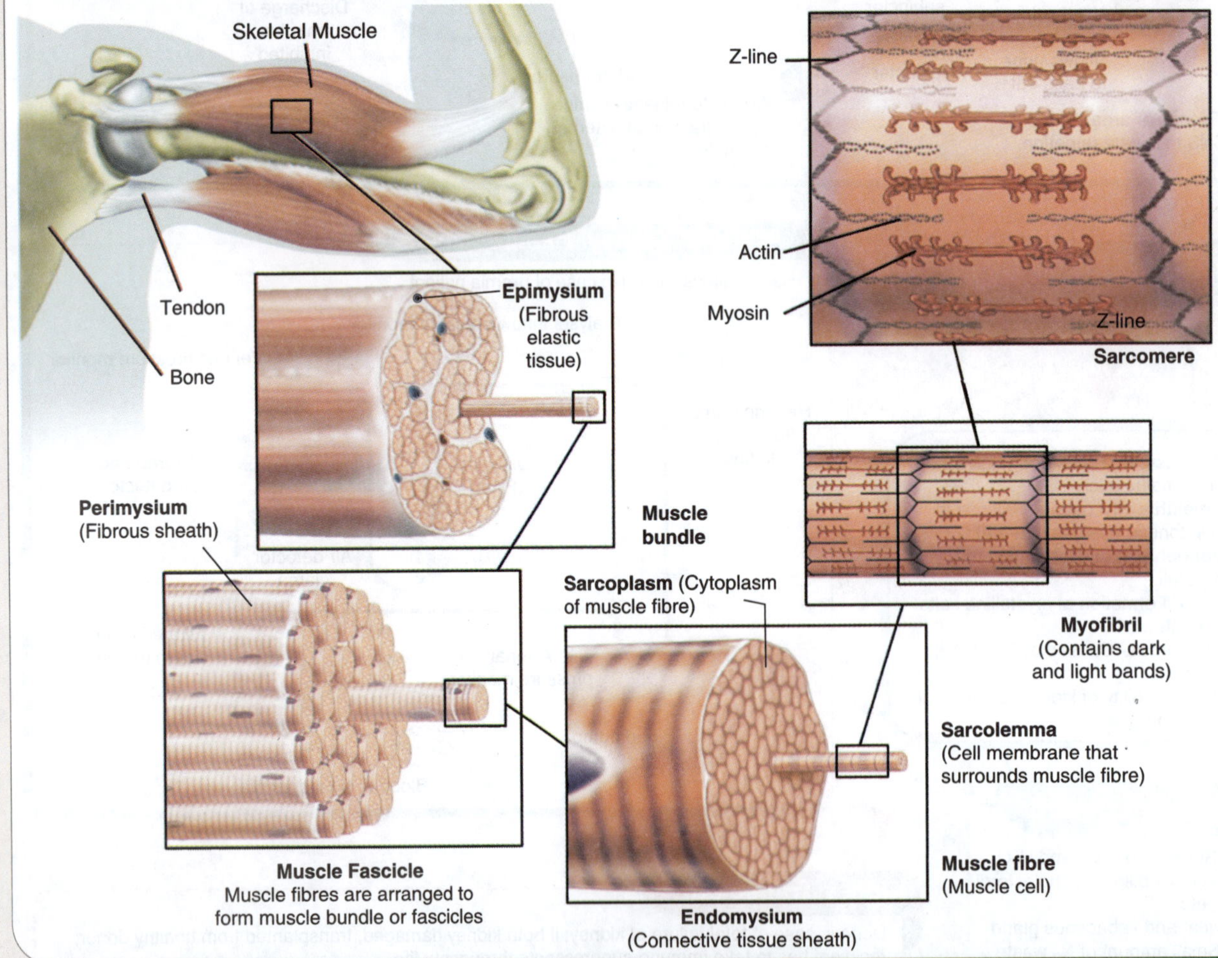

Skeletal Muscle

Tendon

Bone

Epimysium (Fibrous elastic tissue)

Muscle bundle

Perimysium (Fibrous sheath)

Muscle Fascicle
Muscle fibres are arranged to form muscle bundle or fascicles

Sarcoplasm (Cytoplasm of muscle fibre)

Endomysium
(Connective tissue sheath)

Z-line

Actin

Myosin

Z-line

Sarcomere

Myofibril
(Contains dark and light bands)

Sarcolemma
(Cell membrane that surrounds muscle fibre)

Muscle fibre
(Muscle cell)

Sarcomere

Actin
Made up of two hellically wounded F-actins, which are polymer of monomeric G-actins

Troponin complex
Troponin I, troponin T and troponin C.

Z-disc

Desmin

Tropomodulin

Thin filament
Made up of actin, tropomyosin and troponin

Tropomyosin
Double-stranded α-helical rod, attaches to F-actin.

Thick filament made up of meromyosins monomeric proteins

Thin filament

Myosin filament
Two large polypeptide chains, two globular heads and a tail, **Heavy Meromyosin** (HMM), serves as binding site and **Light Meromyosin** (LMM)

Mechanism of Muscle Contraction

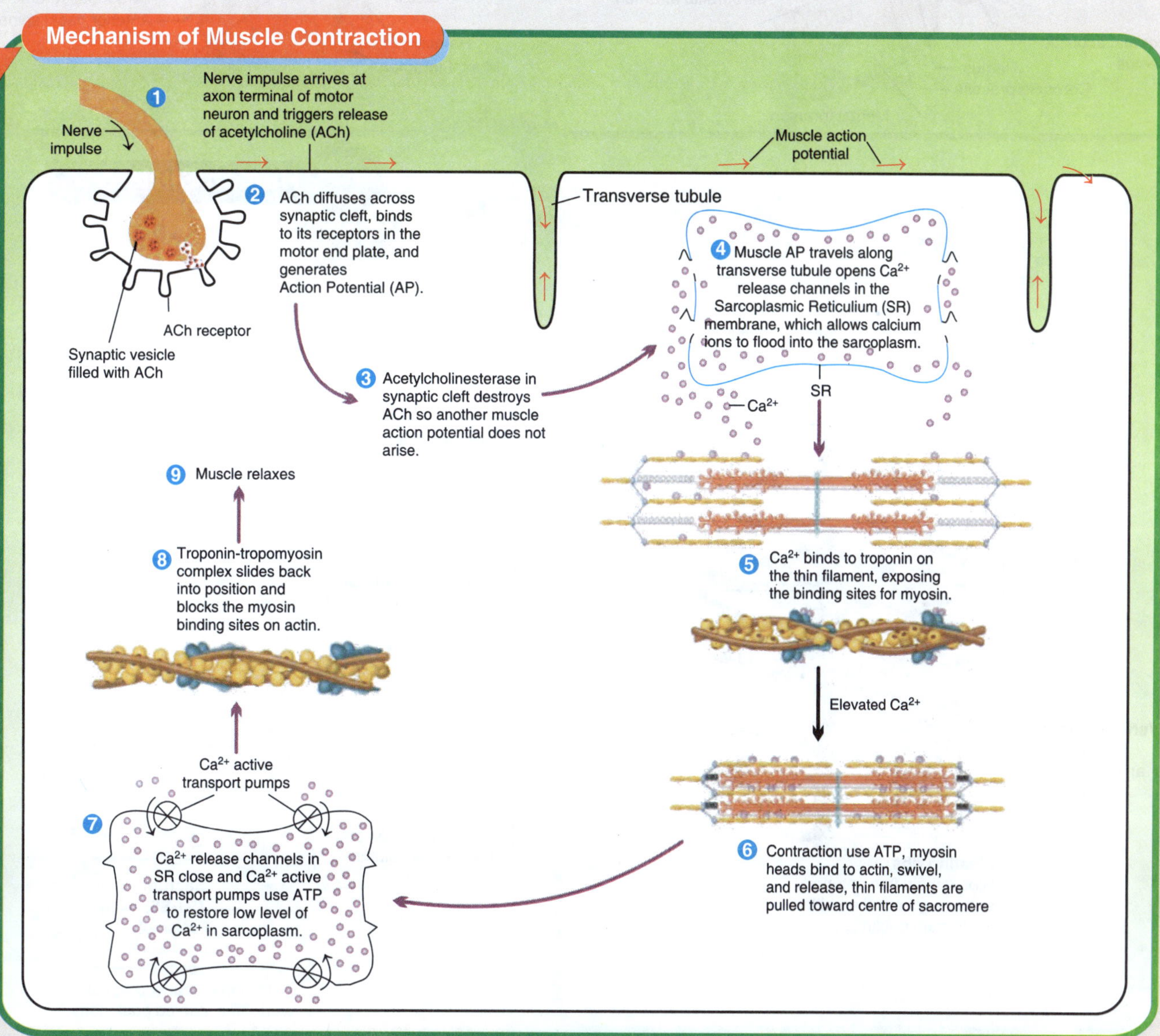

Skull (29)-Dicondylic (2 occipital condyles)

- **Cranium (8)** Sphenoid (1), Temporal (2), Ethmoid (1), Parietal (2), Occipital (1), Frontal (1)
- **Facial (14)** Vomer (1), Nasal (1), Inferior nasal conchea (2), Mandible (1), Maxillae (2), Palatine (2), Lacrimal (2), Zygomatic (2)
- **Eas Ossicle (6)** Malleus (2), Incus (2), Stapes (2)

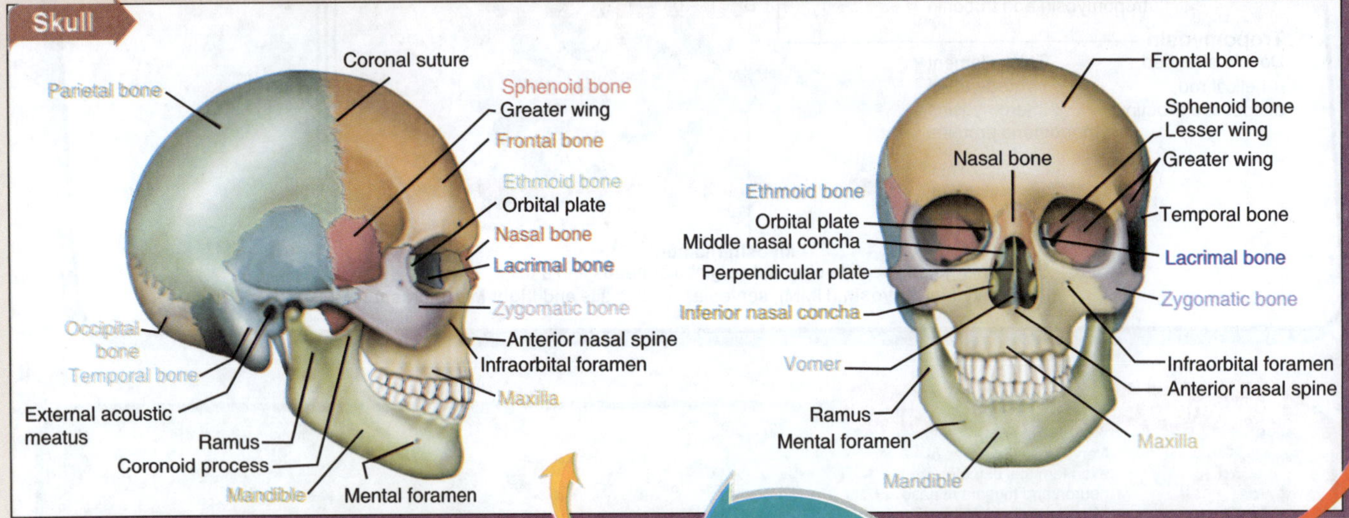

Axial Skeleton

Ribs

- 12 pairs and 1 sternum (Hyaline cartilage)

Thoracic vertebra

True ribs Ribs attached directly with the sternum

1 2 3 4 5 6 7

Sternum

False ribs or Vertebrochondral Ribs do not articulate directly with sternum

8 9 10

Ribs

Costal cartilage

11 12

Floating ribs Ribs remain free anteriorly and are not attached either to sternum or cartilage

Vertebral Column

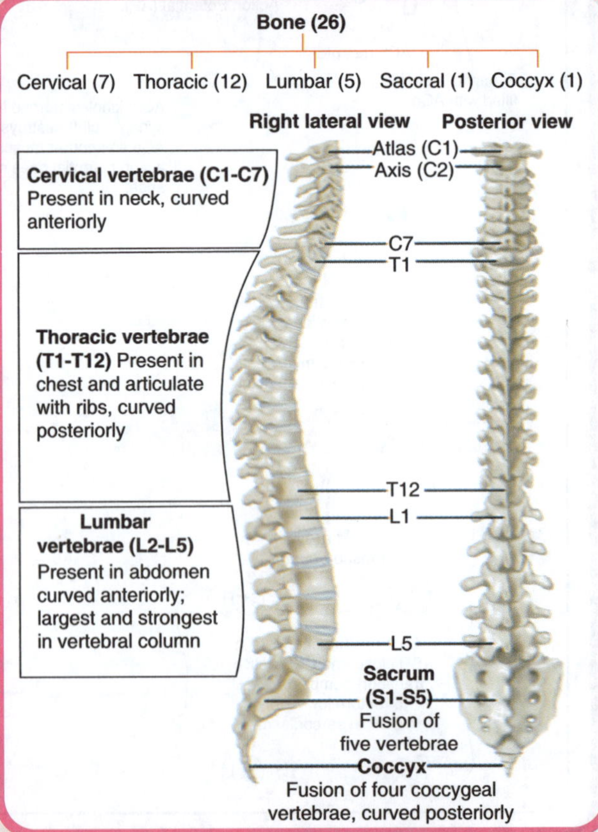

Appendicular Skeleton (126)

- **Girdles : Pectoral** (4)- Scapula (2), Clavicles (2)
  Pelvic (2)- Coxal/Hipbone (2)
- **Limbs : Forelimbs** (60)- Humerus (2), Radius (2), Ulna (2), Carpal (16), Metacarpals (10) and Phalanges (28)
  – **Hind limbs** (60)- Femur (2), Tibia (2), Fibula (2), Patella (2), Tarsal (16), Metatarsal (10) and Phalanges (28)

Appendicular Skeleton

Forelimb

Pectoral girdle

Coracoid process

Acromion Flattened and expanded

Glenoid cavity Head of humerus articulates

Scapula Shoulder blade

Shoulder girdle: Clavicle (Collar bone), Scapula

Upper limb: Arm – Humerus; Forearm – Radius, Ulna; Hand – Carpals, Metacarpals, Phalanges

Hindlimb

Pelvic girdle

Acetabulum Deep depression, head of femur articulates

Ischium Lower elongated bone, running parallel to vertebral column

Ilium Short and straight bone

Pubis (Inner smaller bone)

Pubis symphysis Made up of white fibrous cartilage

Pelvic girdle: Sacrum, Hip bone, Hip joint, Coccyx

Lower limb: Thigh – Femur; Knee – Patella (Knee cap); Leg – Lower leg: Fibula, Tibia; Foot – Tarsal bone, Metatarsal bone, Phalanges

Joints

Fibrous joint/Synarthrosis

- Collagen fibres (Inelastic); immovable

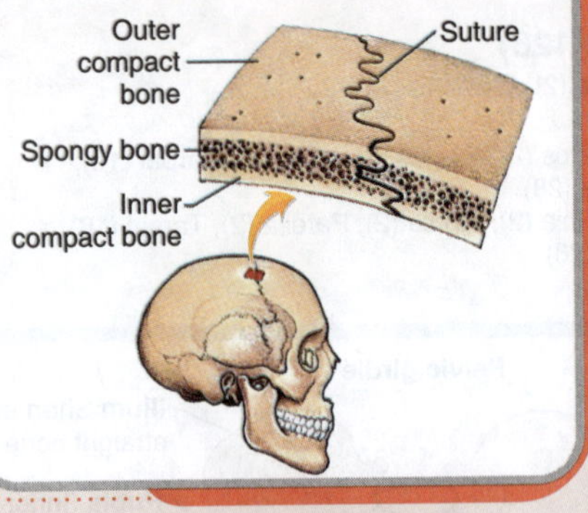

Cartilagenous/Amphiarthrosis

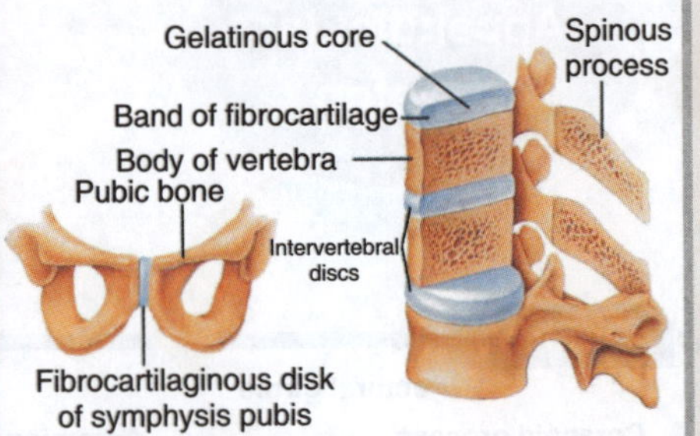

Synovial Joint/Diarthrosis

- Synovial fluid; freely movable

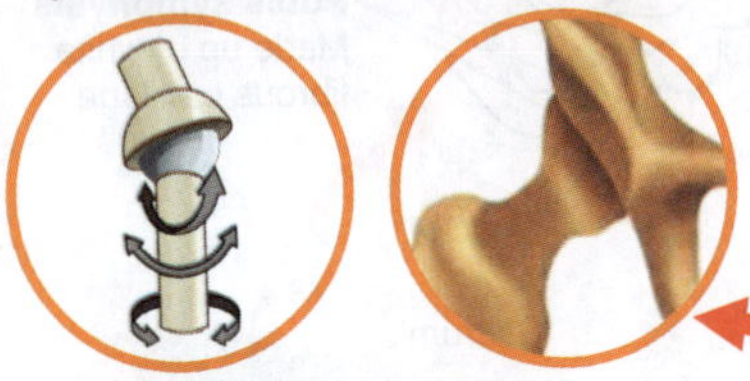

Ball and socket joint
E.g., hip joint and shoulder joint

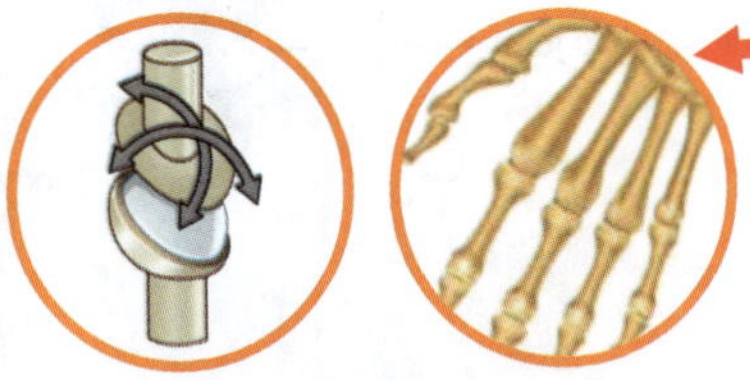

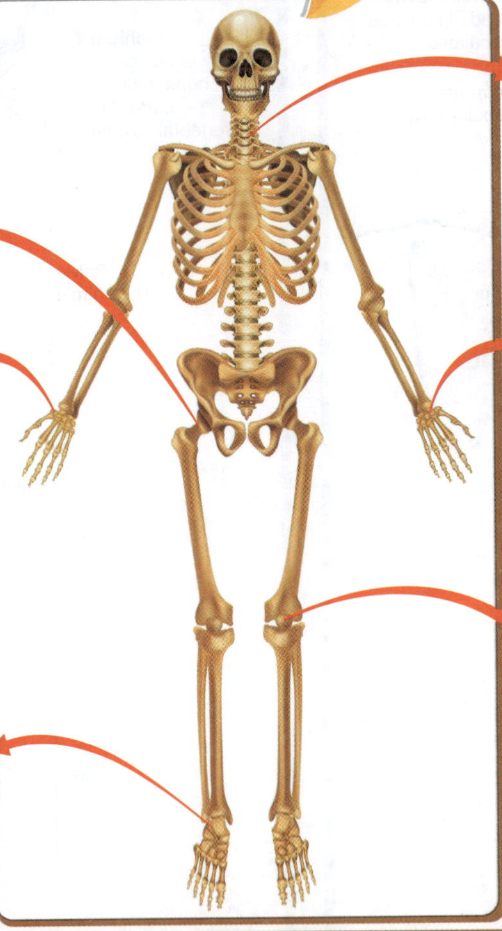

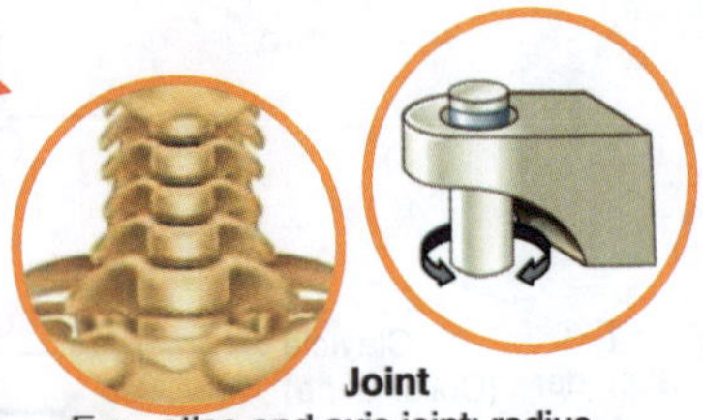

Joint
E.g., atlas and axis joint; radius and ulna

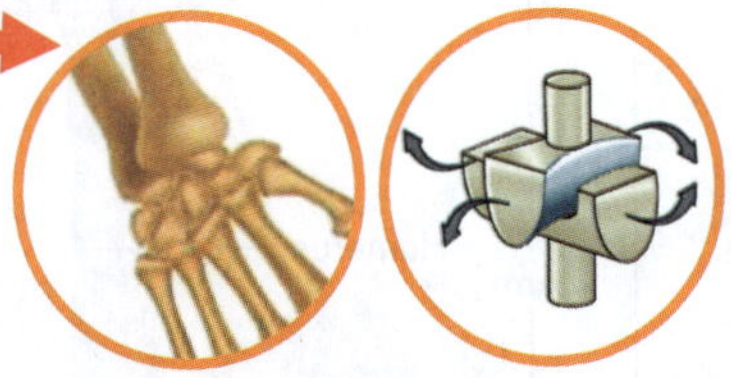

Condyloid joint
E.g. metacarpal and phalanges; Occipital condyle and Atlas

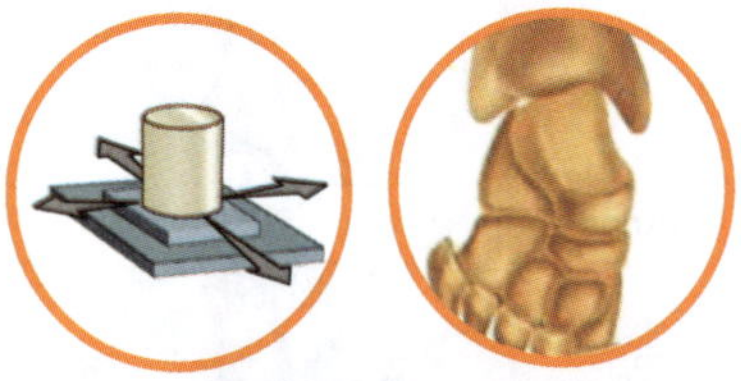

Saddle Joint
E.g., carpal and metacarpal of thumb

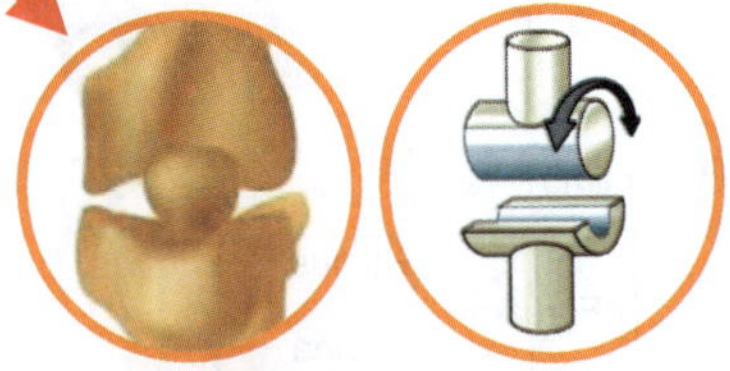

Gliding Joint
E.g., between carpals, tarsals, etc.

Hinge Joint
E.g., elbow, jaw, interpharangeal joint and knee joint

NEET POWER TIPS

Disorders

- **Tetany-** Deficiency of Ca^{2+}; rapid spasms in muscle
- **Osteoporosis-** Deficiency of Ca^{2+} and vitamin-D; bone losses minerals and fibres.
- **Arthritis-** Inflammation of joints
  - – Osteoarthritis- Degenerative joint disease; affects spine, knees and hands
  - – Gouty arthritis- Accumulation of uric acid in joints
  - – Rheumatoid arthritis- Autoimmune disorder; inflammation in synovial membrane of the joints
- **Muscular Dystrophy** Genetic disorder; deficiency of dystrophin (largest protein), progessive degreneration of skeletal muscle
- **Myasthenia Gravis** Autoimmune disorder; affects neuromuscular junction; leads to fatigue.

Chapter 18 Neural Control and Coordination

Human Neural System

- Ectodermal in origin; Consists of highly specialised nerve cells, nerve fibres and organs.
- Function – Send and receive message to and from the body
- Structural and functional unit is neuron

Neuron

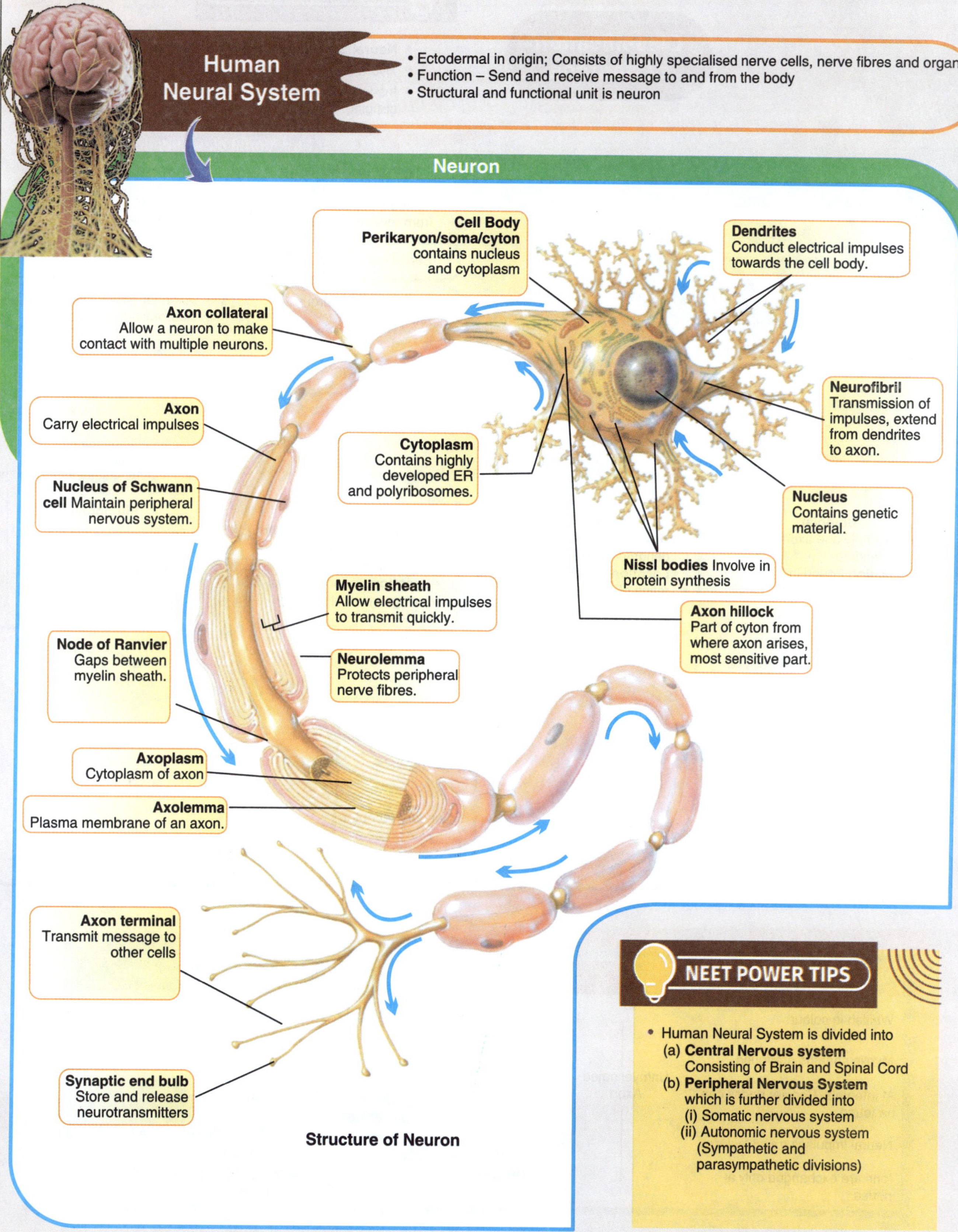

Structure of Neuron

NEET POWER TIPS

- Human Neural System is divided into
  - (a) **Central Nervous system** Consisting of Brain and Spinal Cord
  - (b) **Peripheral Nervous System** which is further divided into
    - (i) Somatic nervous system
    - (ii) Autonomic nervous system (Sympathetic and parasympathetic divisions)

Classification of Neurons

- **Neural System in lower invertebrates**
- *Hydra*-Network of neurons
- Insects- Organised neural system with brain and ganglia.

Functional classification

Afferent Neurons		Efferent Neurons
Conduct impulses from receptors to CNS.	1 	Conduct impulses from CNS to effectors
Sensory in nature	2	Motor in nature
Terminal of dendrons receptors.	3 	Axon terminals form neuromuscular junction.

Structural Classification : Types of Neurons

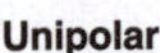

Unipolar
- Have only one axon and no dendrite.
- **Location** Found in embryonic stage

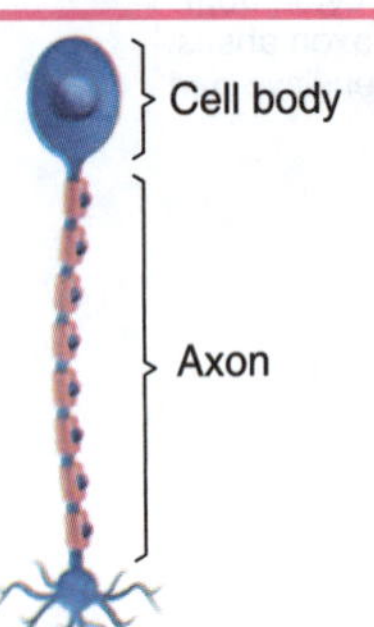

Bipolar
- Have one axon and one dendrite.
- **Location** Present in retina of eye

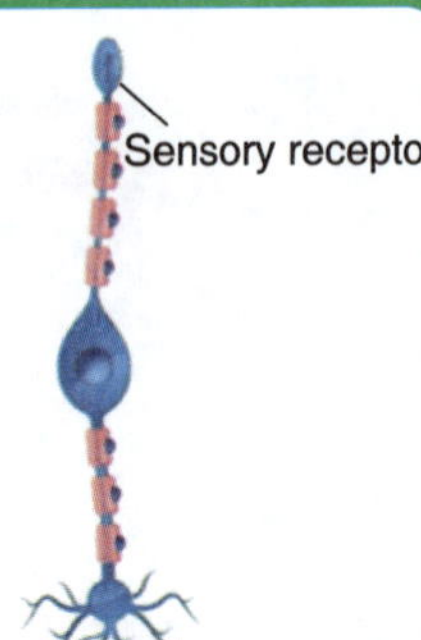

Pseudounipolar
- Single process arises from cyton and then divides into axon and dendrite
- **Location** Found in dorsal root ganglion of spinal nerves.

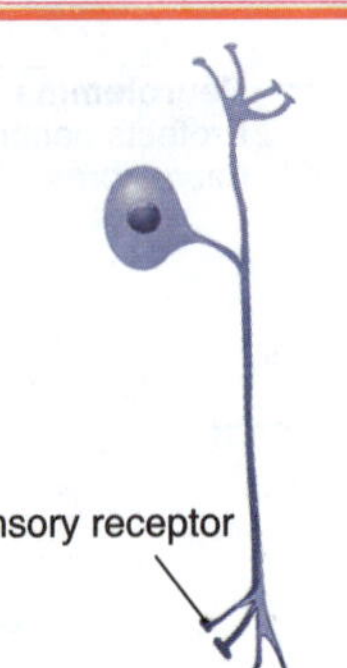

Multipolar
- Have one axon and several dendrites
- **Location** Found in cerebral cortex

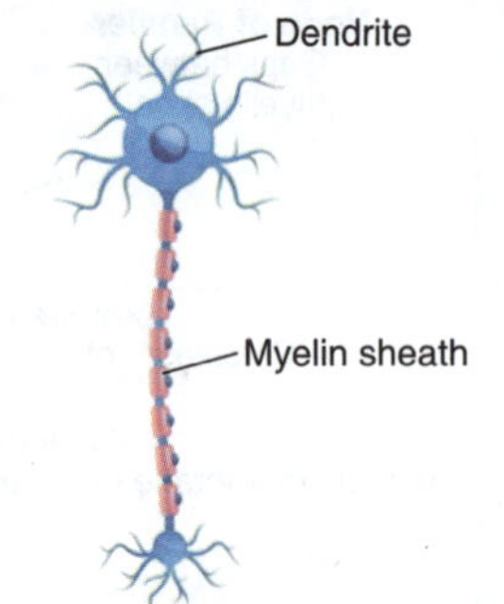

Myelinated Axons	Non-Myelinated Axons
Whitish in colour.	Greyish in colour.
Myelin sheaths are found.	Lacks myelin sheath
At intervals, Ranvier nodes can be found.	No nodes of Ranvier
Neural impulses travel faster.	Nerve impulses are transmitted more slowly
Ions are exchanged only at nodes	A large amount of ion exchange occurs on the surface

Axon terminus
Muscle
Unmyelinated Axon
Axon
Myelin sheath
Nodes of Ranvier
Axon hillock
Cell body
Dendrite

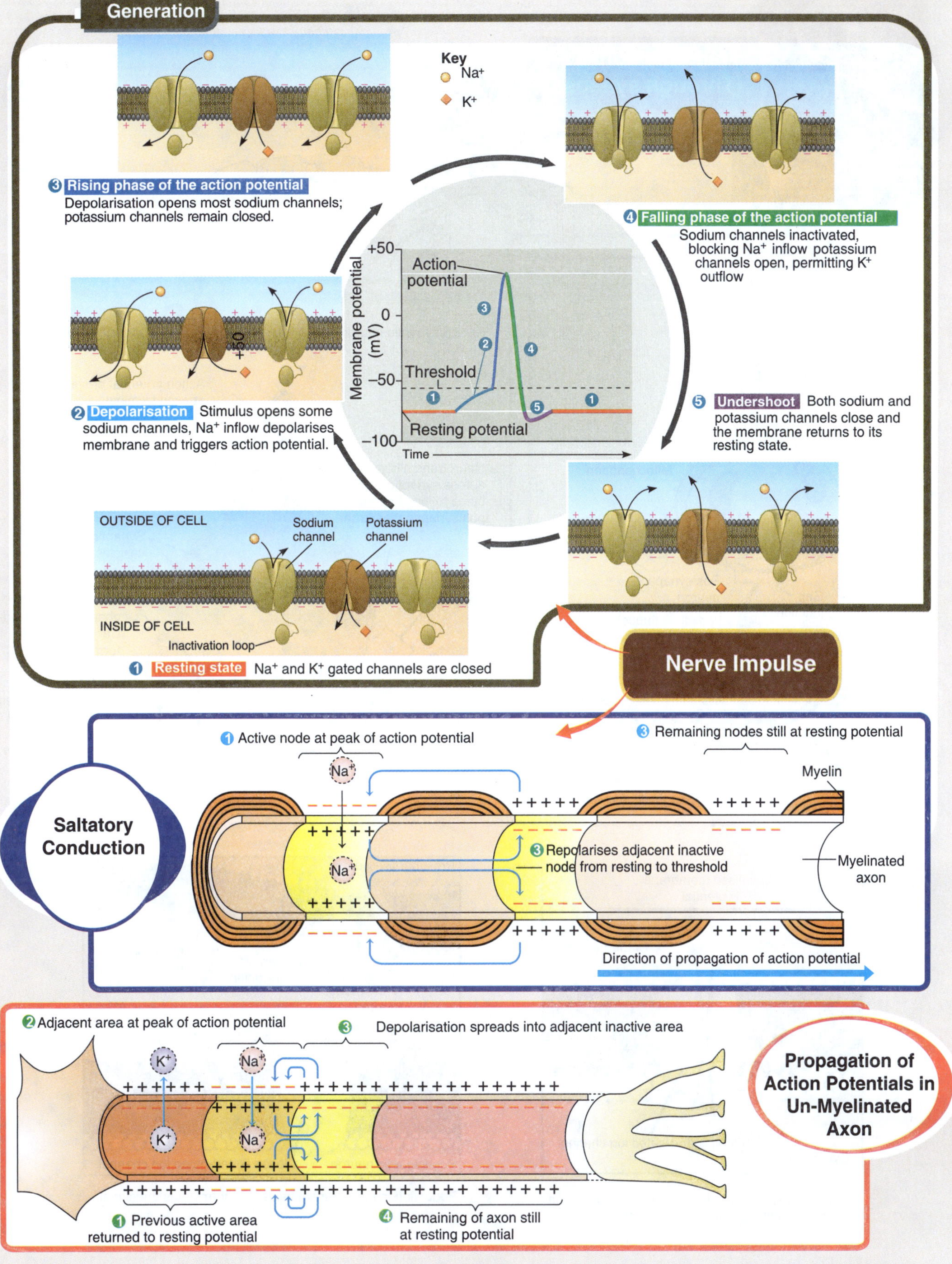
Generation
Key
Na+
K+
3 Rising phase of the action potential
Depolarisation opens most sodium channels; potassium channels remain closed.
4 Falling phase of the action potential
Sodium channels inactivated, blocking Na+ inflow potassium channels open, permitting K+ outflow
2 Depolarisation Stimulus opens some sodium channels, Na+ inflow depolarises membrane and triggers action potential.
5 Undershoot Both sodium and potassium channels close and the membrane returns to its resting state.
+50
0
−50
−100
Membrane potential (mV)
Action potential
Threshold
Resting potential
Time
OUTSIDE OF CELL
Sodium channel
Potassium channel
INSIDE OF CELL
Inactivation loop
1 Resting state Na+ and K+ gated channels are closed
Nerve Impulse
Saltatory Conduction
1 Active node at peak of action potential
3 Remaining nodes still at resting potential
Myelin
3 Repolarises adjacent inactive node from resting to threshold
Myelinated axon
Direction of propagation of action potential
2 Adjacent area at peak of action potential
3 Depolarisation spreads into adjacent inactive area
1 Previous active area returned to resting potential
4 Remaining of axon still at resting potential
Propagation of Action Potentials in Un-Myelinated Axon

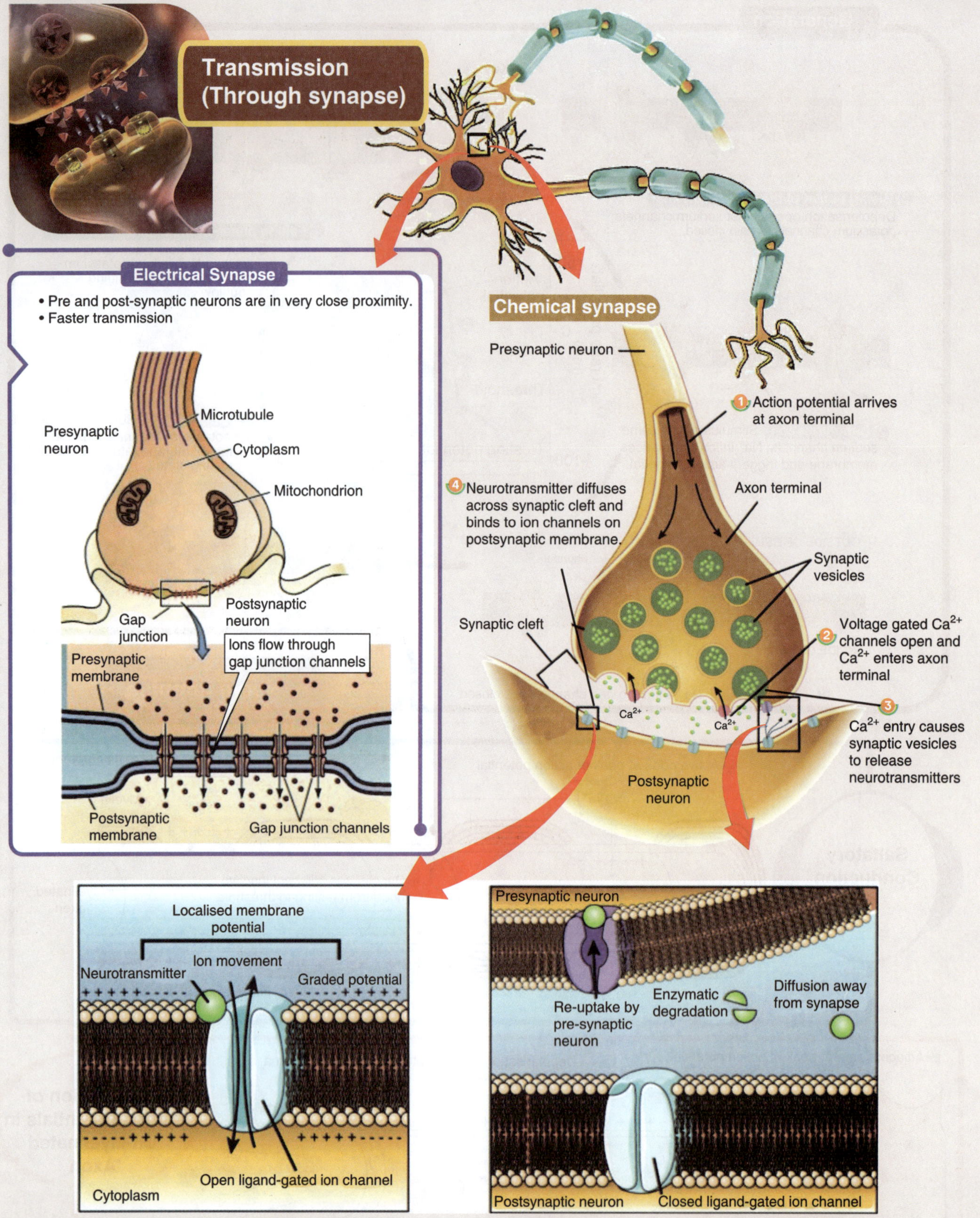

Transmission (Through synapse)

Electrical Synapse

- Pre and post-synaptic neurons are in very close proximity.
- Faster transmission

Chemical synapse

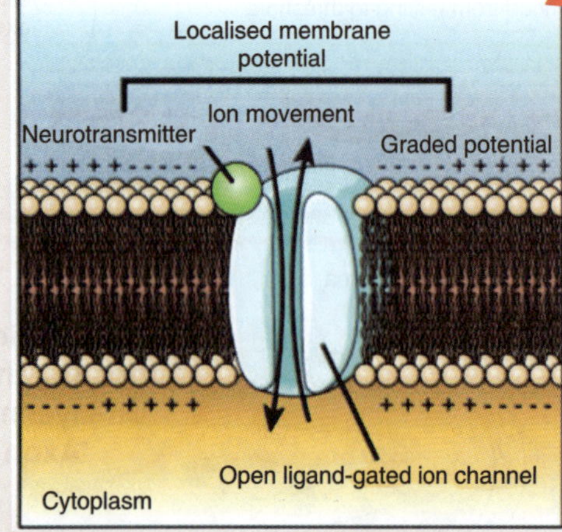

5 Binding of neurotransmitter opens ligand-gated ion channels, resulting in graded potentials.

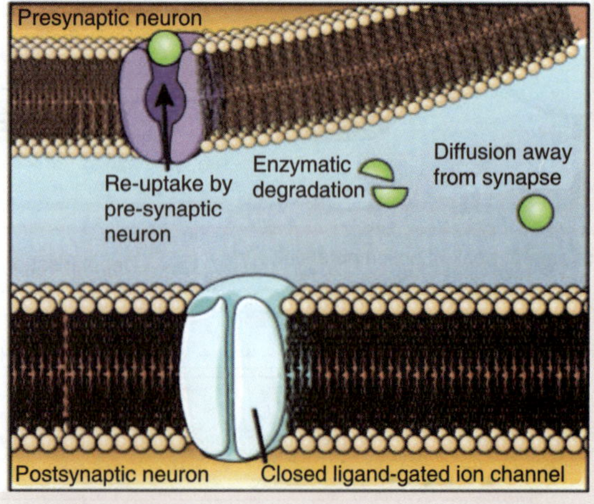

6 Reduction in neurotransmitter levels, terminates the signal.

Meninges of Brain

Bone of Skull
Epidural space
(Space between dura mater and the skull)
Dura mater (Outermost tough, fibrous adhering to inside of skull)
Subdural space
(Space between arachnoid membrane and diva mater)
Arachnoid mater
(Thin spider webley structure)
Subarachnoid space
(Space between arachnoid membrane and pia mater)
Brain
Pia mater
(Innermost thin, delicate vascular membran)

Brain

Central Nervous System

NEET POWER TIPS

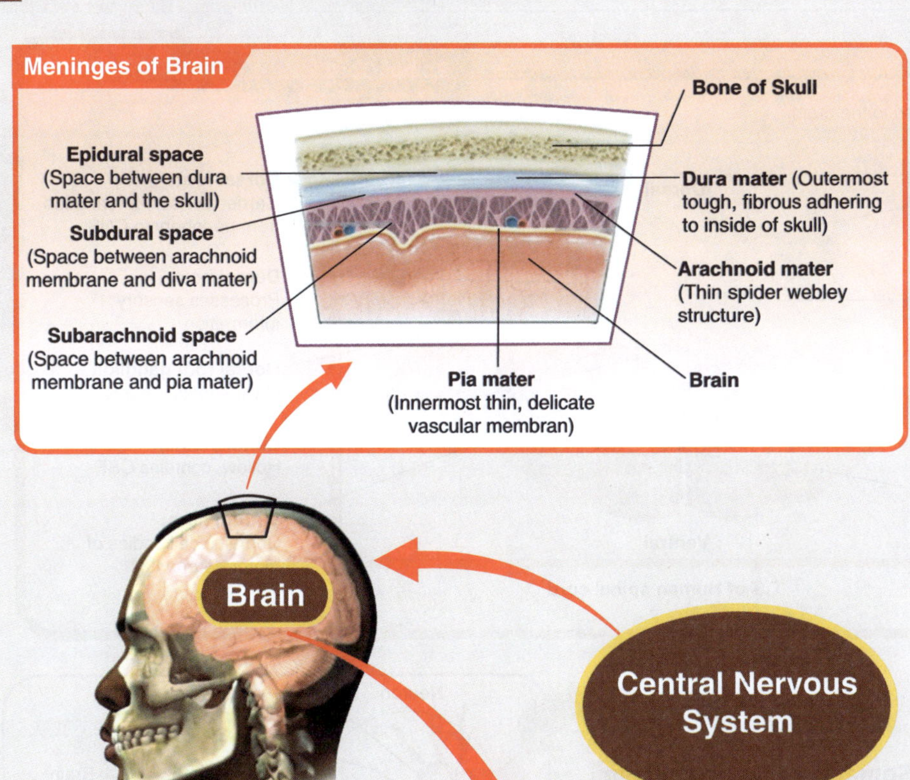

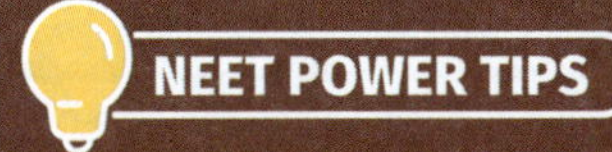

Brain
- Central information processing organ of the body.

Limbic System
- **Hippocampus** Converts short term memory to long term memory.
- **Amygdala** Associated with normal emotions.
- **Mammillary body** Acts as relay centre
- **Septal nuclei** Associated with sexual emotions.

Ventricles of the Brain
- **4 ventricles :** Two lateral ventricle, third and fourth ventricle.
- **CSF**
  - Found in ventricles of brain and spinal cord.
  - Provides shock absorbing medium and protects CNS.

Sagittal view of the brain

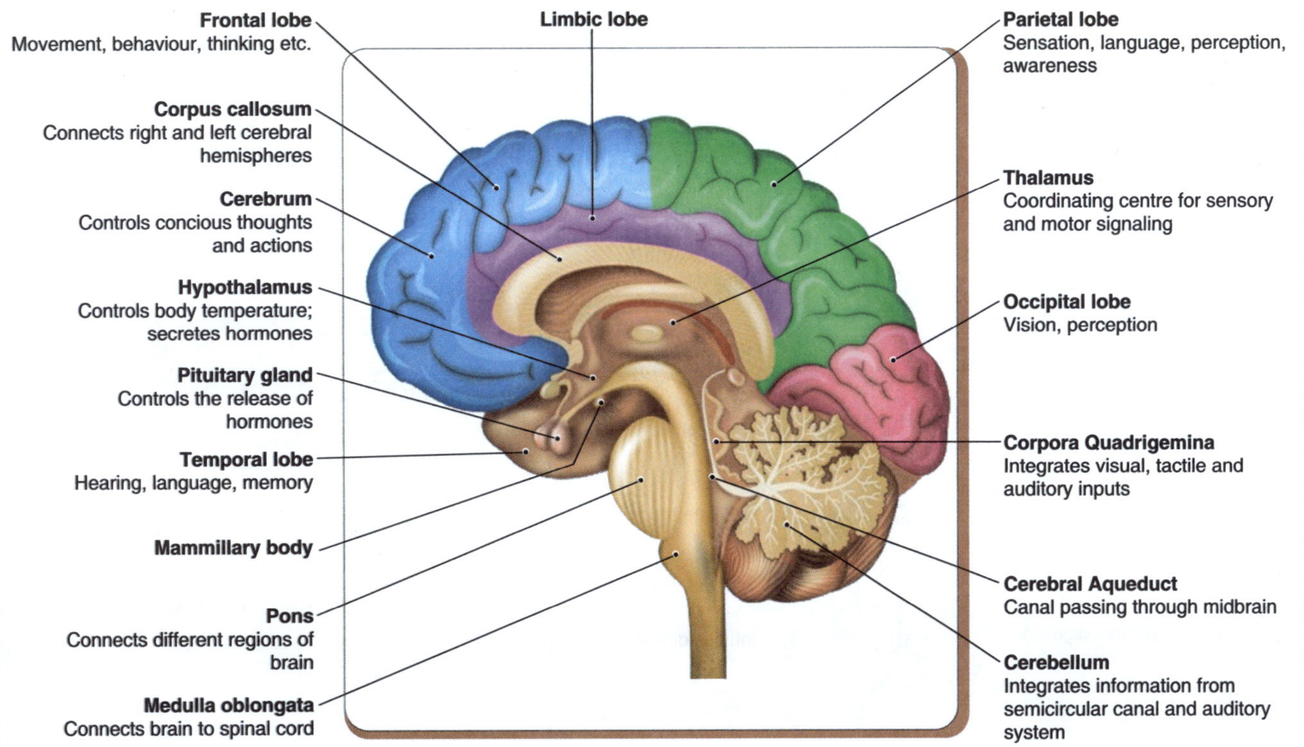

Frontal lobe
Movement, behaviour, thinking etc.
Limbic lobe
Parietal lobe
Sensation, language, perception, awareness
Corpus callosum
Connects right and left cerebral hemispheres
Cerebrum
Controls concious thoughts and actions
Thalamus
Coordinating centre for sensory and motor signaling
Hypothalamus
Controls body temperature; secretes hormones
Occipital lobe
Vision, perception
Pituitary gland
Controls the release of hormones
Corpora Quadrigemina
Integrates visual, tactile and auditory inputs
Temporal lobe
Hearing, language, memory
Mammillary body
Cerebral Aqueduct
Canal passing through midbrain
Pons
Connects different regions of brain
Cerebellum
Integrates information from semicircular canal and auditory system
Medulla oblongata
Connects brain to spinal cord

Spinal Cord

Bundle of nerve fibres that are connected to the brain.

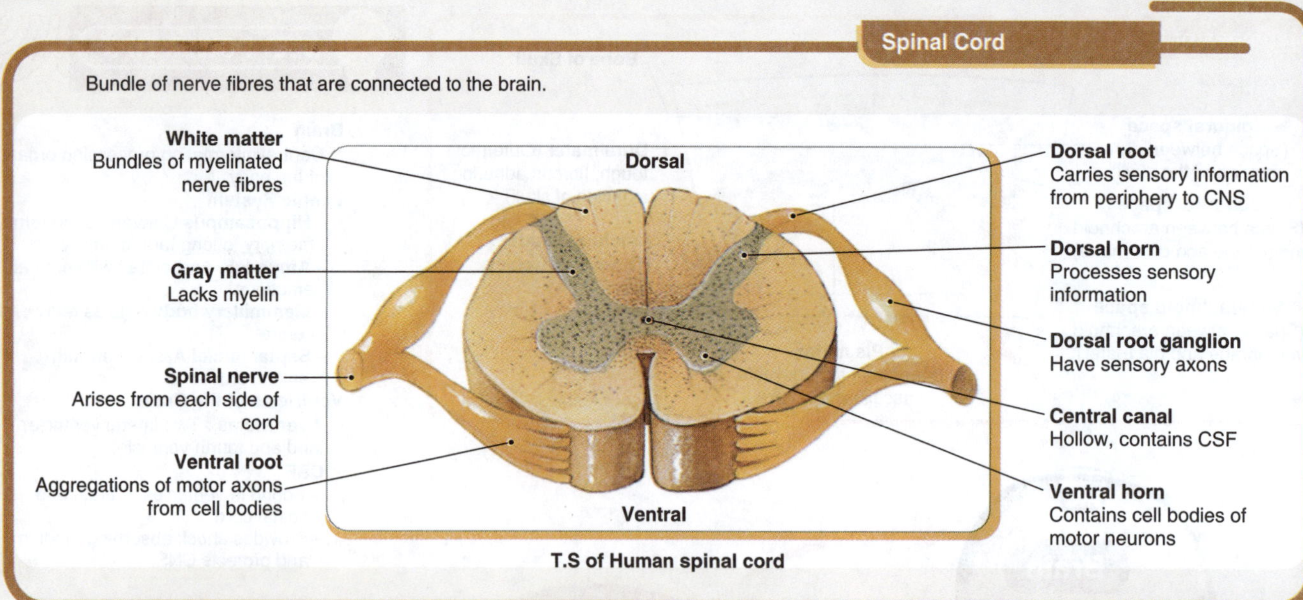

T.S of Human spinal cord

Peripheral Nervous System

Somatic Nervous System

Includes both sensory and motor neurons

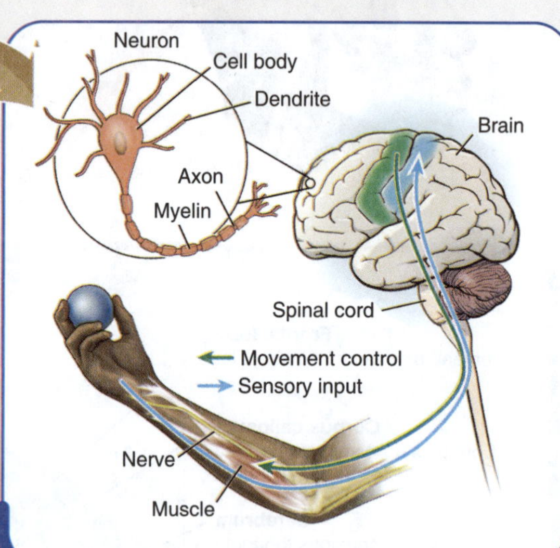

Autonomic Nervous system

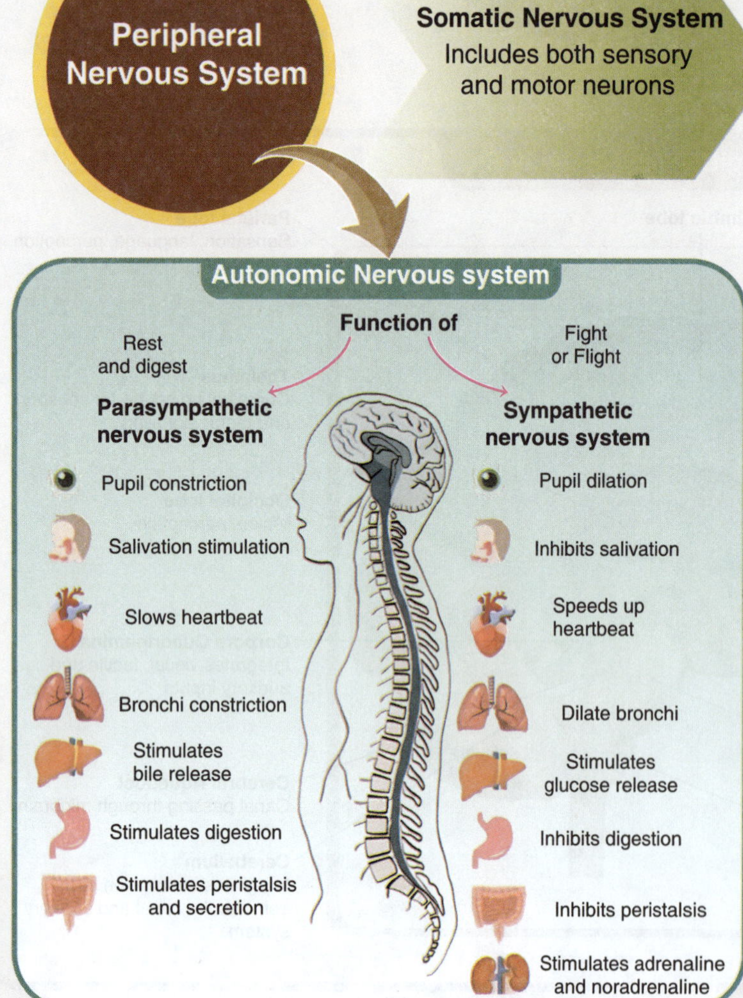

NEET POWER TIPS

- Peripheral Nervous System consists of cranial (12 pairs) and spinal (31 pairs) nerves.
- Somatic nervous system produce both reflexive and voluntary movements.
- ANS includes autonomic sensory neurons, integrating centres in CNS, autonomic motor nervous and the enteric division.

Chapter 19 Chemical Coordination and Integration

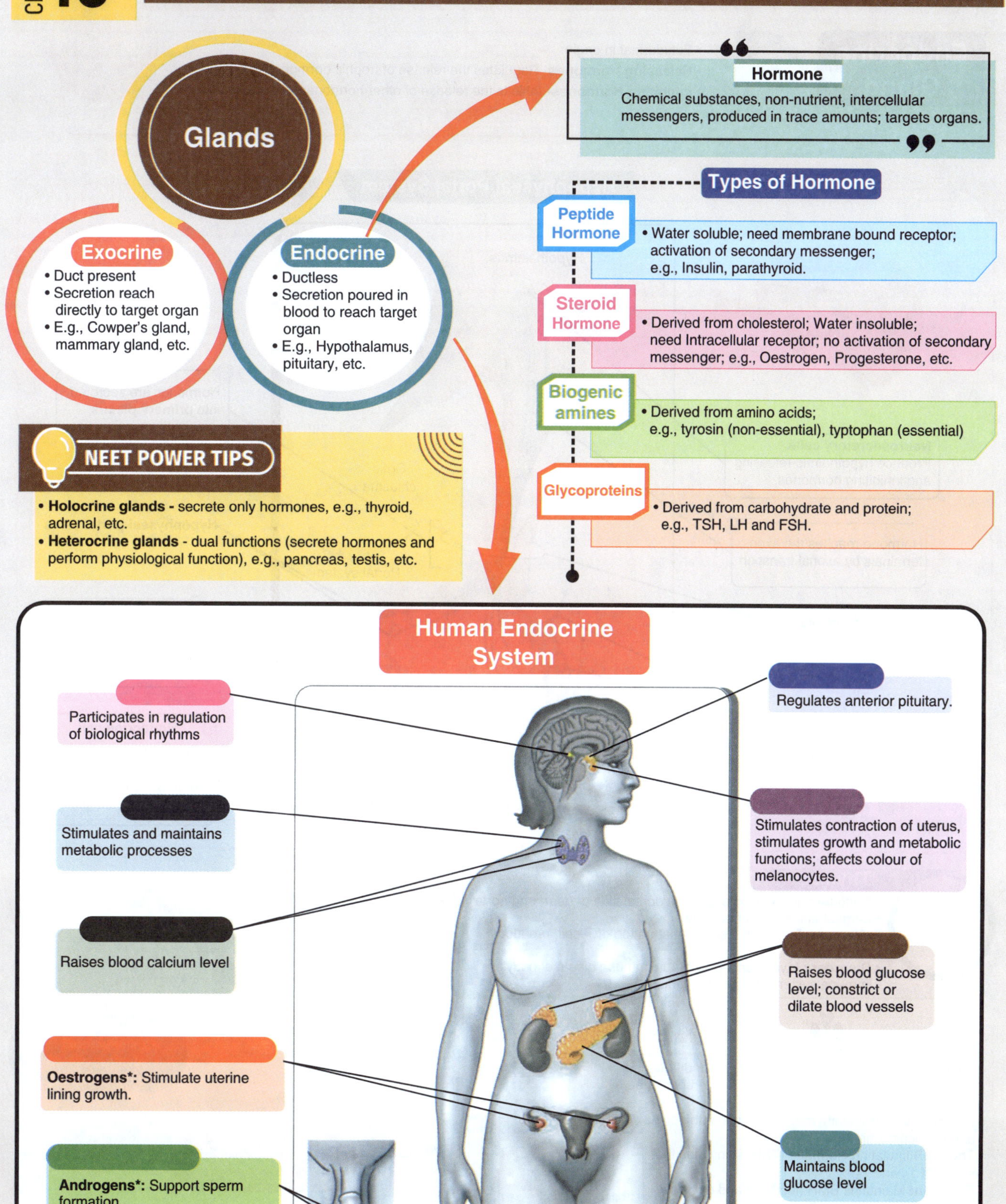

Endocrine Gland

Hypothalamus

- Ectodermal in origin
- **Releasing Hormones**- Regulates the release of trophic hormones, e.g.,GnRH
- **Inhibiting Hormones**- Inhibits the release of other hormones, e.g., Somatostatins.

Hypophyseal Portal System

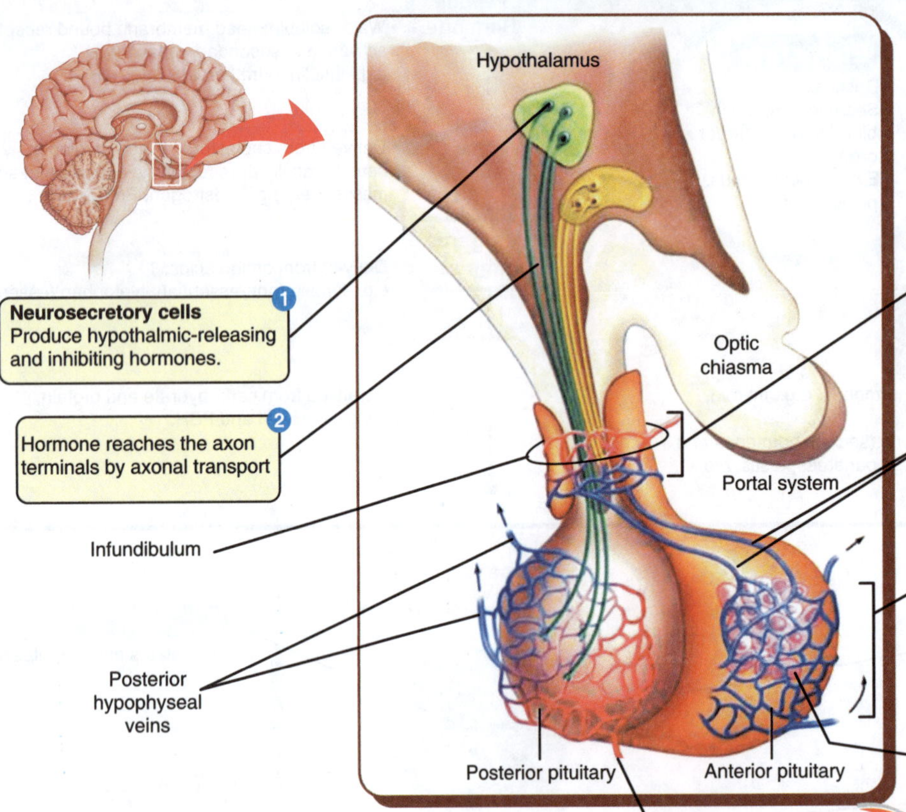

1. **Neurosecretory cells** Produce hypothalmic-releasing and inhibiting hormones.
2. Hormone reaches the axon terminals by axonal transport
3. Hormones are secreted into **primary plexus**
4. Hypothalmic hormone flows with blood then diffuse into **secondary plexus.**
5. **Endocrine cell** Secretes hormones into bloodstream, which delivers them to specific cells, tissues and glands.

Thymus

- Endodermal in origin; located on dorsal side of heart and aorta
- Largest at the time of puberty
- **Hormone** Thymosin, helps in maturation of T-cell, produces antibodies.
- **Disorder :** Myasthenia gravis-Autoimmune disease; body's immune system attacks the gland.

Pituitary Gland

- Adenohypophysis (Anterior lobe)
  - Pars intermedia: MSH
  - Pars distalis: Prolactin, ACTH, FSH, TSH, GHRH
- Neurohypophysis (Posterior lobe)
  - Secretes oxytocin and vasopressin.

Disorder : Hyposecretion (Dwarfism, Diabetes insipidus) and **Hypersecretion** (Gigantism, Acromegaly).

Thyroid Gland

- Endodermal in origin; located ventrally around trachea.
- Two lobes on either side of the trachea, interconnected by isthmus
- **Hormones**: Tetraiodothyronine (T_4), triiodothyronine (T_3) and thyrocalcitonin.
- Thyroid Stimulating Hormone (TSH) stimulates the release of T_3 and T_4.
- **Function:** Maintains BMR (increase and decrease metabolism)
- **Disorder**: Hypothyroidism, Cretinism, Hyperthyroidism, Exopthalmic goitre and Grave's diseases.

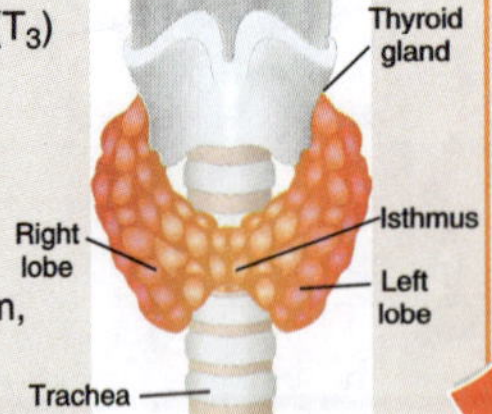

Adrenal Gland

- **Adrenal medulla** Secretes adrenaline (epinephrine) and nor-adrenaline (nor-epinephrine).
- **Adrenal cortex** Secretes androgenic steroids, glucocorticoids and mineralocorticoids
- **Disorders**: Addison's disease- caused due to underproduction of cortisol and aldosterone (adrenal cortex hormone).

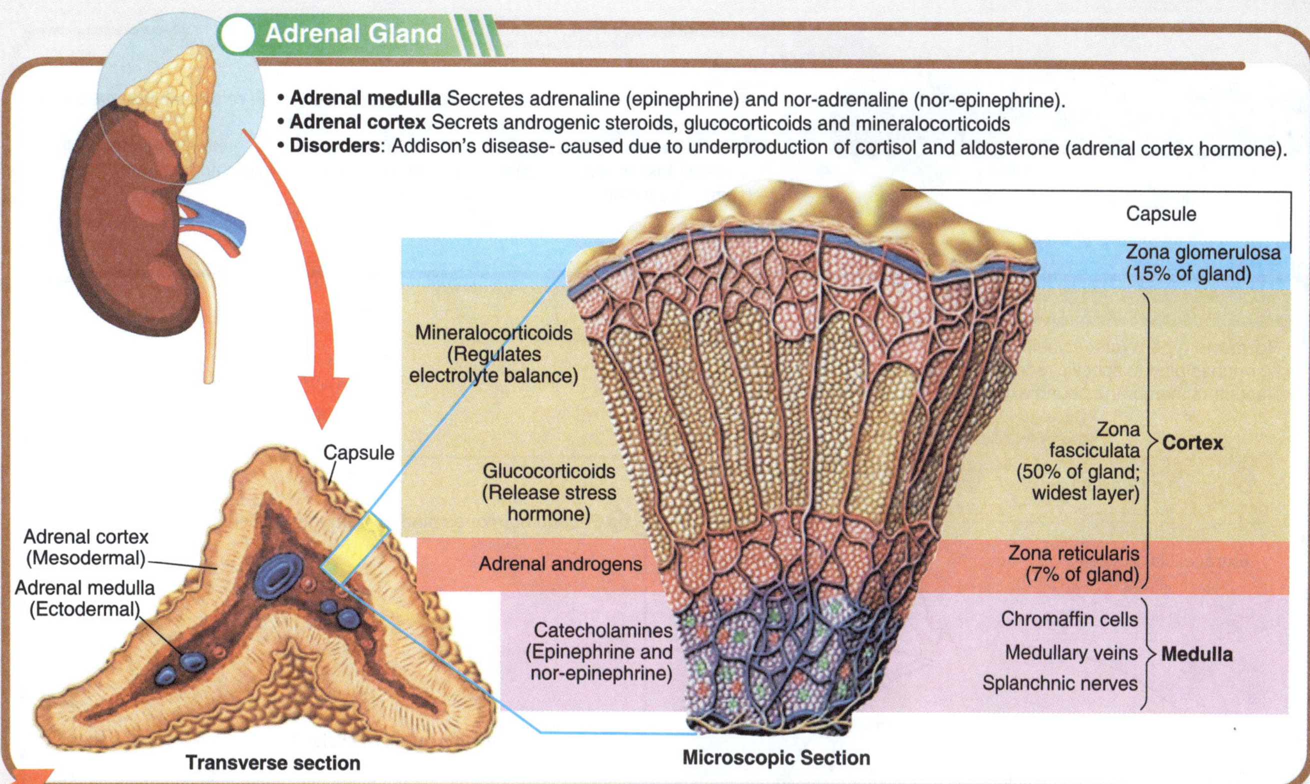

Parathyroid gland

- Endodermal in origin; located on back side of thyroid gland; four dorsal lobes.
- Regulates calcium levels in blood (hyper calcemic hormone)

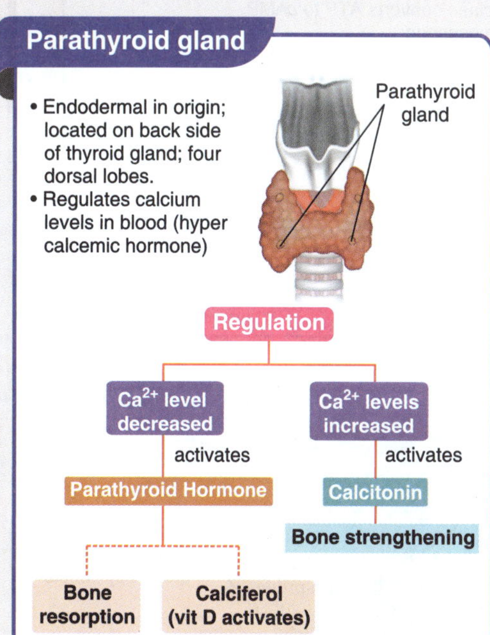

Pancreas

- Endodermal in origin; dual gland-exocrine and endocrine gland (islets of Langerhans)
- Insulin activates GLUT-4, transfer glucose from blood into cell
- **Disorder:** Diabetes Mellitus- Caused due to prolonged hyperglycemia as a result of hyposecretion of insulin.

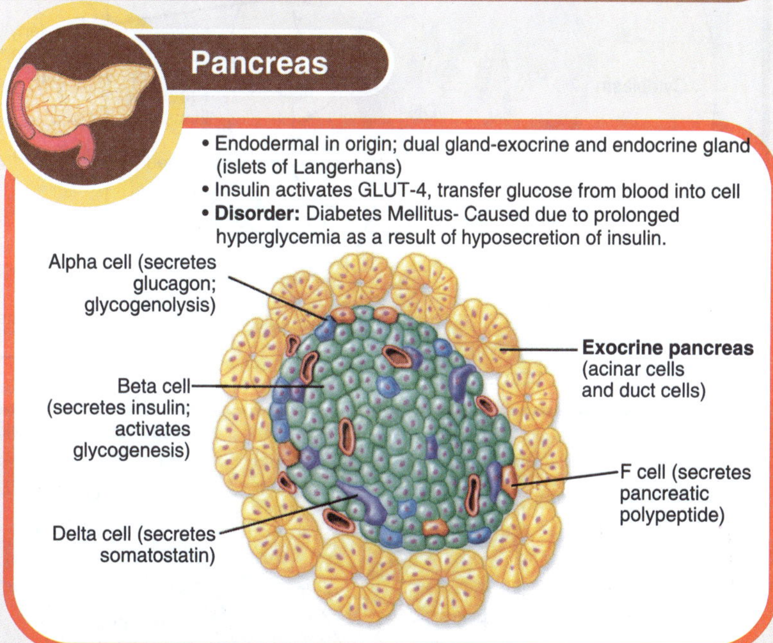

Pineal Gland

- Ectodermal in origin; located on dorsal side of forebrain; smallest gland
- **Hormone** Melatonin- regulates biological clock, pigmentation and delay puberty.

NEET POWER TIPS

- Hypothalamus present below thalamus; connects endocrine and neuro-secretory cells; basal part of diencephalon.
- Master gland located in bony cavity of sella tursica and attach to hypothalamus by stalk.
- Thyroid hormone are essential for metamorphosis of frog and increases the action of neurotransmitters.
- **Gonads** (mesodermal)– Ovaries (Oestrogen and progesterone), Testis (Testesterone)

Mechanism of Hormone Action

Hormones of Heart Kidney and GIT

Tract

- **Heart** (Atrial wall): Releases Atrial Natriuretic Factor (ANF) reduces blood pressure.
- **Kidney** (Juxta glomerular cells) Releases erythropoietin.
- **Gastro-Intestinal Tract** Release gastric inhibitory peptide, gastrin (secretes HCl), Cholecystokinin (secretes pancreatic enzymes and bile juice) and secretin (stimulates water and bicarbonates).

Mechanism of Hormone Action

- **Hormone type**: Water soluble peptide and lipid soluble steroid.
- Hormones bind to specific receptors to produce specific effects on target organ.
- Receptors membrane bound extracellular receptors and Intracellular receptors.

Peptide Hormone Action

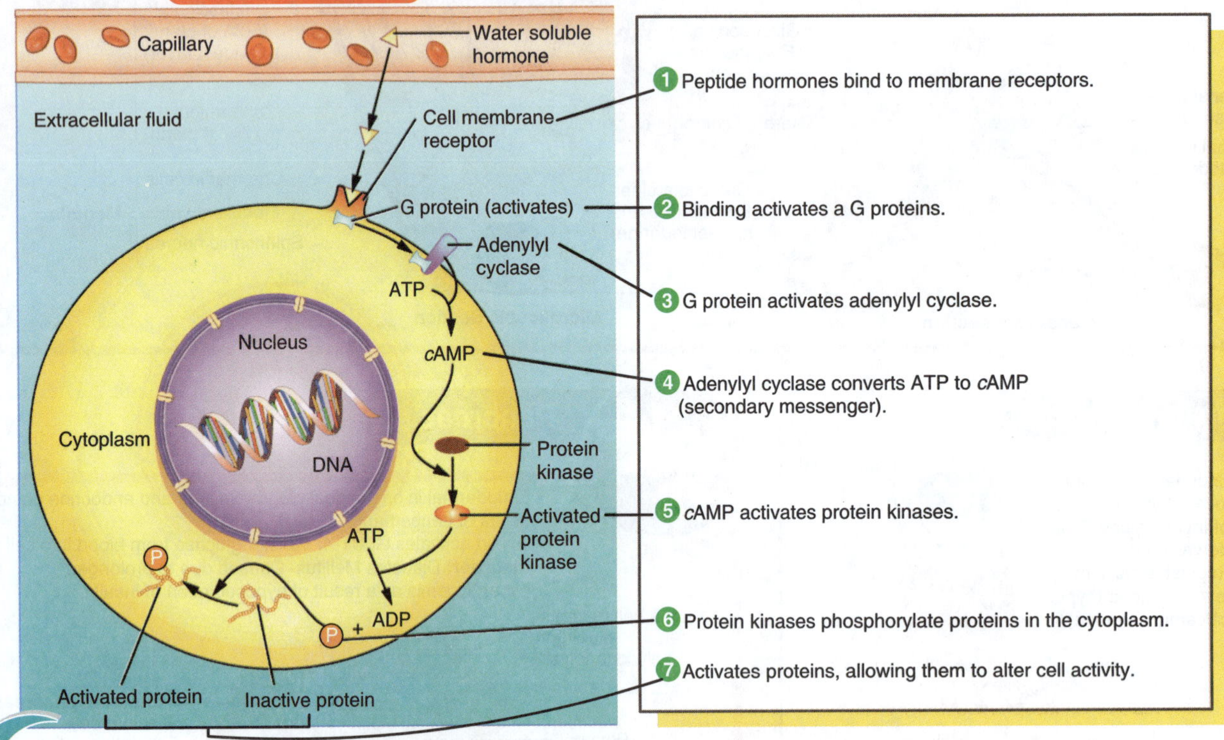

Steroid Hormone Action

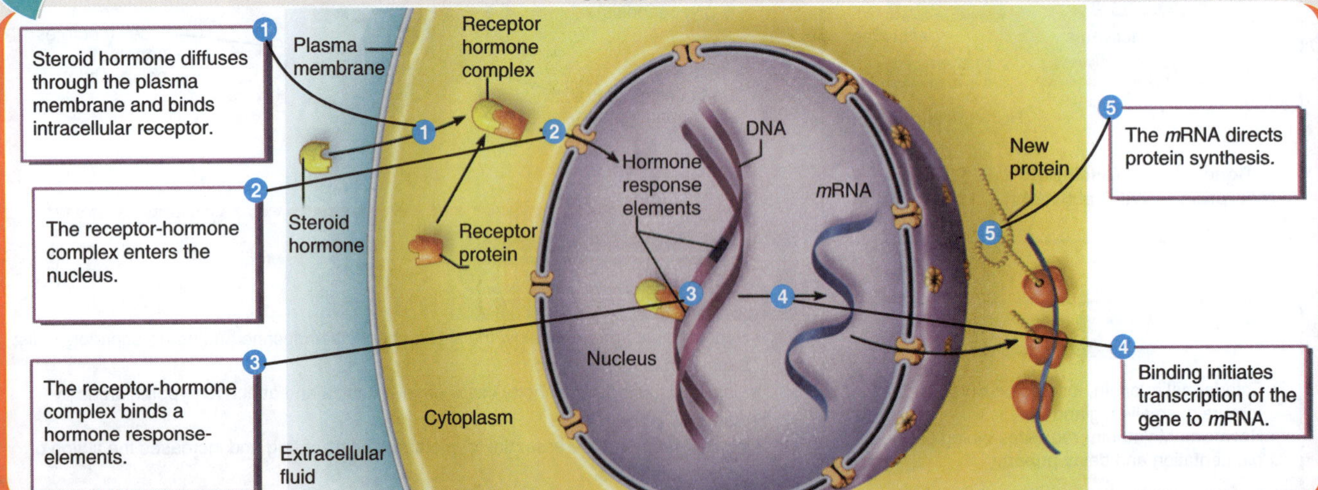

NOTE

Chapter 20

Sexual Reproduction in Flowering Plants

A Diagrammatic Representation of LS of a Flower

Androecium (Male reproductive organ; whorls of stamen)
Anther (Bilobed, dithecous)
Filament (Long and slender stalk)
Corolla (Bright, fragrant, attract pollinators)
Stigma (Captures pollen)
Style (Allows pollen tubes to travel toward ovule)
Ovary (Basal swollen part)
Gynoecium (Female reproductive organ; whorls of carpel)
Ovule (Encloses embryo sac)
Calyx (Protect inner whorls, in bud stage)
Stalk/Pedicel (Support inflorescence)
Receptacle [Thalamus] (Swollen end of the axis where floral leaves are attached)

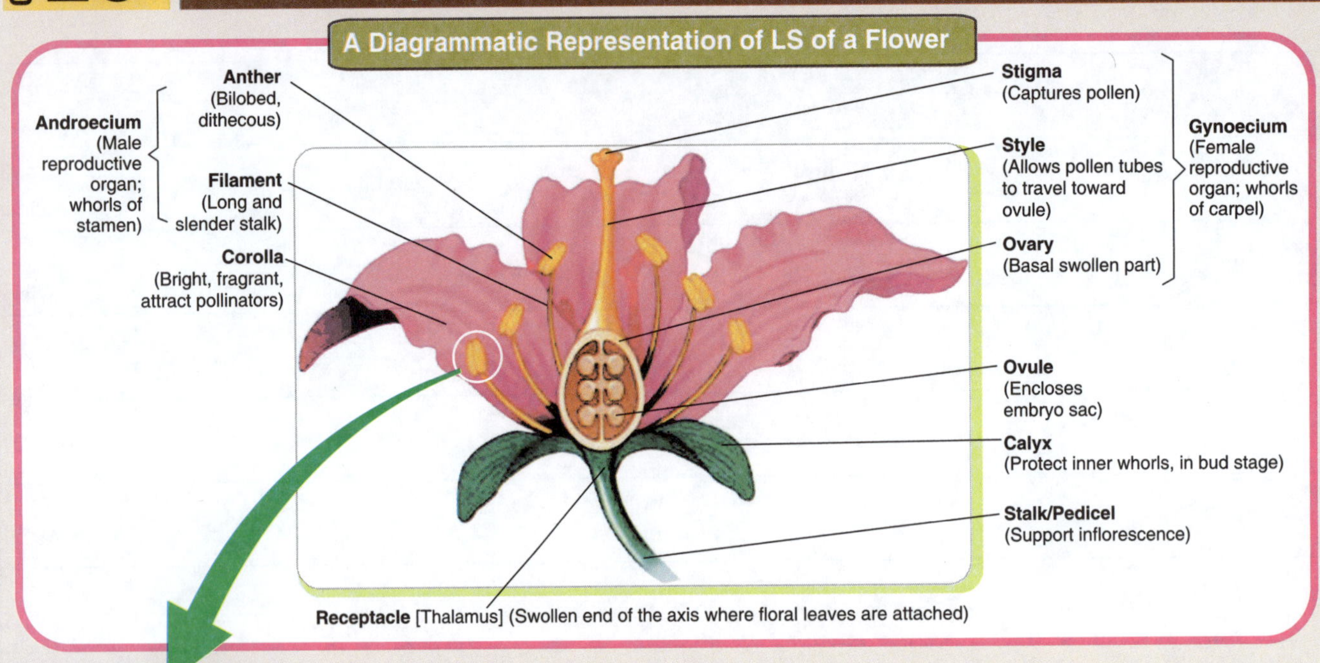

A Typical Stamen

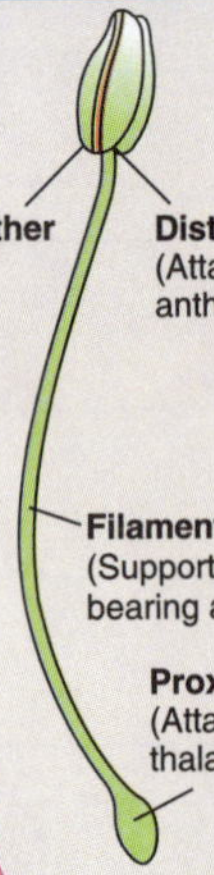

Anther
Distil end (Attach to anther)
Filament (Supports pollen bearing anther)
Proximal end (Attach to thalamus)

Male Gametophyte

3-D Cut Section of an Anther

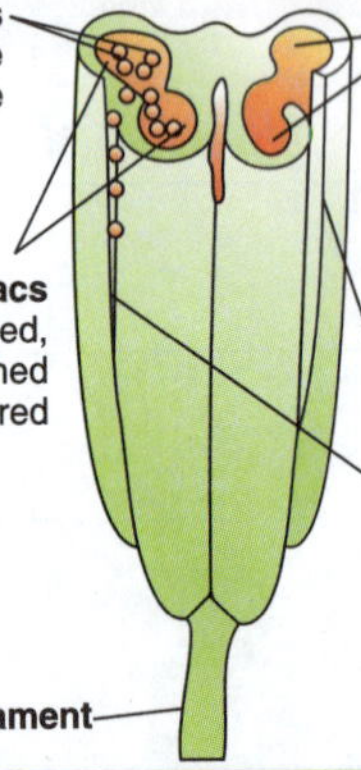

Pollen grains Male gametophyte
Microsporangia Two in each lobe; develop further and become pollen sacs
Pollen sacs Pollens formed, nourished and get matured
Line of dehiscence After maturity, anther releases pollen grains
Filament

Microsporangium

- Microsporangial wall : Epidermis, Endothelium, Middle layer and Tapetum.

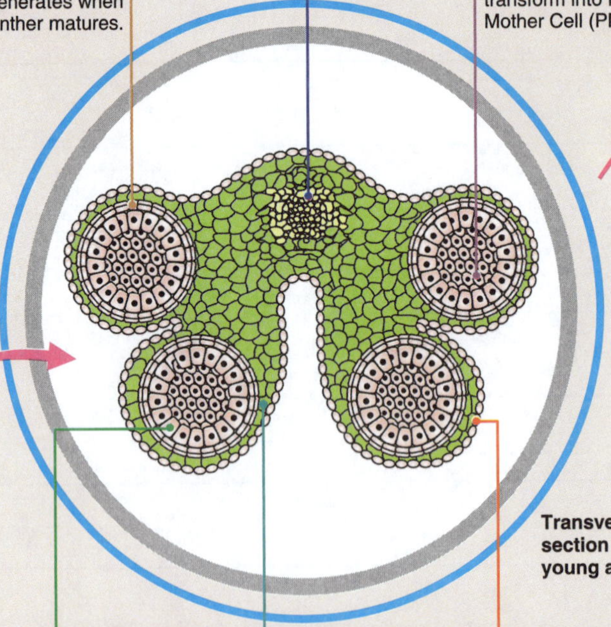

Middle layer Consists 2 or 3 layers of flat parenchymatous cells, stores food and degenerates when anther matures.
Connective
Sporogenous tissue Compactly arranged homogenous cells; transform into Pollen Mother Cell (PMC).
Transverse section of a young anther
Tapetum Innermost layer provide nourishment and secrete enzyme (callase).
Endothecium Lies inner to epidermis; help in the **dehiscence of anthers** as **hygroscopic** in nature.
Epidermis Outermost layer functions as a protective covering.

- In 60% of angiosperms, pollen grains are shed at 2-celled stage.
- Pollen grains are rich in nutrients, used as food supplements, tablets and syrups; increase performance of athletes and race horses.
- In cereal, such as rice and wheat pollen grains lose viability within 30 minutes of their release.
- Rosaceae, Leguminosae and Solanaceae maintain viability for months.
- Pollen grains are stored in liquid nitrogen (-196°C), can be used as pollen banks, in crop breeding programmes.
- **Pollen allergy** Pollen grains of anemophilous plant cause severe allergies and bronchial afflictions, leading to chronic respiratory disorders i.e., asthma and bronchitis, some species like e.g, *Parthenium* (carrot grass), *Amaranthus* and *Chenopodium*.

Types of Microspore Tetrads

- The most common type is **tetrahedral**.
- In some plants, the fusion of all pollen grains of an entire theca is seen, it is called **pollinium**, e.g., *Calotropis*. [Fig.f]
- All other five types of tetrads are found in *Aristolochia elegans*.

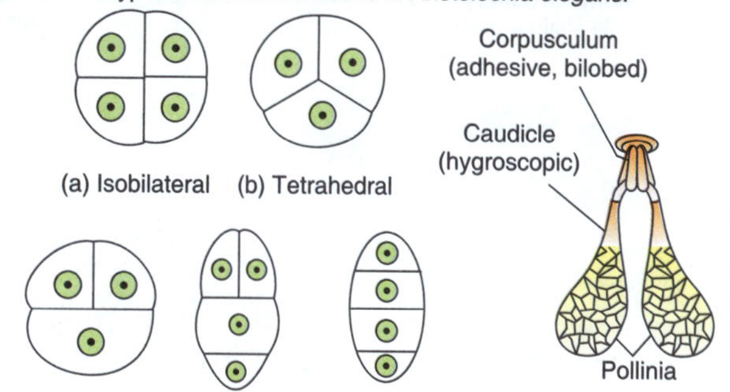

Microsporogenesis

- Sporogenous tissues undergo meiotic divisions to form microspore tetrads.

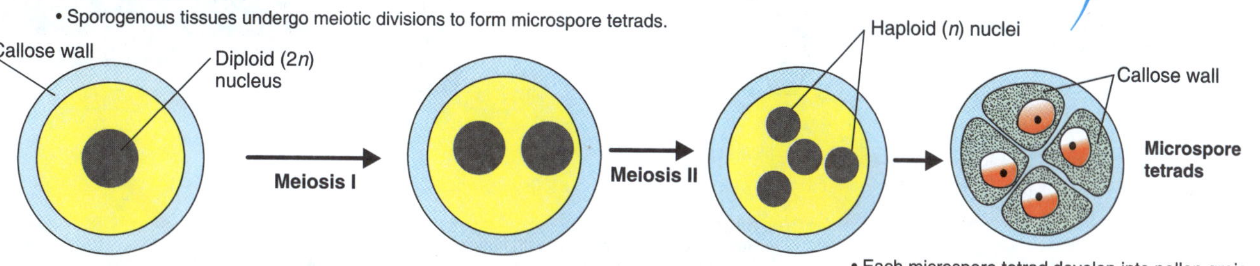

- Each microspore tetrad develop into pollen grain.

Sequential Development of Male Gametophyte

Microsporangia (2*n*)

Sporogenous tissue (2*n*)

Pollen Mother Cell (PMC) (2*n*)

Microspore tetrad (*n*)

Pollen grain (*n*)

Microgametogenesis

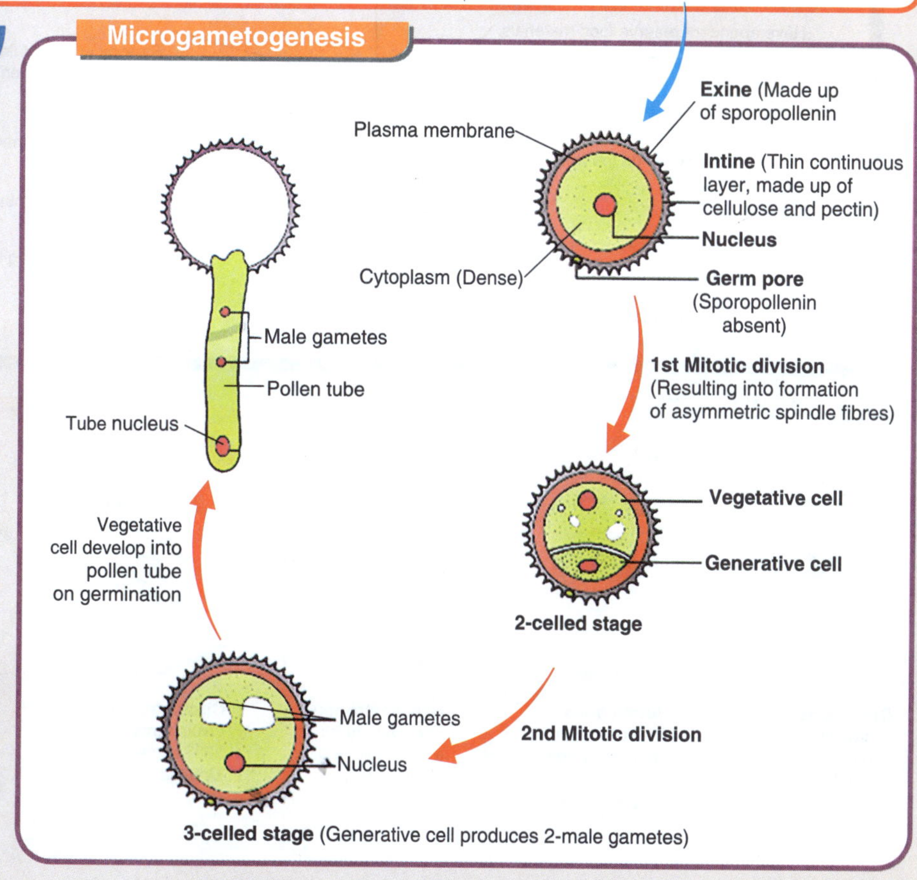

Gynoecium

Stigma (Feathery and sticky)
Style (Neck like structure)
Ovary
Thalamus

Types of Carpel

Monocarpellary (Single pistil) e.g. Pea

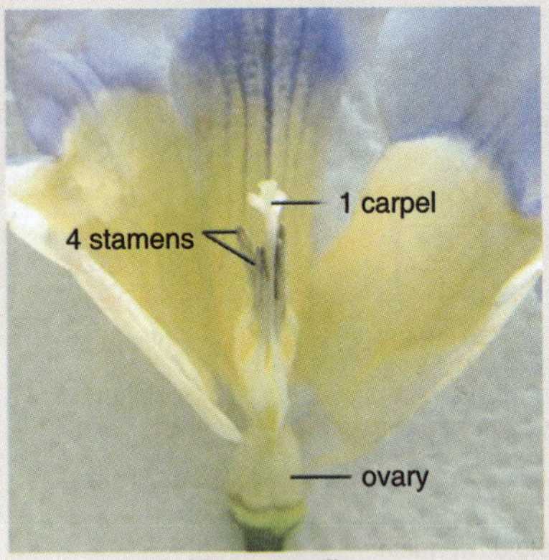

Multicarpellary (More than one pistil)

Syncarpous (Pistils fused) e.g. *Hibiscus, Papaver*

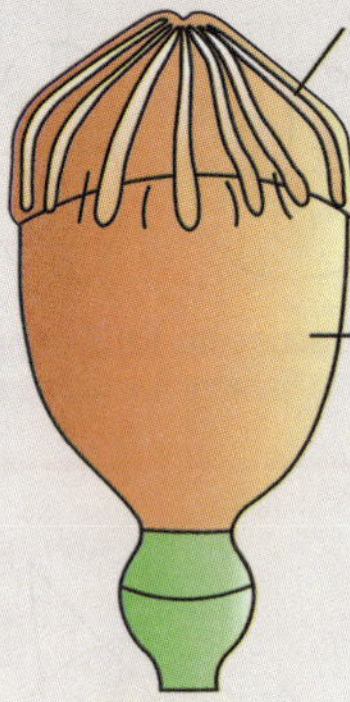

Apocarpous (Pistils free) e.g. *Michelia, Ranunculus*

1 carpel
4 stamens
ovary

Monocarpellary

Stigma
Synacarpous ovary

Carpels

Megasporangium (ovule)

Structure of Megasporangium

Hilum
Region where ovule fuses with funicle.
The extended part of the funicle form a ridge, called **raphe**.

Nucellus
Have abundant reserve food materials.

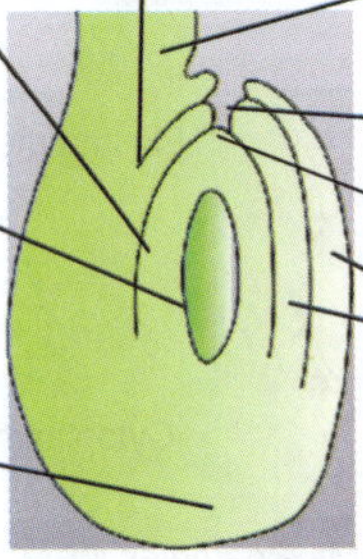

Funicle
Stalk by which ovule is attached to the placenta.
It supply food material from placenta to ovule.

Micropyle
The point, integuments leave a narrow pore.

Embryo sac
Located inside the nucellus.

Micropylar pole
The part of the embryo sac that is closest to the micropyle.

Outer
Inner

Integument
Protective covering of ovule.

Chalazal pole
Basal part of the ovule, opposite to the micropylar end.

Types of Ovules

Orthotropous
Micropyle, chalaza and funicle are in a straight line, e.g. *Polygonum.*

Anatropous
The ovule turns at a 180° angle. e.g. most angiosperms

Hemianatropous
The ovule turns at a 90° angle, e.g. *Ranunculus.*

Circinotropous
Ovule turns at 360° angle, e.g. *Opuntia.*

Amphitropous
The ovule as well as the embryo sac is curved like a horse-shoe, e.g. *Poppy.*

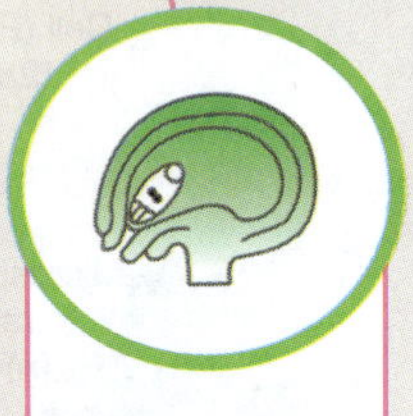

Campylotropous
The ovule is curved more or less at the right angle to the funicle, e.g. *Brassica.*

Megasporogenesis

Ovule diffentiates to form a single MMC

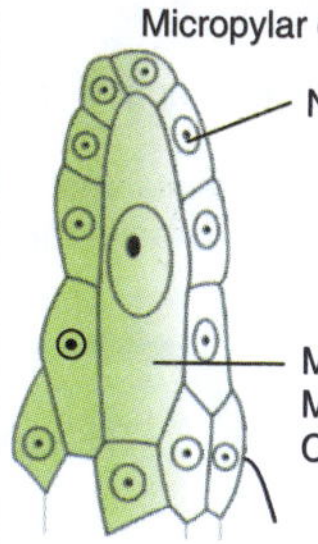

Micropylar end
Nucellus
Megaspore Mother Cell (2*n*)

Meiosis I

MMC undergoes meiotic division

Micropylar end
Nucellus
Megaspore dyad

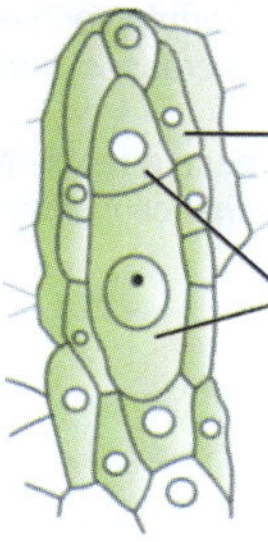

Meiosis II

Meiosis results in the production of 4 megaspore.

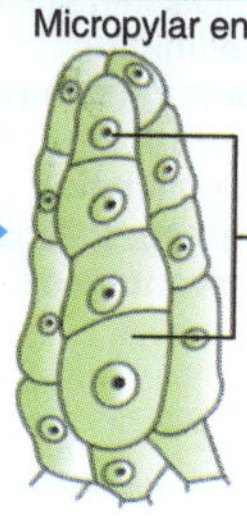

Micropylar end
Megaspore tetrad (Linear)

Out of four megaspores only 1 remain functional (at chalazal end) other 3 degenerates.

Free nuclear division occurs

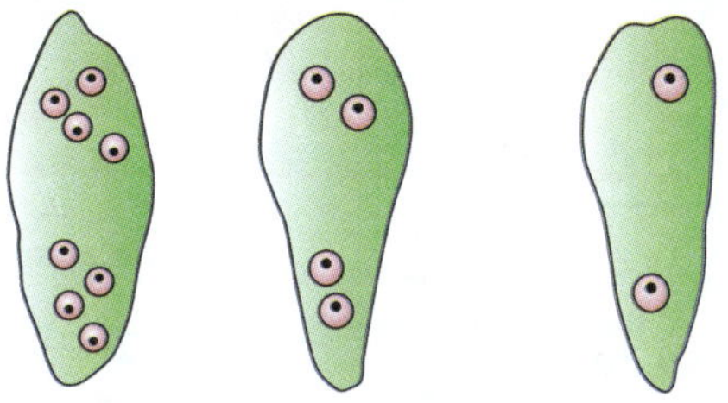

2 nucleate after 1st mitotic division migrate to opposite pole.

4 nucleate after 2 subsequent division

8 nucleate 4 nuclei on each pole

Mature embryo sac, 6 nuclei out of 8 are surrounded by cell wall, remaining two called polar nuclei are situated in central cell.

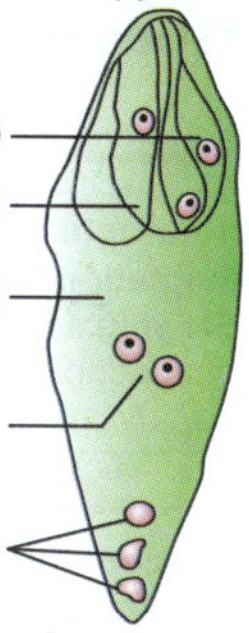

Micropylar end
Synergids (*n*)
Egg (*n*)
Central cell
2 polar nuclei (*n*+*n*)
Antipodals (*n*)
Chalazal end

Digrammatic representation of mature embryo sac (Polygonum type)

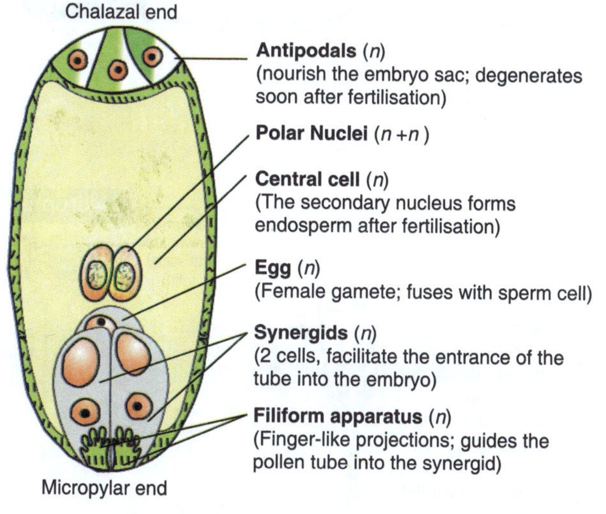

NEET POWER TIPS

- On the basis of number of megaspores involved in development, embryo sac can be monosporic, bisporic or tetrasporic.
- Embryo sac is large and oval structure consisting of seven cells and eight nuclei.
- The nucleus of megaspore undergoes 3 round of mitosis (nuclear division) without cytokinesis (cell division) to form 8 nuclei.
- The three nuclei move towards chalazal end developed into 2 synergids and 1 egg cell.

- Water hyacinth and water lily -Flowers emerge above the water and are pollinated by insects or wind.
- **Self pollination**
  - **Advantages:** Maintain pure lines; eliminate harmful recessive character
  - **Disadvantages:** Vigour and vitality of race decreases; variability and adaptability to changed environment are reduced.
- **Cross pollination**
  - **Advantages** Variations in the progeny; increase adaptability of the offspring; more resistant to disease
  - **Disadvantages** Less economical; factor of chance is always involved; undesirable character may creep in the race.

Types of Pollination

Cleistogamous Flowers
- Closed bisexual flower.
- Self pollinated only
- Produces assured seed-set

Autogamy
Transfer of pollen grain from the anther to stigma of same flower e.g. *Viola, Oxalis* and *Commelina*

Chasmogamous Flowers
- Open flower unisexual
- May be cross pollinated or self pollinated

Geitonogamy
- Transfer of pollen grain to the stigma of different flower of the same plant.
- **Functionally**-Cross pollination
- **Genetically**-Autogamy

Cross Pollination or Xenogamy
Two different plants are involved; need pollinators; genetically different types of pollen grain are invalved.

Biotic agencies

Entomophily (Insects)
Adaptation
- Flowers are large, colourful, fragrant and rich in nectar, e.g., rose, *Hibiscus*, etc.

Chiropterophily (Bats)
Adaptation
- Flowers are large, dull coloured with strong fermenting or foul odour and abundant nectar, e.g., *Bauhinia*, *Kigelia*, etc.

Myremecophily (Ants)
e.g., Family–Rubiaceae

Ornithophily (Birds)
Adaptation
- Flowers are tubular, cup-shaped or urn-shaped, bright coloured, large sized, e.g., *Nicotiana, Callistemon*, etc.

Malacophily (Snails)
e.g., *Arisaema*, *Chrysanthemum*, etc.

Ophiophily (Snake)
e.g., *Santalum*

Abiotic Agencies (Pollinators)

Anemophily

Anemophily (Wind)
- **Pollen grains**-Dry, lightweight, small-sized and non-sticky
- **Flowers**- Small and inconspicuous, colourless, devoid of scent and nectar
- e.g., Sugarcane, maize, *Pinus*, etc.

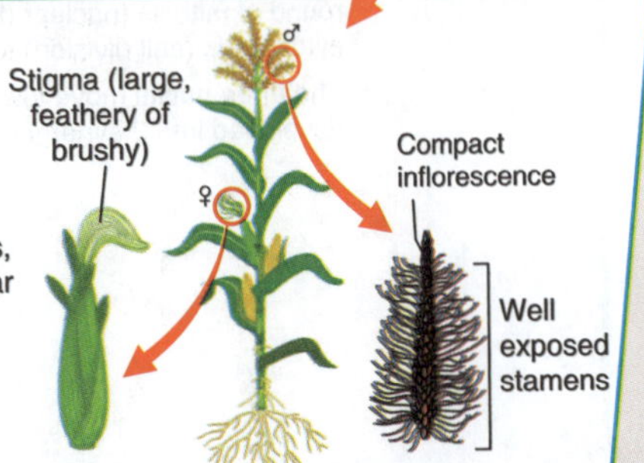

Hydrophily

Hydrophily (Water)
- **Flower**-Small and inconspicuous, nectar and odeur are absent e.g., *Vallisneria* (epihydrophily), *Zostera* (hypohydrophily) etc.

Female flower (solitary)
Long stalk (brings mature female flower to the water surface)
Stigma (Unwettable but sticky trifid)
Female flower
Male flower (Pollen grains long ribbon like protected by mucilage covering)

Pollination in *Vallisneria*

Out-Breeding Devices : Discourage the self-pollination.

1. • **Dicliny** or **Unisexuality** Only one kind of reproductive organ (Unisexual flower).
   • Monoecious (Maize and castor) and Dioecious (Papaya and *Cannabis sativa*)

2. **Dichogamy**
   • Bisexual flower, male and female organs do not mature synchronously
   • **Protandry** Stamen matures earlier (Sunflower).
   • **Protogyny** Carpel matures earlier (*Michelia*)

3. **Heteroanthy/ Heterostyly** Anther and stigma are positioned at different heights, e.g., *Oxalis*, *Primula*, etc.

4. **Herkogamy** Physical barrier between anther and stigma, e.g., *Orchids*.

5. **Self-incompatibility** Genetic barrier, prevents germination of pollen grain on stigma, e.g., potato, *Malva*, etc.

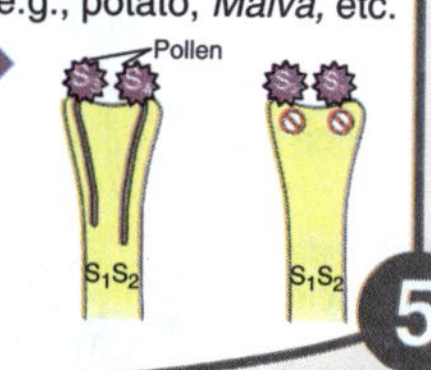

Pollen-Pistil Interaction

- Dynamic process, involves the acceptance of right pollen or rejection of wrong pollen grain by the pistil; as a result of continuous dialogue between pollen grain and pistil.
- **Incompatible pollen** Not allowed to germinate.
- **Compatible pollen** Allows germination and growth of pollen tube.

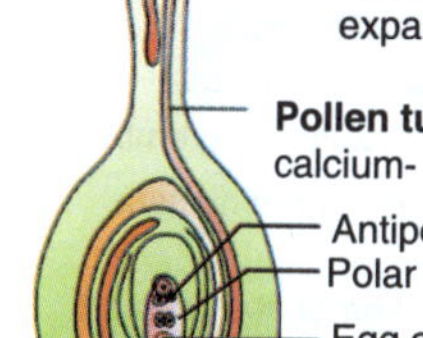

1. Growth of pollen tube

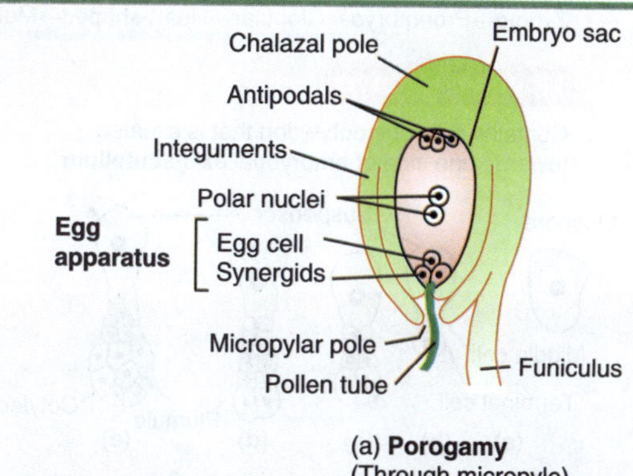

(a) **Porogamy** (Through micropyle)

(b) **Mesogamy** (Through the integuments)

(c) **Chalazogamy** (Through the chalazal tissue)

2. Entry of pollen tube into the ovule

Artificial Hybridisation

Desired pollen grains used for pollination and fertilisation

01 **Emasculation** Removal of anther from the bisexual flower; prevents self-pollination; not required in unisexual flower

02 **Bagging** Prevents the contamination of the stigma within unwanted pollen grain

03 **Pollination** Pollen grains dusted on the stigma when it attains maturity

04 **Rebagging** Till the fruits begin to ripen; latter contain the seed of hybrid variety

Double Fertilisation

- Discovered by **Nawaschin** in 1898.
- Pollen tube releases two male gametes into the cytoplasm of synergids.

Two events

- **Syngamy** - Male gamete (n) + female gamete (n) → Zygote ($2n$) → Embryo ($2n$)
- **Triple fusion** - Second male gamete (n) + 2 polar nuclei ($2n$) → PEN ($3n$) → Endosperm ($3n$) (central cell)

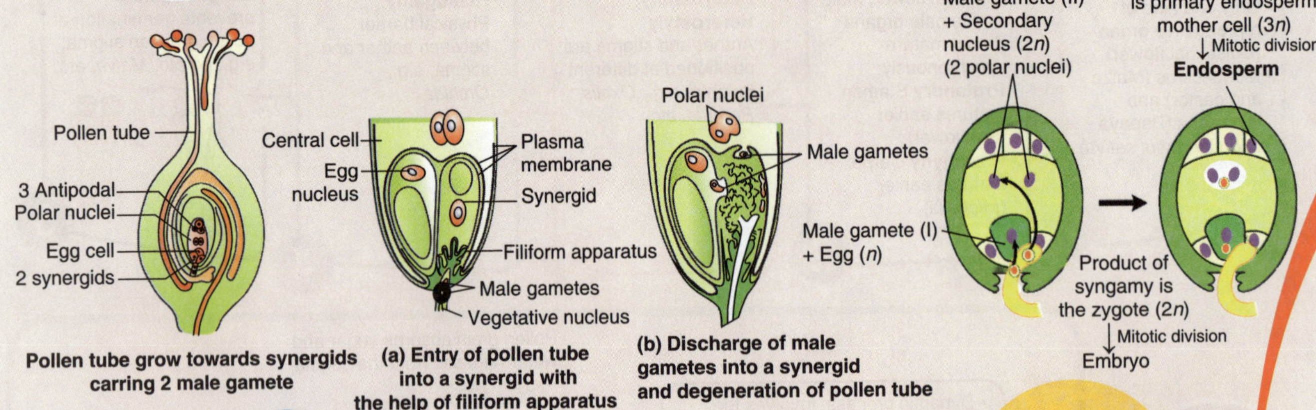

Pollen tube grow towards synergids carring 2 male gamete

(a) Entry of pollen tube into a synergid with the help of filiform apparatus

(b) Discharge of male gametes into a synergid and degeneration of pollen tube

Post-Fertilisation Events

Development of Endosperm

- Nutritive tissue; provides nutrition to the developing embryo.
- PEN → Nuclear divisions → Free nuclei → Free nuclear endosperm (e.g. Coconut water)
- Endosperm become cellular e.g. white kernal of a coconut
- **Types of endosperm**

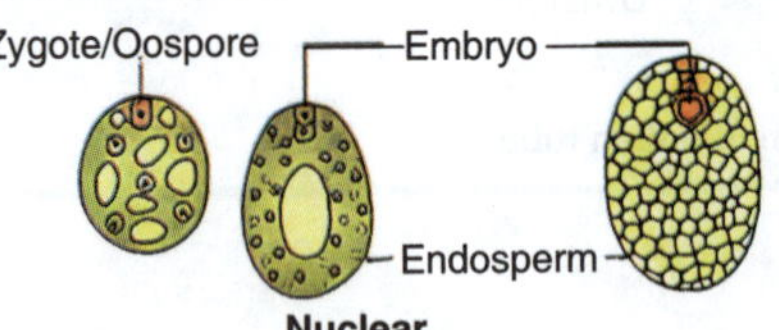

Nuclear

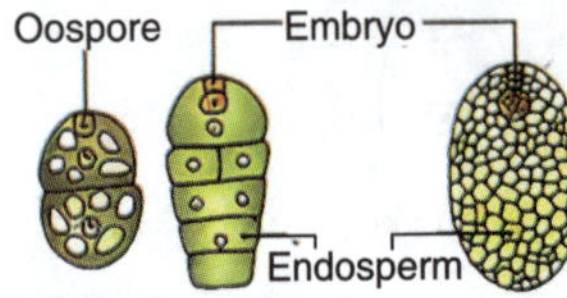

Cellular (e.g. *petunia* and *Datura*)

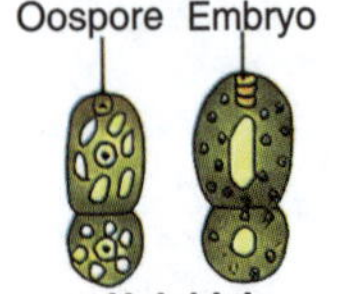

Helobial (e.g. foxtail lilies)

Development of Embryo

- Zygote develops into an embryo - Embryogenesis
- Embryo develops at the micropylar end of the embryo sac.
- Zygote→Proembryo→Globular→Heart-shaped→Mature

Monocot Embryo

Contains only one cotyledon that is situated towards one side of embryonal axis-**scutellum**.

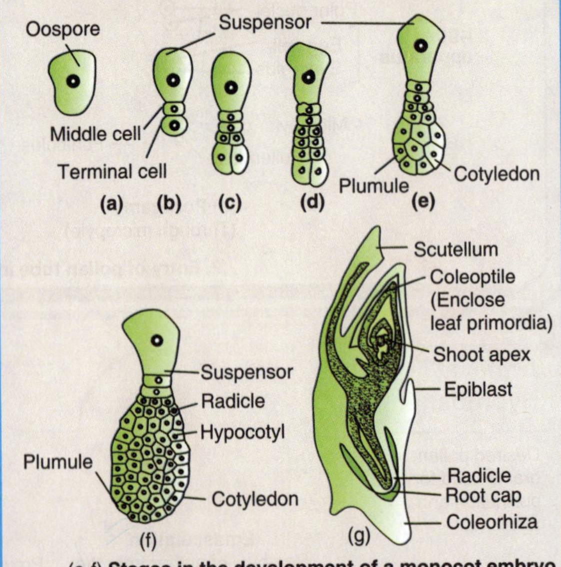

(a-f) Stages in the development of a monocot embryo, (g) A monocot embryo of a grass

Dicot Embryo

01 Consist an embryonal axis and two cotyledons

02 **Epicotyl** portion of the embryonal axis above the level or cotyledon

03 **Hypocotyl** portion below the level of cotyledon.

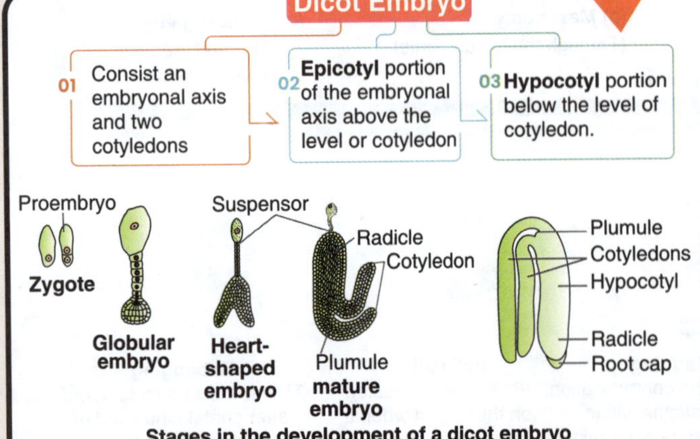

Stages in the development of a dicot embryo

Development of Seed

- **Fertilised** ovule develops into a seed; end product of sexual reproduction
- Consist of seed coat (s), embryo axis and cotyledon with adequate food reserve.

Albuminous

- Endosperm present, not completely consumed
- Usually found in monocot plants, e.g., wheat, maize and barley.

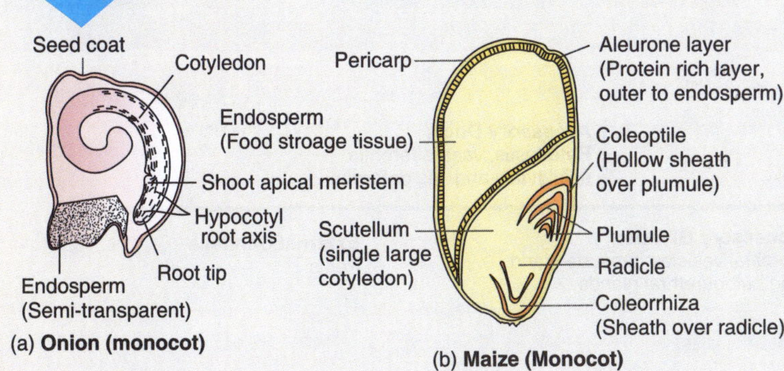

(a) **Onion (monocot)** (b) **Maize (Monocot)**

Non-albuminous/ Ex-albuminous

- Endosperm absent completely; consumed during embryo development
- Food stored in cotyledons
- Dicot plants, e.g., pea, beans, etc.

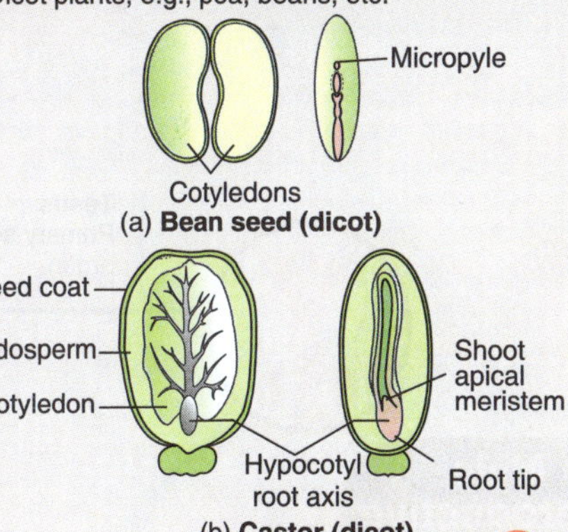

(a) **Bean seed (dicot)**
(b) **Castor (dicot)**

Fruit

Simple (Develops from monocarpellary ovary), **aggregate** (Develops from multicarpellary, apocarpous ovary) and **composite** (Develops from a complete inflorescence).

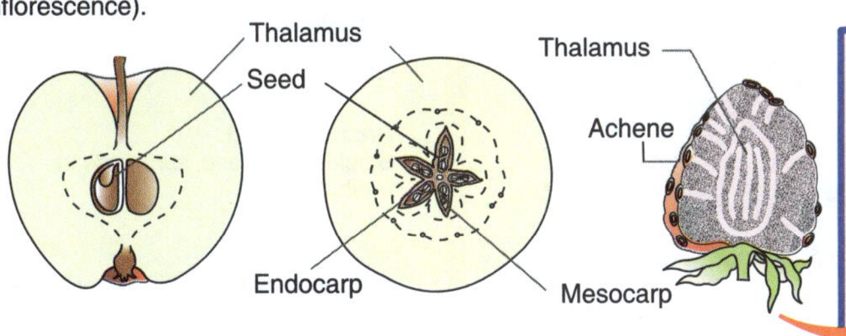

False fruit Apple and Strawberry

Formation of Fruit

(a) Develops from fertilised ovary often.

(b) Pseudocarp or false fruit - derived from tissue outside the ovary i.e., thalamus.

(c) Eucarp or true fruit- developed only from the ovary.

(d) **Pericarp** wall covering the fruit), **epicarp** (Skin of fruits), mesocarp (Fleshy and pulpy part) and **endocarp** (Inner, surrounds the seed)

Special Modes of Reproduction

Parthenocarpy
Formation of fruit without fertilisation; e.g., Banana and seedless grapes.

Apomixis
Production of seed without meiosis and syngamy; e.g., Citrus plants
Types Vegetative, Agamospermy (Recurrent: diplospory and apospory, Adventive, Non-recurrent)

Polyembryony
Having one or more than one embryo in a seed; more common in gymnosperms than angiosperm.
Types Simple polyembryony and adventive polyembryony

NEET POWER TIPS

Fate of floral parts

Ovary ($2n$) → Fruit
Ovary wall ($2n$) → Pericarp
Ovule ($2n$) → Seed
Outer integument ($2n$) → Testa
Inner integument ($2n$) → Tegmen
Zygote ($2n$) → Embryo

PEN ($3n$) → Endosperm
Sepal ($2n$), Petal ($2n$), Stigma ($2n$), Style ($2n$) — Wither away, fall down
Nucellus ($2n$) → Consumed/Present as perisperm
Synergids (n), Antipodal cells (n) — Degenerate

Important facts

- **Perisperm:** Remanats of nucleus that persists e.g., black pepper and beet
- Micropyle remain as a small pore in the seed coat, facilitate entry of oxygen and water during germination.
- Transformation of ovule into seeds and ovary into fruit proceeds simultaneously.

Chapter 21 Human Reproduction

Reproductive Events

Gametogenesis
Formation of gametes

Insemination
Transfer of male gamete into female reproductive tract

Fertilisation
Fusion of male and female gametes to form zygote

Embryogenesis
Cleavage of zygote to form embryo and followed by its development

Parturition
Expelling out fully formed baby from mother's womb.

Male Reproductive System

Testis
Primary sex organ

Accessory Glands
Seminal vesicles, prostate gland and bulbourethral glands.

Accessory Ducts
Rete testis, vasa efferentia, epididymis and vas deferens

External Genitalia
Penis

Urinary bladder
Muscular structure, stores the urine.

Ureter
Convey the urine from kidney to urinary bladder.

Ejaculaory duct
Union of duct, from seminal vesicle and vas deferens to urethra.

Vas deferens
Emerges from cauda epididymis and enters abdominal cavity

Epididymis
Long, narrow, coiled tubules; stores and nourishes sperms.

Testis
Suspended into the scrotum by the spermatic cords.

Scrotum
Pouch of deeply pigmented skin.

Seminal vesicle
Sac-like structure; produces alkaline secretion.

Prostate gland
Single large gland, surrounds the urethra.

Bulbourethral gland/Cowper's gland
Secretes viscous mucus for lubrication of penis.

Corpora cavernosa
Filled with blood during arousal to cause an erection

Spongy erectile tissue
2 dorsal corpora cavernosa and 1 ventral corpus spongiosum.

Corpus spongiosum
Involved in the process of erection.

Glans Penis
Corpus spongiosum's enlargement at the end of penis

Prepuce
Foreskin, covers the glans penis

External genitalia Penis
Male copulatory organ, conduct both urine and semen

Posterior View

Median Longitudinal Section of Mammalian Testis

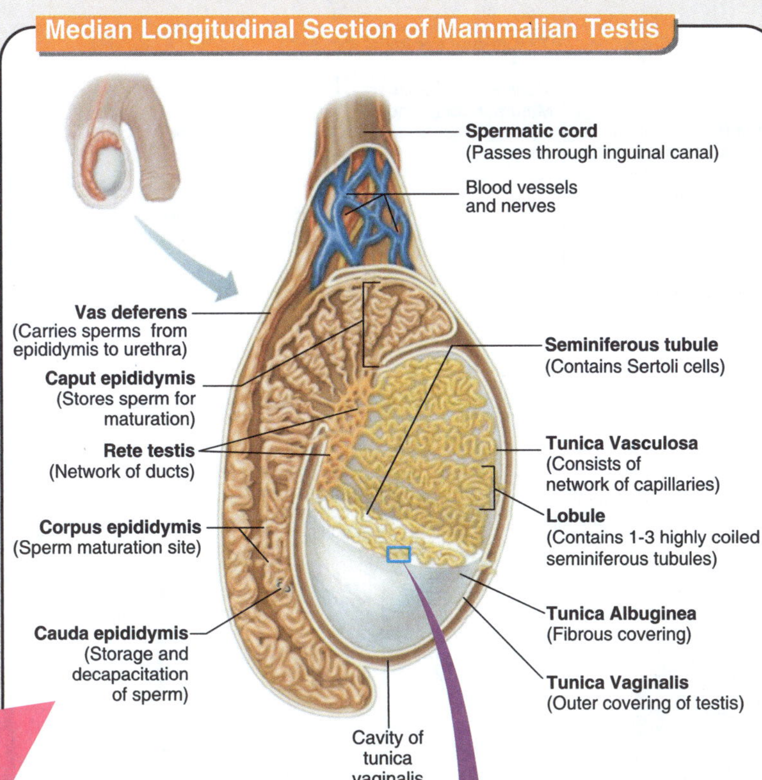

- Semen is collection of secretions from seminal vesicles, prostate gland and Cowper's gland.
- Gubernaculum holds testis in place by fibrous cord.
- Vasa efferentia are 15-20 in numbers in human males.
- In scrotum; septum is made up of **dartos muscle.**
- **Cremaster** muscle covers the testicles and spermatic cords.
- The **cremaster** and **dartos** muscles of the scrotum help to regulate the temperature of the testes.
- Testes descend into scrotum during 7th month of foetal development.
- Dense coverings of testis are tunica vaginalis, tunica albuginea and tunica vasculosa.
- In seminal vesicle, prostaglandins contribute towards sperm motility and muscle contractions within the female reproductive tract.

Section of the Seminiferous Tubule

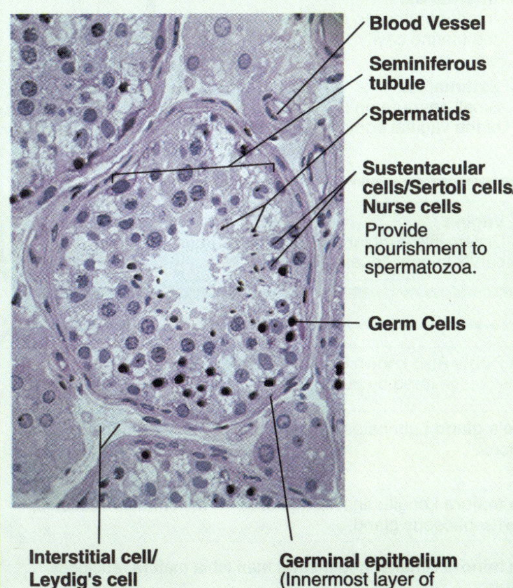

Disorders of Male Reproductive System

Impotence
Inability of adult male to achieve penile erection

Prostatitis
Inflammation of prostate generally caused by infection

Prostate Carcinoma
Cancer of prostate

Inguinal Hernia
Tearing of inguinal tissue, results in the protrusion of a part of intestine into the scrotum

Hydrocele
Enlargement of testicle due to accumulation of fluid

Cryptorchidism
Failure of one or both of the testicles to descend into the scrotum

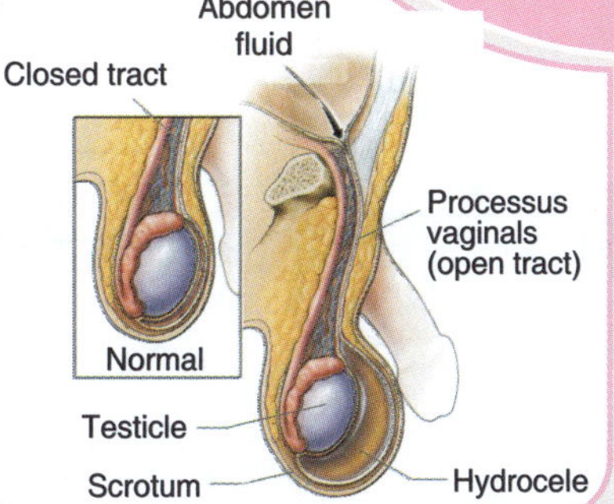

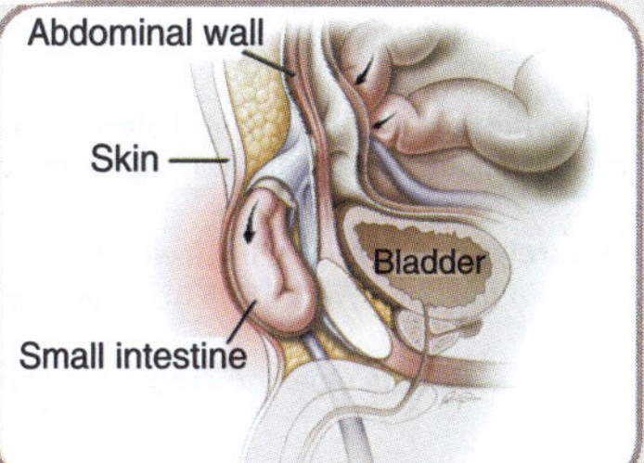

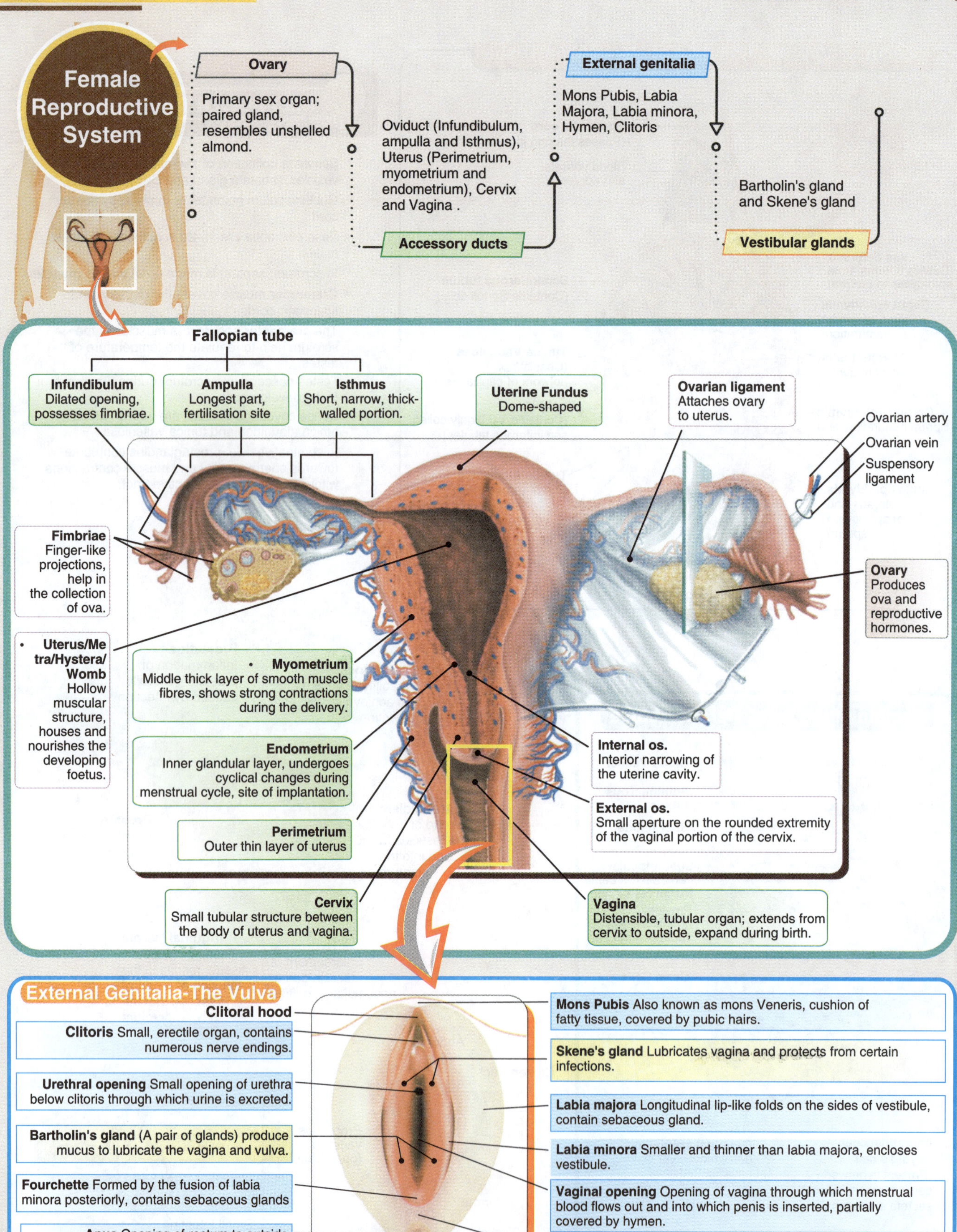
Female Reproductive System
Ovary
Primary sex organ; paired gland, resembles unshelled almond.
Oviduct (Infundibulum, ampulla and Isthmus), Uterus (Perimetrium, myometrium and endometrium), Cervix and Vagina .
Accessory ducts
External genitalia
Mons Pubis, Labia Majora, Labia minora, Hymen, Clitoris
Bartholin's gland and Skene's gland
Vestibular glands
Fallopian tube
Infundibulum Dilated opening, possesses fimbriae.
Ampulla Longest part, fertilisation site
Isthmus Short, narrow, thick-walled portion.
Uterine Fundus Dome-shaped
Ovarian ligament Attaches ovary to uterus.
Ovarian artery
Ovarian vein
Suspensory ligament
Fimbriae Finger-like projections, help in the collection of ova.
Ovary Produces ova and reproductive hormones.
• Uterus/Metra/Hystera/Womb Hollow muscular structure, houses and nourishes the developing foetus.
• Myometrium Middle thick layer of smooth muscle fibres, shows strong contractions during the delivery.
Endometrium Inner glandular layer, undergoes cyclical changes during menstrual cycle, site of implantation.
Perimetrium Outer thin layer of uterus
Internal os. Interior narrowing of the uterine cavity.
External os. Small aperture on the rounded extremity of the vaginal portion of the cervix.
Cervix Small tubular structure between the body of uterus and vagina.
Vagina Distensible, tubular organ; extends from cervix to outside, expand during birth.
External Genitalia-The Vulva
Clitoral hood
Clitoris Small, erectile organ, contains numerous nerve endings.
Urethral opening Small opening of urethra below clitoris through which urine is excreted.
Bartholin's gland (A pair of glands) produce mucus to lubricate the vagina and vulva.
Fourchette Formed by the fusion of labia minora posteriorly, contains sebaceous glands
Anus Opening of rectum to outside.
Mons Pubis Also known as mons Veneris, cushion of fatty tissue, covered by pubic hairs.
Skene's gland Lubricates vagina and protects from certain infections.
Labia majora Longitudinal lip-like folds on the sides of vestibule, contain sebaceous gland.
Labia minora Smaller and thinner than labia majora, encloses vestibule.
Vaginal opening Opening of vagina through which menstrual blood flows out and into which penis is inserted, partially covered by hymen.
Perineum Area which extends from fourchette to anus.

Anatomy of the Breast

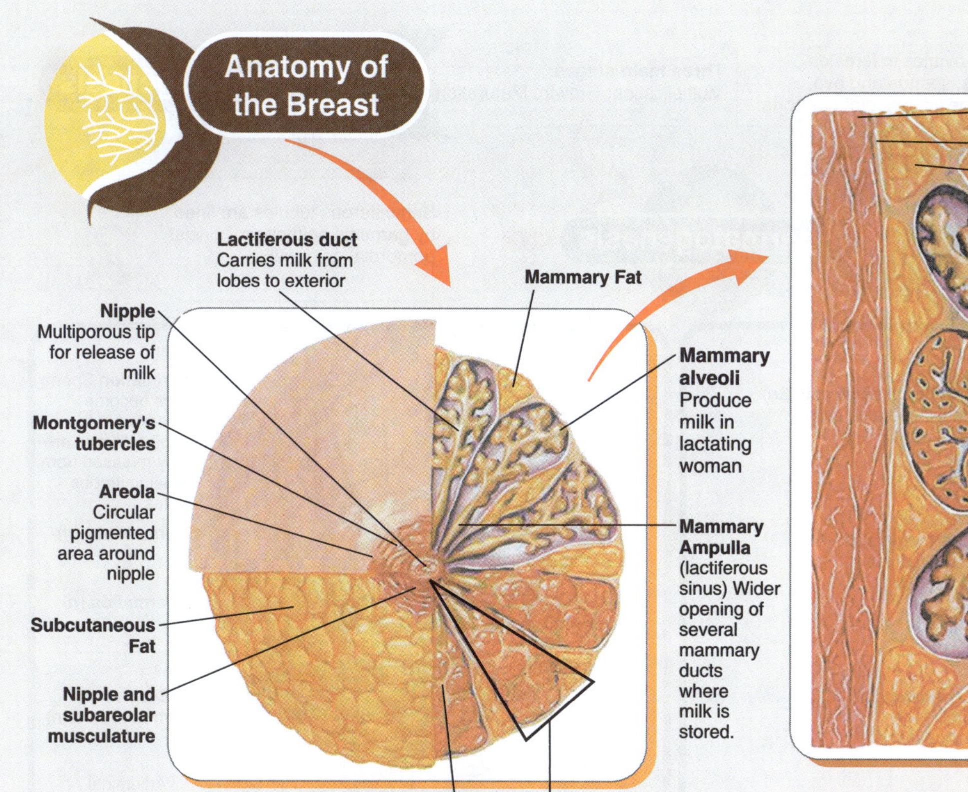

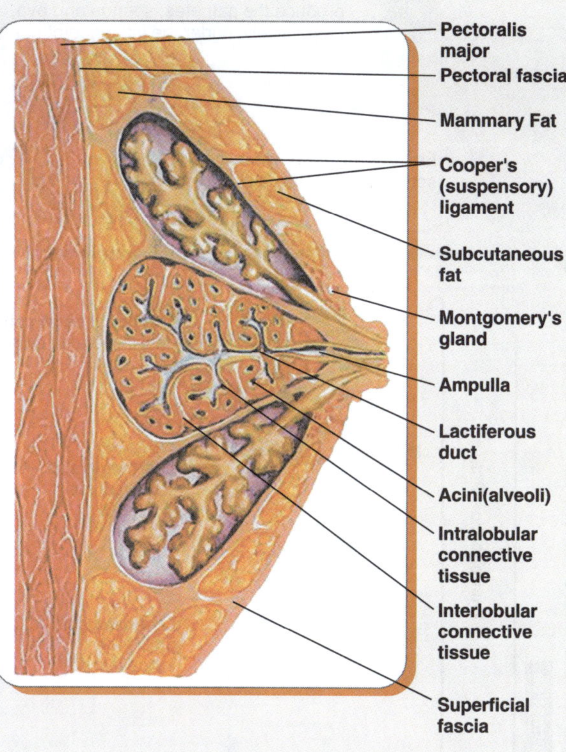

NEET POWER TIPS

Homologous Structures of Female And Male Reproductive Systems

Female	Male
Ovaries	Testes
Ovum	Sperm
Labia majora	Scrotum
Labia minora	Spongy (Penile) urethra
Clitoris	Glans penis
Skene's glands	Prostate
Bartholin's glands	Bulbourethral gland

Facts

- Conduction of ovum or zygote towards the uterus is done by peristalsis and ciliary action by oviducts.
- pH of vagina is acidic due to presence of certain bacteria.
- **Skene's glands** are present around urethral orifice.
- **Bartholin's glands** are present on either side of vaginal orifice.
- Mammary glands are modified sweat glands.
- Production of milk is stimulated by prolactin.
- Ejection of milk is stimulated by oxytocin.
- Milk pathway: Mammary alveolus → Mammary duct → Ampulla → Lactiferous duct → Nipple

Disorders of Female Reproductive System

Breast Cancer Rarely seen before the age of thirty; treated by mastectomy (removal of breast).

Oophorocystosis (Ovarion cysts) Fluid filled tumours of the ovary.

Endometriosis Growth of endometrial tissue outside the uterus, treated by hormone therapy or surgery.

Ectopic Pregnancy Implantation of embryo at a place other than uterus, e.g. oviduct.

Oophoritis Inflammation of ovary.

Cervical Cancer Slow-growing, treated by radiation or surgery.

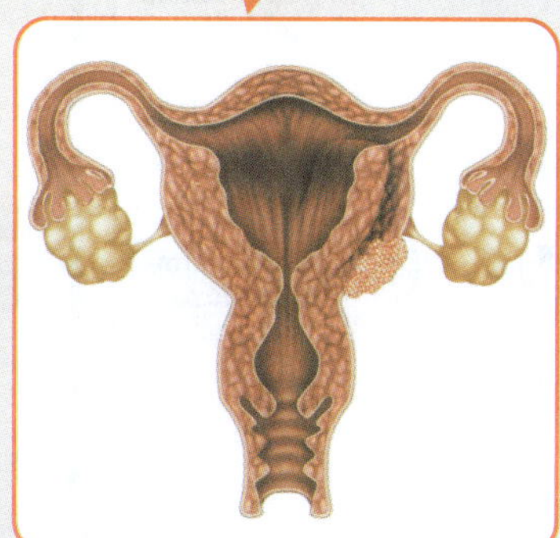

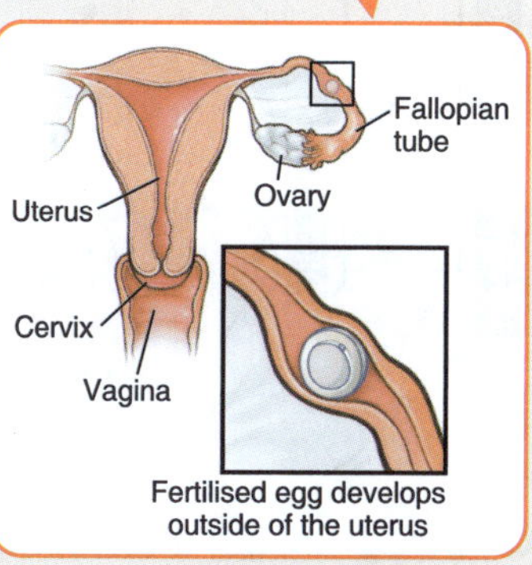

Fertilised egg develops outside of the uterus

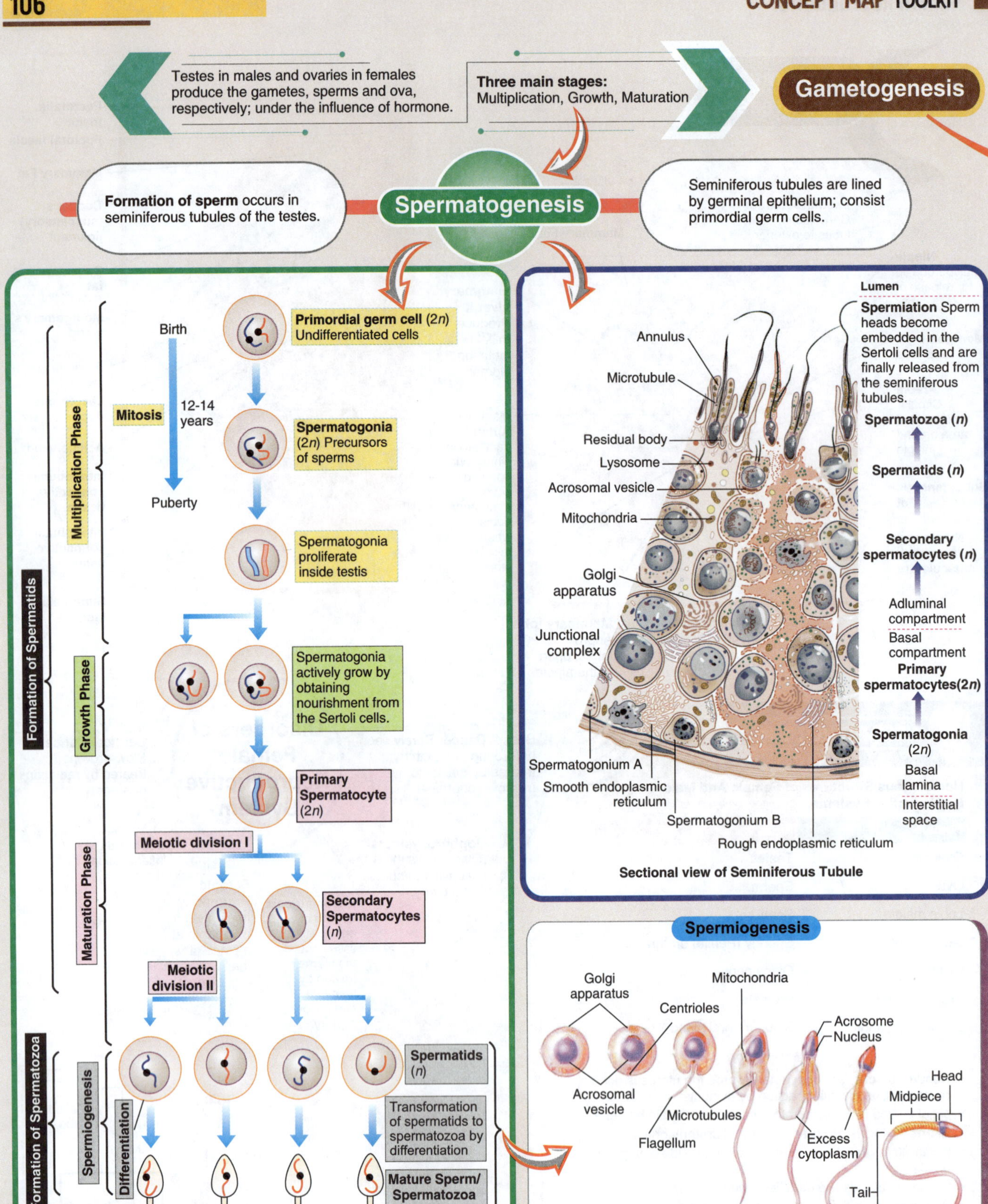
Testes in males and ovaries in females produce the gametes, sperms and ova, respectively; under the influence of hormone.
Three main stages: Multiplication, Growth, Maturation
Gametogenesis
Formation of sperm occurs in seminiferous tubules of the testes.
Spermatogenesis
Seminiferous tubules are lined by germinal epithelium; consist primordial germ cells.
Formation of Spermatids
Multiplication Phase
Birth
Mitosis
12-14 years
Puberty
Primordial germ cell (2n) Undifferentiated cells
Spermatogonia (2n) Precursors of sperms
Spermatogonia proliferate inside testis
Growth Phase
Spermatogonia actively grow by obtaining nourishment from the Sertoli cells.
Maturation Phase
Primary Spermatocyte (2n)
Meiotic division I
Secondary Spermatocytes (n)
Meiotic division II
Formation of Spermatozoa
Spermiogenesis
Differentiation
Spermatids (n)
Transformation of spermatids to spermatozoa by differentiation
Mature Sperm/ Spermatozoa (n)
Lumen
Spermiation Sperm heads become embedded in the Sertoli cells and are finally released from the seminiferous tubules.
Spermatozoa (n)
Spermatids (n)
Secondary spermatocytes (n)
Adluminal compartment
Basal compartment
Primary spermatocytes(2n)
Spermatogonia (2n)
Basal lamina
Interstitial space
Annulus
Microtubule
Residual body
Lysosome
Acrosomal vesicle
Mitochondria
Golgi apparatus
Junctional complex
Spermatogonium A
Smooth endoplasmic reticulum
Spermatogonium B
Rough endoplasmic reticulum
Sectional view of Seminiferous Tubule
Spermiogenesis
Golgi apparatus
Mitochondria
Centrioles
Acrosome
Nucleus
Head
Midpiece
Acrosomal vesicle
Microtubules
Flagellum
Excess cytoplasm
Tail

Oogenesis

- Formation of mature female gametes in the ovaries.
- Germinal epithelium lines the outside of the ovary.
- Ovarian stroma consists of cortex and medulla.

Oogonium $2n$ → (Mitosis) → $2n$ Primary oocyte arrested in prophase I → Primary oocyte $2n$ → Meiosis I → Secondary oocyte n + First polar body (degenerates) n

Secondary oocyte arrested, in metaphase II, ovulated n → Meiosis II (completed only if fertilised) → Zygote $2n$ + Second polar body (degenerates) n

Multiplication Phase (During fetal life before birth)

Growth Phase (Birth to puberty)

Maturation Phase (Puberty to menopause)

NEET POWER TIPS

- Human male ejaculates about 200-300 million sperms during a coitus.
- **Normal fertility** : 60% sperms (normal shape and size); out of this 60%, atleast 40% must show vigorous motility.
- 2 million oogonia (in each ovary) produces by mitosis.
- Oogenesis begins in females even before they are born.
- Human ovum almost free of yolk: Alecithal, spherical, does not contain centrosome.
- Cortical granules are present under the plasma membrane.

Ovaries Showing Different Stages of Oogenesis

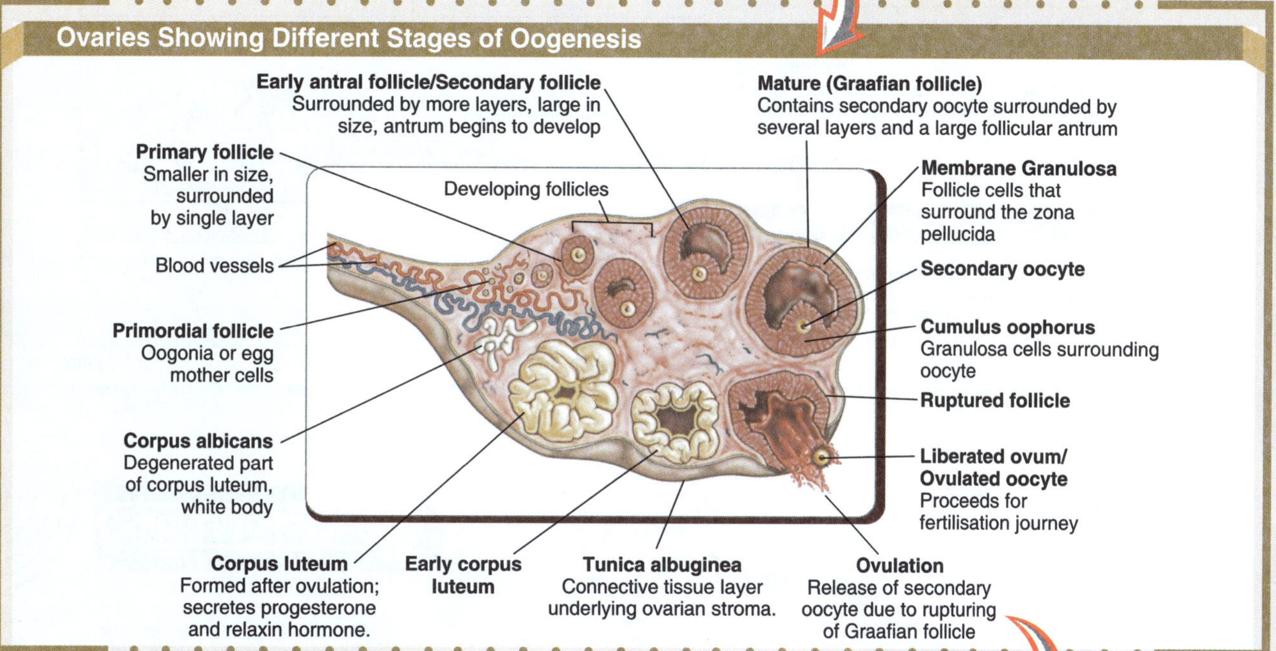

Structure of Sperms

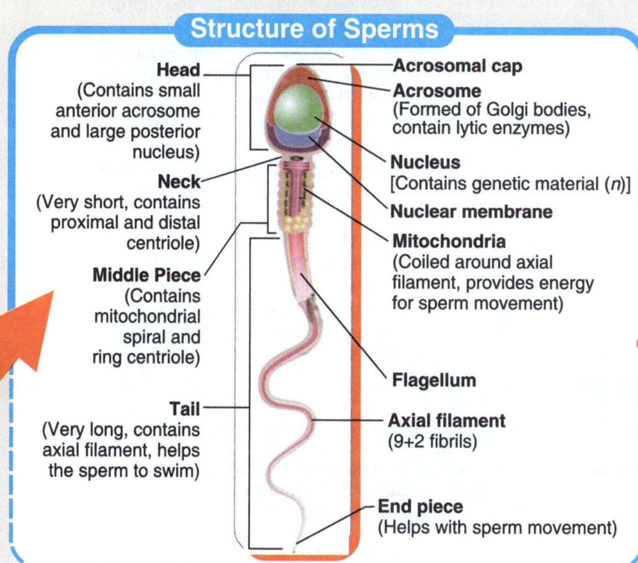

Structure of Human Ovum

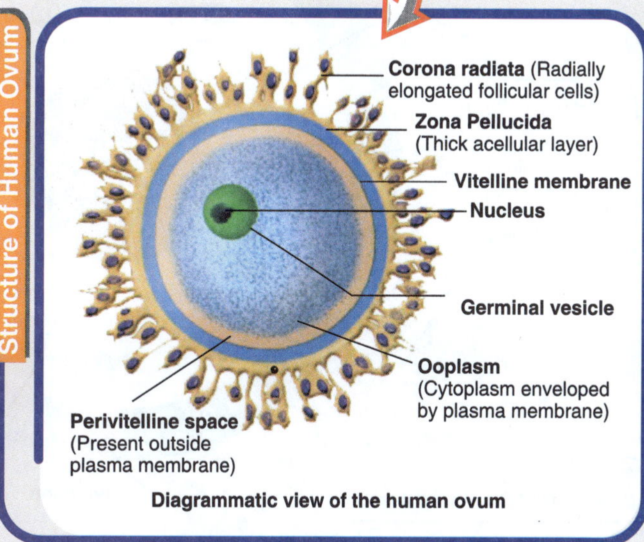

Diagrammatic view of the human ovum

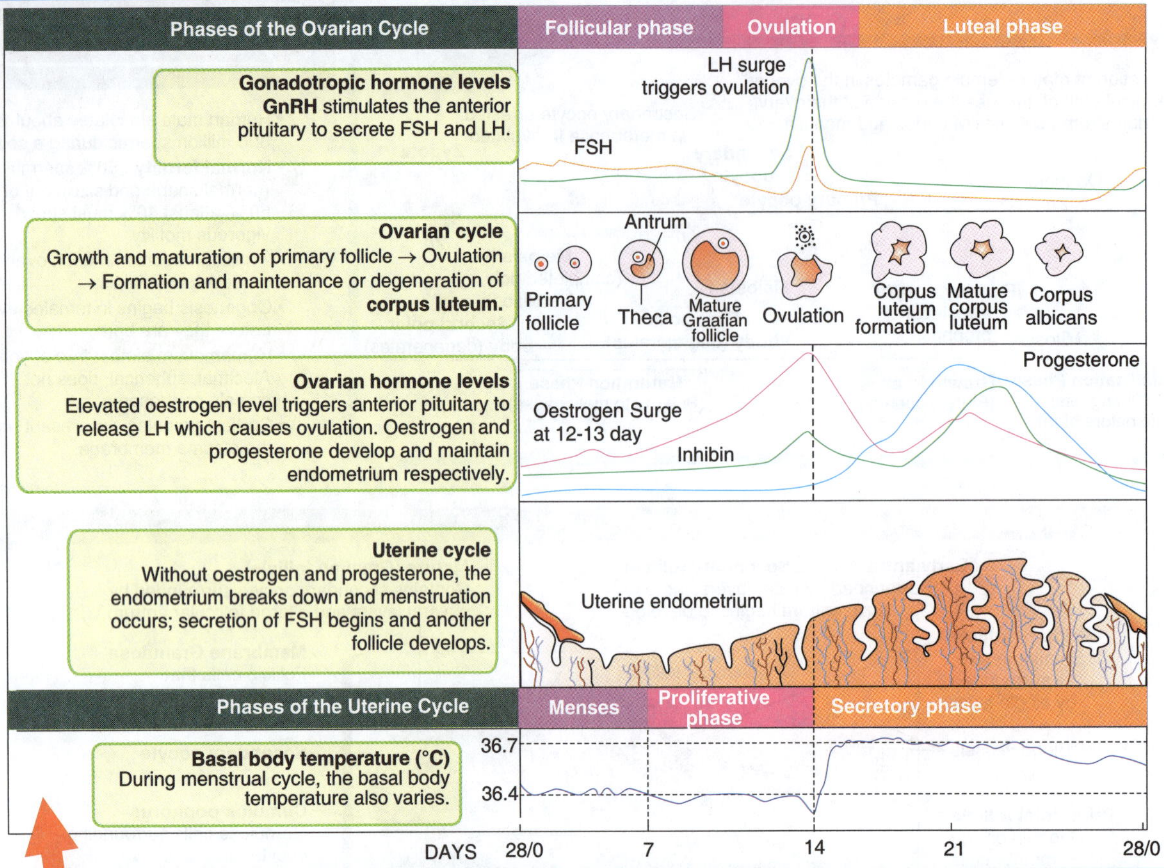

Phases of the Ovarian Cycle
Follicular phase
Ovulation
Luteal phase
Gonadotropic hormone levels
GnRH stimulates the anterior pituitary to secrete FSH and LH.
LH surge triggers ovulation
FSH
Ovarian cycle
Growth and maturation of primary follicle → Ovulation → Formation and maintenance or degeneration of corpus luteum.
Antrum
Primary follicle
Theca
Mature Graafian follicle
Ovulation
Corpus luteum formation
Mature corpus luteum
Corpus albicans
Ovarian hormone levels
Elevated oestrogen level triggers anterior pituitary to release LH which causes ovulation. Oestrogen and progesterone develop and maintain endometrium respectively.
Progesterone
Oestrogen Surge at 12-13 day
Inhibin
Uterine cycle
Without oestrogen and progesterone, the endometrium breaks down and menstruation occurs; secretion of FSH begins and another follicle develops.
Uterine endometrium
Phases of the Uterine Cycle
Menses
Proliferative phase
Secretory phase
Basal body temperature (°C)
During menstrual cycle, the basal body temperature also varies.
36.7
36.4
DAYS
28/0
7
14
21
28/0

Day 1-5
Endometrium breaks down
Menstruation
Menstrual Cycle
Follicular phase
Luteal phase
Ovulation
Day 15-28
Corpus luteum forms and secretes progesterone; endometrium thickens.
Day 14
Both LH and FSH attain a peak level.
Day 6-13
Endometrium rebuilds;FSH and LH secretion increases that stimulates follicular development oestrogen secretion.

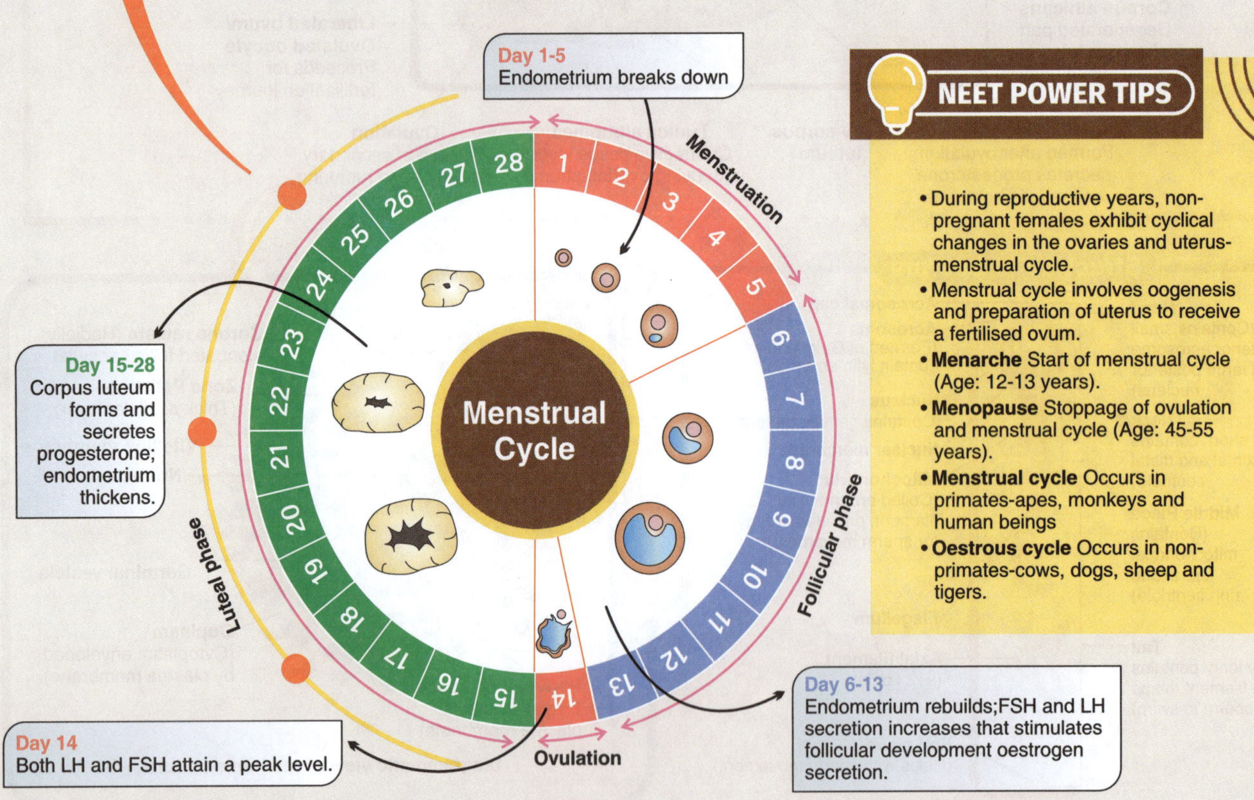

NEET POWER TIPS

- During reproductive years, non-pregnant females exhibit cyclical changes in the ovaries and uterus-menstrual cycle.
- Menstrual cycle involves oogenesis and preparation of uterus to receive a fertilised ovum.
- **Menarche** Start of menstrual cycle (Age: 12-13 years).
- **Menopause** Stoppage of ovulation and menstrual cycle (Age: 45-55 years).
- **Menstrual cycle** Occurs in primates-apes, monkeys and human beings
- **Oestrous cycle** Occurs in non-primates-cows, dogs, sheep and tigers.

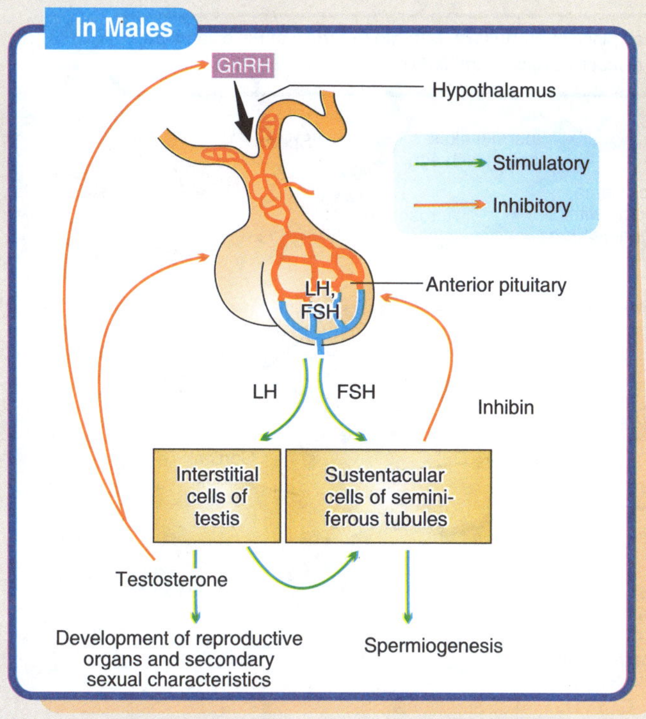

- As the level of progesterone, oestrogen and inhibin decreases, release of GnRH, FSH and LH rises due to loss of negative feedback suppression by ovarian hormones.
- If secondary oocyte is not fertilised corpus luteum degenerates into corpus albicans.
- If secondary oocyte is fertilised, corpus luteum persists and rescued from degeneration by human Chorionic Gonadotropin (hCG).

Hormonal Regulation

In Females

GnRH — Hypothalamus

FSH, LH — Anterior pituitary

FSH stimulates

LH stimulates

Growing follicles

Initial secretion of oestrogens by growing ovarian follicles

Ovaries

Ovulation

Further development of ovarian follicles and secretion of oestrogens, progesterone and inhibin

Corpus luteum

Secretes progesterone, oestrogens, relaxin, and inhibin

Oestrogens

- Promote development and maintenance of female reproductive structures, feminine secondary sex characteristics and breasts.
- High levels stimulate release of GnRH, FSH and LH.

Progesterone

- Works with oestrogens to prepare endometrium for implantation.
- Prepares mammary glands to secrete milk.
- Inhibits release of GnRH and LH.

Relaxin

- Inhibits contractions of uterine smooth muscle.
- During labor, increases flexibility of pubic symphysis and dilates uterine cervix.

Inhibin

- Inhibits release of FSH and to a lesser extent, LH

Inhibitory

Stimulatory

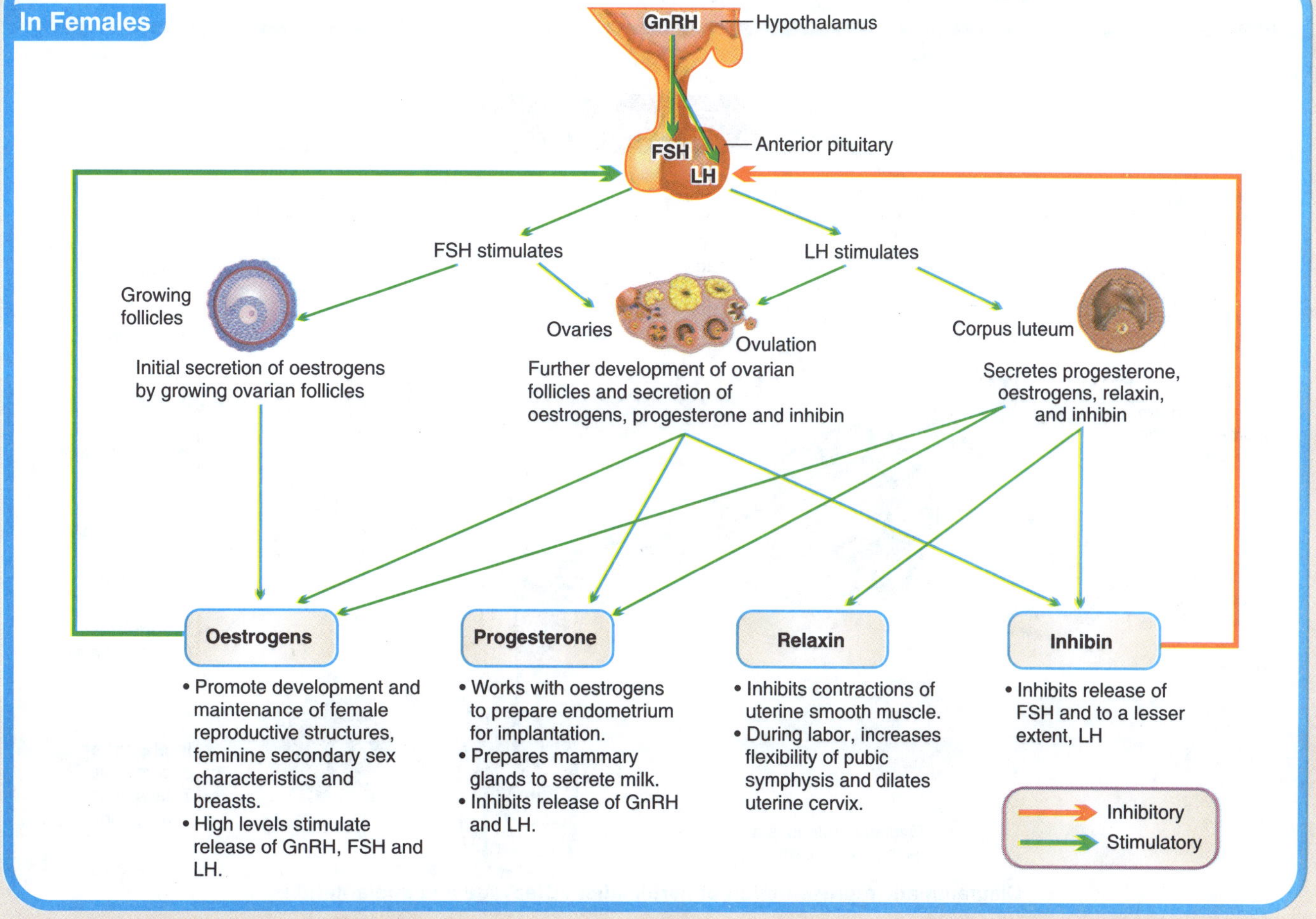

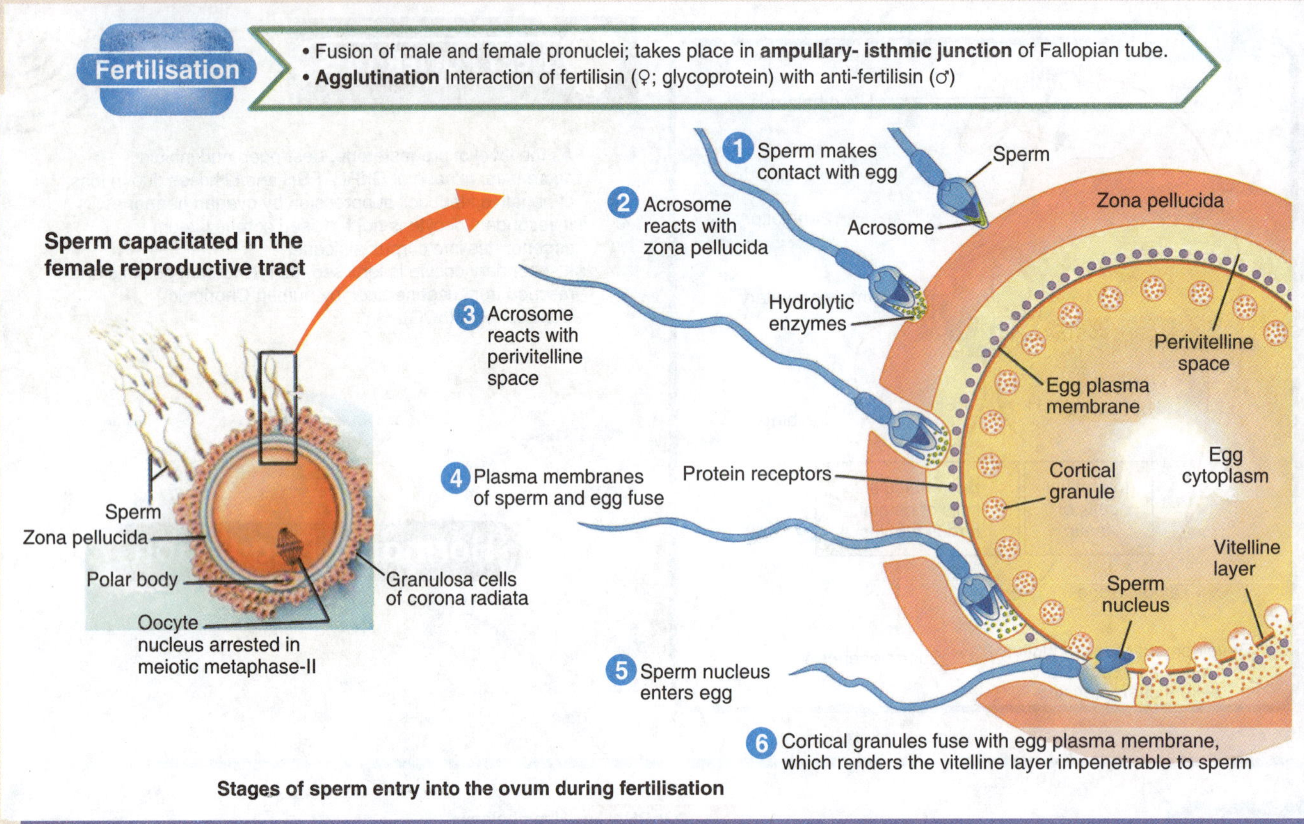

Stages of sperm entry into the ovum during fertilisation

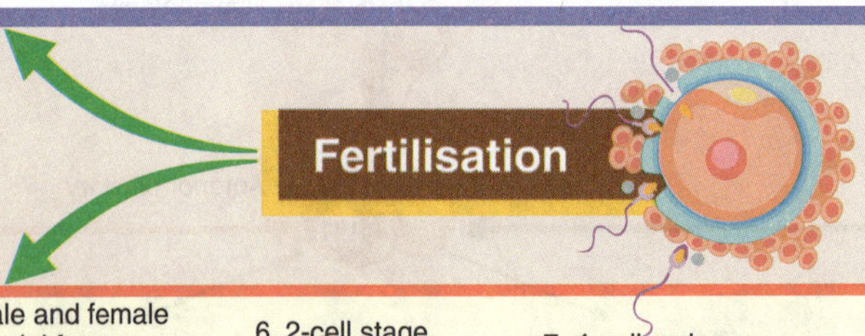

Fertilisation

Implantation

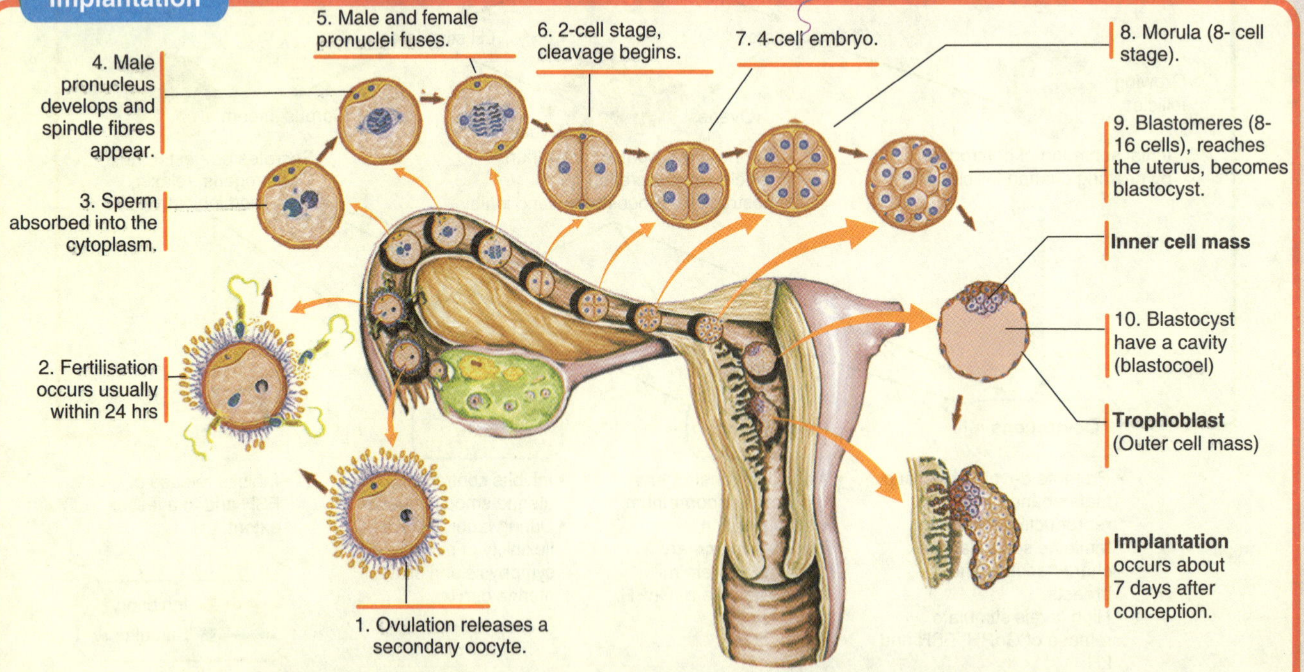

1. Ovulation releases a secondary oocyte.
2. Fertilisation occurs usually within 24 hrs
3. Sperm absorbed into the cytoplasm.
4. Male pronucleus develops and spindle fibres appear.
5. Male and female pronuclei fuses.
6. 2-cell stage, cleavage begins.
7. 4-cell embryo.
8. Morula (8- cell stage).
9. Blastomeres (8-16 cells), reaches the uterus, becomes blastocyst.

Inner cell mass

10. Blastocyst have a cavity (blastocoel)

Trophoblast (Outer cell mass)

Implantation occurs about 7 days after conception.

Diagrammatic representation of Fertilisation, Cleavage and Implantation

Events of Placentation, Early Embryonic Development and Extra Embryonic Membrane Formation

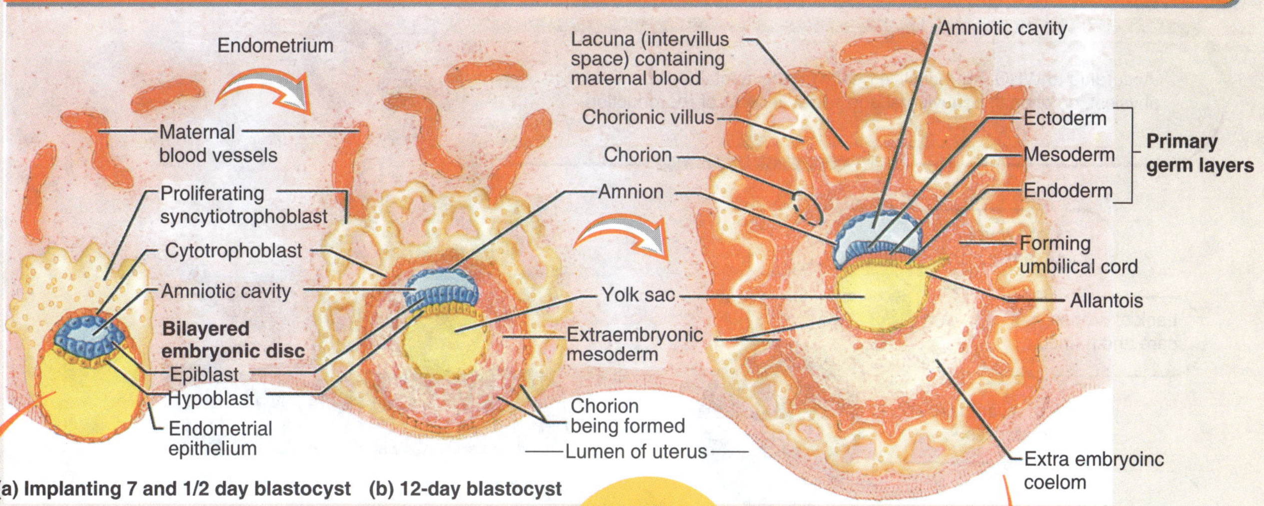

(a) Implanting 7 and 1/2 day blastocyst (b) 12-day blastocyst

(c) 16-day embryo

Post-fertilisation

Developmental changes in Human Embryo

Heart, liver, pancreas, gall bladder (4th week)
↓
Brain, arm and leg buds (5th week)
↓
Eyes and ears starts forming (6th week)
↓
Face, mouth, tongue, internal organs develop (7th week)
↓
Limbs and digits develop (2nd month)
↓
Major organ systems, (Limbs and external genital organs) formed (12th week)
↓
Hair on head (5th month)
↓
Fine hair on body, eye-lids separate, eyelashes are formed (24th week)
↓
Foetus is fully-developed (9th month)

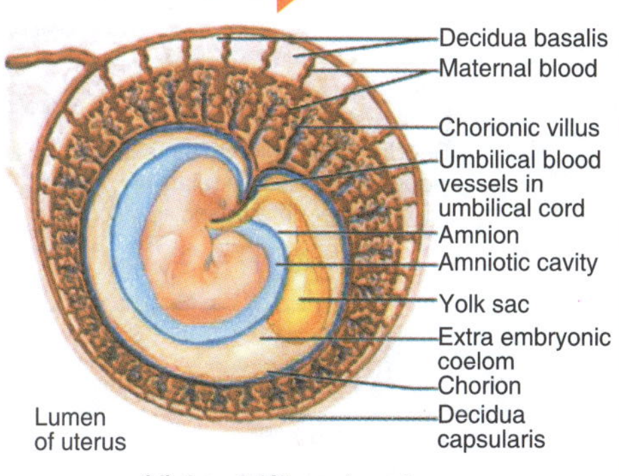

(d) 4 and 1/2 week embryo

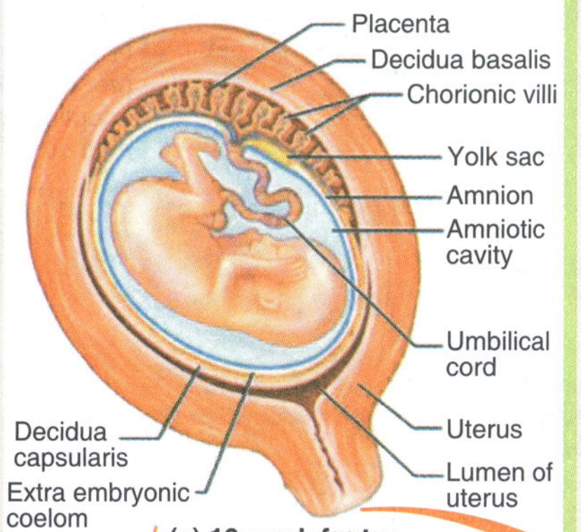

(e) 13 week foetus

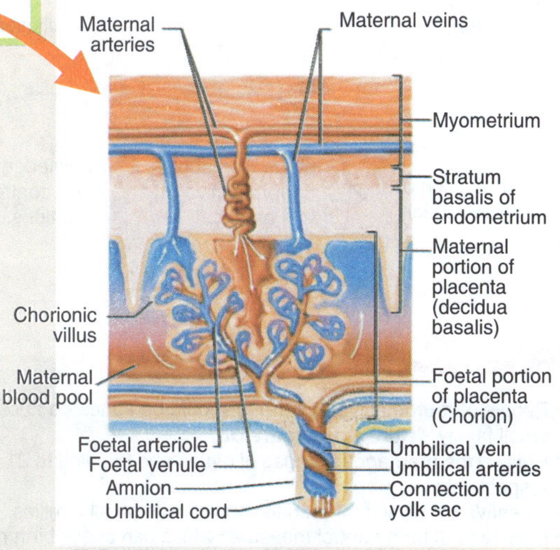

(f) Detailed anatomy of the vascular relationships in the mature decidua basalis

NEET POWER TIPS

- Placenta acts as endocrine tissues.
- hCG, hPL and relaxin are produced only during pregnancy.
- **Parturition**
  - Expulsion/delivery of the foetus. Complex neuroendocrine mechanism; signal originates from fully-developed foetus and placenta.
- **Lactation**
  Release of milk after birth; colostrum (few days); rich in proteins, IgA, etc.
  - hCG is secreted by placental tissues in the chorion of the embryo.
  - LH, hCG stimulates the secretory activity of the corpus luteum.

Placenta

- Chorionic villi and uterine tissue become interdigitated with each other.
- Facilitate the supply of O_2 and nutrients to the embryo, remove CO_2 and excreted waste.
- Connected to the embryo through umbilical cord

Chapter 22 Reproductive Health

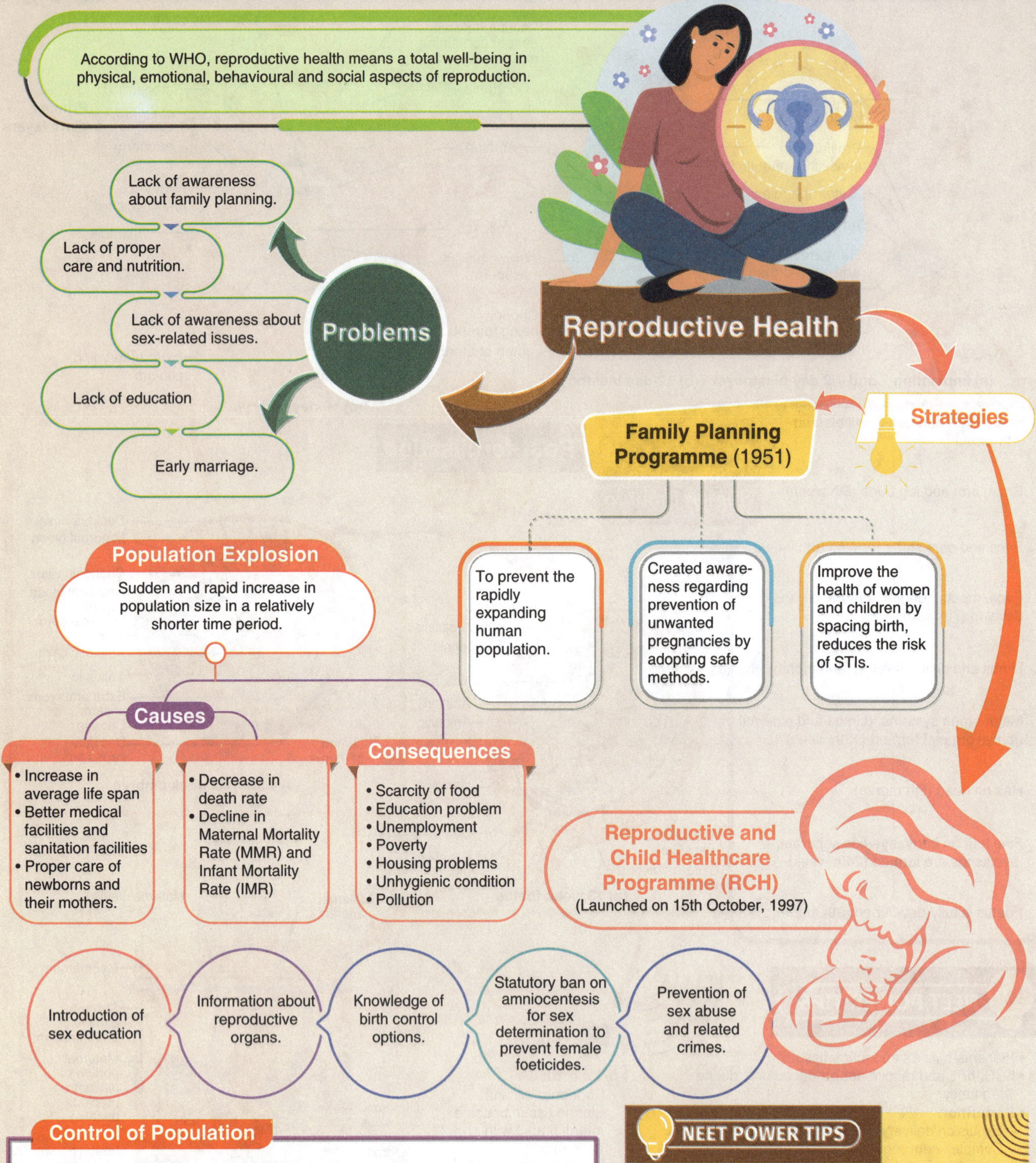

Control of Population

- People of reproductive age group should be educated about the advantages of small family; **"Hum Do Humare Do"**.
- Raising the marriageable ages of males and females to 21 years and 18 years, respectively.
- Incentives are being offered to couples with small families.
- Utilisation of birth control measures which can check birth rate.

NEET POWER TIPS

- **Demography** Scientific study of all aspects of human population.
- Census is an official counting of population which prepare data about age, birth, death, sex-ratio, etc.
- Infant Mortality Rate (IMR) in India 2011 was 44 per 1000 live birth in India.
- Maternal mortality rate was 167 per 100,000 live births.

Birth Control

Temporary Methods

Natural Methods
Principle Avoiding the meeting of sperm and ovum

Periodic abstinence or Rhythm method
Avoid sexual inter-course around ovulation, i.e., from day 10 to17 (fertile period) of menstrual cycle.

Lactational amenorrhoea
High level of prolactin inhibits secretion of gonadotropins, LH and FSH; prevents menstrual cycle (no ovulation).

Coitus interruptus or withdrawal method
Penis is withdrawn from vagina before ejaculation.

Chemical methods
Spermicides
Kill spermatozoa, e.g., boric acid, zinc sulphate, etc.

Sponge
Polyurethane sponge impregnated with spermicide (e.g., Non-oxynol-9).

Barrier Methods
Prevents physically meeting of ovum and sperm.

Condom
Thin, strong rubber sheath (latex); Safeguard against AIDS and other STIs.

Condom of Male

Fem-shield
Thin rubber or polyurethane tube.

Condom of Female

Diaphragm, cervical cap and vaults
Inserted into female reproductive tract to cover the cervix before coitus; are reusable.

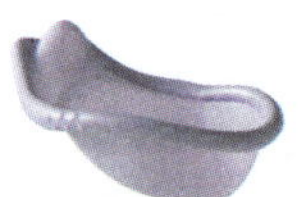
Diaphragm

Cervical Cap

Vaults

Intra-Uterine Devices (IUDs)
Inserted by healthcare professionals in the uterus through vagina.

1 Non-medicated IUDs
Retard sperm motility, also have spermicidal effects e.g., Lippes loop.

2 Copper releasing IUDs
Copper ions suppress the motility and fertilising capacity of sperm e.g., CuT, Cu7, Multiload 375

3 Hormone releasing IUDs
Make the uterus unsuitable for implantation and the cervix hostile to sperm, e.g., progestasert, LNG-20.

Oral Contraceptive Pills
Inhibit ovulation and implantation, alter the quality of cervical mucus.

Combined Pills
- Combination of oestrogen and progestin; inhibits FSH and LH.
  E.g., Mala D and Mala N.

Minipill
- Progestogen only pills (POPs), contain synthetic progestogen; prevent pregnancy.

Saheli (Non-steroidal pill)/Once a week pill
- Non-hormonal pill, contains centchroman, acts by blocking oestrogen receptors in uterus.

Emergency Contraceptives
- Morning after pills, contains RU486 Mifepristone, an antiprogesterone taken within 3 days (72 hours) of sexual intercourse.
  E.g., i-pill, PILL-72 and unwanted 72.

Injectable Contraceptives
Progesterone derivative (progestin) injection, needed in every 3 months.

e.g., Depot Medroxy Progesterone Acetate (DMPA), etc.

Implants
- Inserted under forearm through a small incision; contain progestin; for about 5 years. E.g., Implanon and Nexplanon.

NEET POWER TIPS
Ideal Contraceptive:
Friendly; Easily available; Effective; Affordable; Non-interferable; Reversible.

Permanant Methods or Surgical Methods

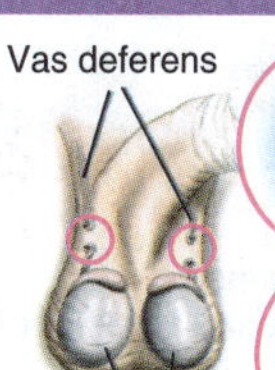

Vasectomy

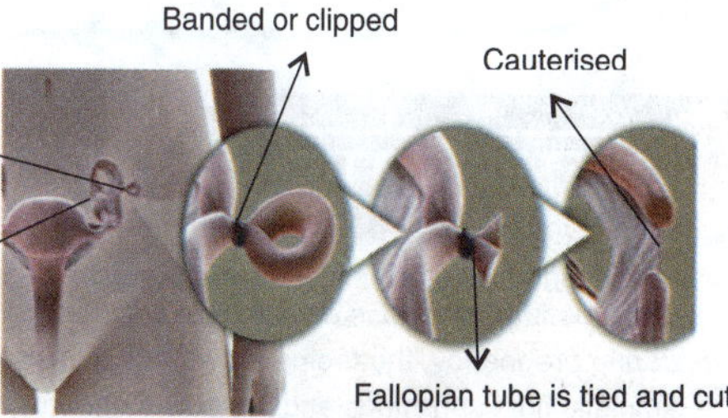

Tubectomy

Amniocentesis

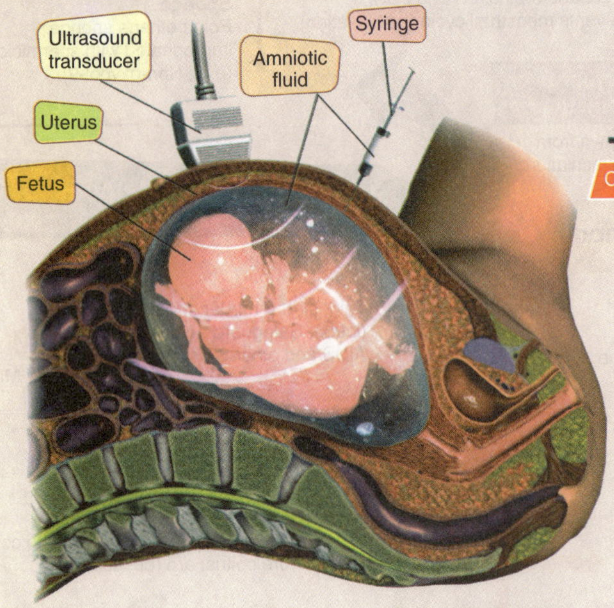

1 Under the guidance of ultrasound, a sterile needle is inserted through the abdominal wall into the amniotic sac. A small amount of amniotic fluid is withdrawn through the needle.

2 The amniotic fluid contains foetal cells, which are separated from the amniotic fluid.

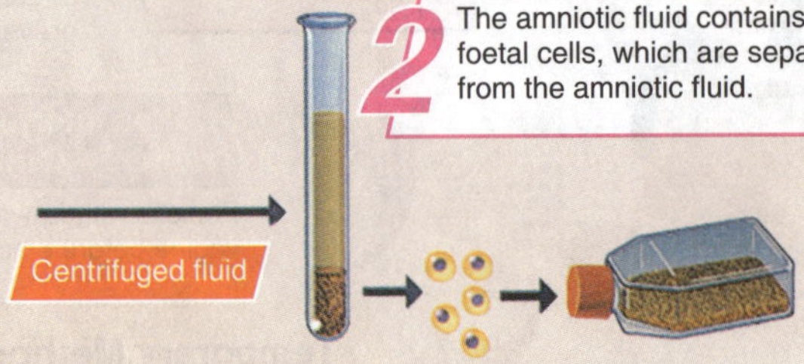

3 These foetal cells are cultured

4 Tests are then performed on the cultured cells.

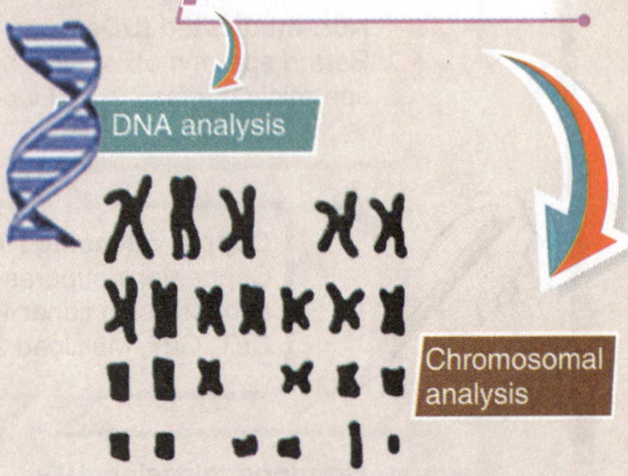

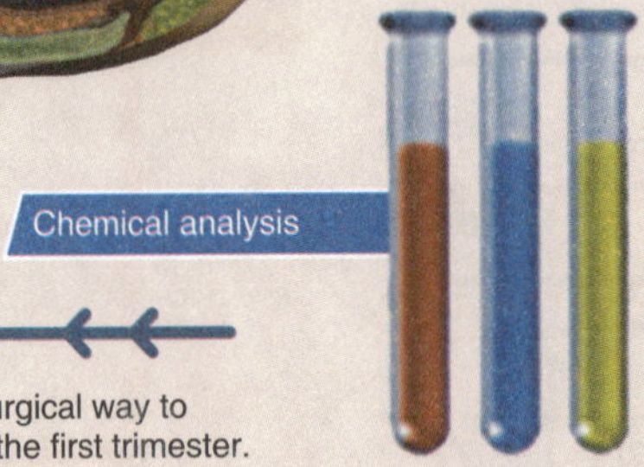

Medical Termination of Pregnancy

01 A medical abortion, nonsurgical way to terminate a pregnancy in the first trimester.

02 Most common regimen involves taking two pills-mifepristone and misoprostol; blocks progesterone, the hormone needed to support a pregnancy.

03 Medical abortion because they're concerned about passing along a congenital or inherited disease.

04 A medical abortion takes about two to six hours after you've taken the second pill.

05 According to the Medical Termination of Pregnancy (MTP) Amendment Act 2021, only one practitioner will be required for the abortion of a foetus up to 20 weeks of gestation and two for the termination of pregnancy from 20 to 24 weeks of gestation.

How Is It Done

- Doctors may use several treatments, surgery, or an amalgamation of both to terminate a pregnancy.
- If abortion is done before 9 weeks, then it only requires medications.
- If done in between 9 to 14 weeks, it requires an operation to remove the embryo.
- The abortions after 14 weeks require labor-inducing treatments.

NEET POWER TIPS

- Amniocentesis is a prenatal testing procedure usually performed during the second or third trimester of pregnancy and is used to diagnose certain chromosomal conditions (such as Down's syndrome) or genetic conditions (such as cystic fibrosis).
- During pregnancy, the foetus grows inside the amniotic sac.
- Amniotic fluid surrounds and protects the foetus inside the amniotic sac; and contains some of the fetal cells.

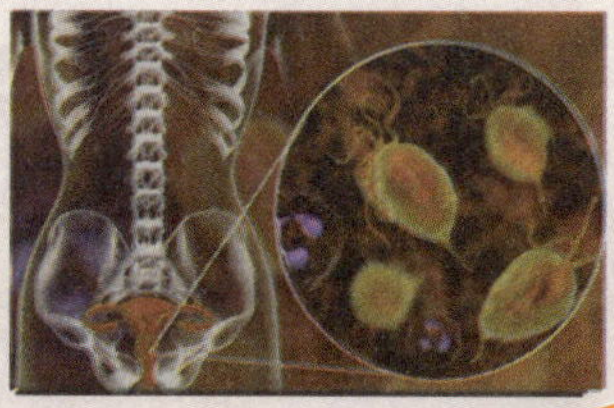

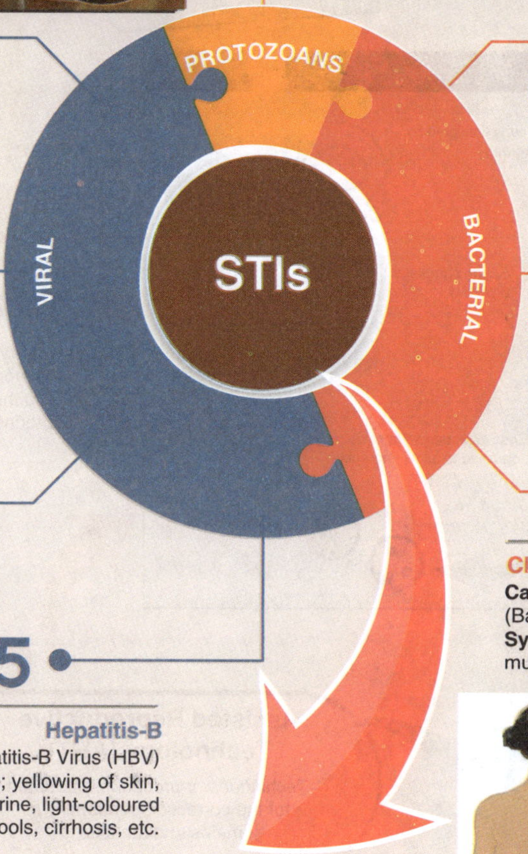

STIs

PROTOZOANS · BACTERIAL · VIRAL

1 Trichomoniasis

Caused by *Trichomonas vaginalis* (protozoan parasite)
Symptoms Vaginitis, urethritis, epididymitis and prostatitis.

2 Gonorrhea

Caused by *Neisseria gonorrhoeae* (Bacteria)
Symptoms Pain around genitalia and burning sensation during urination.

3 Syphilis

Caused by *Treponema pallidum* (Bacteria)
Symptoms Swelling of local lymph glands; painless ulcer.

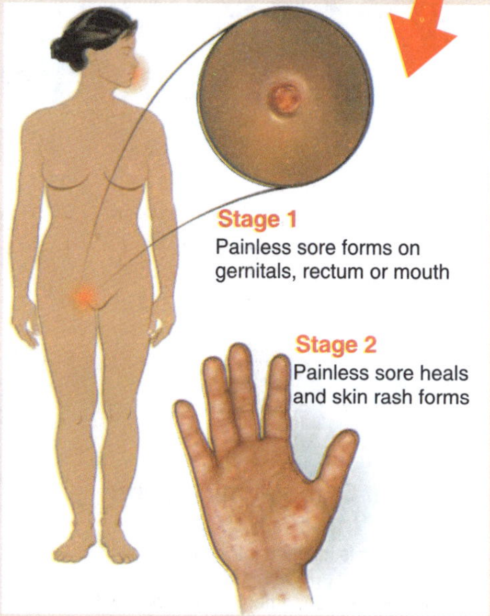

4 Chlamydiasis

Caused by *Chlamydia trachomatis* (Bacteria)
Symptoms Urethritis; epididymitis, mucopurulent discharge; cervicitis.

Stage 1
Painless sore forms on gernitals, rectum or mouth

Stage 2
Painless sore heals and skin rash forms

5 Hepatitis-B

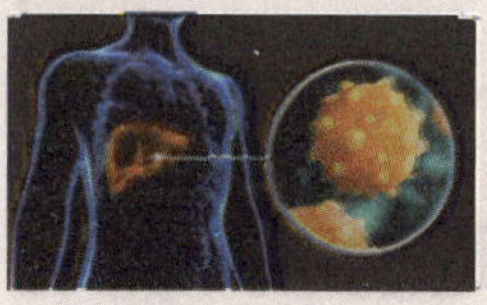

Caused by Hepatitis-B Virus (HBV)
Symptoms Fatigue; yellowing of skin, jaundice, dark urine, light-coloured stools, cirrhosis, etc.

6 Genital warts

Caused by Human Papilloma Virus (HPV)
Symptoms Hard outgrowth with horny surface over mucosal surface of external genitalia.

7 Genital Herpes

Caused by Herpes Simplex Virus type-1 (HSV-1) or type 2 (HSV-2; mostly)
Symptoms Painful genital blisters, vaginal discharge, itching.

8 AIDS

Caused by Human Immunodeficiency Virus (HIV)
Symptoms Weakened immune system, etc.

Modes of Transmission

- Sexual intercourse with infected person.
- From infected mother to foetus.
- Sharing of injections, needles, surgical instruments, etc.
- Transfusion of blood from an infected person to normal person.

Prevention

- Avoid sex with unknown/multiple partners.
- Always use condoms during coitus.
- Use of sterilised needles and syringes during immunisation
- Awareness about sexually transmitted disease.

- **Sexually Transmitted Infections (STIs)** are also known as Venereal Diseases (VD) or Reproductive Tract Infections (RTIs).

Some other STI's are as follows

- **Chancroid**
  Caused by Gram negative *Bacillus* bacteria, *Haemophilus ducreyi*.
- **Scabies**
  Caused by mite *Sarcoptes scabiei* and is characterised by severe itching and patches on the skin.
- **Candidiasis**
  Caused by *Candida albicans* (in human); yeast infection present in the digestive and urogenital tracts.

Test tube Baby Programme

- Involves *In Vitro* Fertilisation (IVF) of male and female gametes outside the body followed by Embryo Transfer (ET).

Embryo upto 8 blastomeres is transferred into the Fallopian tube (ZIFT-Zygote Intra Fallopian Transfer); enters into uterus after 24 hours.

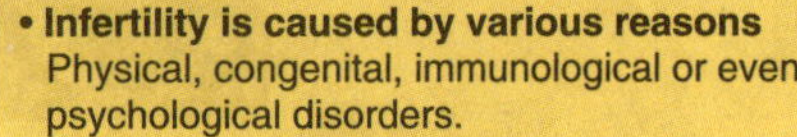

- **Infertility is caused by various reasons** Physical, congenital, immunological or even psychological disorders.
- **In males** Oligospermia (low sperm count), azoospermia (absence of sperm), asthenozoospermia (low sperm motility), cryptorchidism (failure of testes to descent from the abdomen into the scrotum), etc.
- **In females** Irregular menstrual cycle, Polycystic Ovarian Disease (PCOD), blockage of Fallopian tube, vaginal and cervical infections, etc.

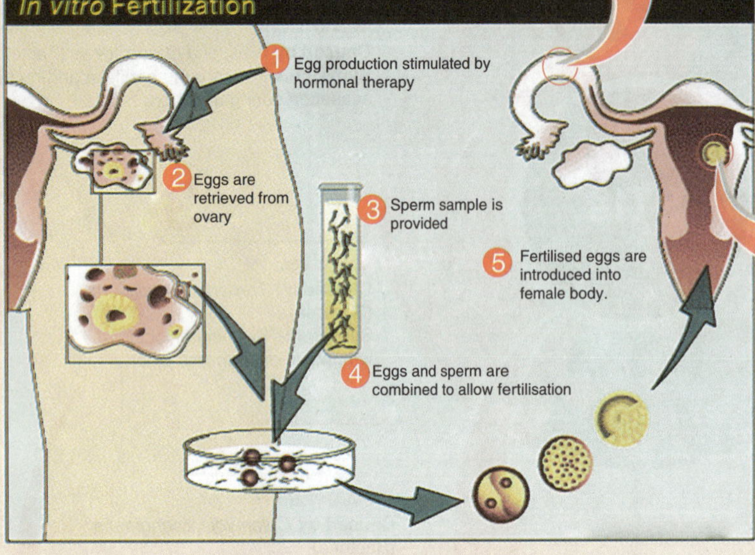

Embryo with more than 8 blastomeres, is transferred into the uterus (IUT-Intra Uterine Transfer).

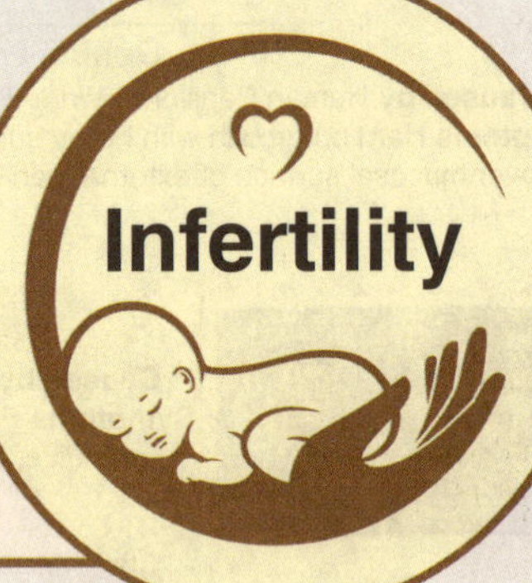

Gamete Intra Fallopian Transfer (GIFT)

Used in female; who cannot produce ova but can provide suitable environment for fertilisation and development of embryo.

Assisted Reproductive Technology (ART)

Techniques or procedures adopted for the correction of infertility in males and females.

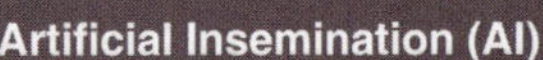

- When male partner is unable to inseminate.
- Medication stimulates ovulation before IUI (Intrauterine Insemination) or AI.
- Semen is introduced artificially into the vagina or uterus.

STAGES OF ARTIFICIAL INSEMINATION

1. Ovarian stimulation.
2. Control of the size and number of follicles.
3. Release of an egg from the follicle.
4. Preparation of the semen sample.
5. Insemination. on the day of ovulation.

Intra Cytoplasmic Sperm Injection (ICSI)

The sperm is injected into the cytoplasm of an egg with a needle.
After fertilisation, embryo is placed inside uterus as done in IVF.

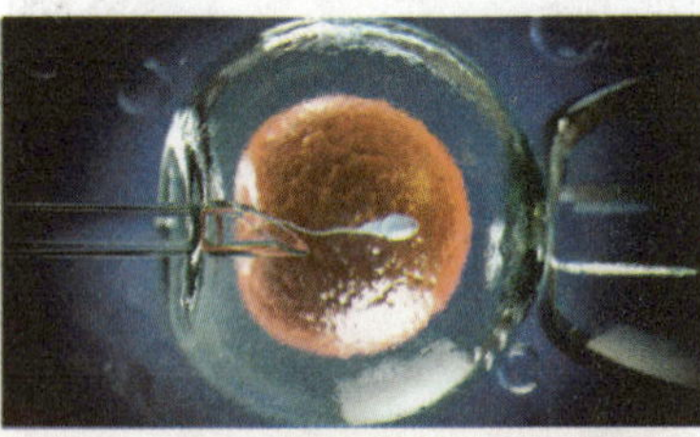

Chapter 23

Principles of Inheritance and Variation

Mendelian Inheritance

He represented his rules of inheritance in 1865 based on hybridisation experiments on *Pisum sativum* for 7 years (1856-1863).

S. No.	Characters	Dominant Traits	Recessive Traits	Chromosome locations
1.	Flower Colour	Purple	White	1
2.	Seed Colour	Yellow	Green	1
3.	Seed Shape	Round	Wrinkled	7
4.	Pod Colour	Green	Yellow	5
5.	Pod Shape	Inflated	Constricted	4
6.	Flower Position	Axial	Terminal	4
7.	Stem Length	Tall	Dwarf	4

Historical Aspect

- **William Bateson** (1905) used the term, genetics.
- **Gregor Johann Mendel** (1822-84) is the Father of Genetics; proposed that inheritance is caused by factors (genes).
- **Archibald Garrod** is considered as the Father of Human Genetics.
- **Genetics** Deals with the study of heredity and variations.
- **Heredity** Transmission of characters from parents to offsprings, from one generation to another.
- **Variations** Difference in characteristics of a species and their offsprings.
- **Characters** Morphological or physiological features of an organism.
- **Trait** Distinguishing feature of a character.

Advantages of Selecting Pea Plant

- Self-pollination.
- Bisexual flowers.
- Well-defined contrasting characters.
- F_1 hybrids are fertile.
- Purelines easily available.
- It is an annual plant, short life span.
- Produces large number of seeds.

Mendel's Work

Reasons Behind Mendel's Success

- Garden pea was easy to grow, can be hybridised artificially.
- Different varieties of pure breeding pea had contrasting expression of traits.
- Restricted his examination.
- Characters showed complete independent assortment.
- Maintained the statistical records of all the experiments and analysed them carefully.

- **Allele** A pair of contrasting characters or alternate forms of same gene.
- **Dominant allele** The allele which can express itself in both homozygous and heterozygous state.
- **Recessive allele** The allele which can express itself only in homozygous state.

Crossing Pea Plant Experiment (Gregor Mendel)

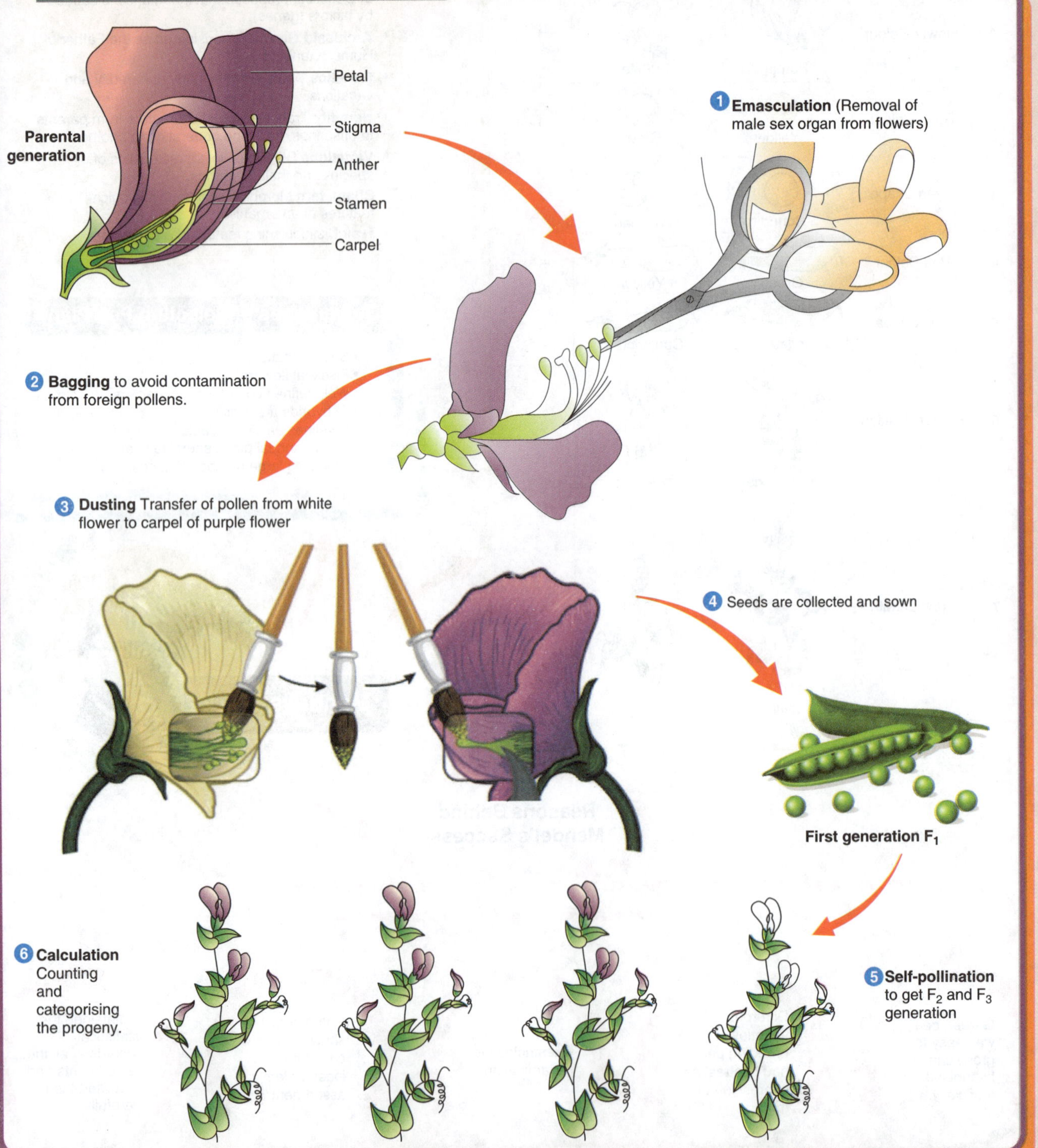

Parental generation

Petal
Stigma
Anther
Stamen
Carpel

1 **Emasculation** (Removal of male sex organ from flowers)

2 **Bagging** to avoid contamination from foreign pollens.

3 **Dusting** Transfer of pollen from white flower to carpel of purple flower

4 Seeds are collected and sown

First generation F_1

5 **Self-pollination** to get F_2 and F_3 generation

6 **Calculation** Counting and categorising the progeny.

Mendel's Monohybrid Cross

Simultaneous inheritance of a single pair of Mendelian factors.

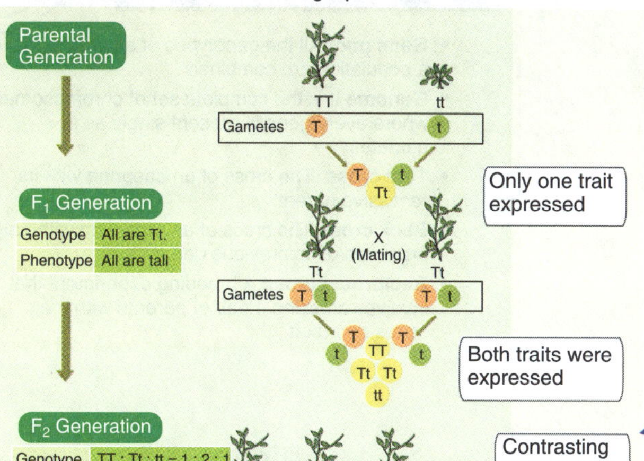

TT (Tall) Tt (Tall) Tt (Tall) tt (Dwarf)

Contrasting traits did not show any blending.

NEET POWER TIPS

- **Monohybrid cross** Only one allelic pair is considered in cross breeding.
- **F_1 generation** Offsprings obtained from a cross made between two different parents.
- **F_2 generation** Offsprings obtained from the cross of F_1 generation.
- **Genotype** Genetic constitution of an individual.
- **Phenotype** External features of an organism.
- **Homozygous condition** The condition wherein the organism has two similar genes or alleles for a specific character, e.g., TT.
- **Heterozygous condition** The condition in which the organism has two different alleles for a character, e.g., Tt.
- **Punnett square** A checker board invented by RC Punnett, used to show the result of a cross between two organisms.

Inheritance of One Gene

Mendel's laws

Law of Dominance
Characters are controlled by discrete units (factors) that occur in pairs. When both contrasting alleles are present, only one is expressed (dominant) and the other remains suppressed (recessive).

Multiple allelism

- More than two alternative alleles of a gene in a population occupying the same locus on a chromosome.
- Produced due to repeated mutations of the same gene; absence of crossing over.

Blood types	Genotypes	Antigens	Antibodies
A	I^AI^A or I^AI^O	A	B
B	I^BI^B or I^BI^O	B	A
AB* (Universal acceptor)	I^AI^B	Both A and B	Neither A or B
O* (Universal donor)	I^OI^O	Neither A or B	Both A and B

* AB^+ is the universal acceptor; on the other hand O^- is universal donor.

Deviation from Law of Dominance

Pleiotropic Gene

Ability of a gene to have multiple phenotypic effects, simultaneously.

Pleiotropy is due to effect of the gene on two or more inter-related metabolic pathways.

Sickle cell anaemia and phenylketonuria.

Incomplete Dominance

- None of the two alleles of a gene is dominant over the other.
- F_1 hybrids exhibit a mixture or blending of character of two parents. E.g., Inheritance of flower colour in the 4O' clock plant (*Mirabilis jalapa*) and snapdragon (*Antirrhinum majus*).

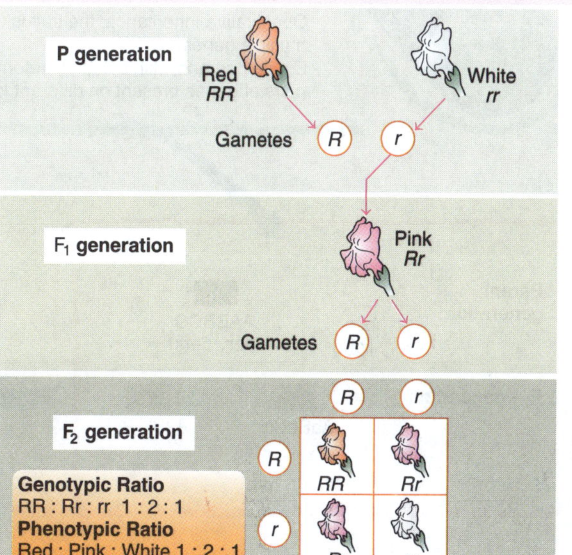

Codominance

- Phenomenon of expression of both the alleles in a heterozygote.
- Alleles do not show dominant-recessive relationship, but are able to express their traits independently.
- Mainly observed in ABO blood grouping system in human-discovered by **Karl Landsteiner**.

	Group A	Group B	Group AB	Group O
Red Blood Cell Type	A (Antigen, RBC)	B	AB	O
	A antigen on RBC's surface	B antigen on RBC's surface	A & B antigens on RBC's surface	No antigen on RBC's surface

Dihybrid Cross

Inheritance of two pairs of Mendelian factors or genes.

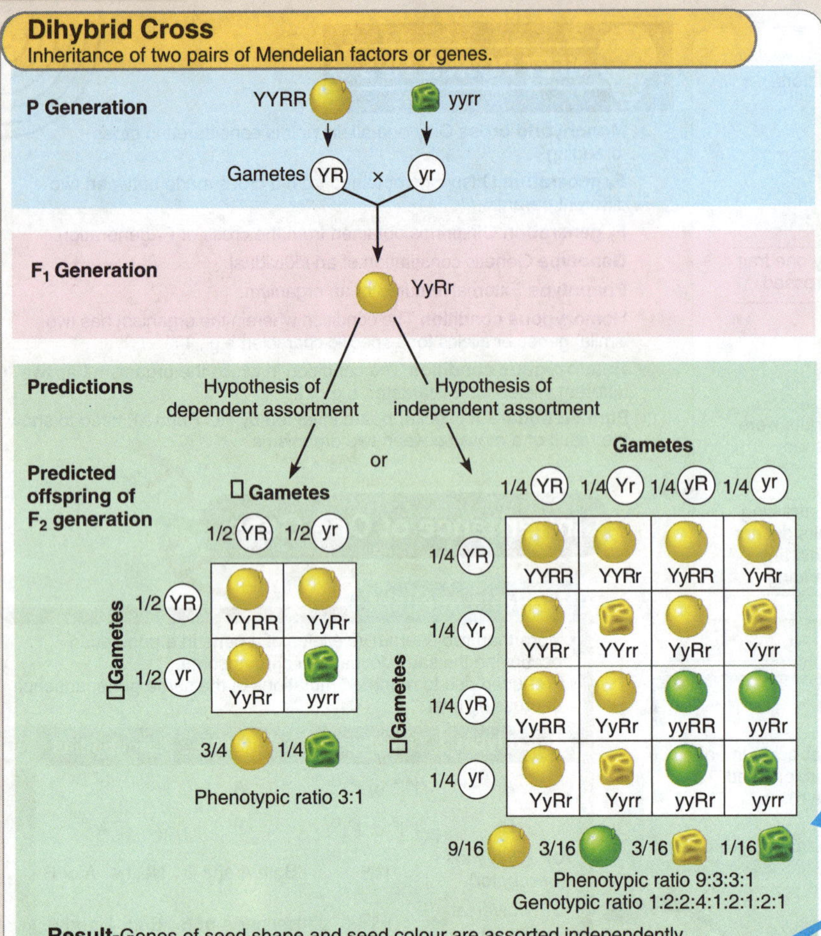

Result-Genes of seed shape and seed colour are assorted independently.

- **Gene pool** All the genotypes of all organisms in a population are combinely.
- **Genome** It is the complete set of chromosomes where every gene is present singly as in gamete.
- **Test cross** The cross of an offspring with its recessive parent.
- **Back cross** The cross of an organism with only organism of its previous generation.
- **Reciprocal cross** A breeding experiment that involves crossing a pair of parents with the sexes reversed.

Gene Interaction

- Modification of normal phenotypic expression of a gene due to either of its alleles or other non-allelic genes.

Epistasis

- One gene complements, masks, inhibits or suppresses the expression of the other non-allelic gene.

Inheritance of Two Genes

Law of Independent Assortment

- When two pairs of traits are combined in a hybrid, segregation of one pair of trait is independent of the other pair of trait.

Polygenic Inheritance

- Quantitative inheritance; the trait is controlled by multiple genes.
- E.g. In humans, skin colour is determined by three pairs of genes present on different loci.

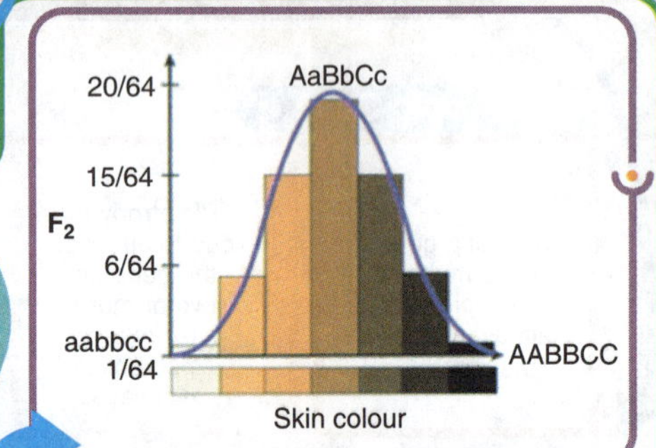

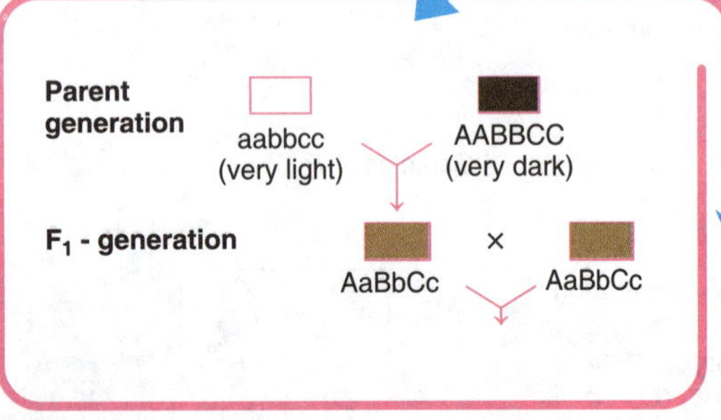

F2-generation

Gametes (Egg \ Sperm)	ABC	ABc	AbC	Abc	aBC	aBc	abC	abc
ABC	6	5	5	5	4	4	4	3
ABc	5	4	4	4	3	3	3	2
AbC	5	4	4	4	3	3	3	2
Abc	5	4	4	4	3	3	3	2
aBC	4	3	3	3	2	2	2	1
aBc	4	3	3	3	2	2	2	1
abC	4	3	3	3	2	2	2	1
abc	3	2	2	2	1	1	1	0

Chromosomal Theory

- Proposed by **Sutton** and **Boveri** in 1902.
- Behaviour of chromosomes was parallel to the behaviour of gene.
- Used chromosome movement to explain Mendel's laws.
- Experimental verification was done by **TH Morgan** and his colleagues.
- He worked with ***Drosophila melanogaster***.

Law of Segregation

When a pair of contrasting factors are brought together in a hybrid; these factors do not blend or mix up but remain together and separate at the time of gamete formation.

Chromosomal Explanation of Law of Segregation

Formation of four germ cells from one cell (with four chromosomes) by meiosis.

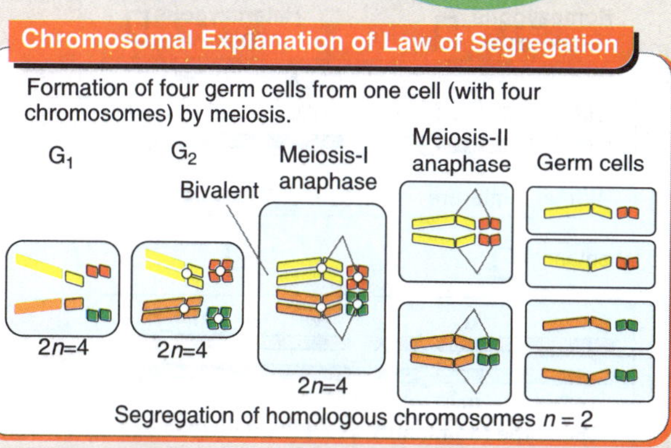

Segregation of homologous chromosomes $n = 2$

Comparison Between Gene and Chromosome

Gene
- Occur in pairs
- Segregate at the time of gamete formation such that only one of each pair is transmitted to a gamete.
- Independent pairs segregate independently of each other.

Chromosome
- Occur in pairs.
- Segregate during gamete formation and only one of each pair is transmitted to a gamete.
- One pair segregates independently of another pair.

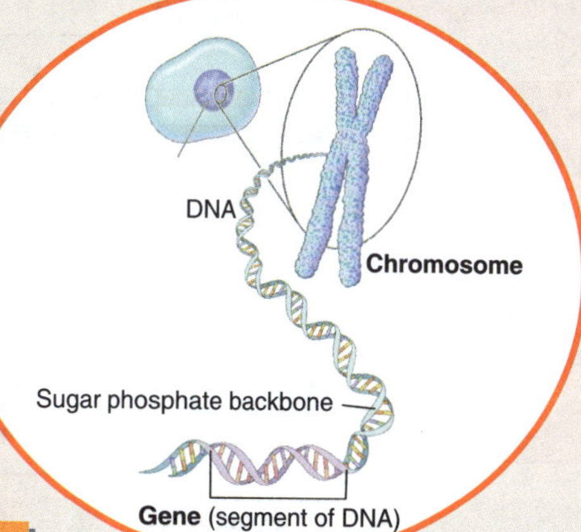

Chromosomal Explanation of Law of Independent Assortment

- During anaphase-I of meiosis-I, the two chromosome pairs, aligned at metaphase plate, separate out independently.

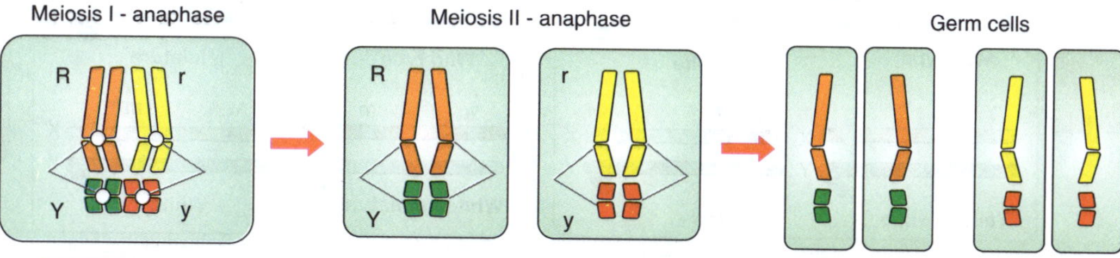

Possibility 1: One long orange and short green chromosome and long yellow and short red chromosome at the same pole.

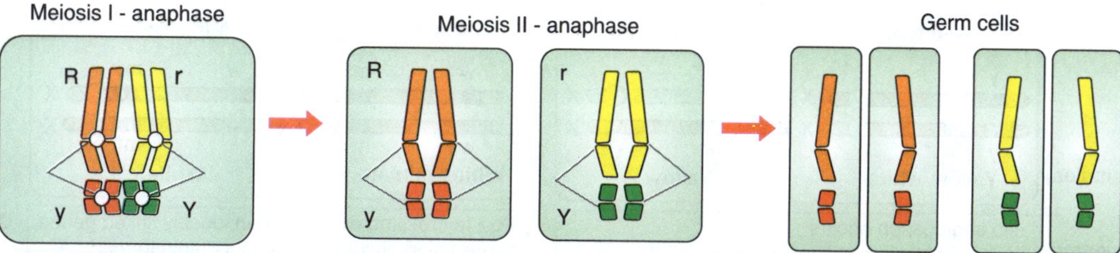

Possibility 2: One long orange and short red chromosome and long yellow and short green chromosome at the same pole. pole.One long orange and short red chromosome and long yellow and short green chromosome at the same pole.

Linkage

- Genes are arranged in a linear fashion on the chromosome.
- Linkage between two genes is inversely proportional to the distance between the two.

Crossing Over

- Exchange of genetic material between two synapsed homologous chromosome; Occurs in pachytene of meiosis-I.

NEET POWER TIPS

- **Complete Linkage** Linkage which is not altered, inherited without any cross-over.
  - Parental percentage is always 100% and recombinant is 0%.
- **Incomplete Linkage** one or more alleles replaced by other alleles.
  - Parental types more than 50%, recombinant types are less than 50%.
- 1st chromosomal map was given by **Sturtevant** and **Morgan**.
- Centi Morgan (CM) or 1 map unit: 1% crossing over between two linked genes.

Linkage Maps or Chromosome Maps

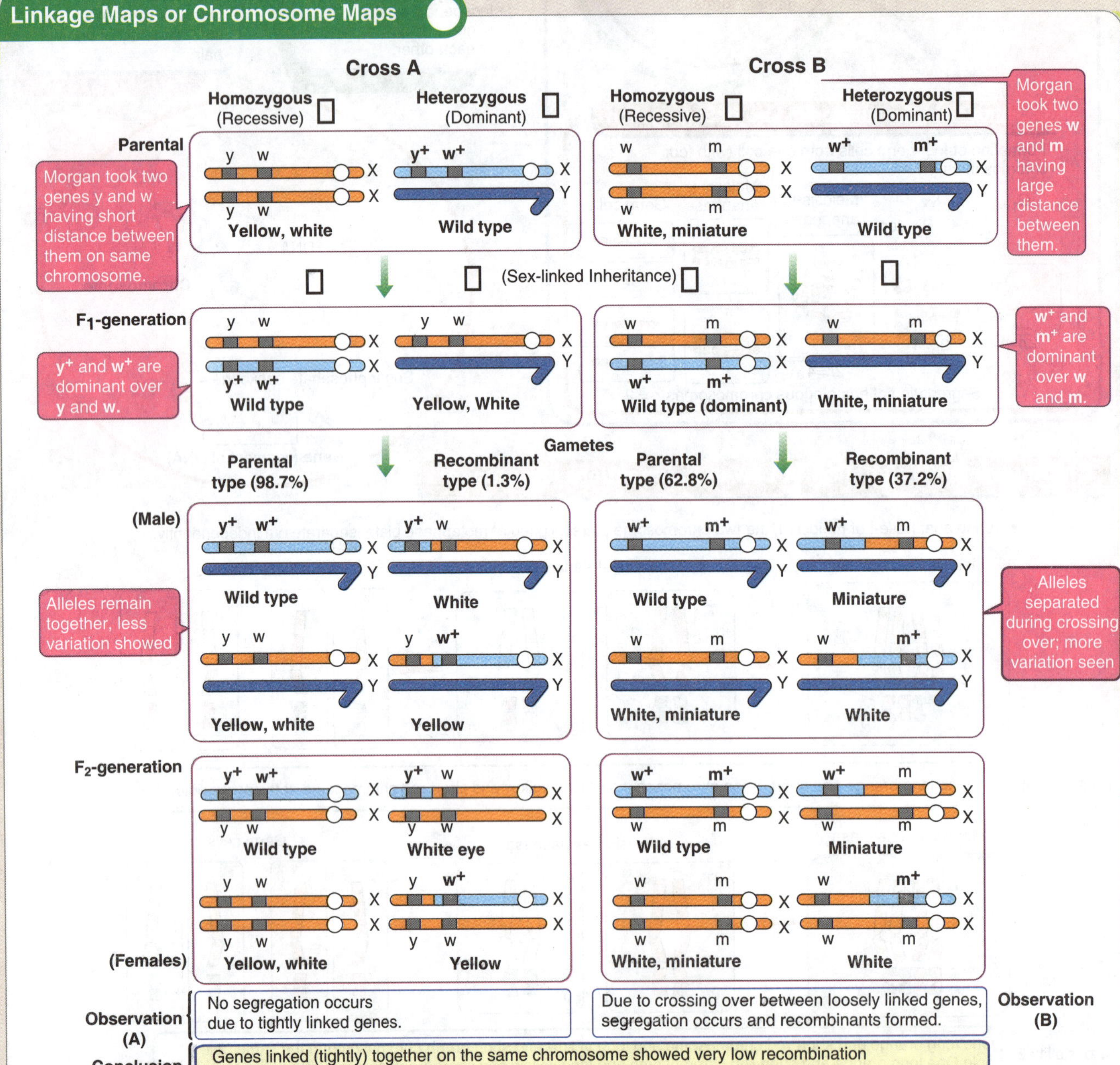

Chromosomal Sex Determination

XX-XY Type

- Female is homogametic (XX) and male is heterogameti (X or Y)
- Found in mammals and some insects.

Parents	Male AA + XY	×	Female AA + XX	
Gametes	A+X	A+Y	A+X	A+X
Offsprings	AA+XX Female	AA+XX Female	AA+XY Male	AA+XY Male

ZW-ZZ Type

- Male is homogametic (ZZ) while female is heterogametic (ZW) - Found in birds and some reptiles.

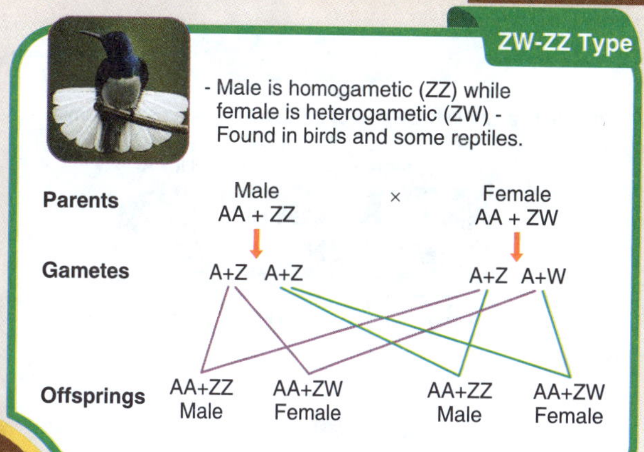

Parents	Male AA + ZZ	×	Female AA + ZW	
Gametes	A+Z	A+Z	A+Z	A+W
Offsprings	AA+ZZ Male	AA+ZW Female	AA+ZZ Male	AA+ZW Female

XX-XO Type

- Female is homogametic (XX); while male is heterogametic (XO; androsperms
- Found in some insects e.g., grasshopper, cockroach, and roundworms.

Parents	Male AA + XO	×	Female AA + XX	
Gametes	A+X	A+O	A+X	A+X
Offsprings	AA+XX Female	AA+XX Female	AA+XO Male	AA+XO Male

ZO-ZZ Type

- Female is heterogametic (ZO); while the male is homogametic (ZZ)
- Occurs in certain butterflies and moths.

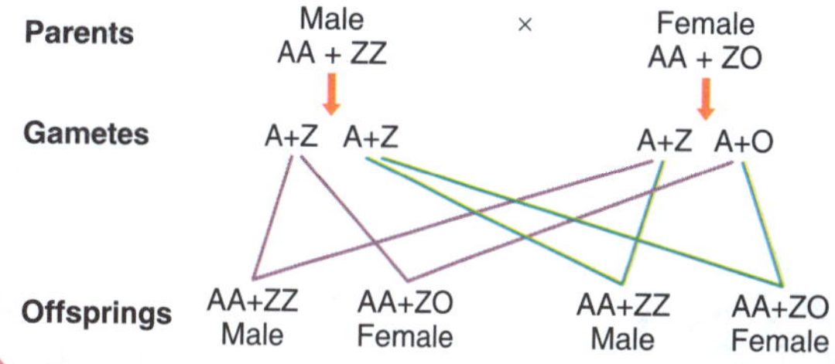

Parents	Male AA + ZZ	×	Female AA + ZO	
Gametes	A+Z	A+Z	A+Z	A+O
Offsprings	AA+ZZ Male	AA+ZO Female	AA+ZZ Male	AA+ZO Female

Haplodiploidy

Honeybee (Apis mellifera)

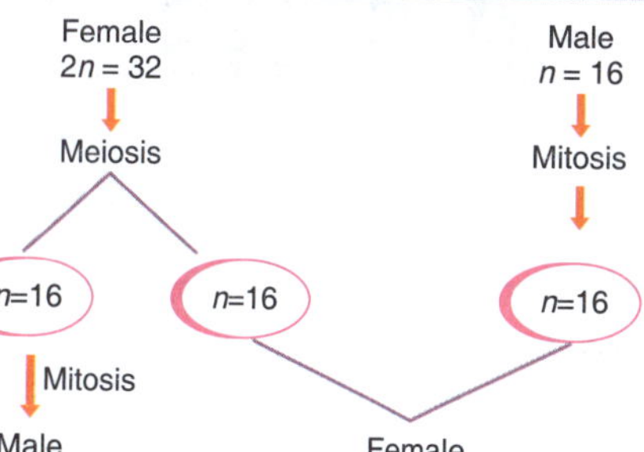

- Present in Honeybee, wasps, etc.
- Unfertilised egg develops into a drone (male; $n = 16$ chromosomes) and fertilised egg develops into a queen or worker bee (female; $2n = 32$ chromosomes).

NEET POWER TIPS

- **X-linked genes**-Sex linked genes located on X-chromosome.
- Holandric genes-Sex linked genes only located on Y-chromosome
- **Allosomes**-Sex determination by specific chromosome
- X body/chromosome, nuclear structure discovered by **Hermann Henking** in 1891.

Point Mutation

Change in a single base pair of DNA, e.g., sickle cell anaemia.

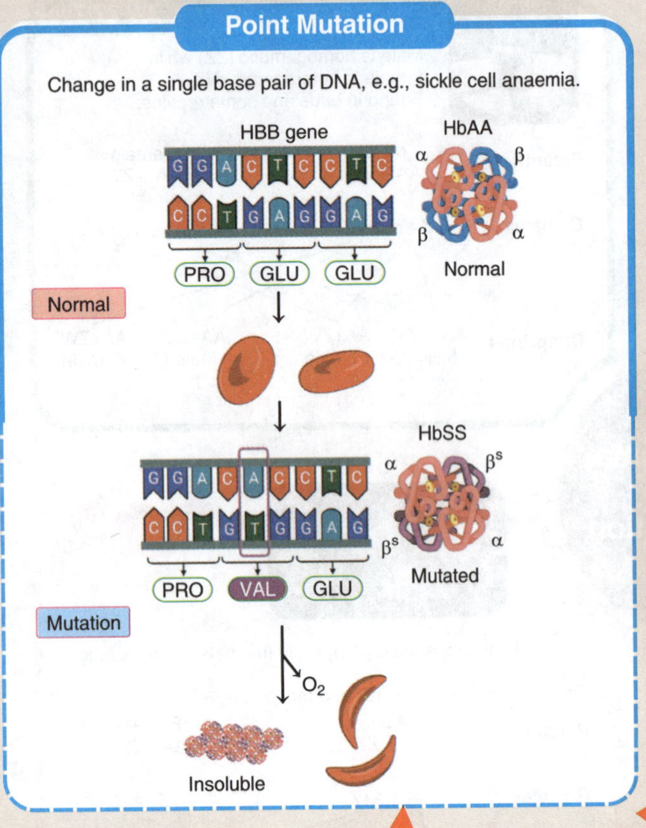

- Mutation is sudden alternation of DNA sequences; results in changes in the genotype and phenotype.
- Chromosomal aberrations are commonly observed in cancer.
- **Mutagens** Chemical and physical factors that induce mutations, i.e., UV radiations, etc.
- **Pedigree Analysis** Record of inheritance of certain traits for two or more ancestral generations.
- Mendelian disorders mainly determined by mutation in the single gene.

Frame-shift Mutation

Deletion and insertion of base pairs in DNA.

Base pair deletion

Missing U

*m*RNA 5' A U G A A G U U G G C U A A ... 3'

Protein MET LYS LEU ALA ...

Mutation

Base Pair Insertion

Extra U

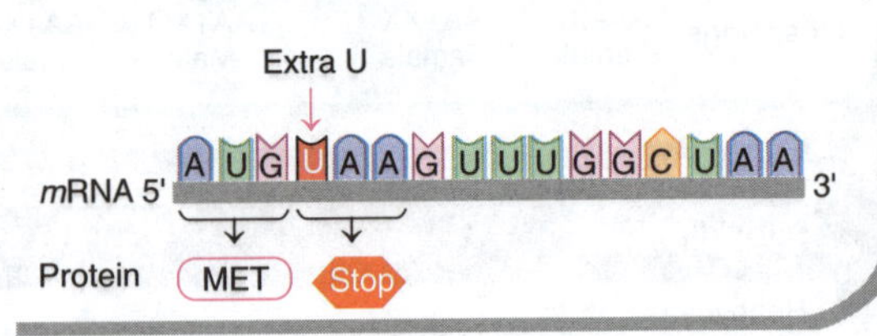

Chromosomal Aberrations

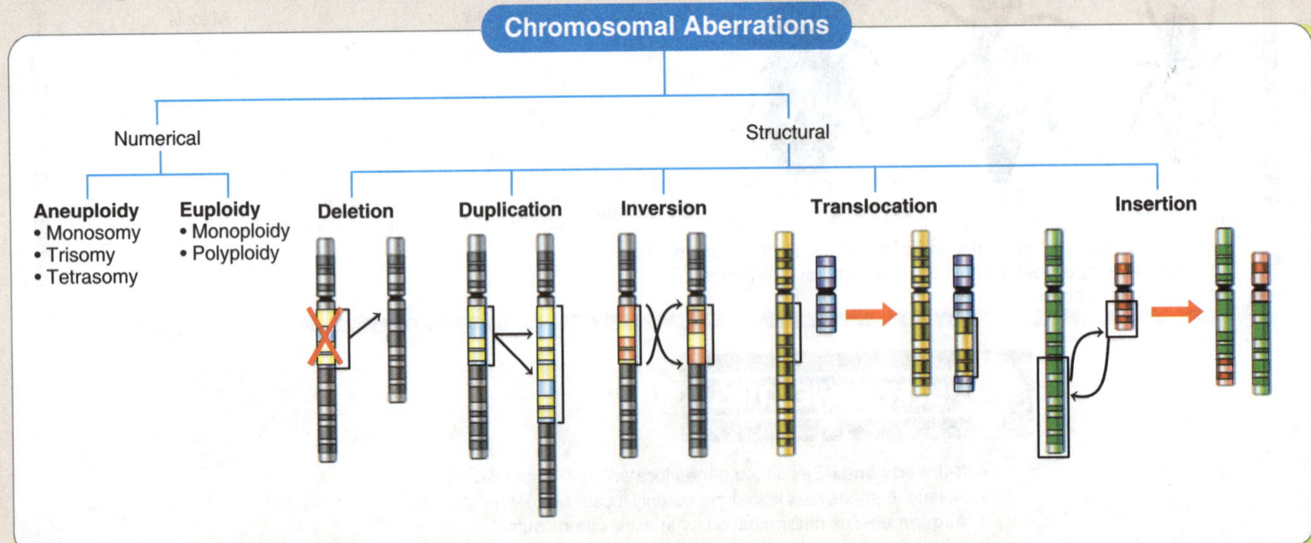

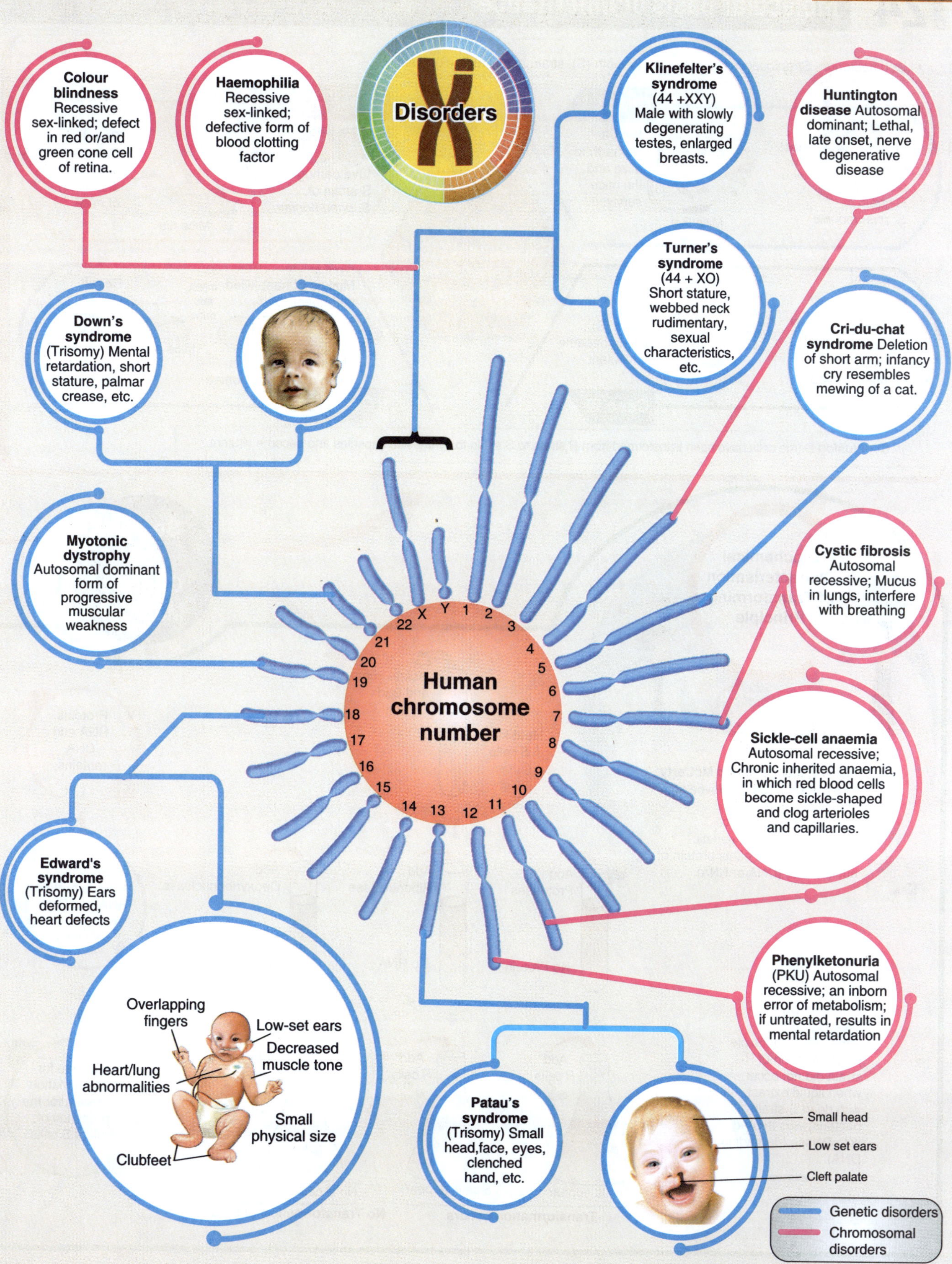
Disorders
Colour blindness Recessive sex-linked; defect in red or/and green cone cell of retina.
Haemophilia Recessive sex-linked; defective form of blood clotting factor
Klinefelter's syndrome (44 +XXY) Male with slowly degenerating testes, enlarged breasts.
Huntington disease Autosomal dominant; Lethal, late onset, nerve degenerative disease
Turner's syndrome (44 + XO) Short stature, webbed neck rudimentary, sexual characteristics, etc.
Down's syndrome (Trisomy) Mental retardation, short stature, palmar crease, etc.
Cri-du-chat syndrome Deletion of short arm; infancy cry resembles mewing of a cat.
Myotonic dystrophy Autosomal dominant form of progressive muscular weakness
Cystic fibrosis Autosomal recessive; Mucus in lungs, interfere with breathing
Human chromosome number
X Y 1 2 3 4 5 6 7 8 9 10 11 12 13 14 15 16 17 18 19 20 21 22
Sickle-cell anaemia Autosomal recessive; Chronic inherited anaemia, in which red blood cells become sickle-shaped and clog arterioles and capillaries.
Edward's syndrome (Trisomy) Ears deformed, heart defects
Phenylketonuria (PKU) Autosomal recessive; an inborn error of metabolism; if untreated, results in mental retardation
Overlapping fingers
Low-set ears
Decreased muscle tone
Heart/lung abnormalities
Small physical size
Clubfeet
Patau's syndrome (Trisomy) Small head,face, eyes, clenched hand, etc.
Small head
Low set ears
Cleft palate
Genetic disorders
Chromosomal disorders

Chapter 24

Molecular Basis of Inheritance

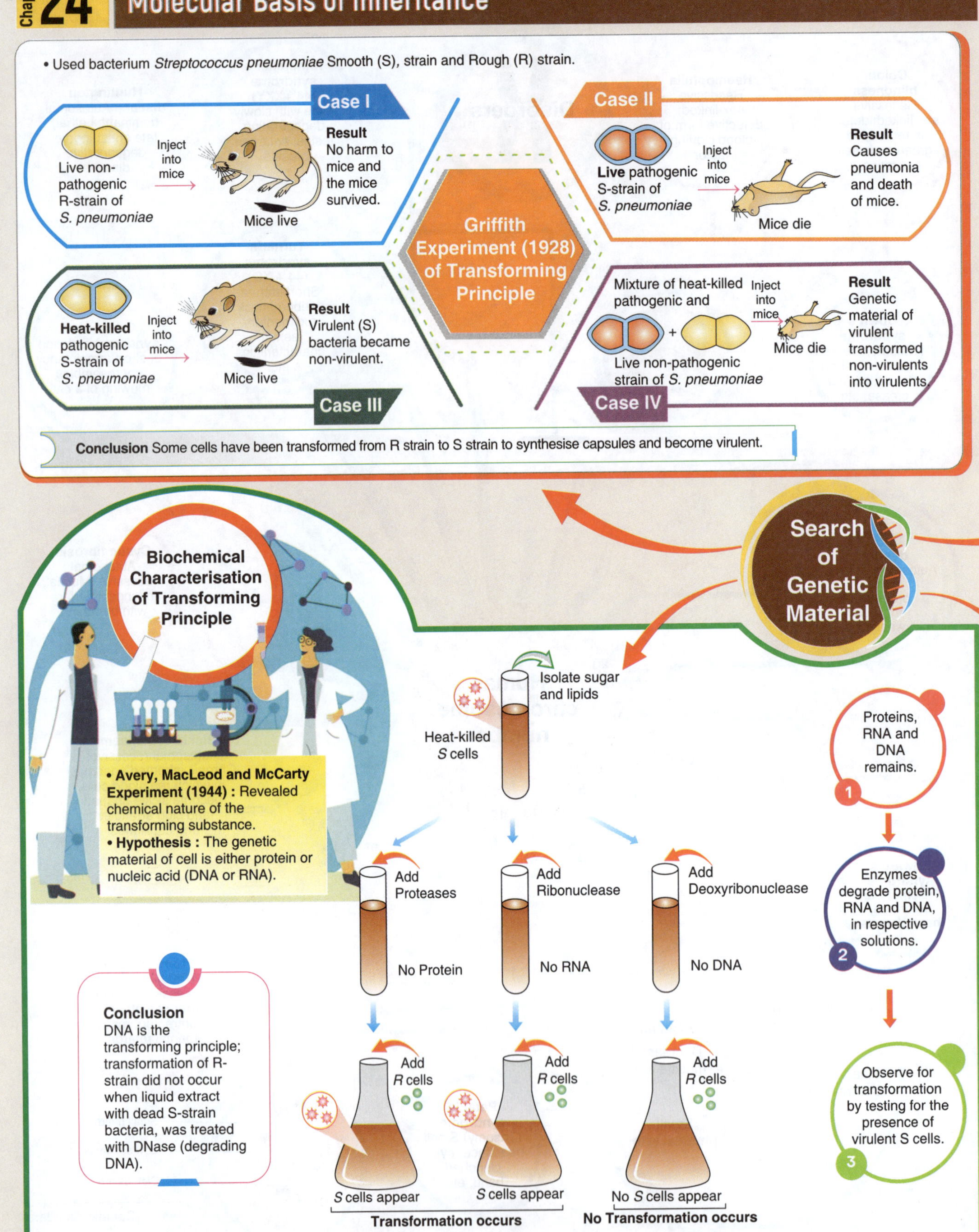

Hershey and Chase Experiment/ Blender's Experiment

- Provides the unequivocal proof that DNA is genetic material.
- **Steps :** Radiolabeling infection, blending and centrifugation.

1. Radioactively labelled T2 phages infected the bacterial cells.
2. Phages were detached from the bacterial cells.
3. Bacteria formed a pellet at the bottom of the test tube.
4. Radioactivity was measured in the pellet and the liquid.

Experiment 1

T2 phages grown with radioactive ^{35}S.

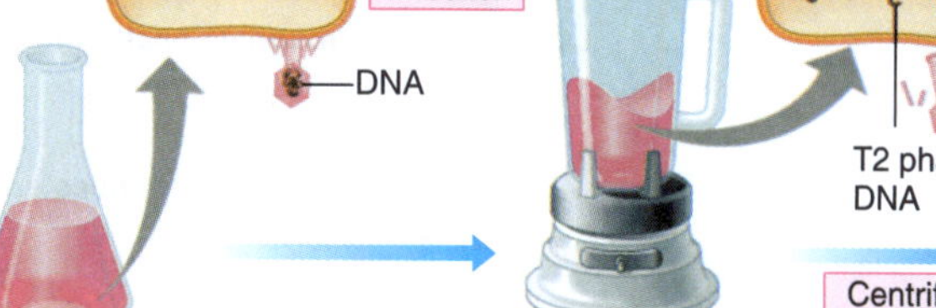

Experiment 2

T2 phages grown with radioactive ^{32}P.

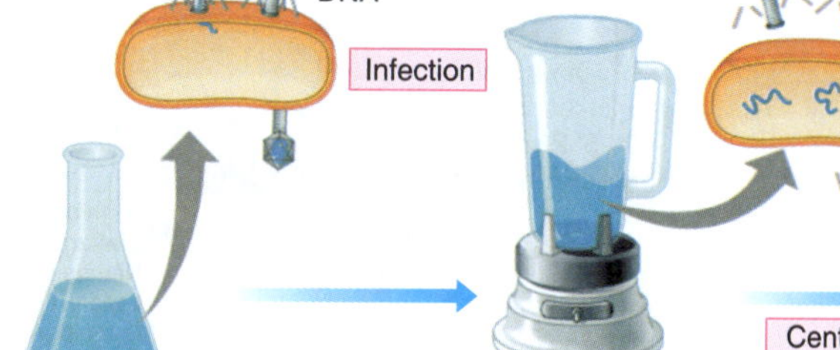

Conclusions

- Viral DNA enters into the host cell, whereas protein coat remains outside the cell.
- Progeny contains ^{32}P (present in DNA), but not the ^{35}S (present in protein coat) and thus concluded DNA as the genetic material.

DNA vs RNA as Genetic Material

DNA	RNA
Can replicate on their own (base pairing and complementarity)	Can replicate on their own (base pairing and complementarity)
More stable and less reactive (thymine instead of uracil)	Easily degradable and labile (2–OH group); catalytic and reactive
Mutates at slower rate	Mutates and thus evolve at faster rate; short life span
Stable in storing genetic information	More important in transmitting the genetic information
Found in most of the organism	Found in most of the viruses

NEET POWER TIPS

- R strain (non-virulent) lacks a capsule, produces rough colonies.
- S strain (virulent) has a polysaccharide capsule and produces smooth shiny colonies.
- ^{32}P and ^{35}S are radioactive isotopes.
- RNA was the first genetic material and biocatalyst.
- Bacteriophage T2 composed of about 50% DNA and 50% protein.

The DNA : Structure and Packaging

The DNA

- Discovery of nuclein: Friedrich Miescher (1869).
- Nucleic acid term: Altmann (1889)
- Nucleic acid: DNA and RNA.
- Nucleus: Formed of chromatin (mostly)
- Nucleoid and plasmid (prokaryotes); nuclear DNA and organellar DNA (eukaryotes).

Length of DNA in Different Organisms

Organisms	Number of nucleotides/ Base pairs
ϕ × 174 bacteriophage	5386 nucleotides
Bacteriophage lambda	48502 bp
Escherichia coli	4.6×10^6 bp
Haploid human DNA	3.3×10^9 bp

Structure of Polynucleotide Chain

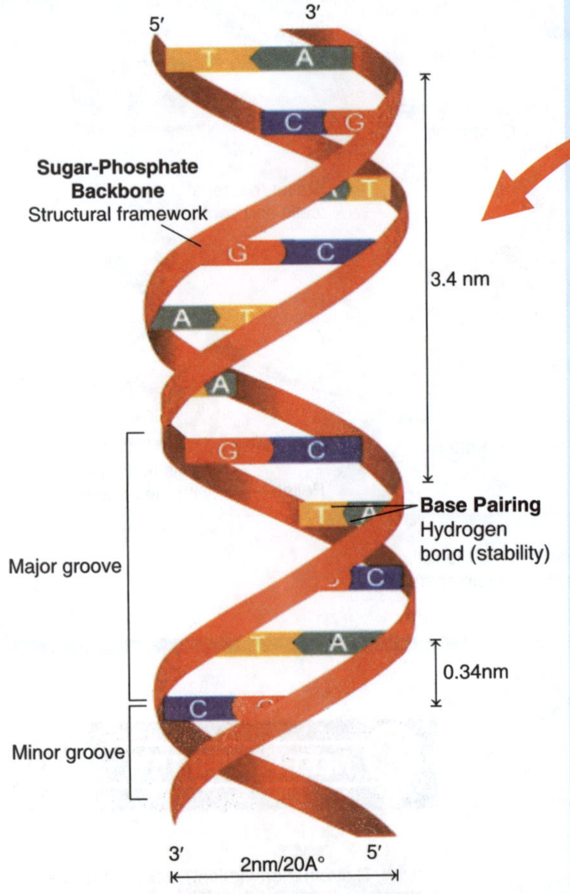

Double-helix structure of DNA.

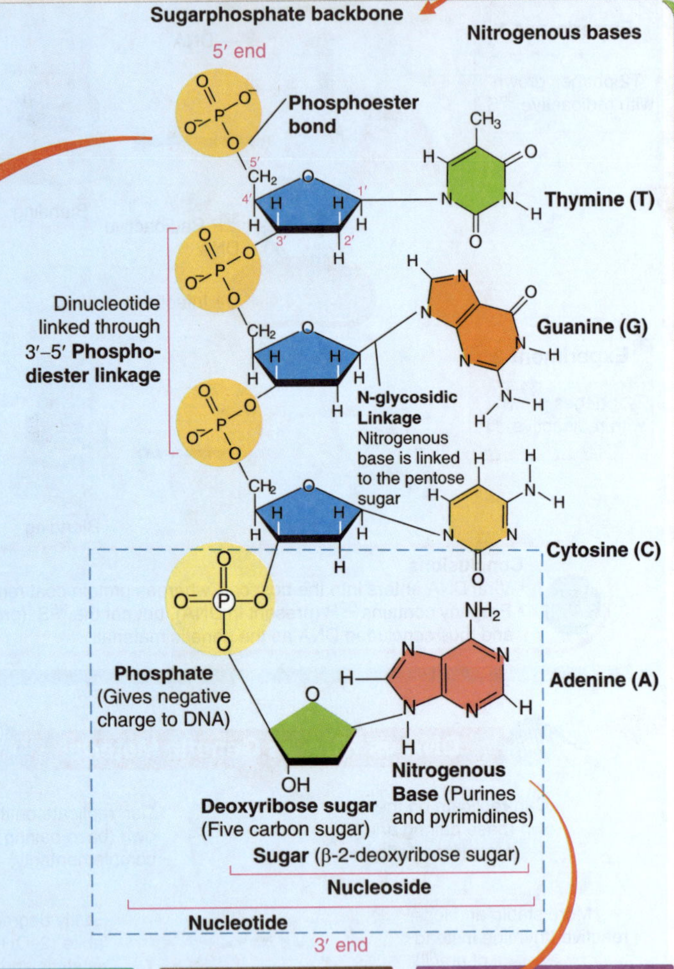

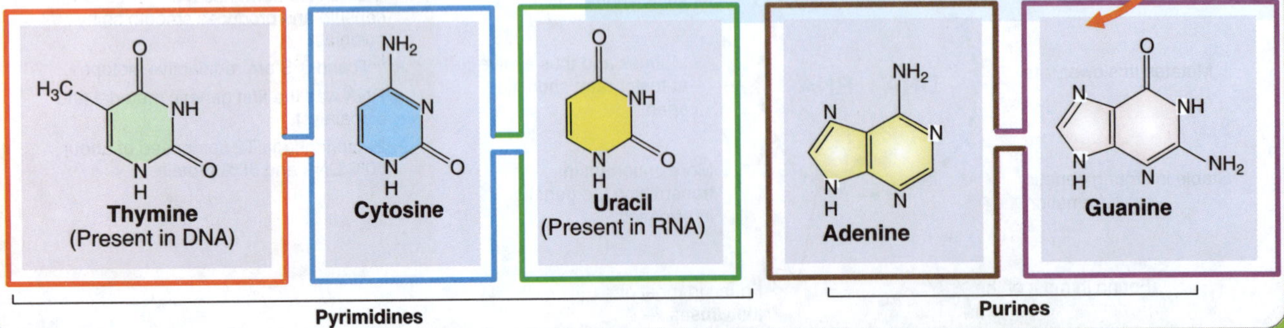

Salient Features of DNA

- Sugar-phosphate backbone
- Anti-parallel chains
- Bases pair through hydrogen bond
- Mostly chains coiled in right handed fashion (A, B, C and D; except Z, left handed fashion)
- Dimension of DNA: Pitch = 3.4 nm; 10 bp per turn; distance between a bp 0.34 nm (approx.)
- H-bond confers the stability of helical structure.

Central Dogma

- Proposed by **Francis Crick** for the flow of genetic information.

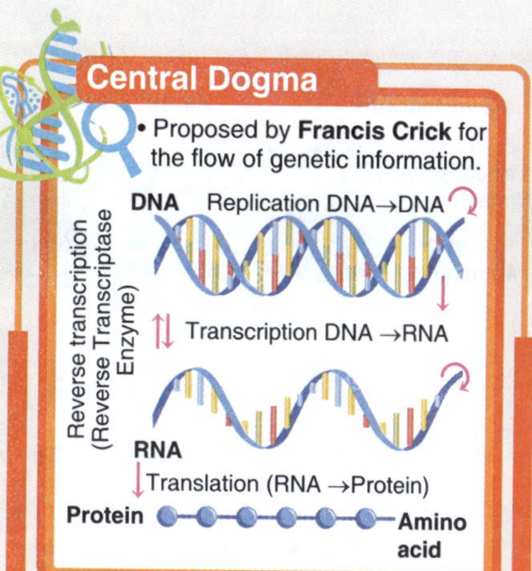

NEET POWER TIPS

- **Rosalind Franklin**, studied the structure of DNA using X-rays.
- **James Watson** and **Francis Crick** proposed 3-D structure of DNA.
- **Chargaff's Rule:** Erwin Chargaff found that, Purines (A+G) = Pyrimidines (T+C).
- Ratio of A+T/ G+C is constant for a species.
- **Heterochromatin:** Transcriptionally inactive chromatin, darkly stained and condensed DNA.
- **Euchromatin:** Transcriptionally active chromatin, lightly stained and loosely packed.

Packaging of DNA Helix in Eukaryotes

- Human DNA (2*n*) is about 2.2 metres.
- Histones (basic) are rich in lysine and arginine.

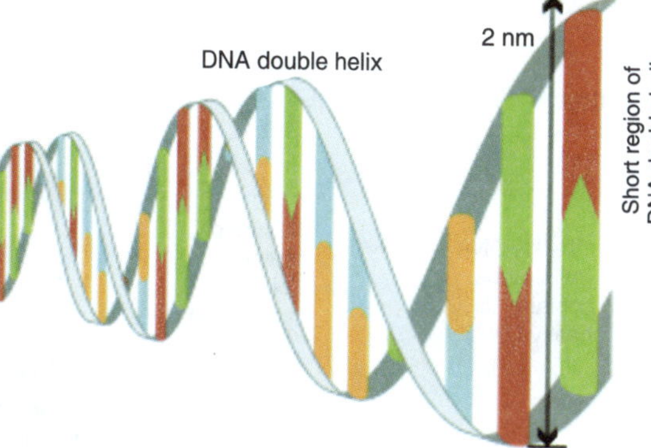

1. **Chromatin** is a double-stranded helical structure of DNA.

2. DNA is complexed with histones to form **nucleosomes**.

3. Each **nucleosome** consists of eight histone proteins around which the DNA wraps 1.65 times.

Nucleosome core of eight histone molecules (2 molecules of each H_2A, H_2B, H_3 and H_4)

Histone H_1, linker binds DNA of two adjacent nucleosomes

10 nm

4. A chromatosome consists of a nucleosome plus the H_1 histone.

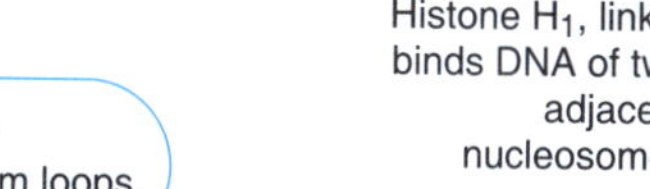

6. **Solenoid** further condenses to form loops.

5. The nucleosomes fold up to produce a 30 nm fibre.

Solenoid
30 nm

250 nm wide fibre

Extended scaffold associated chromatin.

Metaphase chromosome

1400 nm

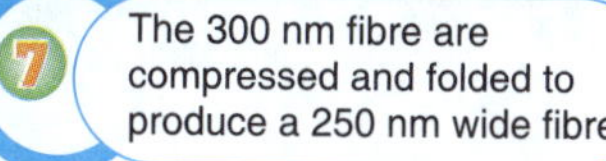

7. The 300 nm fibre are compressed and folded to produce a 250 nm wide fibre.

8. Tight coiling of the 250 nm fibre produces the chromatid of a chromosome.

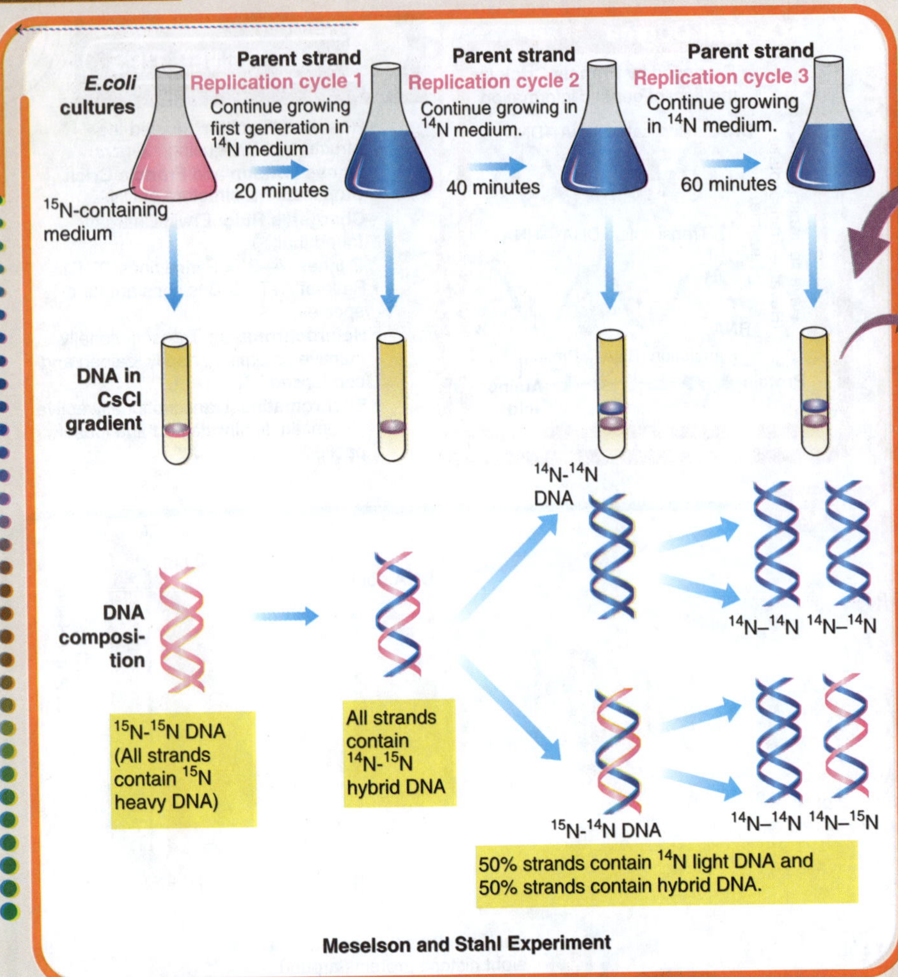

Meselson and Stahl Experiment

Semiconservative DNA replication

- Formation of one parental and one newly synthesised strand.
- Taylor and colleagues use radioactive thymidine to detect newly synthesised DNA in the chromosome of *Vicia faba* (faba beans).

Conclusion

- Subsequent increase in amount of lighter DNA and constancy in hybrid DNA demonstrates that DNA replication is a semiconservative process.

Replication

- In eukaryotes, the replication of DNA takes place at S-phase of the cycle.
- Failure in cell division after DNA replication results into polyploidy.

Prokaryotic DNA Replication	Eukaryotic DNA Replication
Occus in cytoplasm	Occurs in nucleus
Single *Ori*	Numerous *Ori*
Large Okazaki fragments	Short Okazaki fragments
Rapid replication	Slow replication

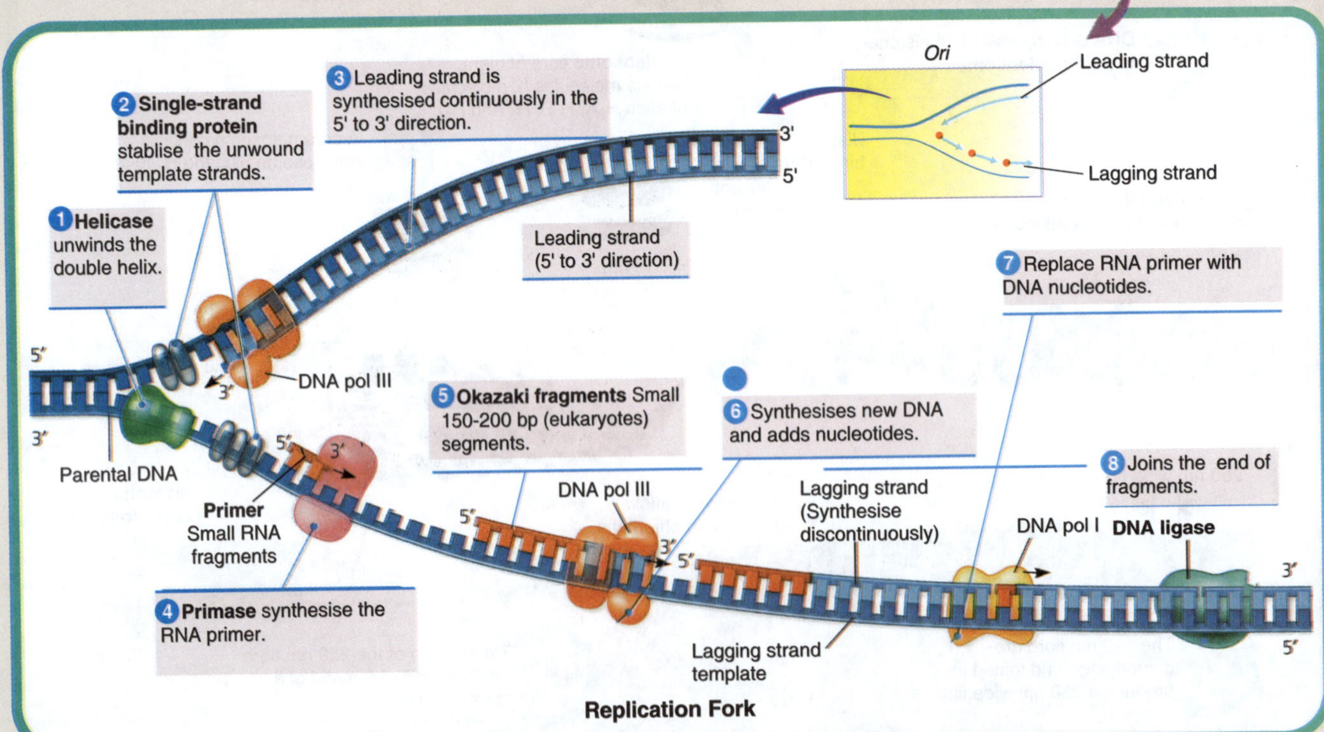

Replication Fork

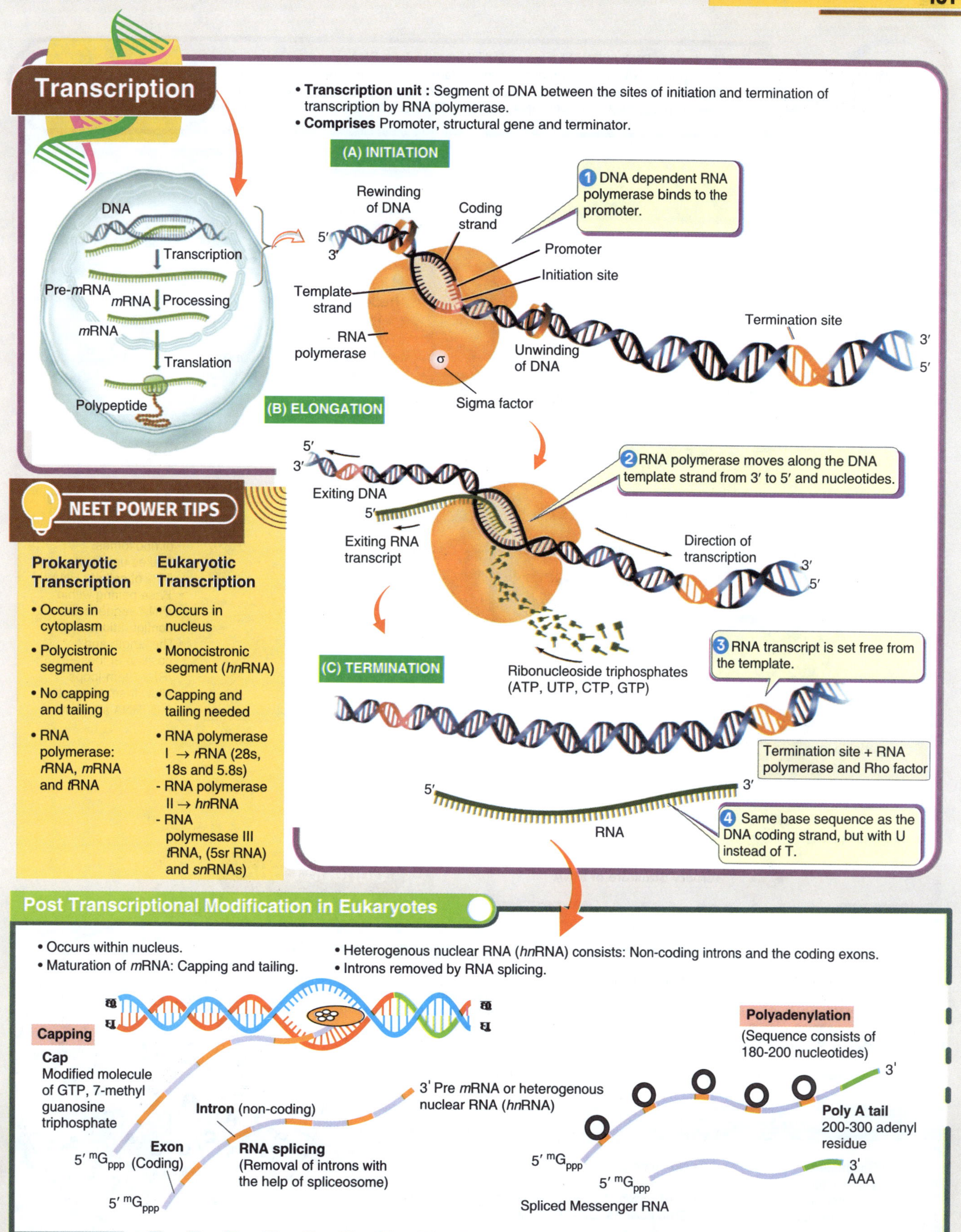

Post Transcriptional Modification in Eukaryotes

- Occurs within nucleus.
- Maturation of *m*RNA: Capping and tailing.
- Heterogenous nuclear RNA (*hn*RNA) consists: Non-coding introns and the coding exons.
- Introns removed by RNA splicing.

Types of RNA

- **Messenger RNA** (*m*RNA) brings coded information from DNA.
- **Ribosomal RNA** (*r*RNA) attract and provide large surface for spreading of *m*RNA.
- **Transfer RNA** (*t*RNA) transfers an amino acid from cytoplasm to the site of protein synthesis.
- Other forms of RNA: Catalytic RNA, Genomic RNA, small nuclear RNA (*sn*RNA), small cytoplasmic RNA (*sc*RNA).

t-RNA or soluble RNA

- Synthesised in nucleus on DNA template.
- **Function:** Carry amino acid for protein synthesis.

OH 3′ end

Amino acid acceptor (Amino acid covalently attach to 3'-OH terminal of t-RNA)

Hydrogen bonds

5′ end

Acceptor stem

TψC loop (Ribosomal binding loop)

T-arm

D-arm

DHU loop (Amino-acyl synthetase binding loop)

Variable loop

Anticodon arm

Anticodon loop

Anticodon (For attachment with *m*RNA)

Clover Leaf Structure

T loop

5′

CCA terminus

3′

Acceptor stem

Variable loop

DHU loop

Anticodon loop

Tertiary Structure of *t*RNA

*m*RNA or Messenger RNA

- A single stranded molecule of RNA.
- Corresponds to the genetic sequence of a gene.
- Read by a ribosome during the process of protein synthesis.

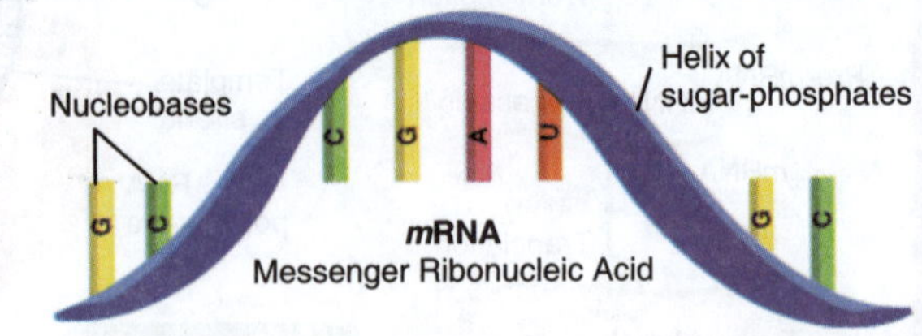

*r*RNA or Ribosomal RNA

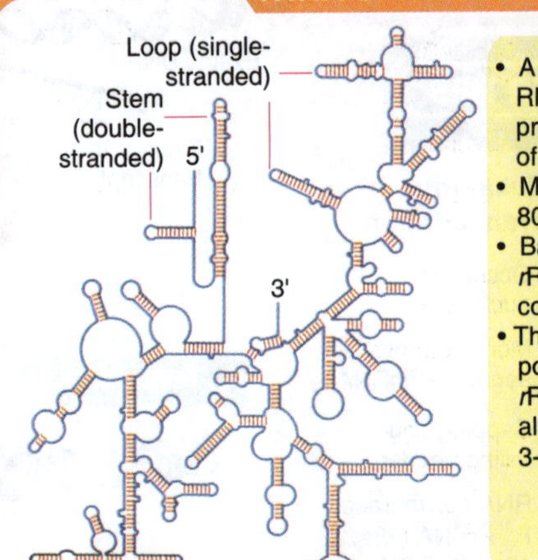

- A type of non-coding RNA which is the primary component of ribosomes.
- Makes up about 80% of cellular RNA.
- Base pairing within *r*RNA sequences configurations.
- The length and position of these *r*RNA stem-loops allow them to create 3-D *r*RNA structures.

Genetic Code

- Information in RNA is decoded in a polypeptide chain
- **George Gamow** : 1 codon-3 nucleotides and 20 amino acids; 4^3 would generate 64 codons.
- **Har Gobind Khorana** : Derived artificially synthesised *m*RNA; Defined combination of bases.
- **Nirenberg and Matthaei :** Proved triplet code existence; synthetic poly-U sequence.
- **Severo Ochoa Enzyme** (Polynucleotide phosphorylase) helpful in enzymatic synsthesis of RNA.

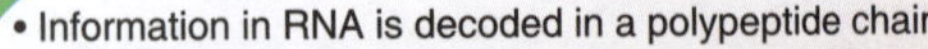

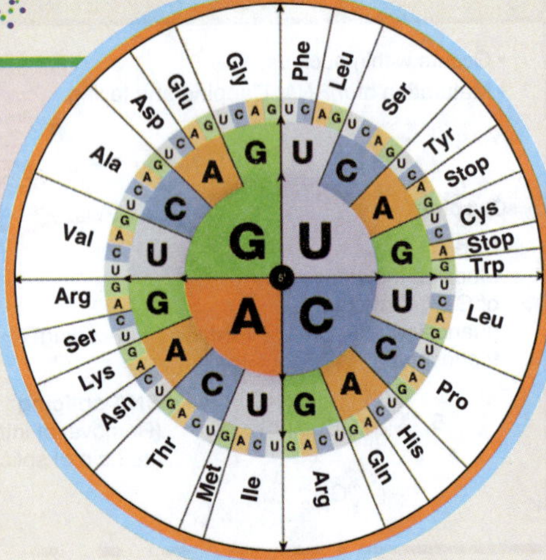

Characteristics of Genetic Code

- Commaless
- Triplet code
- Degenerate
- Non-overlapping
- Non-ambiguous
- Universal
- **Start codon**: AUG (methionine),rarely, GUG (valine)
- **Stop codons**: UAA, UAG and UGA

Aminoacylation of *t*RNA or charging of *t*RNA

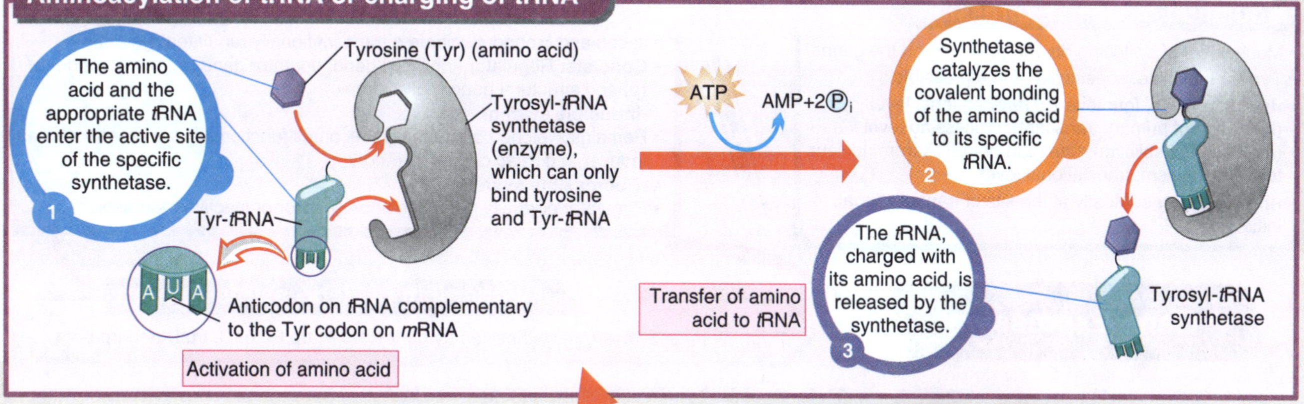

1 The amino acid and the appropriate *t*RNA enter the active site of the specific synthetase.

Tyrosine (Tyr) (amino acid)

Tyrosyl-*t*RNA synthetase (enzyme), which can only bind tyrosine and Tyr-*t*RNA

Tyr-*t*RNA

A U A

Anticodon on *t*RNA complementary to the Tyr codon on *m*RNA

Activation of amino acid

ATP → AMP+2Ⓟ$_i$

2 Synthetase catalyzes the covalent bonding of the amino acid to its specific *t*RNA.

3 The *t*RNA, charged with its amino acid, is released by the synthetase.

Transfer of amino acid to *t*RNA

Tyrosyl-*t*RNA synthetase

Translation

Mechanism of Translation

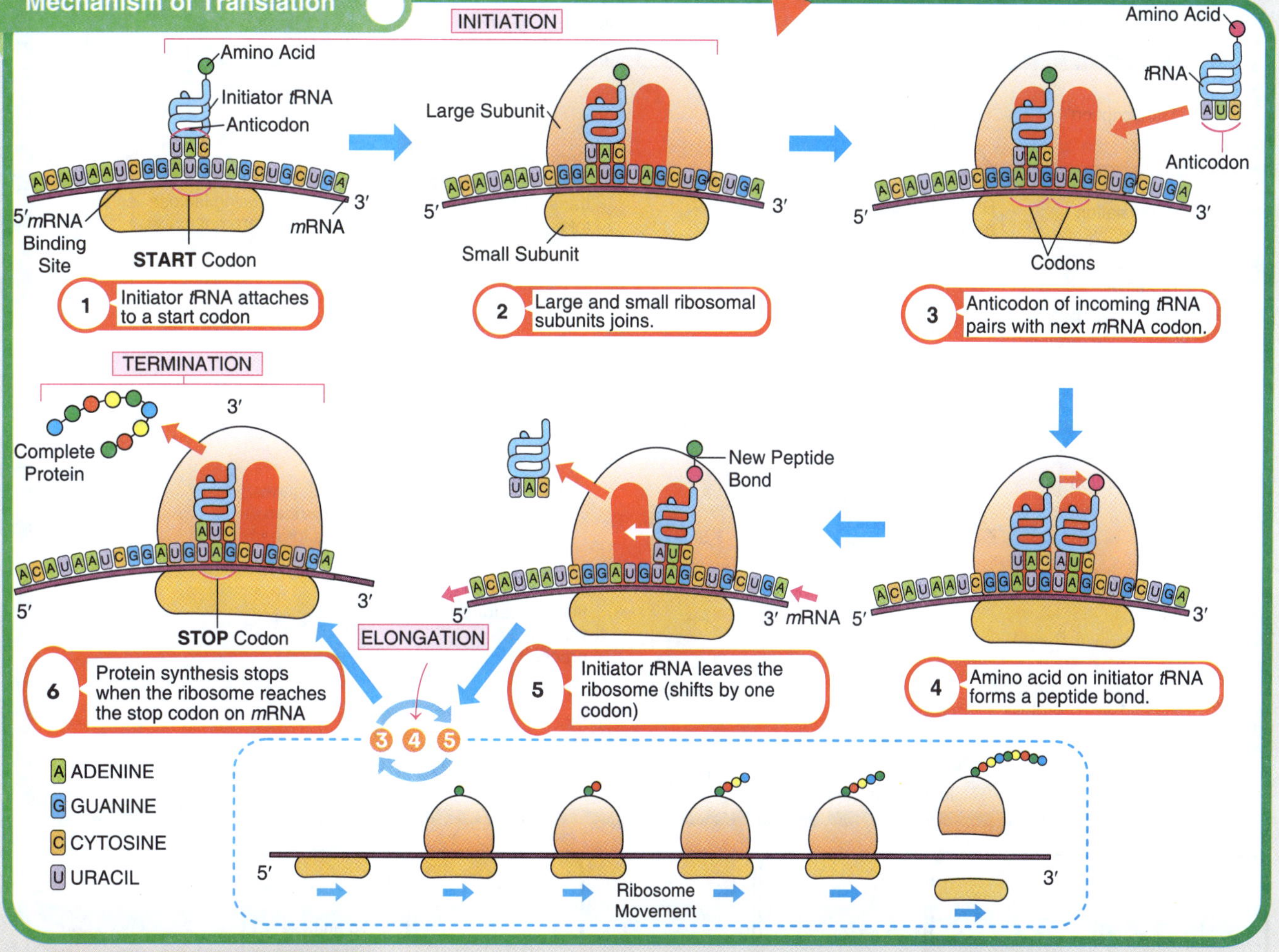

INITIATION

Amino Acid

Initiator *t*RNA

Anticodon

UAC

ACAUAAUCGGAUGUAGCUGCUGA

5′ *m*RNA Binding Site

*m*RNA 3′

START Codon

1 Initiator *t*RNA attaches to a start codon

Large Subunit

Small Subunit

2 Large and small ribosomal subunits joins.

Amino Acid

*t*RNA

AUC

Anticodon

Codons

3 Anticodon of incoming *t*RNA pairs with next *m*RNA codon.

4 Amino acid on initiator *t*RNA forms a peptide bond.

New Peptide Bond

5 Initiator *t*RNA leaves the ribosome (shifts by one codon)

ELONGATION

TERMINATION

Complete Protein

STOP Codon

6 Protein synthesis stops when the ribosome reaches the stop codon on *m*RNA

3 4 5

Ribosome Movement

A ADENINE

G GUANINE

C CYTOSINE

U URACIL

- 61 codons code for the 20 amino acids.
- *t*RNA is specific to each amino acid.
- **Untranslated Regions** (UTRs): Sequence before 5′ end and after 3′ end of mRNA.
- Magnesium ions helps in binding of two units of ribosomes.

Regulation of Gene Expression

- Mechanism of switching off and switching on the genes.
- **Types:** Inducible, constitutive and repressible.

→**In eukaryotes,** four levels: Transcriptional level (formation of primary transcript), processing level (regulation of splicing), transport of *m*RNA from nucleus to the cytoplasm; translational level.

→**In prokaryotes:** Mostly at the site of transcriptional initiation.

Operon System

- Jacob and Monod elucidate a transcriptionally regulated system.
- **Consists:** Regulator (inhibitor) gene, operator gene (o), promoter gene (p) and structural gene (polycistronic).

→**Inducible system**

- Remains switched off normally, becomes functional in the presence of an inducer, e.g., *Lac* operon in *E.coli.*

→**Repressible system**

- Regulator normally produces aporepressor or inactive repressor.

Gene Expression

Mechanism of Repressible Operon

Tryptophan, enzymes are synthesised by genes; trp A, trp B, trp C, trp D and trp E.

Mechanism of *Lac* Operon (Inducible operon)

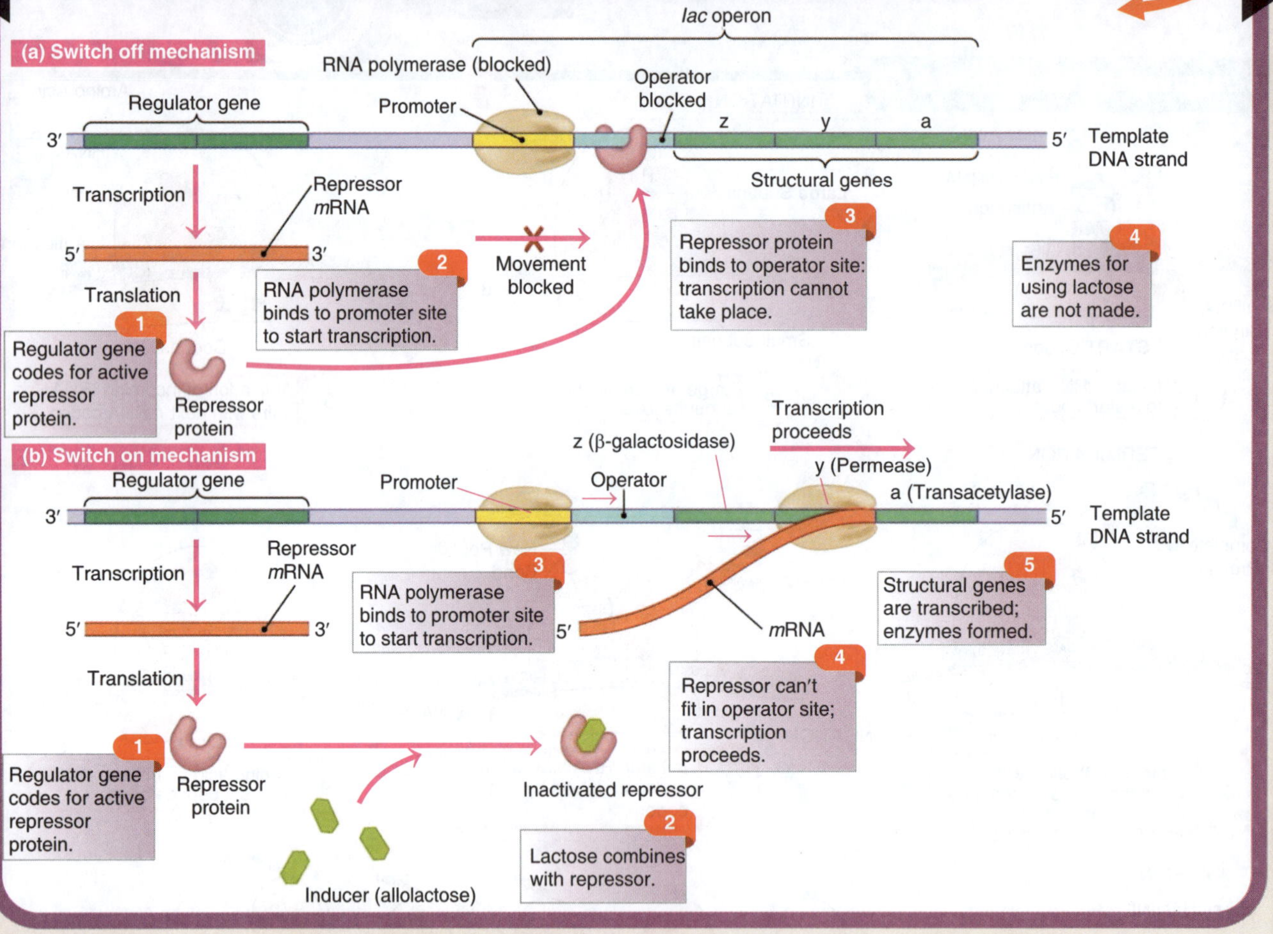

(a) Switch off mechanism

lac operon

RNA polymerase (blocked)

Operator blocked

Regulator gene

Promoter

3′ z y a 5′ Template DNA strand

Structural genes

Transcription

Repressor *m*RNA

5′ 3′

Movement blocked

Translation

Repressor protein

1. Regulator gene codes for active repressor protein.
2. RNA polymerase binds to promoter site to start transcription.
3. Repressor protein binds to operator site: transcription cannot take place.
4. Enzymes for using lactose are not made.

(b) Switch on mechanism

Regulator gene

Promoter

Operator

z (β-galactosidase)

Transcription proceeds

y (Permease)

a (Transacetylase)

3′ 5′ Template DNA strand

Transcription

Repressor *m*RNA

5′ 3′

5′ *m*RNA

Translation

Repressor protein

Inactivated repressor

Inducer (allolactose)

1. Regulator gene codes for active repressor protein.
2. Lactose combines with repressor.
3. RNA polymerase binds to promoter site to start transcription.
4. Repressor can't fit in operator site; transcription proceeds.
5. Structural genes are transcribed; enzymes formed.

Human Genome Project

Goals

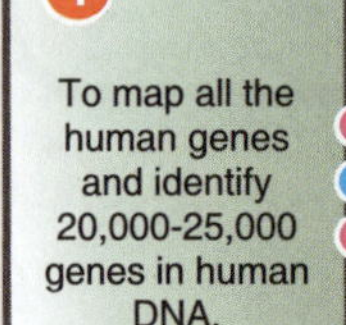

1. To map all the human genes and identify 20,000-25,000 genes in human DNA.
2. To determine the nucleotide sequences of 3 billion base pairs.
3. To store all information in databases.
4. To improve data analysis tools.
5. To transfer the related technologies to relevant industries.
6. To analyse and address ethical, legal and social issues arising from the project.

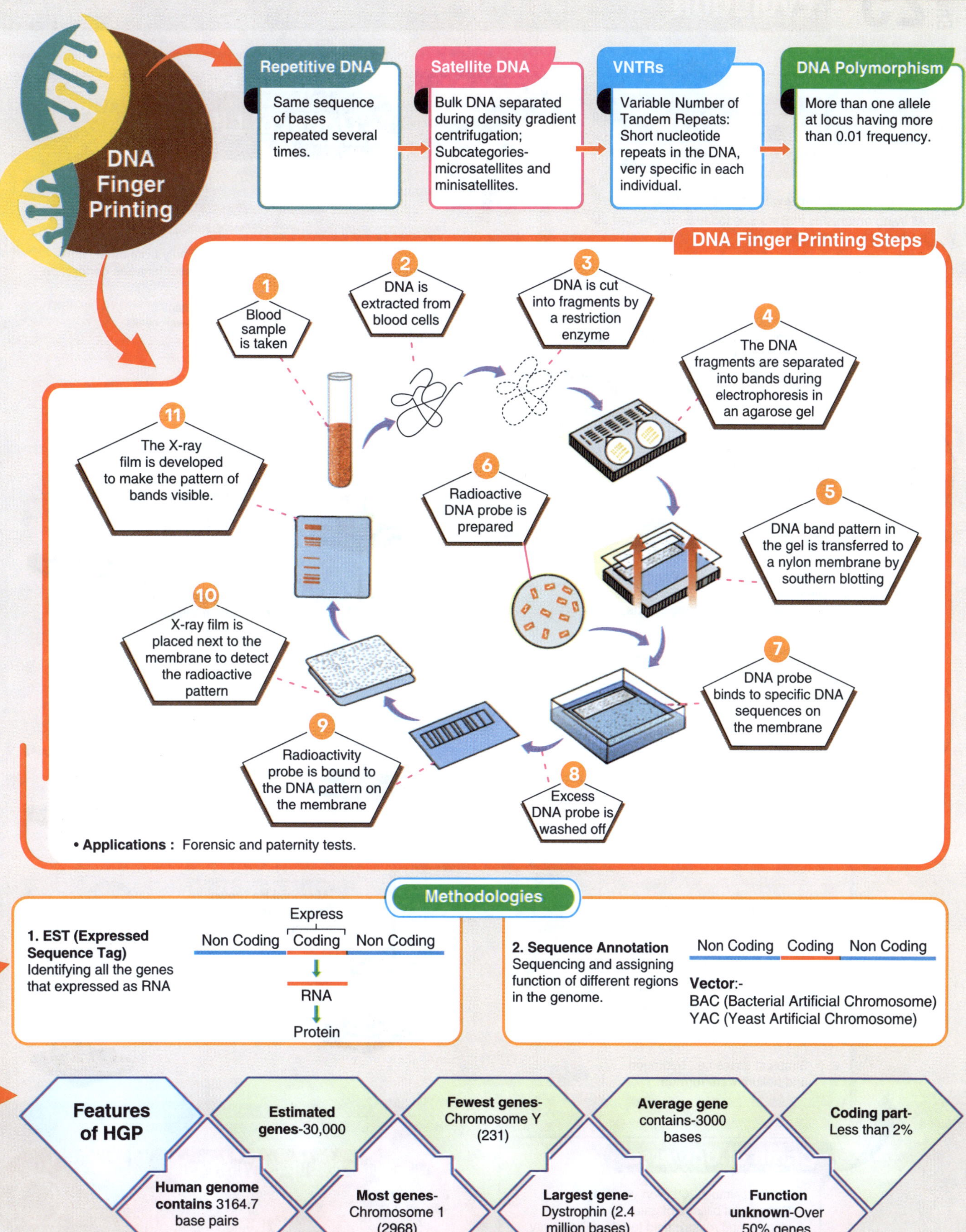
DNA Finger Printing
Repetitive DNA
Same sequence of bases repeated several times.
Satellite DNA
Bulk DNA separated during density gradient centrifugation; Subcategories- microsatellites and minisatellites.
VNTRs
Variable Number of Tandem Repeats: Short nucleotide repeats in the DNA, very specific in each individual.
DNA Polymorphism
More than one allele at locus having more than 0.01 frequency.
DNA Finger Printing Steps
1 Blood sample is taken
2 DNA is extracted from blood cells
3 DNA is cut into fragments by a restriction enzyme
4 The DNA fragments are separated into bands during electrophoresis in an agarose gel
5 DNA band pattern in the gel is transferred to a nylon membrane by southern blotting
6 Radioactive DNA probe is prepared
7 DNA probe binds to specific DNA sequences on the membrane
8 Excess DNA probe is washed off
9 Radioactivity probe is bound to the DNA pattern on the membrane
10 X-ray film is placed next to the membrane to detect the radioactive pattern
11 The X-ray film is developed to make the pattern of bands visible.
• Applications : Forensic and paternity tests.
Methodologies
1. EST (Expressed Sequence Tag)
Identifying all the genes that expressed as RNA
Express
Non Coding
Coding
Non Coding
RNA
Protein
2. Sequence Annotation
Sequencing and assigning function of different regions in the genome.
Non Coding
Coding
Non Coding
Vector:-
BAC (Bacterial Artificial Chromosome)
YAC (Yeast Artificial Chromosome)
Features of HGP
Estimated genes-30,000
Fewest genes- Chromosome Y (231)
Average gene contains-3000 bases
Coding part- Less than 2%
Human genome contains 3164.7 base pairs
Most genes- Chromosome 1 (2968)
Largest gene- Dystrophin (2.4 million bases)
Function unknown-Over 50% genes

Chapter 25 Evolution

Origin of Life

Ancient Theories

01 Theory of Special Creation

- Given by **Father Saurez**; life created by God.
- All living organisms that we see today were created as such and will be same in future.
- Proposed earth is about 4000 years old.

02 Theory of Panspermia

- Supported by **Arrhenius**; extension of theory of cosmozoic origin (protoplasm reached on earth from other parts of universe).
- Transfer of spores from other planets, supposedly brought to earth *via* asteroids or meteors.

03 Theory of Catastrophism

- Proposed by **Cuvier.**
- Earth passed through many ages, at the end of each age a catastroph occurred.

04 Theory of Spontaneous Generation

- Supported by **Aristotle**, **Van Helmont**, etc.
- Life originated from non-living material, also known as **theory of abiogenesis**.

05 Theory of Biogenesis

Life was originated from pre-existing life.

Louis Pasteur's Experiment

Hypothesis →Microorganisms come only from other microorganisms and cannot arise by spontaneous generation.

Origin of Universe

- Formed almost 20 billion years ago.
- Consists of billions of galaxies (stars, planets and rocks); held together by gravity.

Big Bang Theory

- Thermonuclear explosion (unimaginable in physical terms).
- Expansion of universe brought down temperature.
- Gases condensed under the influence of gravity.
- Simplest gases i.e., hydrogen and helium were formed

Solar Nebular Hypothesis

- About 4.6 billion years ago, solar system created from gas.
- Started to collapse under the influence of gravity.

Modern Theory

Also known as abiogenesis given by **Oparin** and **Haldane**.

Life comes from pre-existing, non-living organic molecules (RNA, protein, etc).

Urey-Miller's Experiment

Hypothesis Organic chemical compounds can be generated under conditions similar to the atmosphere of primitive earth.

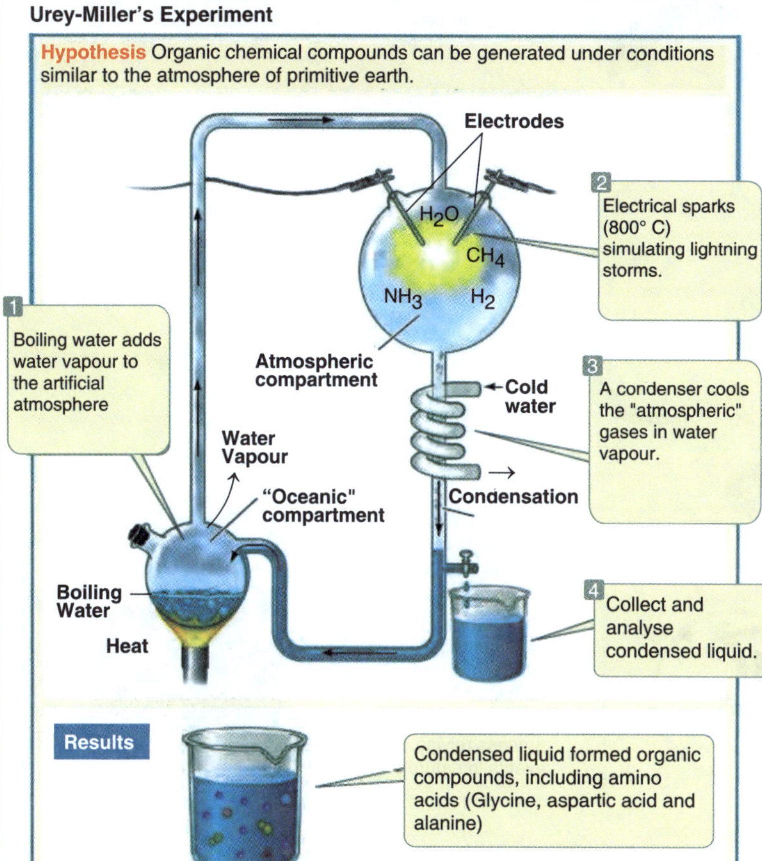

Results Condensed liquid formed organic compounds, including amino acids (Glycine, aspartic acid and alanine)

Conclusion The chemical building blocks of life could have been generated in the reducing/primitive atmosphere of early earth.

Origin of Universe

- Big Bang Theory (1931)
- Solar Nebular Hypothesis (1753)

Origin of Life

- **Ancient Theories**
  From theory of special creation to theory of Biogenesis
- **Modern Theories**
  Abiogenesis given by Oparin and Haldane (Urey-Miller experiment 1953)

Chemical Evolution/Chemogeny

- Atomic Phase
- Formation of Early Molecules
- Formation of Simple Organic Molecules
- Formation of Large Organic Molecules
- Formation of Complex Organic Compounds

Biological Evolution/Biogeny

- Formation of Coacervates and Microspheres
- Formation of Protocells or Eobionts or Protobionts
- Origin of Prokaryotes (≈3.5-3.8 billion years ago)
- Origin of Eukaryotes (1.5 billion years ago)
- Origin of Multicellular Organisms

Origin of Earth

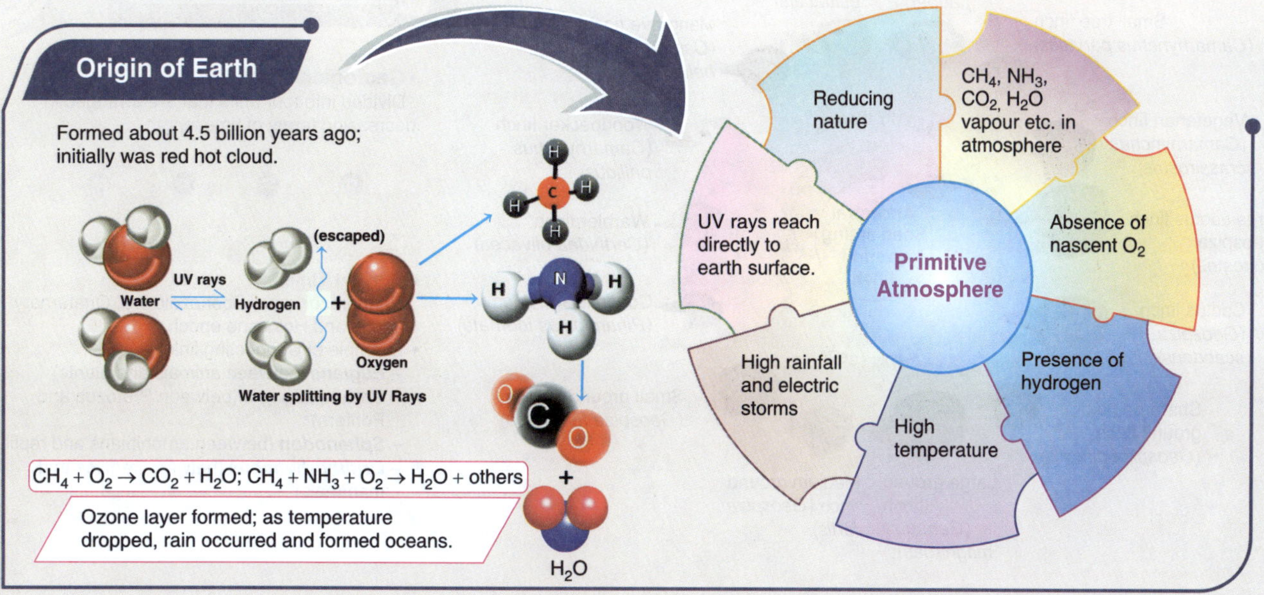

Evolution of Life Forms

Alfred Wallace

- Worked on Malay Archipelago
- Existing life form share similarities and common ancestor.
- Geological history correlates with biological history of earth.

Natural Selection: Mechanism of Evolution

- Leave more progeny than others
- Variation in characteristics
- Survive better in natural condition
- Reproductive fitness
- Better fit in an environment

Charles Darwin

- A. Sea voyage in HMS Beagle.
- B. Living forms share similarities with each other and those from the past.
- C. These similarities vary in degree.

Industrial Melanism

- Peppered moths (*Biston betularia*), existed into two varieties, *viz*, light coloured (white) and dark coloured (black).
- Evolution is a stochastic process relying on chance events in nature and mutation.

Adaptive radiation in Galapagos finches

- Development of different functional structures from a common ancestral form.
- Adaptive Convergence: Development of similar adaptive functional structures in unrelated groups of organism.
- Homologous organ shows adaptive radiation.

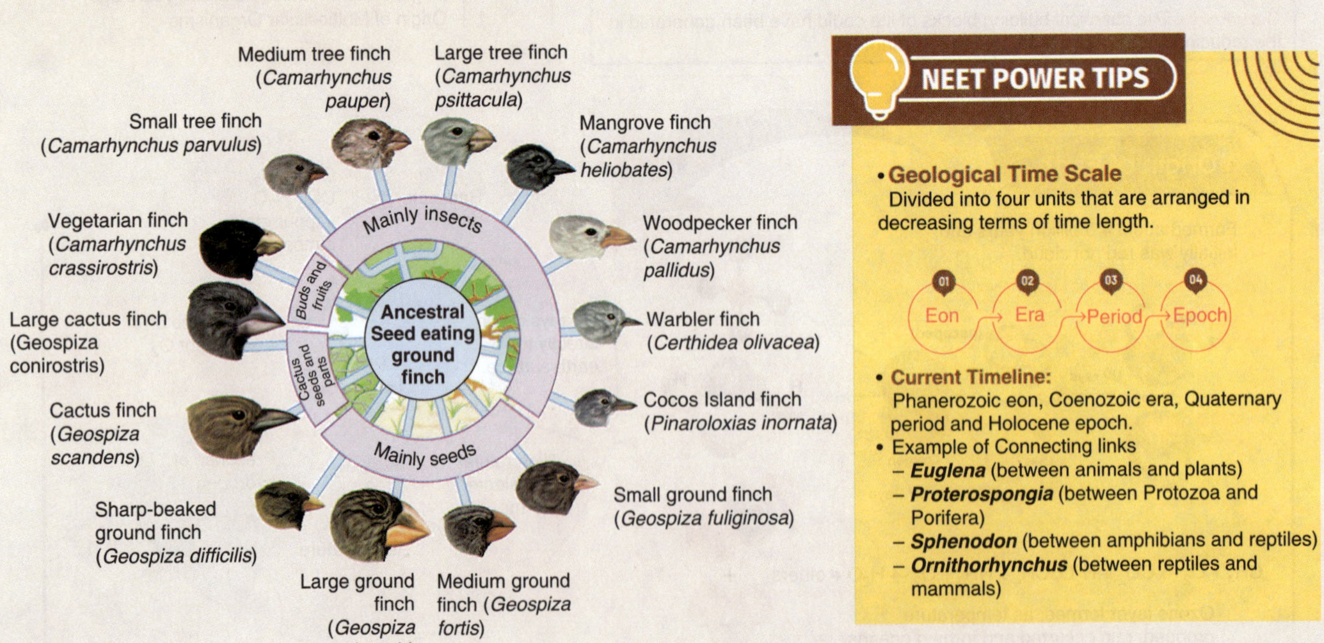

NEET POWER TIPS

- **Geological Time Scale**
  Divided into four units that are arranged in decreasing terms of time length.
  01 Eon → 02 Era → 03 Period → 04 Epoch
- **Current Timeline:**
  Phanerozoic eon, Coenozoic era, Quaternary period and Holocene epoch.
- Example of Connecting links
  - ***Euglena*** (between animals and plants)
  - ***Proterospongia*** (between Protozoa and Porifera)
  - ***Sphenodon*** (between amphibians and reptiles)
  - ***Ornithorhynchus*** (between reptiles and mammals)

Missing link

Archaeopteryx (Connecting link between both reptiles and birds)

***Archaeopteryx* Fossil**

Evidences

Palaeontological Evidence

Determination of the Age of Fossils

- **Uranium-lead technique** (calculate amount of lead in rock)
- **Radioactive carbon** (C^{14}) dating (determine age of an object containing organic material)
- **Potassium-argon method** (calculate time of origin of rock by measuring ratio of Ar to K in the rock.)
- **Electron Spin Resonance** (ESR) method (most precise and accurate method of dating; mostly to date calcium carbonate in lime stone, corals, egg shells, etc.)

- Based on fossil study or records.
- Sedimentary layers shows different geological period.
- Fossilisation is a continuous process.
- **Fossil types**: Trace fossil, moulds and casts, replacement, petrified, amber, original material.

Embryological Evidences

- Based on comparative study of the embryos
- **Recapitulation Theory:** Ernst Haeckel modified biogenetic law, Ontogeny recapitulates phylogeny; disapproved by **Karl Ernst von Baer**

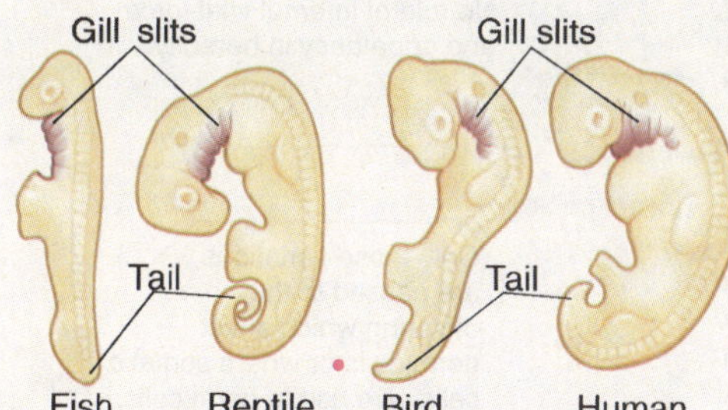

Similarity in the early embryos of some vertebrates

Anthropogenic Evolution

- Evolutionary changes or processes under the influence of human activities.
- Through artificial selection; selectively bred certain plants and animals.
- Overuse of chemicals led to selection of resistant varieties.

Vestigial Organs

e.g., vermiform appendix, wisdom teeth, muscles of pinna, nictitating membrane in humans

Atavism

Reappearance of certain ancestral characters. Short tail in some babies, power of moving pinna etc.

Evidences from Morphology and Comparative Anatomy

1 Homologous Organs

Same embryonic origin and fundamental structure but different in functions; result of divergence evolution

2 Analogous Organs

Similar functions, but different in their structural details and origin; results of convergent evolution.

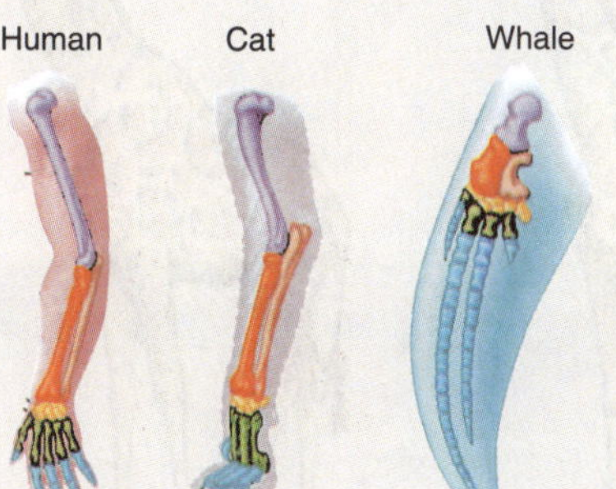

Homology of the forelimbs in vertebrates

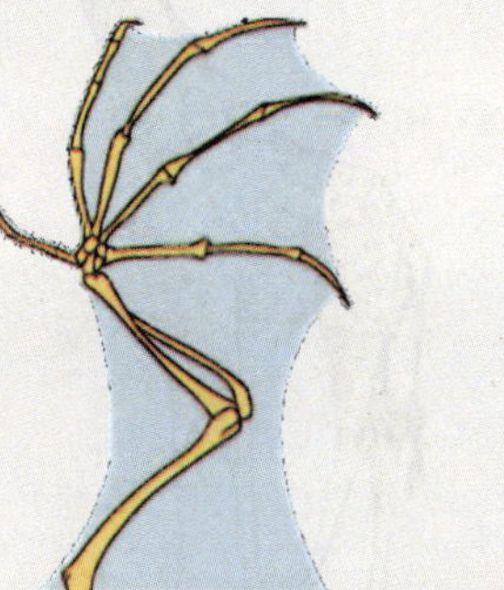

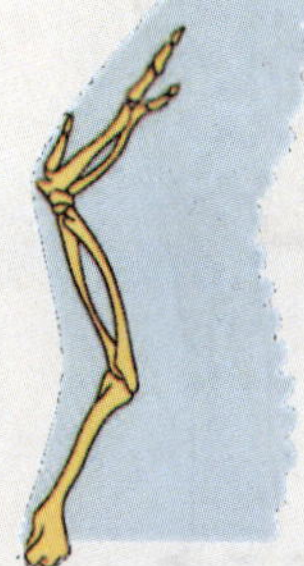

Analogy of the forelimbs of bat and bird.

Darwin Theory

Two Key Concept: Branching descent and Natural selection

Darwin Evolution	de Vries Mutation
Minor variation	Major variation
Slow and directional	Random, sudden and directionless
Gradual evolution	Speciation by saltation

Mechanism of Evolution

Hugo de Vries Mutation Theory

Sudden appearance of variations, named as **mutations**; causes **speciation**.

Saltation Single step Large Mutation

Synthetic Theory: Only genetic variations (mutations) are inherited.

Biological Evolution

Theories of Evolution

Lamarckism (1744-1829)

- Internal vital force for growth
- Changes in environment giving rise to new needs.
- Use and disuse of organ
- Inheritance of acquired characters

Neo-Lamarckism

1. Environment influences an organism and change its heredity.
2. No role of internal vital force and appetency in heredity.
3. Variations acquired by an individual passed onto the offspring.
4. Only those variations are passed to the offspring which affect germ cells or where somatic cells give rise to germ cells.

Diagrammatic representation of Lamarck's theory

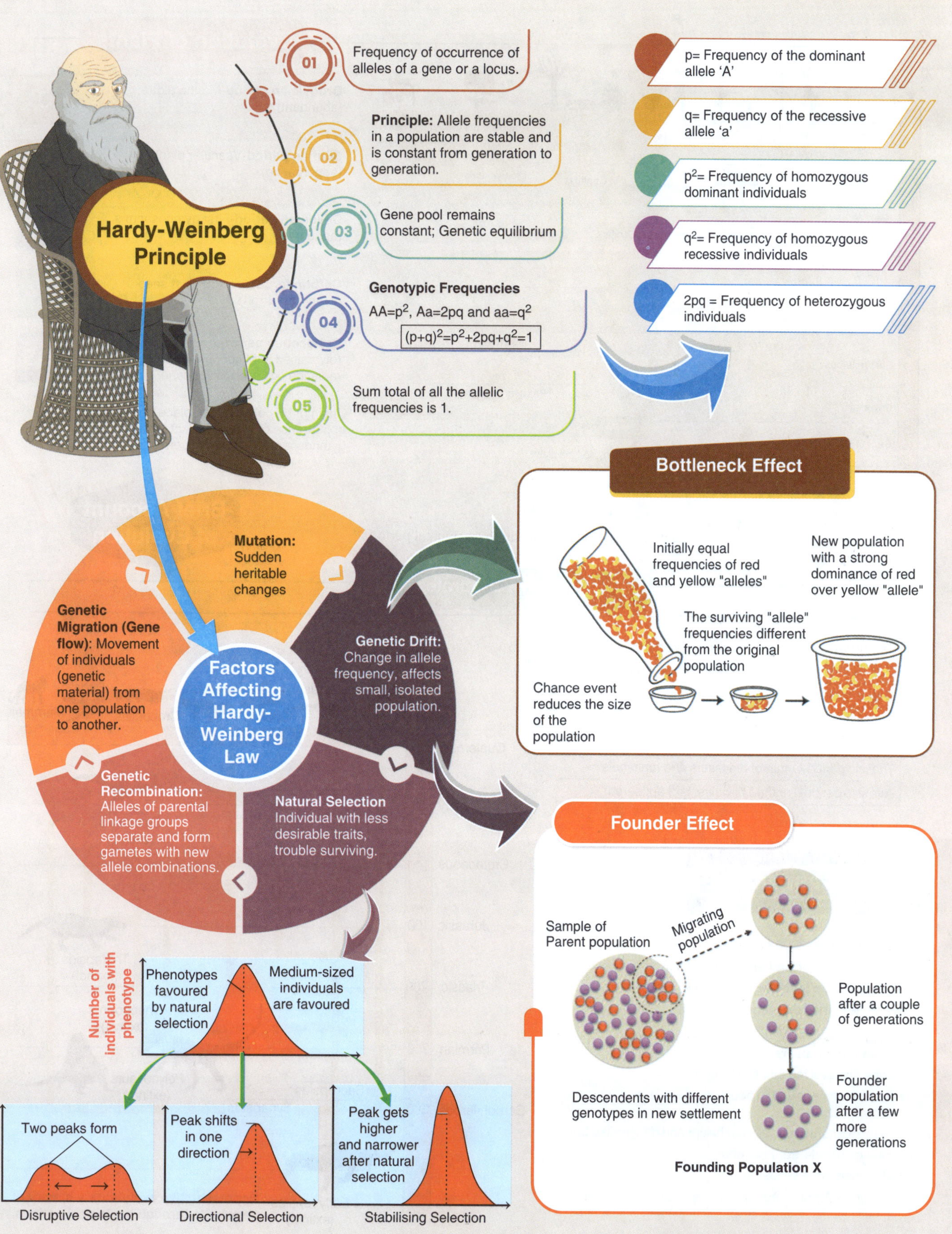
Hardy-Weinberg Principle
01
Frequency of occurrence of alleles of a gene or a locus.
02
Principle: Allele frequencies in a population are stable and is constant from generation to generation.
03
Gene pool remains constant; Genetic equilibrium
04
Genotypic Frequencies
AA=p^2, Aa=2pq and aa=q^2
$(p+q)^2=p^2+2pq+q^2=1$
05
Sum total of all the allelic frequencies is 1.
p= Frequency of the dominant allele 'A'
q= Frequency of the recessive allele 'a'
p^2= Frequency of homozygous dominant individuals
q^2= Frequency of homozygous recessive individuals
2pq = Frequency of heterozygous individuals
Factors Affecting Hardy-Weinberg Law
Mutation: Sudden heritable changes
Genetic Drift: Change in allele frequency, affects small, isolated population.
Natural Selection Individual with less desirable traits, trouble surviving.
Genetic Recombination: Alleles of parental linkage groups separate and form gametes with new allele combinations.
Genetic Migration (Gene flow): Movement of individuals (genetic material) from one population to another.
Bottleneck Effect
Initially equal frequencies of red and yellow "alleles"
New population with a strong dominance of red over yellow "allele"
The surviving "allele" frequencies different from the original population
Chance event reduces the size of the population
Founder Effect
Sample of Parent population
Migrating population
Population after a couple of generations
Descendents with different genotypes in new settlement
Founder population after a few more generations
Founding Population X
Number of individuals with phenotype
Phenotypes favoured by natural selection
Medium-sized individuals are favoured
Two peaks form
Peak shifts in one direction
Peak gets higher and narrower after natural selection
Disruptive Selection
Directional Selection
Stabilising Selection

Brief Account of Evolution

Evolution of Plants

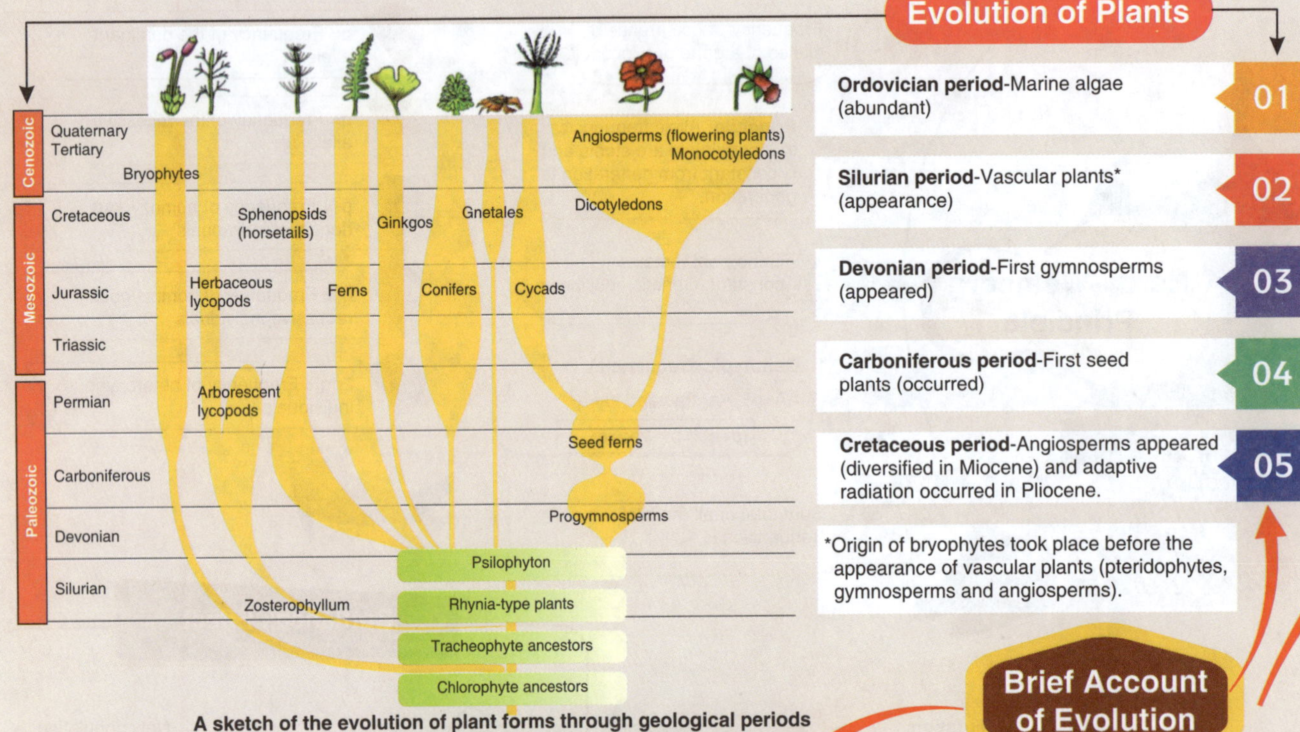

A sketch of the evolution of plant forms through geological periods

01 **Ordovician period**-Marine algae (abundant)

02 **Silurian period**-Vascular plants* (appearance)

03 **Devonian period**-First gymnosperms (appeared)

04 **Carboniferous period**-First seed plants (occurred)

05 **Cretaceous period**-Angiosperms appeared (diversified in Miocene) and adaptive radiation occurred in Pliocene.

*Origin of bryophytes took place before the appearance of vascular plants (pteridophytes, gymnosperms and angiosperms).

Evolution of Vertebrates

Cambrian period origin of most invertebrate phyla
- Ordovician period-Origin of vertebrates (jawless)
- Late Silurian-Acanthodians (vertebrates with lower jaw)
- Devonian period-Origin of amphibian
- Carboniferous period-Reptiles (appeared)
- Triassic period-Origin of dinosaurs and mammals
- Jurassic period-Toothed bird (first bird appeared)

1st cellular life: 2000 mya
Invertebrates (formed and active) : 500 mya
Jawless fishes (evolved) : 350 mya
Sea weeds and few plants : 320 mya
Reptiles : 200 mya (*Ichthyosaurs*)
Dinosaur disappeared : 65 mya

- Lobe fins evolved into first amphibians.
- Amphibians evolved into reptiles, giant ferns forms coal deposits slowly
- *Tyrannosaurus rex* : 20 feet height and dagger-like teeth
- First mammals were like shrews
- Mammals were viviparous
- Fishes → Amphibians → Reptiles → Birds → Mammals

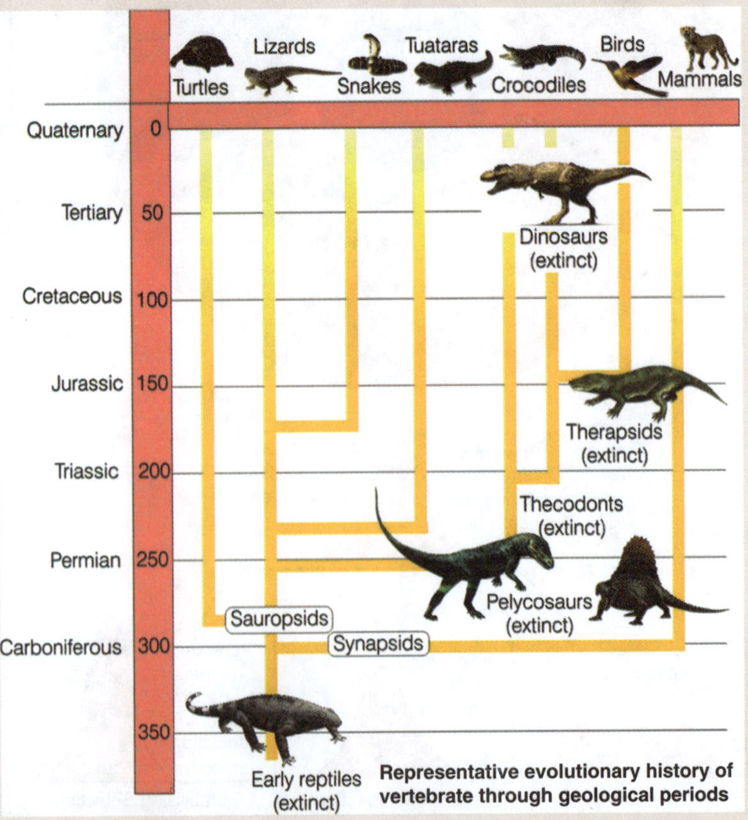

Representative evolutionary history of vertebrate through geological periods

Human Evolution

Period: 15 Mya; Miocene

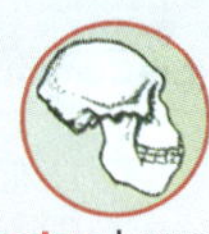

Brain size: Large (Unknown)

Characteristics: Arboreal and ate soft fruits and leaves; arms and legs are of same length, knuckle walker

Period: 15 mya; Miocene to Pliocene

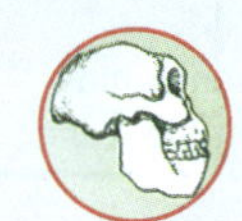

Brain size: Unknown

Characteristics: Walked erect, teeth (small canines and large molars); Ate hard nuts.

Period: 3-4 mya; Pliocene

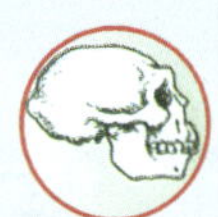

Brain size: 400-600 cc

Characteristics: Tall, walked straight, ate fruits; fossils found in Tanzania and Ethiopia.

Period: 1.5-2 mya; Pleistocene

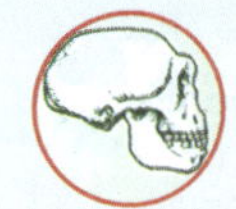

Brain size: 650-800 cc

Characteristics: Bipedal; absence of chin, herbivores and fossils fund in East Africa.

Period: 1.5 mya; Middle Pleistocene

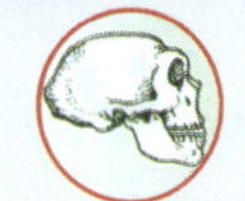

Brain size: 900 cc

Characteristics: Erect posture, omnivorous; made elaborate tools of stones and bones; fossils found in Java.

Period: 1,00,000-40,000 years ago

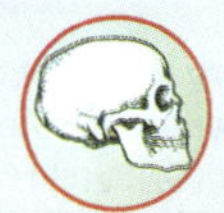

Brain size: 1400 cc

Characteristics: Used hides to protect body and body buried after death; fossils found in East and central Asia; omnivorous.

Dryopithecus (Ape-like) → ***Ramapithecus*** (Man-like) → ***Australopitheus*** (First ape men) → ***Homo habilis*** (Human-like) (Toolmaker/Handy man) → ***Homo erectus*** (Java man; Pecking man) → ***Homo sapiens neanderthalensis*** (Primitive man)

Homo sapiens fossilis (Cro-Magnon)

Period: 40,000-10,000 years ago; Holocene

Brain size: 1650cc

Characteristics: Walk and run faster, omnivorous, direct ancestor of living modern man; carving and paintings in caves.

Homo sapiens sapiens

Period: 25,000 years ago (Holocene)

Brain size: Approx 1450 cc.

Characteristics: Reduction in cranial capacity and cultural evolution; prominent chin, reduction in tooth and facial bone size.

Chapter **26**

Human Health and Diseases

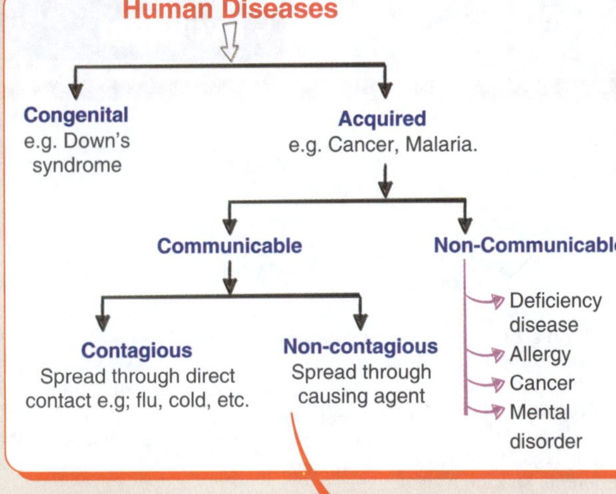

Common Communicable Diseases

Bacterial Diseases

Typhoid (*Salmonella typhi*)

- **Organs Affected** Intestinal tract
- **Symptoms** Continuous high fever, abdominal pain, vomiting
- **Modes of Transmission** Through contaminated food and water
- **Diagnosis:** Widal test

Pneumonia (*Streptococcus pneumoniae, Haemophilus influenzae*)

- **Organs Affected** Lungs
- **Symptoms** Accumulation of mucus and lymph in alveoli and bronchioles, difficulty in breathing.
- **Modes of Transmission** Inhaling droplets released by an infected person.

Tuberculosis (TB) (*Mycobacterium tuberculosis*)

- **Organs Affected** It could affect any part of the body; bones, brain, lungs, lymph nodes, joints
- **Symptoms** Constant cough, sputum with blood in severe case, pain in chest while coughing; low grade fever.
- **Modes of Transmission** Through the air from one person to another.
- **Diagnosis**: Montoux test
- **Vaccine** BCG

Diphtheria (*Corynebacterium diphtheriae*)

- **Organs Affected** Respiratory tract, pharynx, larynx, throat
- **Symptoms** Fever, sore throat, hoarseness, difficulty in breathing
- **Modes of Transmission** Droplet infection, sharing contaminated objects.
- **Diagnosis**: Schick test
- **Vaccine:** DPT

Tetanus (Lock jaw) (*Clostridium tetani*)

- **Organs Affected** Muscles of jaw and face
- **Symptoms** Muscular spasm, Lock jaw condition, convulsions and paralysis of muscles.
- **Modes of Transmission** Wound infection
- **Diagnosis** : Spatula test
- **Vaccine**: DTP, TT, DT

Viral Diseases

Diseases	Pathogens	Organs Affected	Symptoms	Modes of Transmission
Common cold (Rhinitis)	Rhino virus	Nose and upper respiratory passage	Nasal congestion, sore throat, cough, slight fever	Droplets from cough and sneeze of infected persons
Mumps	Paramyxo virus, Myxovirus sp.	Inflammation of parotid glands	Swelling of parotid glands	Droplet infection
Dengue fever (Breakbone fever)	Flavi-ribo virus	Liver, spleen, lymph nodes	High fever, muscle and joint pains, nausea and vomiting, etc.	*Aedes aegypti* (mosquito)
Poliomyelitis	Enterovirus (polio virus)	Nervous system	Stiffness of the neck, paralysis of skeletal muscles.	Faecal-oral route
Hepatitis	Hepatitis virus	Liver	Fever, nausea, vomiting, pains in muscles and joints	Through blood, body secretion, sexual contact
Chikungunya	Chikungunya virus	Limbs, joints	Fever, crippling joint pains, conjunctivitis	Through mosquitoes, *Aedes aegypti* and *Aedes albopictus* (Asian tiger mosquito)
Chickenpox	Varicella zoster virus	Liver, skin, brain	Rashes on chest, face and whole body, fever, itching, body aches	Droplet infection, direct contact

Helminthic Diseases

Ascariasis
- Caused by *Ascaris lumbricoides*
- **Infection site**: Small intestine
- **Mode of transmission**: Ingestion of fruits and vegetable contaminated with eggs.
- **Symptoms:** Internal bleeding, muscular pain, anemia, blockage of intestinal passage.

Filariasis (Elephantiasis)
- **Caused by** *Wuchereria bancrofti* and *W.malayi*, *Culex* mosquito (host).
- **Infection site:** Lymphatic system
- **Mode of transmission**: Bite of *Culex* mosquito
- **Symptoms**: Swelling of lymph nodes.

NEET POWER TIPS

Health: According to W.H.O, health is a state of complete physical, mental and social well-being.

Disease: Discomfort or disability in the body, interrupts the performance of vital functions.

Pathogens: Disease causing organisms, like bacteria, virus, fungi, protozoans, worms, etc.

Protozoan Diseases

Amoebiasis
- **Causative agent:** *Entamoeba histolytica*
- **Host** : Human
- **Symptoms:** Abdominal pain, mild diarrhoea, mucus and blood in faeces, etc.

African sleeping sickness/ Trypanosomiasis
- **Causative agents:** *Trypanosoma gambiense*
- **Hosts:** Human and tse-tse fly

Kala azar
- **Causative agents:** *Leishmania donovani*
- **Hosts:** Human and sand fly

Malaria
- **Causative agents:** *P. vivax*, *P. malariae*, *P. ovale* and *P. falciparum* (fatal)
- **Hosts:** Human and female *Anopheles* mosquito

Stages in the Life Cycle of *Plasmodium*

Some Important Facts about Malaria

01 Rupture of RBCs is associated with release of **haemozoin** (toxic substance), responsible for chills and high fever.

2 Gametocytes fertilize and develop in mosquito's stomach

03 **Treatment:** Chloroquine (drug)

Fungal Diseases

Tinea or Ringworm
- **Causative agents:** *Microsporum*, *Trichophyton* and *Epidermophyton*.
- **Transmission:** Using towels, clothes and comb of the infected persons.
- **Symptoms:** Dry scaly lesions on skin, nails and scalp.

Non-Communicable Diseases
- Cardiovascular diseases
- Diabetes mellitus
- Arthritis
- Gout
- Cancer
- Osteoporosis.

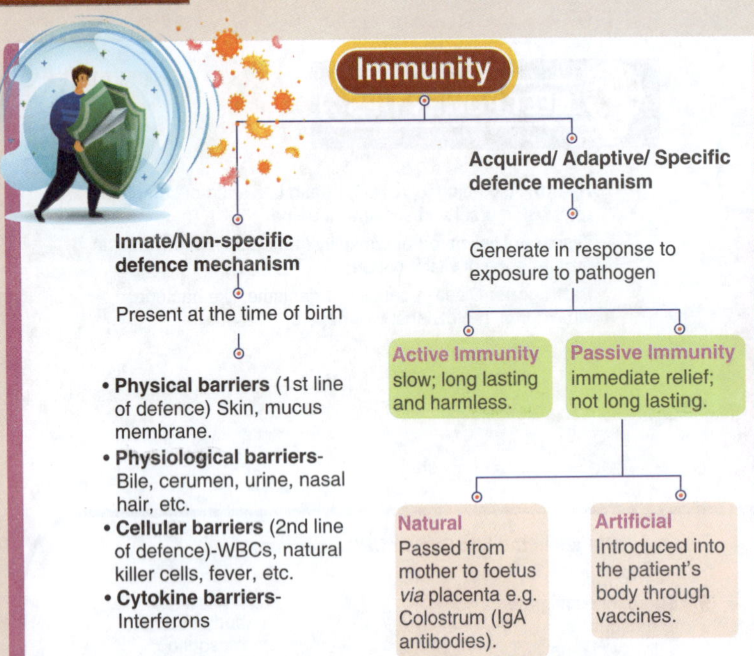

NEET POWER TIPS

- Ability of an organism to fight against disease causing agents is called **immunity**.
- **Edward Jenner** (1749-1823)-Father of Immunology.
- Active immunity is developed when person's own cells produce antibodies in response to infection.
- Passive immunity is developed when ready made antibodies are directly injected into a person.

Cell Involved in Acquired Immunity

B-cells

Produced and get matured in bone marrow

Humoral Immunity

- Produce antibodies or immunoglobulins.
- Types of B-cells.
  - Plasma B-cells and Memory B-cells.

T-cells

Produced in bone marrow but get matured in thymus

Cell-Mediated Immune System

- Activates phagocytosis
- Antigen specific
- No antibodies involved
- Responsible for graft rejection
- Types of T-cells : Helper T-cells, memory T-cells, cytotoxic.

Structure of Immunoglobulins (Ig)

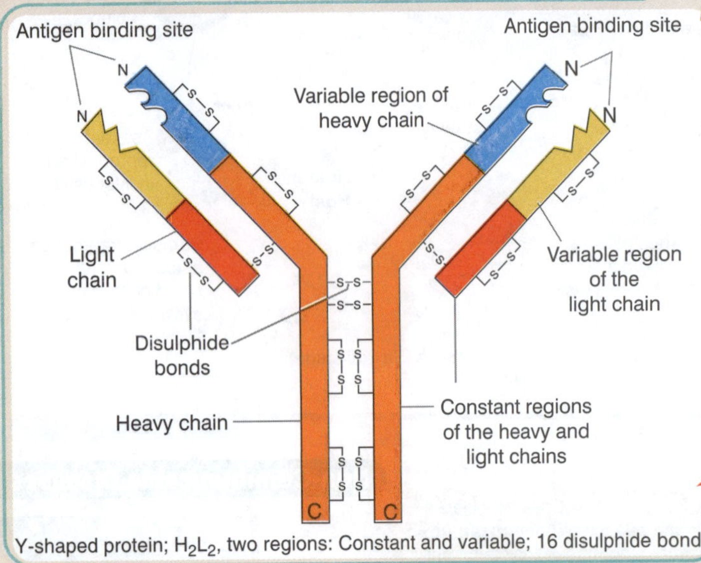

Y-shaped protein; H_2L_2, two regions: Constant and variable; 16 disulphide bonds.

Five Types of immunoglobulins

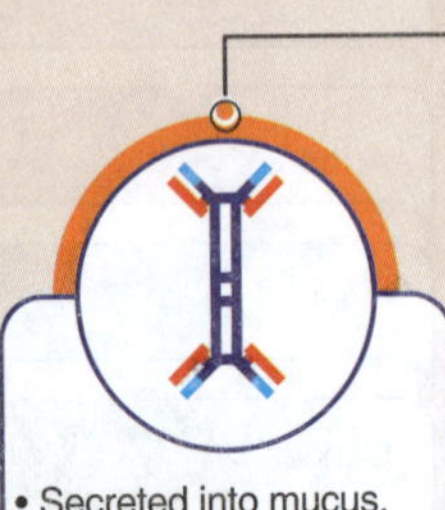

- Secreted into mucus, saliva, tears, colostrum.
- Tags pathogens for destruction.

IgA

- B-cell receptor.
- Stimulates release of IgM.

IgD

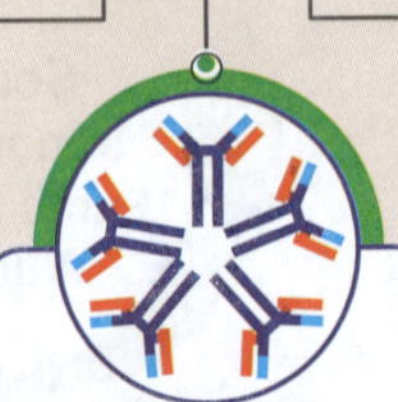

- Main antibody of primary responses.
- B-cell receptor.

IgM

- Binds to phagocytes.
- Main blood antibody for secondary responses.
- Crosses placenta.

IgG

- Binds to mast cells and basophils.
- Allergy and antiparasitic activity.

IgE

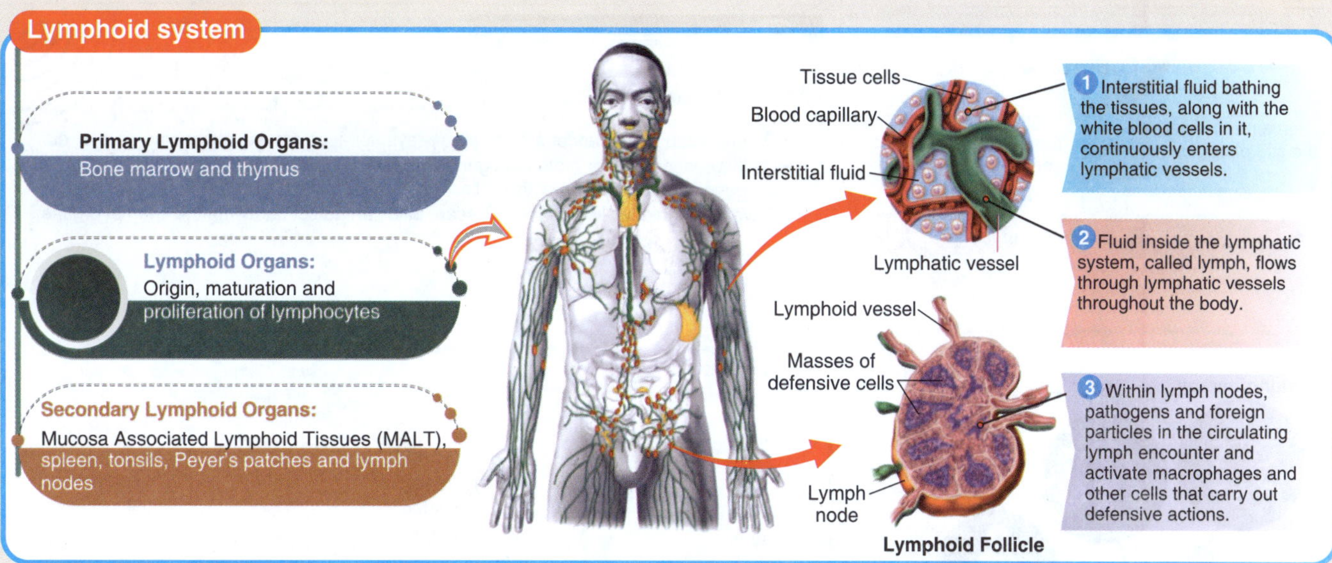

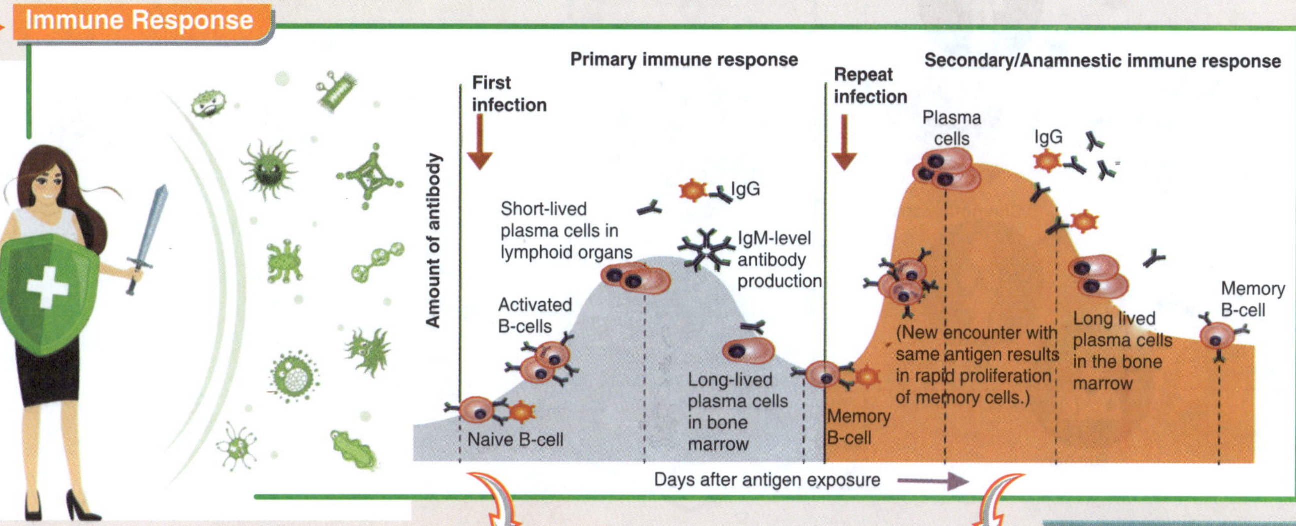

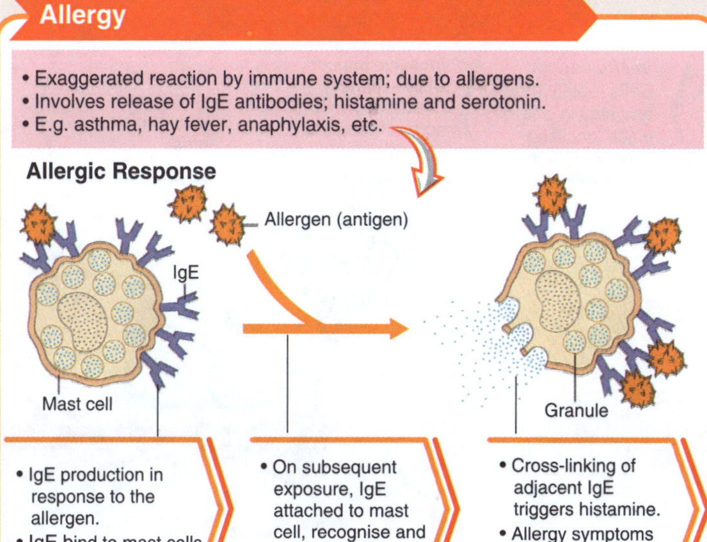

- IgE production in response to the allergen.
- IgE bind to mast cells.

- On subsequent exposure, IgE attached to mast cell, recognise and bind the allergen.

- Cross-linking of adjacent IgE triggers histamine.
- Allergy symptoms appear.

Autoimmunity

- Immune system fails to recognise self cells from foreign cells, start to destroy body's own proteins.
- Caused due to genetic factor, environmental factor etc.
- Examples : Grave's disease, Addison's disease, rheumatoid arthritis, rheumatic fever, diabetes mellitus, etc.

Vaccination and Immunisation

Vaccination: Introduce pathogens in body to produce antibodies.

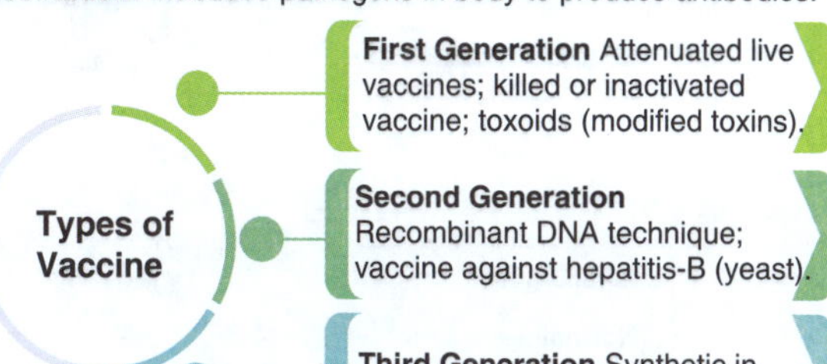

Immunisation: Body produces antibodies against the vaccine preventable disease through administration of specific vaccines.

Types of Tumour

Benign Tumour: Remains confined to the site of origin.

Malignant tumour: Migrate to other sites of the body (Metastasis); continues to divide.

NEET POWER TIPS

- Different causes of cancer are- X-rays, γ-rays, tobacco smoke, oncogenic viruses, etc.
- Cellular oncogenes or proto-oncogenes, in normal cells when activated can lead to oncogenic transformation of the cells.
- Several techniques like x-rays, CT scan, MRI can detect cancer of the internal organs.

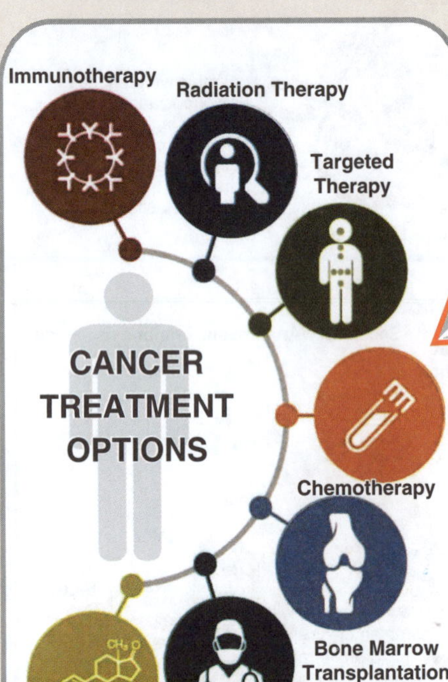

Cancer

No differentiation, invade and destroy the surrounding tissues.

An abnormal and uncontrolled proliferation of cells resulting into tumour or neoplasm

Differences between Normal Cells and Cancer Cells

Normal Cell
- Definite lifespan
- Show contact inhibition
- Divide in regulated manner

Cancer Cell
- Cells divide in uncontrolled manner
- No definite life-span
- Do not show contact inhibition

Metastasis

Initiation Oncogene activation in the altered cell

Hyperplasia Cells divides more rapidly than normal

Dysplasia Altered cells with increased growth potential

***In situ* cancer** Cells rapidly grow and stay in one place localised cancerous tumours

Invasive cancer Cells secrete chemical, invade normal tissue and enter blood and lymph

Metastasis Metastases form at distant sites

Genetically mutated epithelial cell

Epithelium (Normal epithelium)

Early stage of tumor genesis

Blood vessel

Metastasis
- Invasion
- Intravasation
- Dissemination
- Extravasation
- Colonisation

Structure of HIV

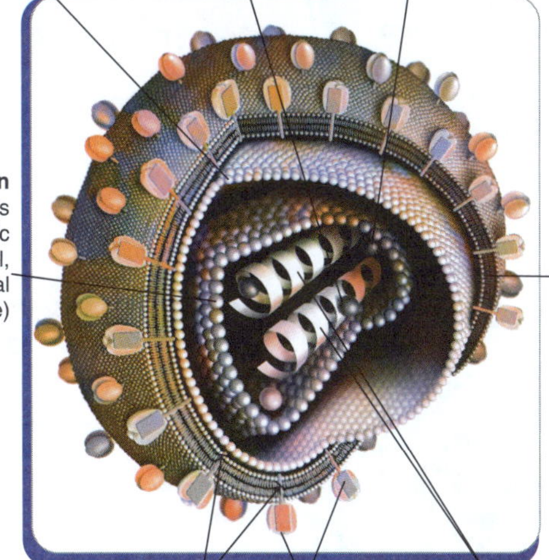

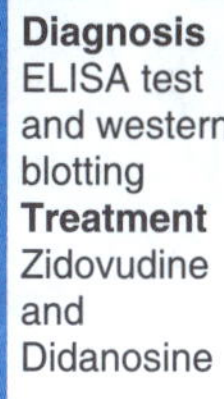

Disorder of cell mediated immune system. **Causative agent** Human immunodeficiency virus (HIV); Reduces number of helper T-cells.

Incubation period 6 months-10 years **Symptoms** Fever, lethargy, nausea. headaches, rashes, etc.

Diagnosis ELISA test and western blotting **Treatment** Zidovudine and Didanosine

AIDS (Acquired Immuno Deficiency Syndrome)

Replication of Retrovirus

1. **Binding** HIV to receptors.
2. **Fusion** of HIV envelope and the CD4 cell membrane.
3. **Reverse Transcription** Convert HIV RNA-into HIV DNA.
4. **Integration** secretion of an HIV enzyme (integrase) to insert its viral DNA into the CD4 cell.
5. **Replication** begins to make long chains of HIV proteins.
6. **Assembing** of New HIV proteins and HIV RNA into immature (non-infectious) HIV.
7. **Budding** Newly formed HIV releases, protease which breaks up the long protein chains in the immature virus, creating the mature (infectious) virus.

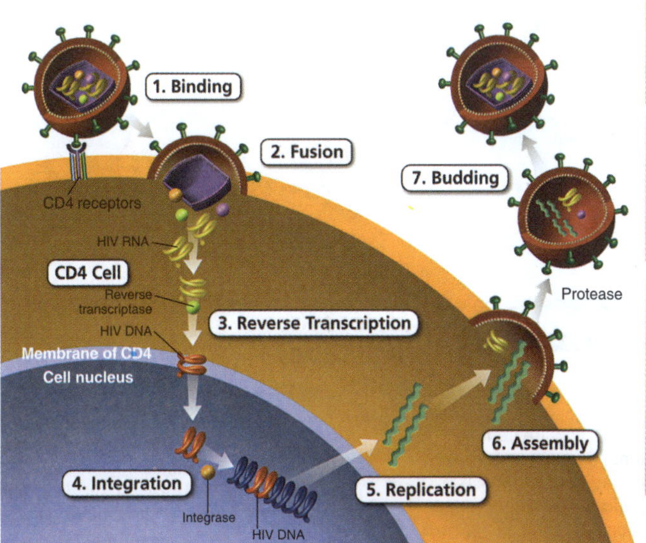

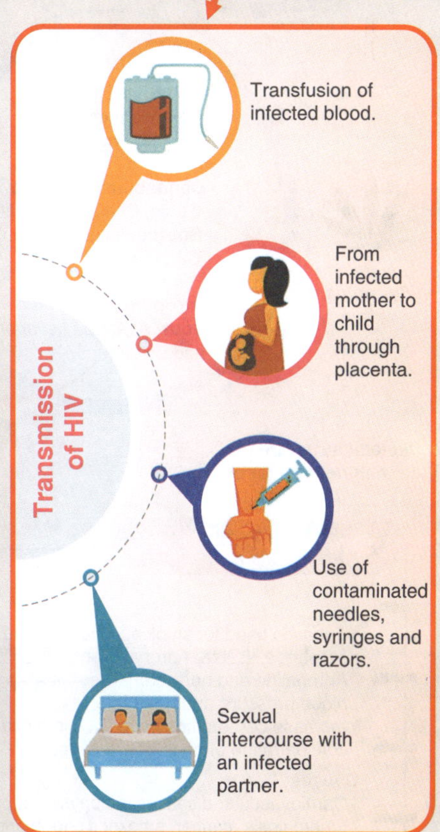

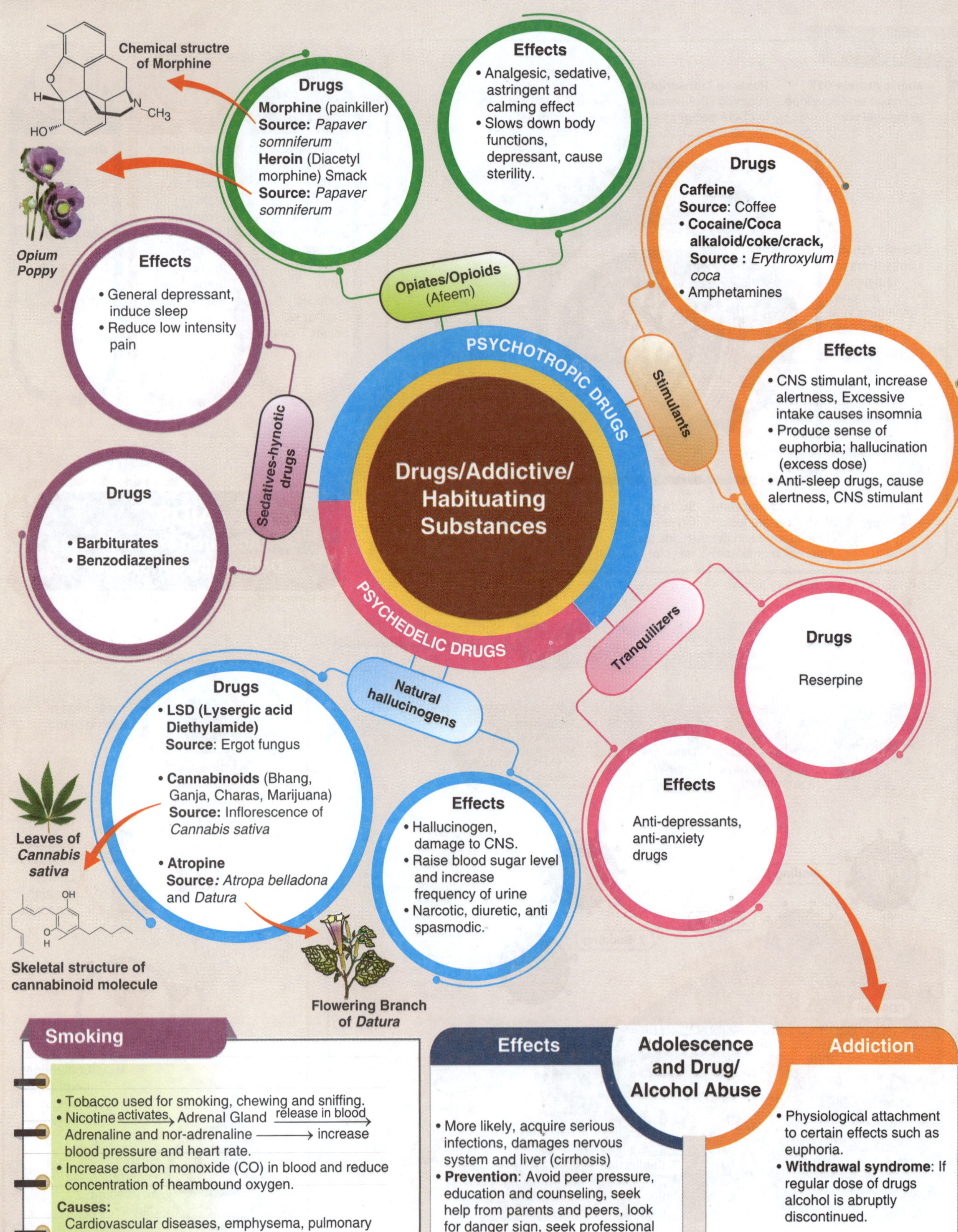

Smoking

- Tobacco used for smoking, chewing and sniffing.
- Nicotine $\xrightarrow{\text{activates}}$ Adrenal Gland $\xrightarrow{\text{release in blood}}$ Adrenaline and nor-adrenaline $\longrightarrow$ increase blood pressure and heart rate.
- Increase carbon monoxide (CO) in blood and reduce concentration of heambound oxygen.

Causes:
Cardiovascular diseases, emphysema, pulmonary tuberculosis, cancer, smoker's cough and bronchitis.

Adolescence and Drug/ Alcohol Abuse

Effects

- More likely, acquire serious infections, damages nervous system and liver (cirrhosis)
- **Prevention**: Avoid peer pressure, education and counseling, seek help from parents and peers, look for danger sign, seek professional and medical help.

Addiction

- Physiological attachment to certain effects such as euphoria.
- **Withdrawal syndrome**: If regular dose of drugs alcohol is abruptly discontinued.

Chapter 27 Microbes in Human Welfare

Curd

- Prepared by action of *Lactobacillus*, Lactic Acid Bacteria (LAB).
- Lactase enzyme produced by LAB coagulate and partially digest the milk proteins.
- Improves nutritional quality by increasing vitamin-B_{12}.
- LAB plays beneficial role in checking the growth of disease causing microbes in our stomach.

Cheese

- Formed by coagulation of the milk protein, **casein.**
- Large holes in **Swiss cheese,** due to the production of large amount of CO_2 by *Propionibacterium shermanii*
- **Roquefort cheese** Ripened by growing *Penicillium roqueforti*, gives particular taste.

Bread

- *Saccharomyces cerevisiae* (baker's yeast) used in baking bread.
- Converts sugar present in dough into CO_2.
- Yeast acts as a leavening agent by secreting enzymes, such as amylase, maltase and zymase.

Household Products

Idli, Dosa, Uttapam

- Fermentation of rice and black gram in the presence of air by *Leuconostoc* and *Streptococcus*
- CO_2 produced during fermentation causes puffing up of the dough.

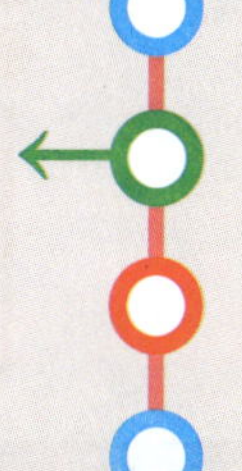

- Toddy traditional, refreshing drink made by fermentation of sap of palms (South India).

Other Foods

- Tempeh (Indonesia), Tofu (Japanese) and Sufu (Chinese) are fermented food obtained from soybeans.
- ***Tender bamboo*** shoots are used as vegetable (after fermentation).
- Sausages are prepared by fermentation and curing of meat.

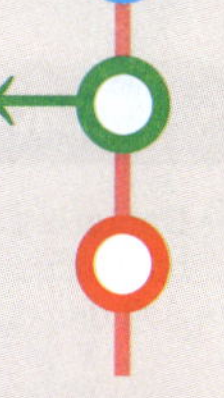

Industrial Products

Microbes as

(Household and Industrial Products, Antibiotics, Organic Acids Production, Bioactive Molecules)

Fermented beverages, their sources and alcohol content

	Beverages	Sources	Alcoholic contents
Without distillation	Beer	Barley malt	3-6%
Without distillation	Wine	Grapes	9-12%
With distillation	Gin	Rye	40%
With distillation	Rum	Molasses of sugarcane	40%
With distillation	Whisky	Fermented cereals	50%
With distillation	Vodka	Potato	60-80%
With distillation	Brandy	Fruit juices	60-70%

Bioreactors/Fermentors:

- Production on an industrial scale, requires growing microbes in very large vessels.

Alcoholic fermentation

- Involves *Saccharomyces cerevisiae* (brewer's yeast).
- Sugar is inoculated with a pure culture of yeast.

$$C_6H_{12}O_6 + \text{Yeast} \longrightarrow 2C_2H_5OH + CO_2 + \text{Energy}$$

- Different types of alcoholic drinks are produced depending on the types of raw materials used and type of processing.

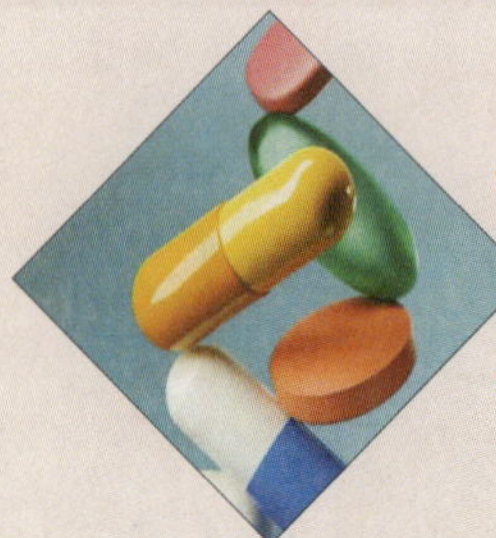

Antibiotics

- Kill or retard the growth of harmful microbes.

- **Penicillin** was the first antibiotic to be discovered.
- It was discovered by Alexander Fleming from *Penicillium notatum* mould.
- **Fleming**, **Chain** and **Florey** were awarded Nobel prize in 1945 for their discovery.

Steps involved in the Production of Antibiotics

Step 01
Suitable strain of microorganism is cultivated on a sterilised nutrient medium provided with optimum pH, aeration, temperature, antifoaming agent and antibiotic precursor.

Step 02
When sufficient antibiotic has diffused into medium, the microorganism is separated.

Step 03
The antibiotic is extracted from medium by precipitation, absorption or solvent.

Step 04
Finally the antibiotic is purified, concentrated and bioassayed before packing.

Organic Acids Production

Lactic acid
- **Bacteria** *Lactobacillus bulgaricus*
- Soft drinks, pickles

Citric acid
- **Fungus** *Aspergillus niger*
- Natural preservative for food.

Butyric acid
- **Bacteria** *Clostridium acetobutylicum*
- Preparation of butyrate esters, food and perfume additives

Acetic acid
- **Bacteria** *Acetobacter aceti*
- **Uses :** Vinegar

Enzyme Production

Enzymes	Microorganisms	Uses
Protease	*Bacillus licheniformis*, *Aspergillus* sp.	In detergents to digest protein present in stains, clearing of fruit juices
Lipase	*Candida lipolytica*, *Geotrichum candidum.*	In detergents for digestion of lipids present in stains.
Amylase	*Aspergillus* sp.	Detergents to digests starch present in stains; in baking
Pectinase	*Aspergillus niger*	Pectin hydrolysis in fruit juices, retting of fibre.
Streptokinase	*Streptococcus* sp.	Clearing blood clots inside the blood vessels.

Bioactive Molecules

Cylclosporin-A
- Produced by *Trichoderma polysporum* (fungus)
- Immunosuppressive agent-organ transplant patients.

Statins
- Produced by *Monascus purpureus* (yeast).
- Blood cholesterol lowering agent-inhibit cholesterol synthesising enzyme.

Sewage Treatment

Microbes in Sewage Treatment

Treatment of wastewater done by heterotrophic microbes.

Primary Treatment

Filtration: Removal of floating particles (debris) by sequential filtration.

Sedimentation: Grit settle down (primary sludge) and supernatant form **effluent**.

Secondary Treatment/ Biological Treatment

- Primary effluent passed to **aeration tanks**.
- Growth of aerobic microbes into **flocs**.

- Effluent digestion by microbes and reduces BOD.
- Effluent passed into a settling tank, flocs sediment (activated sludge).

- Activated sludge as inoculum, pumped back into aeration tank.
- Remaining part is pumped into **anaerobic sludge digesters**.

- Anaerobic bacteria organic matter and aerobic microbes in sludge.
- Produce a mixture of gases, CH_4, H_2S and CO_2.

Tertiary Treatment

Treat effluent before discharged to the environment.

Reduces phosphorus and ammoniacal nitrogen, removes chlorine

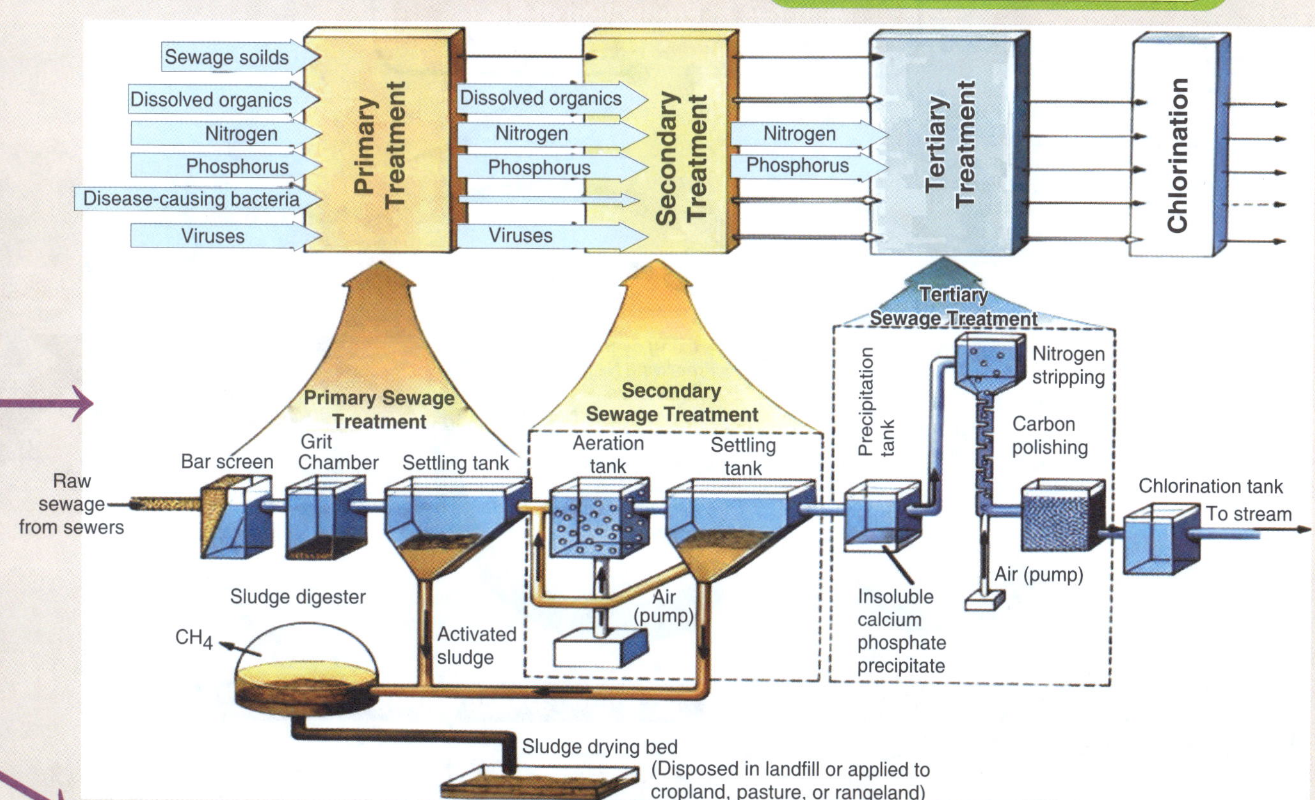

River Action Plan

Ministry of Environment and Forests initiated development of sewage treatment plants.

Aim: Protect the major rivers of India from sewage pollution.

Ganga Action Plan (GAP), **Yamuna Action Plan**, (YAP) Sutlej Action Plan, Gomti Action Plan, etc.

NEET POWER TIPS

- Flocs is masses of bacteria associated with fungal filaments to form mesh like structures.
- **BOD** (Biochemical Oxygen Demand) refers to the amount of the O_2 consumed when all the organic matter in 1L of water is oxidised by bacteria.

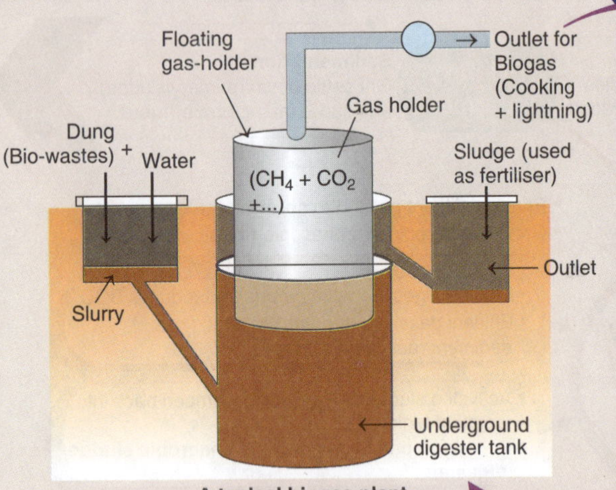

Floating gas-holder
Outlet for Biogas (Cooking + lightning)
Gas holder
Dung (Bio-wastes) + Water
($CH_4 + CO_2$ +...)
Sludge (used as fertiliser)
Outlet
Slurry
Underground digester tank

A typical biogas plant

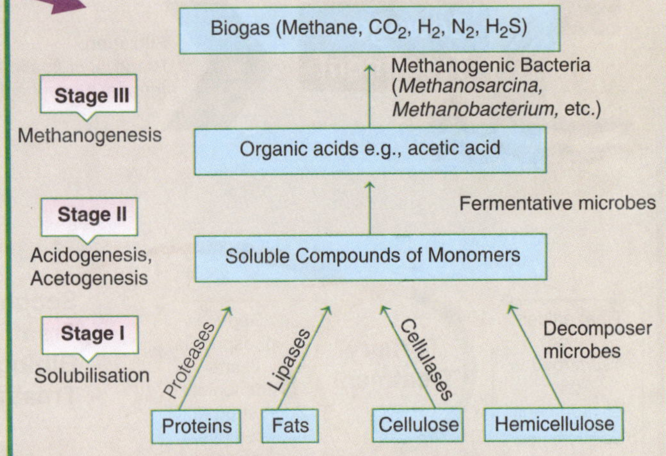

Stage	Process
Stage III Methanogenesis	Organic acids e.g., acetic acid → (Methanogenic Bacteria (*Methanosarcina, Methanobacterium,* etc.)) → Biogas (Methane, CO_2, H_2, N_2, H_2S)
Stage II Acidogenesis, Acetogenesis	Soluble Compounds of Monomers → (Fermentative microbes) → Organic acids e.g., acetic acid
Stage I Solubilisation	Proteins (Proteases), Fats (Lipases), Cellulose (Cellulases), Hemicellulose (Decomposer microbes) → Soluble Compounds of Monomers

Stages in Production of Biogas

Microbes in Production of Biogas

Microbes in Agriculture

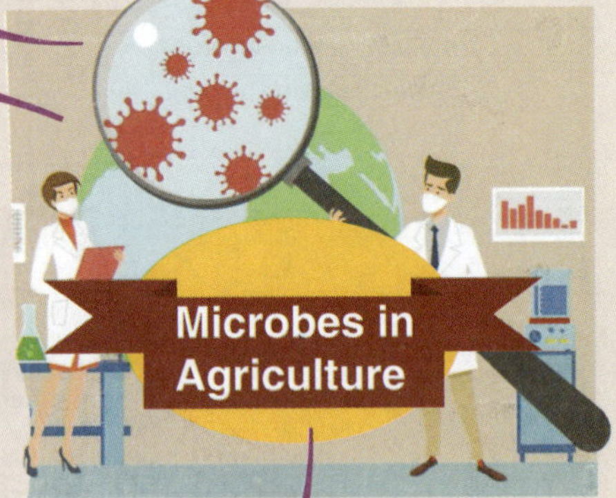

Biofertilisers

N_2 fixing bacteria
- Symbiotic N_2 fixing bacteria. e.g. *Rhizobium* in roots of leguminous plants.
- Free-living N_2 fixing bacteria, e.g., *Azotobacter, Bacillus, Clostridium, Beijerinckia*, etc.
- N_2 fixing Actinomycetes, e.g. *Alder, Frankia, Purshia*, etc.

N_2 fixing cyanobacteria
- Free living N_2 fixing cyanobacteria e.g. *Anabaena, Nostoc, Aulosira*, etc.
- Symbiotic N_2 fixing cyanobacteria e.g. cycad roots, lichens, liverworts, *Azolla*.

Mycorrhiza
Mutualistic association of fungus *Glomus* sp. and higher plant roots; absorb phosphorus from soil.

NEET POWER TIPS

- **Biogas**: Mixture of gases (predominantly CH_4)
- **Methanogens** Produces CH_4 along with CO_2 and H_2; found in anaerobic sludge; present in rumen of cattle.
- **Technology of Biogas Production**: Indian Agriculture Reseasch Institute (IARI) and Khadi and Village Industries Commission (KVIC).
- *Nucleopolyhedrovirus* are excellent candidates for species-specific, narrow insecticidal applications.

Biocontrol Agents

Biopesticides
Natural or biological agents, i.e. animals, plants, bacteria, viruses, fungi, etc.

Bioherbicide
Organism controls or destroys unwanted plant growth, i.e. *Alternaria*.

Bioinsecticides
Used to control harmful insects.

- Ladybird and dragonflies to get rid of aphids and mosquitoes.
- Baculovirus attack insect pests.
- *Trichoderma* controls several plant pathogens.
- *Bacillus thuringiensis* to control butterfly caterpillars.

Chapter 28 Biotechnology: Principles and Processes

Principles of Biotechnology

Core Techniques

Genetic Engineering
- Change genetic makeup.
- Modifies the host's phenotype

Bioprocess Engineering
- Grow only desired microbes
- Ensures protection of product (e.g. antibiotics, enzymes, etc.) from contamination.

Biotechnology

NEET POWER TIPS

- Defined by EFB as, "the integration of natural science and organisms, cells, parts thereof and molecular analogues for products and services."
- **Recombinant DNA:** Desired gene + Vector (gene taxi)
- First recombinant DNA, produced by **Stanley cohen** and **Herbert boyer** in 1972, by isolating antibiotic resistance gene from plasmid of *Salmonella typhimurium*.
- ***Hind* II** recognition sequence- 6 base pairs (GAATTC).
- **Endonucleases** break phosphodiester bond slightly away from their restriction site.
- Vector and source DNA need to be cut with the same restriction enzyme to form a recombinant vector.
- **Plasmid** is an extra-chromosomal, self-replicating, circular, *ds*DNA found in prokaryotes, without histone protein.

Steps of Genetic Engineering

A Identification of DNA with Desirable Gene
- **Traditional hybridisation** Inclusion and multiplication of undesirable genes along with desired gene.
- **Genetic engineering** Inclusion and multiplication of only desired genes.

B Introduction of Identified DNA (Alien DNA) into the Host

Using vector DNA such as plasmid.

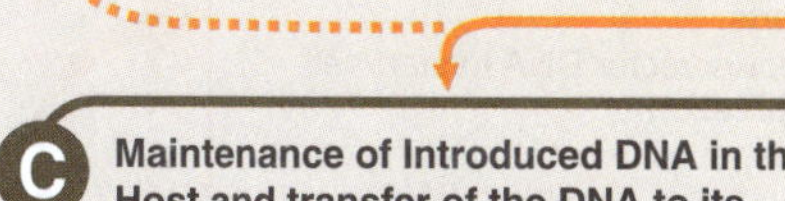

C Maintenance of Introduced DNA in the Host and transfer of the DNA to its Progeny
- Alien DNA → no *ori* (origin of replication) cannot multiply itself.
- Alien DNA recipient genome (with *ori*) → multiplies itself.

Tools of RDT

Restriction Enzymes (Molecular Scissors)

- Belongs to nuclease group
- Cut DNA at specific sites into fragments.
- *Hind* II, is first restriction enzyme extracted from *Haemophilus influenzae*.

- More than 900 restriction enzymes isolated from 230 strains of bacteria.
- **Nomenclature:**

Genus → ***Eco*** **RI** → Order of isolation

Genus ↓ *Escherichia*; Species ↓ *coli*; Strain ↓ RY13; Order of isolation ↓ First

Sticky / Overhanging / Staggering ends produced by enzymes like *Eco*RI, form hydrogen bonds with their complementary cut counterparts; stickiness facilitate action of enzyme DNA ligase. **Blunt / even ends** produced by *Sma*I, *Hind* III, *Eco*RV.

Two types of nuclease enzymes : Endonucleases Cut at specific position within the DNA. It acts on palindromic sequences. **Exonucleases** Remove nucleotides from end of DNA.

Separation and Isolation of DNA fragments

Technique Gel electrophoresis.

Principle Separation of DNA on gel according to their size when electric field is applied.

Agarose Produce sieving effect on DNA.

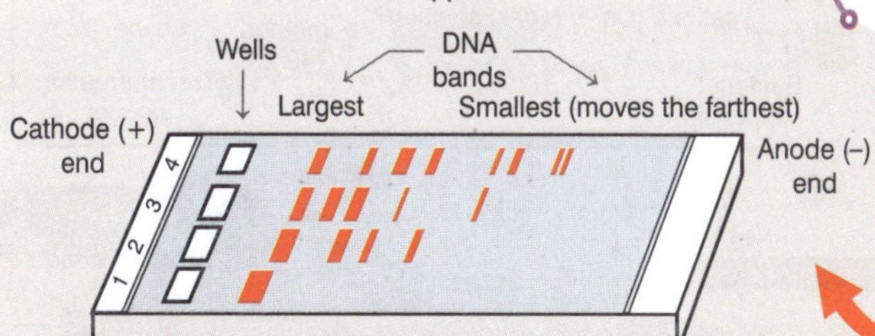

A typical agarose gel electrophoresis showing migration of undigested (lane 1) and digested set of DNA fragments (lane 2 to 4)

DNA fragment at Anode (-) end → **Ethidium Bromide** (EtBr) staining → **Orange DNA bands** → **Elution** (Separation of DNA fragments from gel) → **Desired DNA fragment**

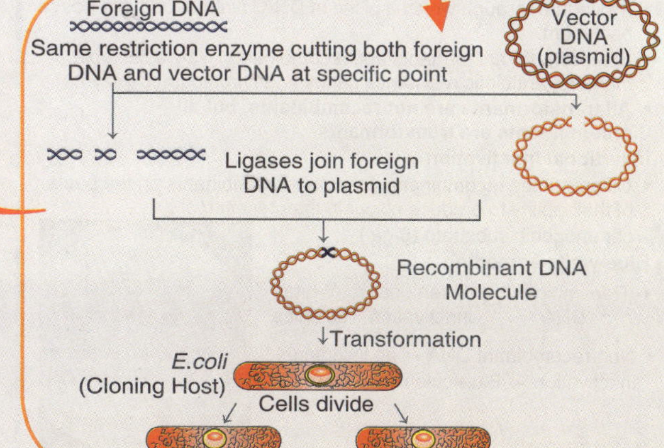

Diagrammatic representation of Recombinant DNA technology

pBR322 (*E.coli* cloning vector)

- **Nomenclature** p-plasmid, B-Boliver, R-Rodriguez, 322-order of synthesis.

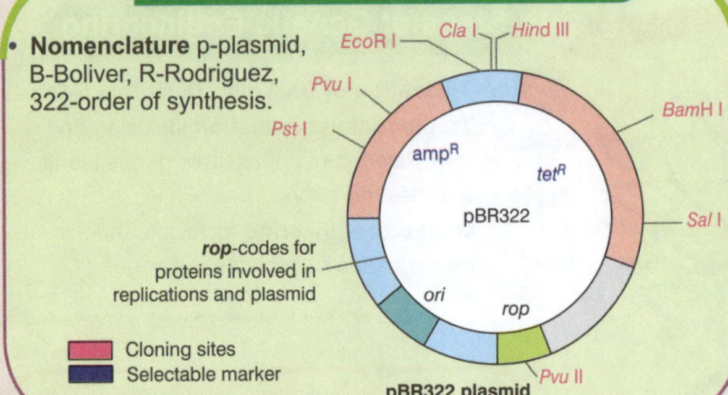

Retroviruses

Disarmed forms used as vectors to deliver desirable genes into animals cells

Cloning/Restriction sites

- Preference of single recognition site for a restriction enzyme within a vector.
- Ligation of gene of interest done at restriction site present in one of the antibiotic resistant genes.

Origin of replication (*ori*)

- Sequence from where replication starts.
- Allows vector DNA to start self-replication.
- Responsible for controlling copy number of the linked DNA.

NEET POWER TIPS

Properties of good vector

- Replicate autonomously
- Able to deliver gene into host cell
- Small size
- High copy number
- Easy to isolate and purify
- Suitable selectable marker
- Unique target site for restriction enzymes

Cloning Vector (Vehicle to deliver foreign DNA into the host cell)

Ti plasmid (Tumor inducing plasmid) (Help in cell division)

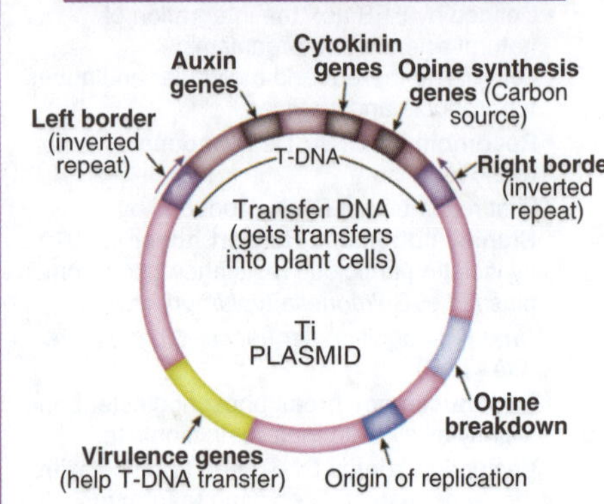

- Naturally transferred from *Agrobacterium tumefaciens* to plant cells. Can also enter other eukaryotes cells like yeast, fungi, etc.
- **Disarmed Ti plasmid** (not pathogenic) used to deliver gene of interest into plants.

Selectable Markers

- Allows the selection of transformants from non-transformants.
- E.g., Antibiotic resistant genes (Tet^R, Amp^R etc.) and chromogenic enzyme (β-galactosidase)

Transformation

- Procedure through which a piece of DNA is introduced in a host bacterium.
- Selection of transformants and recombinants → by selectable markers (antibiotic resistance genes and chromogenic enzyme).
- **All transformants are not recombinants, but all recombinants are transformants.**

Insertional inactivation

- Differentiates recombinants from non-recombinants on the basis of their ability to produce colour in the presence of a chromogenic substrate (β-gal).

Blue-white screening

- Recombinant DNA → Insertional inactivation → White colonies
- Non-recombinant DNA → no insertional inactivation → Blue-colonies

blue-white colonies

Competent Host (For transformation with Recombinant DNA)

- DNA (hydrophilic) cannot pass through cell membrane, thus needs to be made competent for transformation.

For Bacterial cell

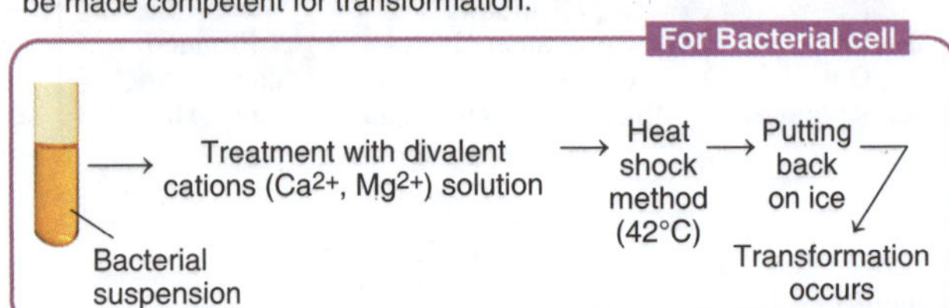

Methods of Transformation

For Animal cell

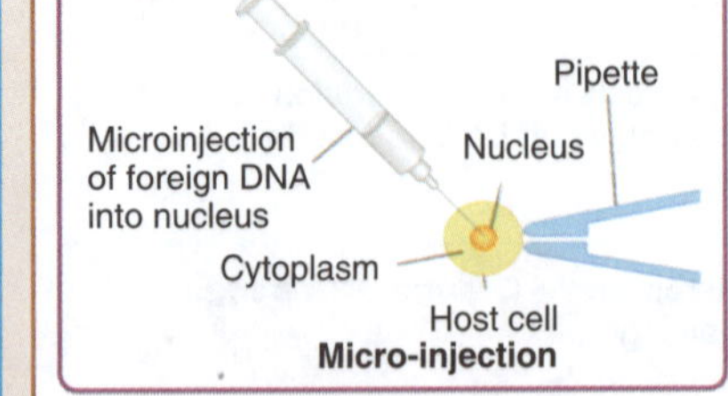

Micro-injection

- Use of **'disarmed pathogen'** vectors to infect the cell and transfer the *r*DNA into the host.

For Plant cell

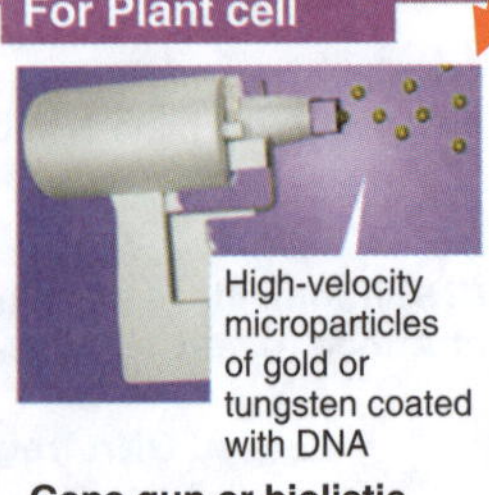

High-velocity microparticles of gold or tungsten coated with DNA

Gene gun or biolistic

01

- Isolation of the genetic material.
- This include digestion of membranes enclosing DNA.
- Membranes and their digesting enzymes are as follows
  - For plasma membrane (lipid bilayer): Lipase
  - For RNA: RNAse; For proteins: Protease
  - For cell wall
    Bacteria (Peptidoglycan) → Lysozyme
    Fungal (Chitin) → Chitinase
    Plant (cellulose) → Cellulase.

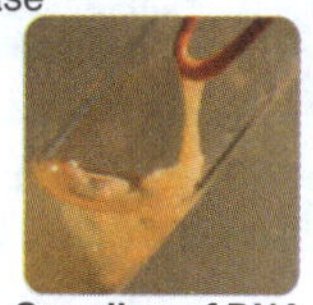
Spooling of DNA

02

Cutting of DNA at specific locations, by restriction enzymes at optimal condition

03

Isolation of desired DNA fragment by Agarose Gel electrophoresis

04

Amplification of the gene of interest using Polymerase chain Reaction (PCR).

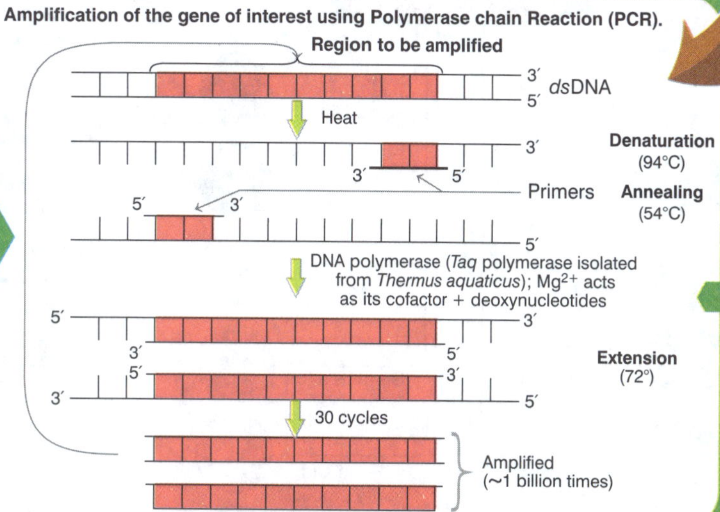

05

Ligation of DNA fragment into a vector using DNA ligase enzyme

06

Transferring the Recombinant DNA into host cell by making host cell competent followed by transfer of desired gene.

07

Culturing the host cells in a medium at large scale (Bioreactors / Fermenters)
Using sterile condition, optimum nutrition, temperature condition, proper O_2 supply.

Two types of Bioreactors

Acid/Base for pH control
Motor
Foam breaker
Flat bladed impeller
Culture broth
Steam (for sterilisation)
Sterile air

(a) Simple stirred tank bioreactor

Bubbles/dramatically increase the oxygen transfer area

Increased surface area for oxygen transfer
Gas entrain-ment

(b) Sparged stirred-tank bioreactor

08

Downstream Processing

- Separation and purification of the desired product from bioreactor.
- Formulations of preservatives and strict quality control testing, (that varies from product to product).

NEET POWER TIPS

- PCR, discovered by **Kary Mullis**.
- Number of DNA copies upon *n* number of PCR cycle = 2^n.
- **Applications** Forensics, diagnosis of diseases, checking mutation, DNA fingerprinting, evolutionary studies.

Components of Bioreactor Agitator system, oxygen delivery system, a foam control system, a temperature control system, pH control system and sampling ports.

Type of Batches in Bioreactor's are as follows

- **Closed Batch–** Nutrient and sample added once; product extracted once
- **Open / Continuous Batch–** Nutrition, samples continuously added, product extracted continuously.
- **Fed Batch–** Nutrient and sample added to once; products extracted at regular interval.

Chapter 29

Biotechnology and Its Application

Biotechnology

Research Areas of Biotechnology

- Providing best catalyst (microbe or pure enzyme)
- Creating optimal condition for catalyst
- Downstream process to purify protein

Types of Biotechnology

- **Red biotechnology:** Medical processes, e.g., antibiotic production
- **White biotechnology:** Industrial processes
- **Green biotechnology:** Agricultural processes
- **Grey biotechnology:** Environmental applications
- **Blue biotechnology:** Exploitation of sea resources.

Applications of Biotechnology

Vaccines

Antibiotics

Vitamins

Alcoholic and non-alcoholic beverages

Monoclonal antibodies

Tissue culture

Agriculture

Biofertilisers

Organic acids

Steroids and Hormones

Food and dairy product

Genetic engineering

Biotechnological Application in Agriculture

- Three options for increasing food production
  - Agrochemical based agriculture
  - Organic agriculture
  - Genetically engineered crop-based agriculture

NEET POWER TIPS

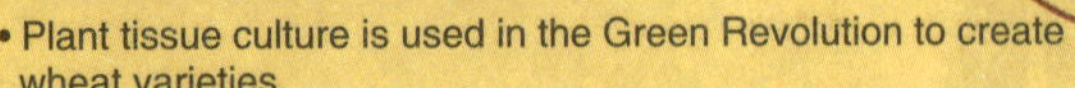

- Plant tissue culture is used in the Green Revolution to create wheat varieties.
- **Micro-propagation:** Produce thousand of plants.
- **Somaclones:** Plants grown are genetically identical to the original plant.
- **Meristem:** Apical or axillary (free of virus.)

Somatic Hybridisation

- Process of producing somatic hybrids.
- **Somatic hybrid:** Fusion of somatic cells of two varieties.
- **Pomato:** First intergeneric somatic hybrid; fusion of protoplasm (tomato and potato).
- **Steps:** Isolation of naked protoplast (cellulase and pectinases) and fusion of protoplast (PEG).

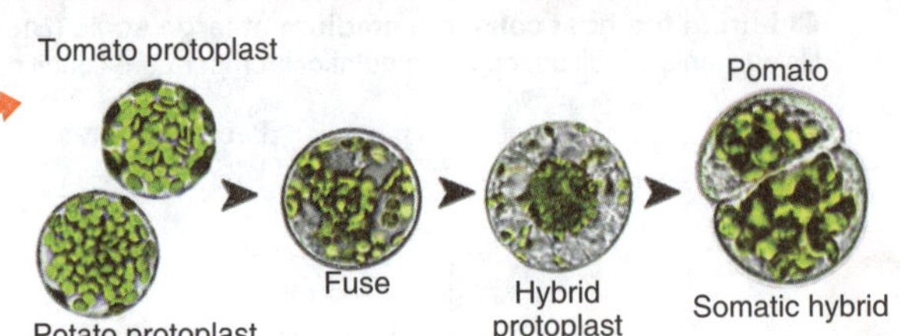

Procedure of Plant Tissue Culture

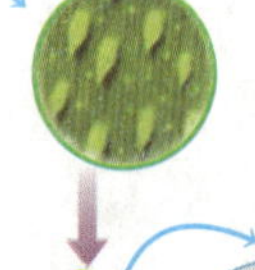

1. **Initiation stage**
   Explant grown in a special nutrient media.
2. **Multiplication stage**
   Multiplication of tissue through repeated subcultures

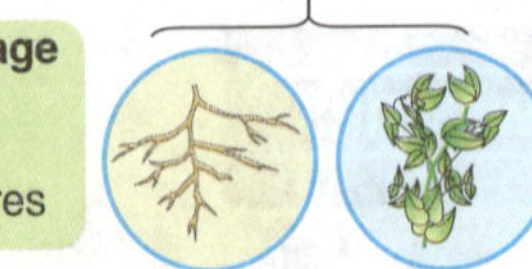

Undifferentiated callus formed

3. **Root and shoot formation**
   Root and shoot emerged from explants due to totipotency.

4. **Acclimatisation**
   The plant is transferred into a greenhouses for development.

5. Plant is transferred to a nursery.

Production of Transgenic Plant

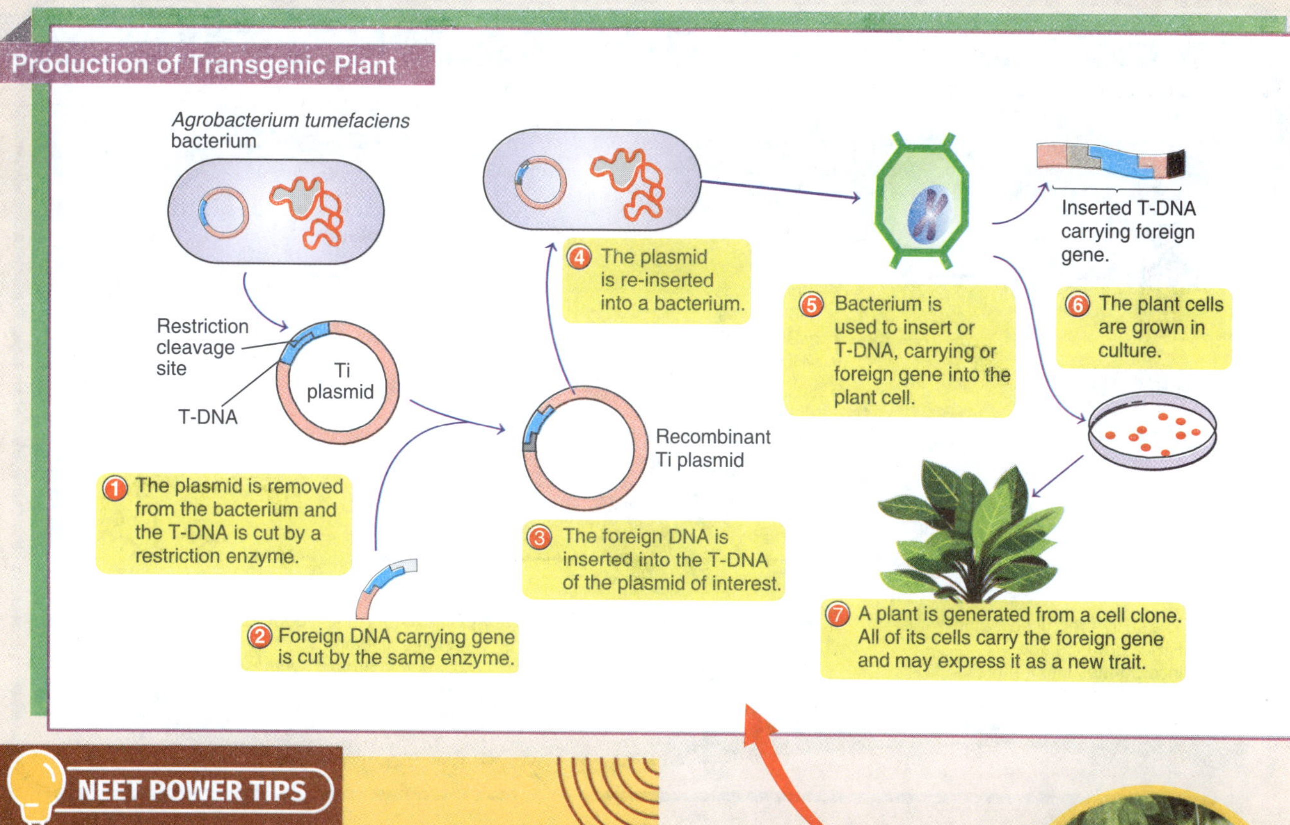

Genetically Modified Organisms (GMOs)

- Importance of GMOs
  - Developing tolerance to abiotic stresses.
  - Pest resistant crops.
  - Reduce post harvest losses.
  - Increase efficiency of mineral usage by plants.
  - Enhance nutritional value of food (golden rice).
- Some strains of *Bacillus thuringiensis* produce proteins that kill certain insects such as lepidopterans (tobacco budworms, armyworm), coleopterans (beetles) and dipterans (flies and mosquitoes).
- *Bt* tobacco was first cultured to kill hornworm (*Manduca sexta*).

GMO for Insect Resistance in Plants

- Toxin is coded by *cry* gene.
- Cotton bollworms controlled by *cryIAc* and *cryIIAb*.
- Corn borer controlled by *cryIAb*.

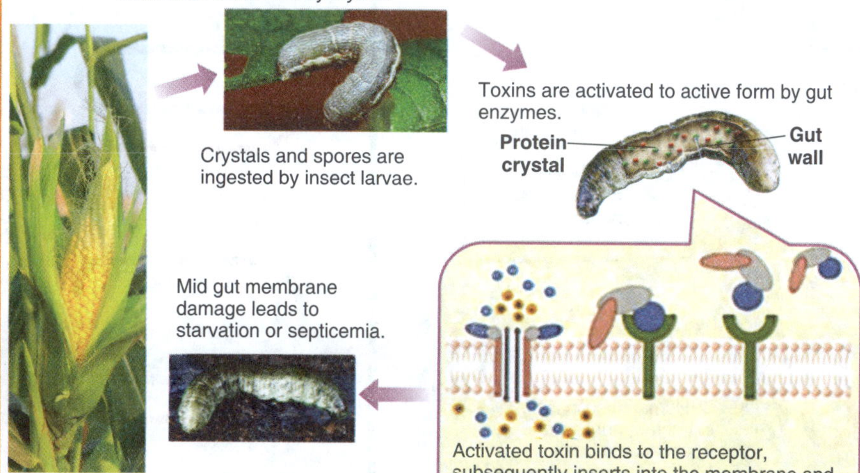

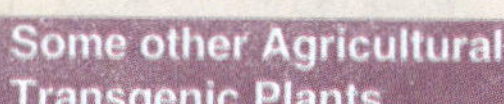

- *Hirudin* (protein) present in leech prevents blood clotting, is chemically synthesised in *Brassica napus* and extracted by downstream process.
- ***Flavr savr***, first transgenic variety of tomato *via* inactivation of polygalacturonase enzyme that prevents over-ripening and increases the shelf-life.
- **Golden rice**, a transgenic variety of rice (*Oryza sativa*) contains beta carotene (pro-vitamin), good source of vitamin-A.

Pest Resistance in Plants (RNAi Pathway)

Used to prevent the infestation of tobacco plants by nematode, *Meloidegyne incognita*.

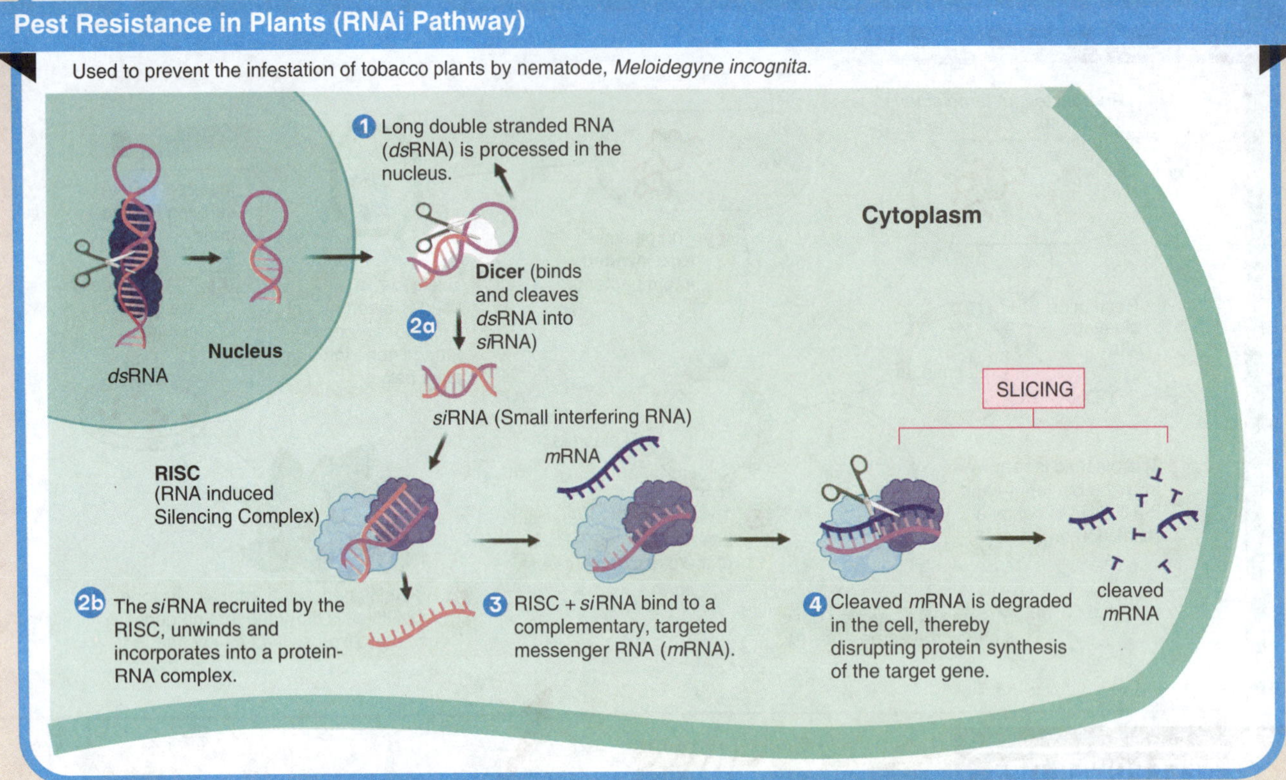

Vaccines

- Suspensions or killed or modified pathogenic microorganism.
- **Types of vaccines** Conventional vaccines, Purified antigen, Recombinant vaccines.

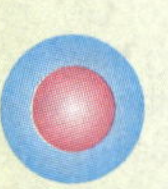
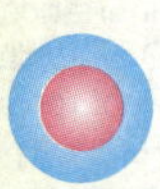

Genetically Engineered Insulin

- **Humulin:** Genetically engineered by **Eli Lilly** (1983).
- Insulin secreted by β-cells of islets of Langerhans.

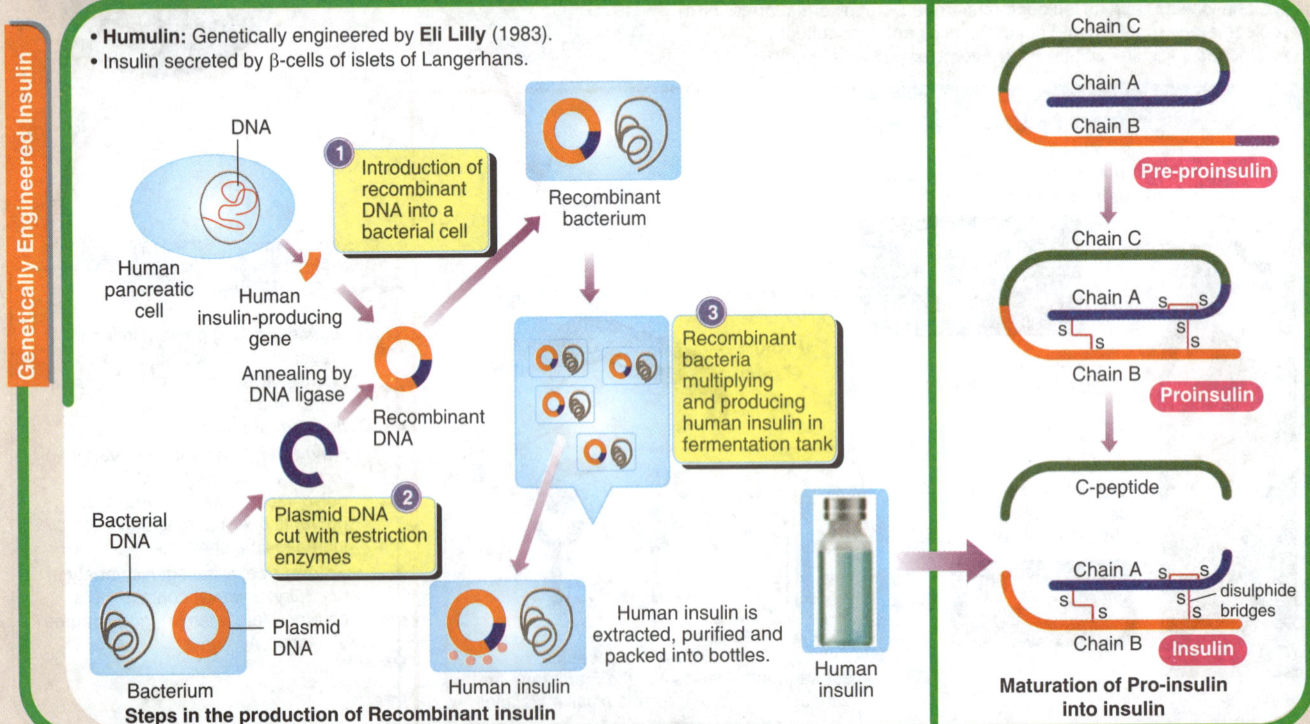

Gene Therapy

- Replace a faulty gene by a normal, healthy and functional gene.
- **SCID** (Severe Combined Immunodeficiency Disease)
- Performed on 4 year old girl with Adenosine Deaminase (ADA) deficiency in 1990.
- Caused by mutation (deletion) in the gene coding for enzyme Adenosine Deaminase (ADA).
- ADA enzyme provides immune response against invading pathogen.

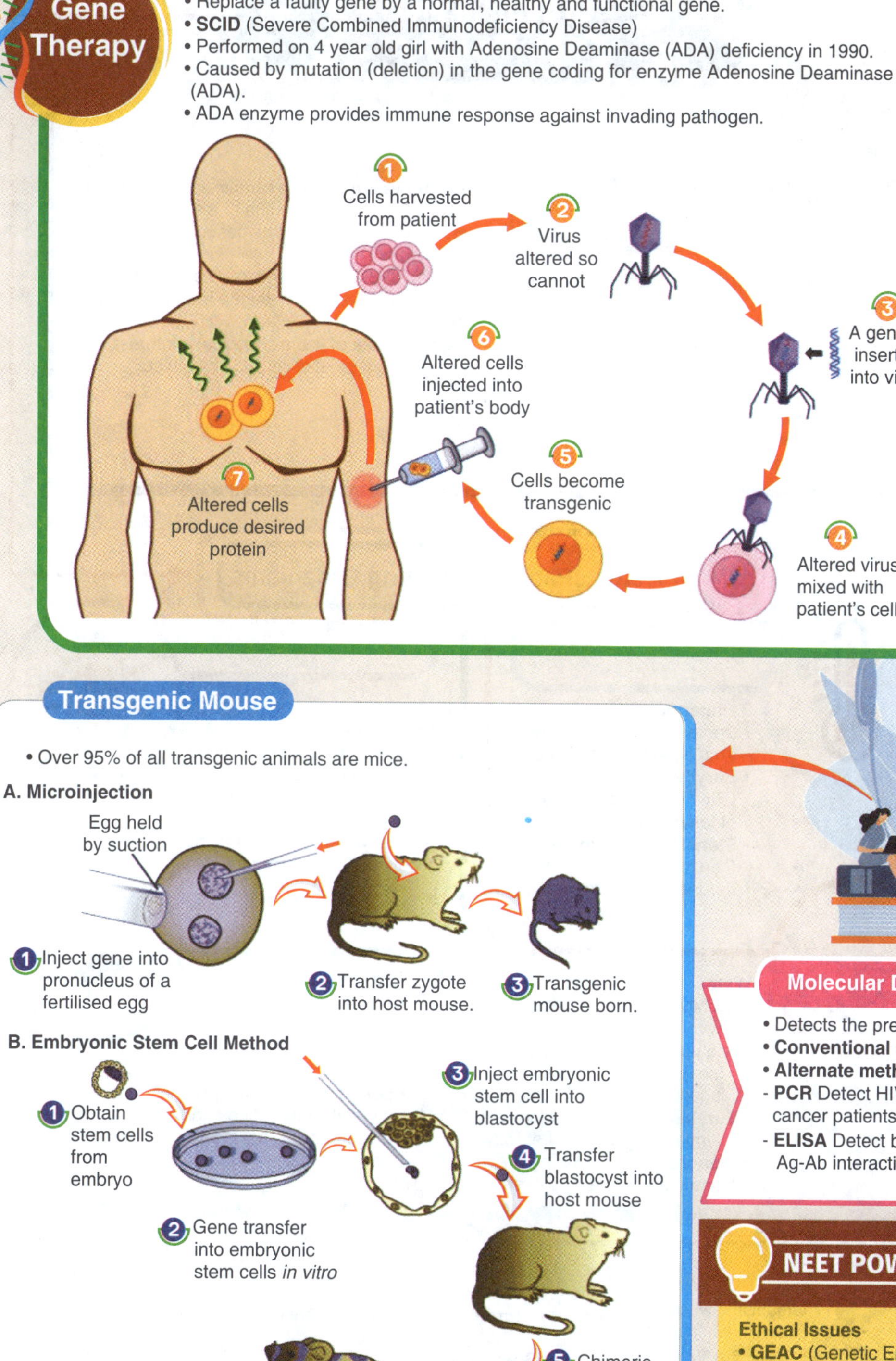

Transgenic Mouse

- Over 95% of all transgenic animals are mice.

Transgenic Animals

Benefits of Transgenic Animals

1. Study of normal, physiology and development, e.g., metabolism, blood cell production, etc.
2. Study of diseases, e.g., Cancer, cystic fibrosis, etc.
3. **Biological Products**
   - Human protein (α-1-antitrypsin) to treat emphysema.
   - Rosie (first transgenic cow) produced human protein-enriched milk (2.4 grams/litre)
4. **Vaccine safety** testing before human trial
5. **Chemical safety testing**, e.g., effects of toxic substances on organisms.

Molecular Diagnosis

- Detects the presence of pathogen.
- **Conventional methods** serum and urine analysis.
- **Alternate methods**
  - **PCR** Detect HIV, genetic mutations in suspected cancer patients, genetic disorders.
  - **ELISA** Detect by the presence of antigens; principle Ag-Ab interaction.

NEET POWER TIPS

Ethical Issues

- **GEAC** (Genetic Engineering Approval Committee): Make decisions regarding the validity of GM research and the safety of introducing GMO for public services, e.g., Basmati rice, turmeric, neem, etc.
- **Biopatent** Right granted by the government to an inventor to prevent others to make commercial use of one's invention.
- **Biopiracy** Use of bioresources by multinational companies and other organisation without proper authorisation from the countries and people concerned without compensatory payment.

Chapter 30 Organisms and Populations

Organism and Its Environment

Ecological Hierarchy

BIOSPHERE

BIOME

ECOSYSTEM

COMMUNITY

ORGANISM

Biomes

Mean annual temperature (°C): 30, 25, 20, 15, 10, 5, 0, -5, -10, -15

Mean annual precipitation (cm): 50, 100, 150, 200, 250, 300, 350, 400, 450

Desert; Grassland; Tropical forest; Temperate forest; Coniferous forest; Arctic and Alpine tundra

Biome distribution with respect to annual temperature and precipitation

- **Factors determining a biome**-annual variations in the intensity and duration of temperature.
- Increasing order of biomes based on their productivity
  Desert < Arctic and Alpine Tundra < Grassland < Coniferous forest < Temperate forest < Tropical forest
- **Major biomes of India :** Tropical rainforest, deciduous forest, Desert and sea coast.

Major Abiotic Factors Affecting Organisms

Temperature
- Decreases progressively from equator towards pole.
- **Eurythermal Organism** (can tolerate wide ranges of temperature)
- **Stenothermal Organism** (can tolerate narrow ranges of temperature)

Light
- **Effects of Light**
  Photosynthesis, productivity, photoperiodism, cues for foraging pattern in animals.
- Red algae inhabiting the deepest waters due to presence of phycoerythrin pigment.

Water
- Salinity ranges in aquatic environment
  - 5 ppt (inland water); 30-35 ppt (sea); > 100 ppt (hypersaline lagoons).
- **Euryhaline Organism** (can tolerate wide ranges of salinity)
- **Stenohaline Organism**(can tolerate narrow ranges of salinity)

Soil
- Properties of soil are determined by soil composition, grain size and aggregation.
- **Soil characteristics** pH, mineral composition and topography determine vegetation in any area.

Responses to Abiotic Factors

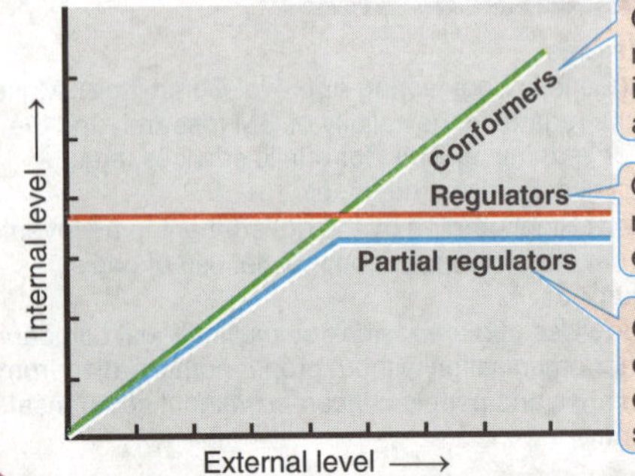

Conformers: Organisms who cannot maintain a constant internal environment, e.g. aquatic animals

Regulators: Organisms who can maintain their internal environment, e.g. mammals

Partial regulators: Organisms constant internal environment but up to a certain level, e.g. ground squirrel.

Alternative response for stressful conditions that are localised or remain for short duration.
- **Migrate:** Seasonal movement of animals from one habitat to another, e.g., birds
- **Suspend:** A period of dormancy

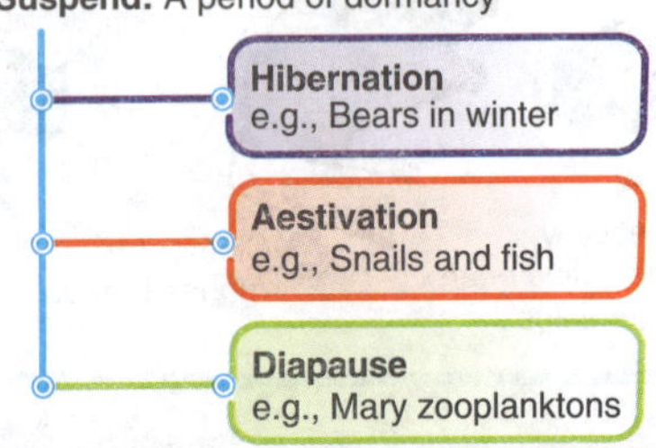

Adaptations in Organisms

Plants

Morphological Xerophytes- Thick cuticle on leaf surface, sunken stomata, flat green stem, leaves reduced to spines (e.g. *Opuntia*)

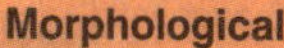

Morphological Hydrophytes- Large floating leaves,elongated petioles, reduced root system, presence of aerenchyma (e.g. water lily)

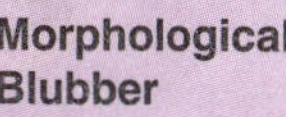

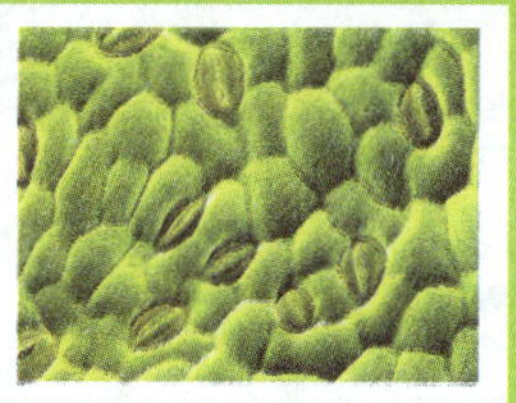

Physiological

- Plant growing is arid environments CAM pathway.
- e.g. Closure of stomata during day and exchange of gases during night.

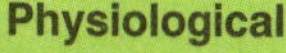

Biochemical

- Increase in antioxidants in plants upon stress.
- e.g. Decreased photosynthesis during water stress.

Behavioural

- Trapping of insects by venus flytrap
- Phototropism, geotropism in plants e.g., sunflower

Animals

Morphological e.g. Shorter ears and limbs of mammals in colder climates to minimise heat loss (Allen's rule)

Morphological Blubber Thick layer of fat under the skin of some animals e.g. polar seals.

Physiological e.g. Increase in RBCs during decrease in O_2 in humans to compensate altitude sickness

Biochemical

- Internal fat oxidation in some animals for water requirement, e.g. kangaroo.
- Desert animal excreting very concentrated urine to conserve water.

Behavioural Thermoregulation in desert animals during temperature change, e.g. desert lizards

Attributes of Population

Birth rate and Death rate

- **Birth rate**-per capita birth

Example

Drosophila

Original population = 20
Birth (after 1 week) = 8
Death (after 1 week) = 10

- **Death rate**-per capita death
  - **Birth rate**
    = Birth/Original population
    = 8/20 = 0.4 offsprings per housefly per week
  - **Death rate**
    = Death/Original population
    = 10/20 = 0.5 offsprings per housefly per week

Age Distribution

- Percent individuals of given age or age group
- **Age-Pyramid**-Plots the age distribution for a population

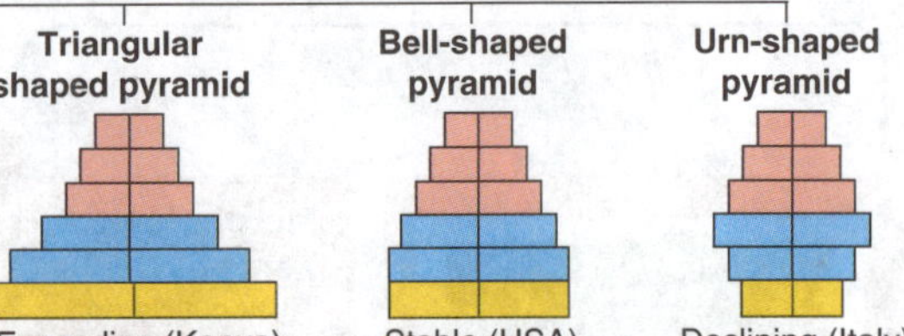

- **Demographic dividend** Occurs when working population is larger than non-working population; India's demographic dividend is expected to persist at least until 2055-56.

Sex Ratio

- Ratio of males to females in a population.
- Sex ratio Males/ Females = 50/100 or 50 males to 100 females
- Calculated as ratio of females to males in a population in India.

Population Density (N)

- Need not necessarily be measured in numbers only.
- When number of a species is less (due to its large size) in comparison to other species, percent biomass or cover should be used.
- When population is huge and counting is impossible, relative densities are used.
- Mostly estimate population sizes indirectly, e.g., tiger census involves counting based on pug marks and fecal pellets.

Population Growth

- Fluctuates due to changes in four basic processes: natality, mortality, immigration and emigration.

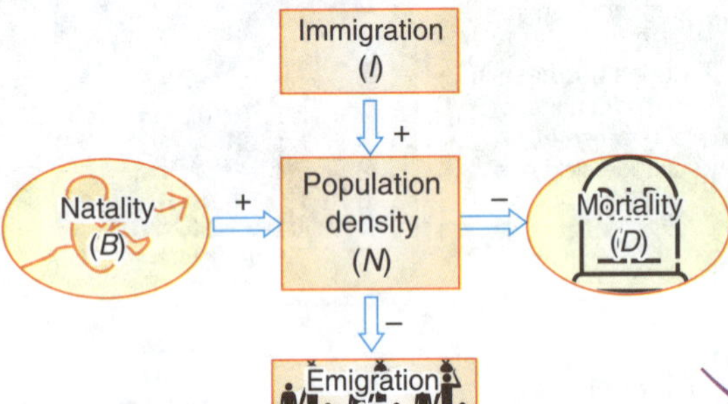

- If N is the population density at time t , then its density at time is at time t+1 is $N_{t+1} = N_t + [(B+I) - (D+E)]$

NEET POWER TIPS

- Under a particular set of selection pressures, organisms evolve towards the most efficient reproductive strategy.
- **Semelparity** Breeding only once in the lifetime and then dies, e.g. Pacific salmon fish, bamboo.
- **Iteroparity** Reproducing many time in the lifetime, e.g. most birds and mammals.

Growth Models

Population density (N) ⟶
Time (t) ⟶

$\frac{dN}{dt} = rN$ — a

K

Asymptote

b $\frac{dN}{dt} = rN\left(\frac{K-N}{K}\right)$

Deceleration

Acceleration

Exponential Growth
- Unlimited resources
- Unrestricted growth
- No competition
- J-shaped curve
- Less realistic

Logistic Growth
- Limited resources
- Restricted growth
- Competition present
- S-shaped curve
- More realistic

Life History Variation

K-selection (birds, mammals) — I

Mortality constant — II

r-selection (Oyster, pelagic fishes) — III

Number of survivors (log scale): 1,000; 100; 10; 1

Percentage of maximum life span: 0; 50; 100

r-selection:
- Large number of offsprings with small size
- Minimal parental care
- Short-life
- Fast reproduction

K-selection:
- Few number of offsprings with large size
- High level of parental care
- Long-life
- Good competitors

Survivorship curves of r and K-selected Species

COMPETITION (+, –)

- Occurs in closely related species (not always) wherein they share the same type of habitat and food resources.
- Interspecific competition-Potent force in organic evolution
- Few examples

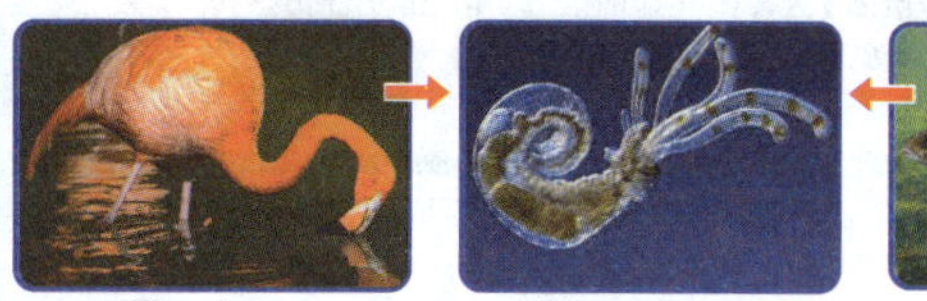

Flamingo Zooplankton Native fishes

An example of interspecific competition (not closely related) in American Lakes

Extinction of Abingdon tortoise in Galapagos islands after introduction of goats (Here, resources are not limiting factor)

- **Competitive Release** A species restricted to a small geographical area expands its distributional range dramatically on removal of a the competing species.

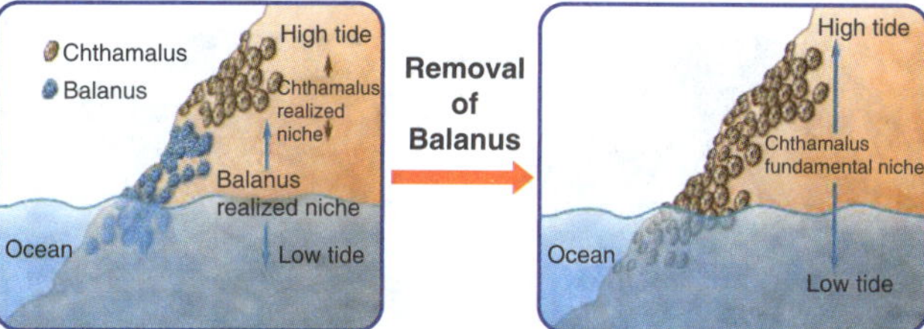

Connell's elegant Field Experiment on Barnacles

Gause's 'Competitive Exclusion Principle':
Two closely related species competing for the same resources cannot coexist indefinitely.

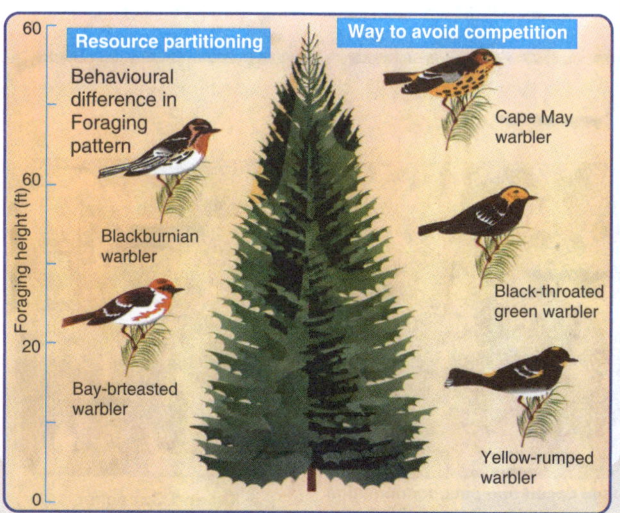

Concept of Resource Partitioning Explained by MacArthur

PREDATION (+, –)

- Feeding of lower trophic level organisms (prey) by organisms of higher trophic level (predator).
- **Role of Predators** Passage of energy transfer across trophic level; keeping prey population under control.

Prickly Pear cactus and prickly pear moth

Removal of *Pisaster* starfish led to extinction of more than 10 species of invertabrates

- **Defenses developed by prey against predators**

PLANTS

Cardiac glycosides produced by *Calotropis*

ANIMALS

Distasteful taste of Monarch butterfly due to chemical produced by it

Population Interactions
(Competition, Predation, Amensalism, Parasitism Commensalism, Mutualism)

AMENSALISM (–, 0)

- One organism harmed, other remains neutral.
- Few examples: Allelopathy by *Eucalyptus* plant (0) (inhibiting growth of other vegetation-near its base), inhibition of bacteria-by *Penicillium* (0).

Black walnut
(Release juglone from roots)

Penicillium
(Inhibits the growth of bacteria)

PARASITISM (+, –)

- One partner benefitted due to residing inside/outside the host body and getting shelter and nutrition, other harmed
- **Adaptations of Parasites**
  - Loss of unnecessary sense organs
  - Presence of adhesive organs or suckers
  - Loss of digestive system
  - High reproduction capacity
  - Having more than one intermediate hosts.

NEET POWER TIPS

- **Intraspecific interactions** Individuals of the same species cooperate or compete with each other.
- **Mimicry** is a defensive mechanism the includes deceiving the prey.
- **Protocooperation** is a non-obligatory relationship; both species are mutuauy benefited.

Types of Parasitism

Ectoparasitism

Cuscuta (+) on hedge plant (–)

Marine fish (–) infested with copepods (+)

Endoparasitism

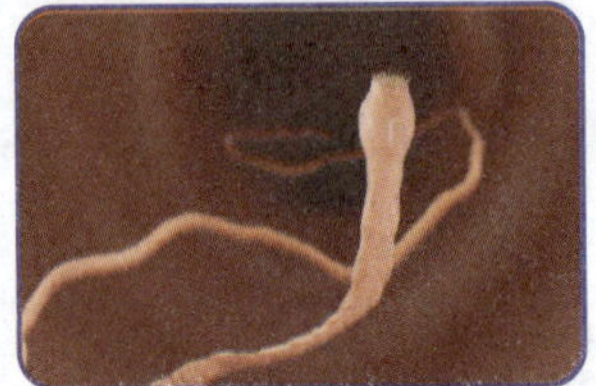

Tapeworm (+) in human intestine (–)

Brood parasitism

Cuckoo, (+) laying its eggs in crow's nest (–)

Commensalism (+, 0)

- One partner benefits, other neither benefits nor harmed
- **Few examples**

Clown fish (+) living among tentacles of sea anemone (0)

Cattle Egret (+) and grazing cattle (0)

Orchids (+) growing on mango (0)

Barnacles (+) on back of whale (0)

MUTUALISM (+, +)

- Both the partners benefits
- **Few examples**

Fig fruit and wasps

Lichen algae (+) fungi

Sexual deceit and pseudocopulation exhibited by *Ophrys* plant*

Ox and Oxpecker

*Not a true example of mutualism

Chapter 31

Ecosystem

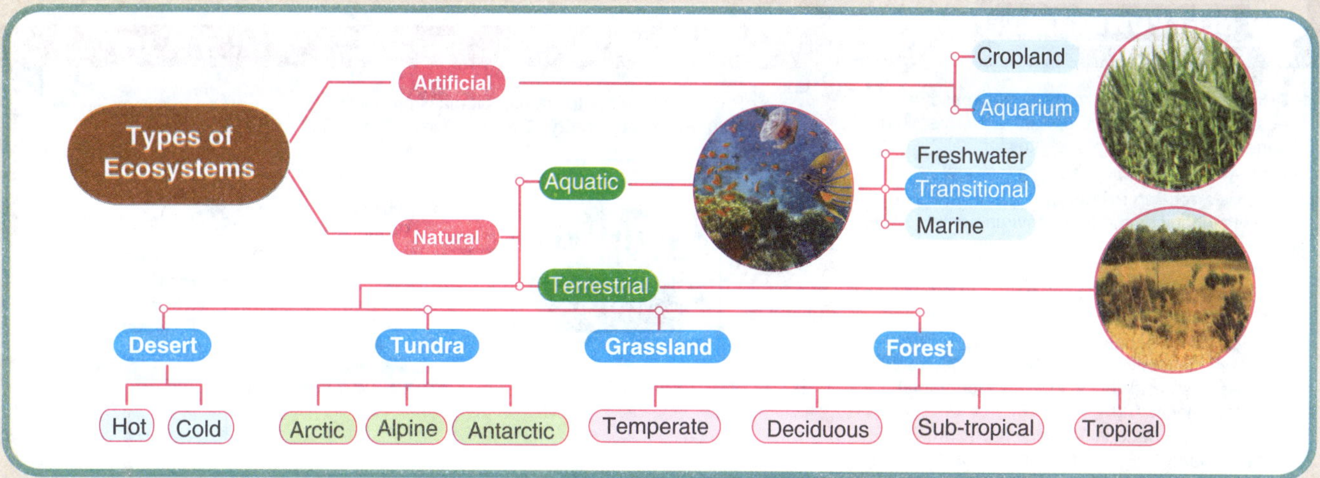

Ecosystem: Structure and Function

Structure of Ecosystem

- **Species composition** Determined by identification and enumeration of plant and animal species of an ecosystem.
- **Stratification:** Vertical distribution of different species occupying different levels; maximum strata is found in tropical forest.

Stratification in Tropical Forest

Function of Ecosystem

- Energy flow
- Decomposition
- Productivity
- Nutrient cycling

Pond as an Ecosystem

- **Abiotic factors** - Water, air, soil, temperature, etc.
- **Biotic factors**

Producers

Phytoplanktons

Algae

Floating, sub-merged and marginal plants

Consumers

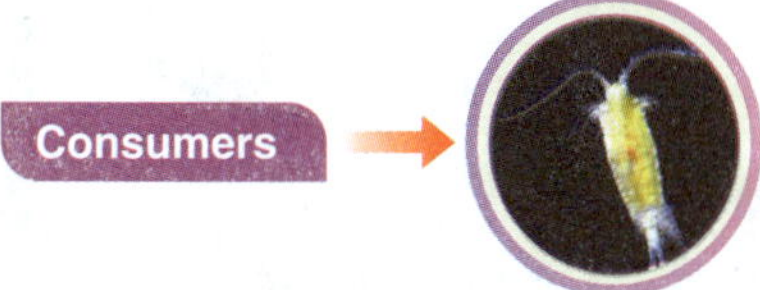

Zooplanktons

Free swimming form

Bottom dwelling forms

Decomposers

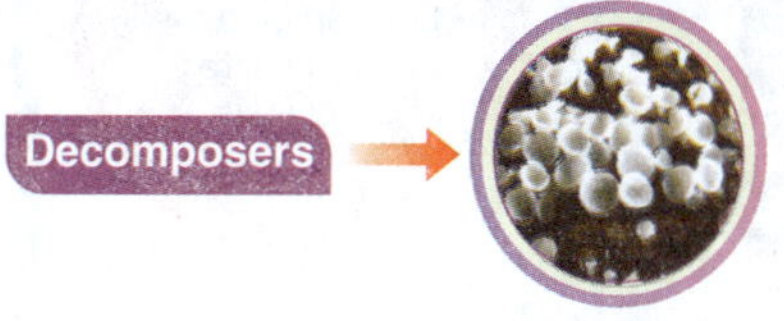

Fungi

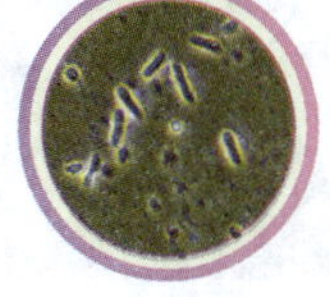

Bacteria

Flagellates

NEET POWER TIPS

- **Ecology** Study of relationship between organism and its environment.
- Father of Ecology-**Alexander von Humboldt**
- Father of Indian Ecology-**Ramdeo Mishra**
- **Branches of Ecology**
  - **Autecology** (Ecology of individuals)
  - **Synecology** (Concerned with communities)
  - **Genecology** (Concerned with genetic variations)
  - **Paleoecology** (Ecology of the past)
- **Ecosystem** Functional unit of nature where living organisms interact among themselves and also with their surrounding environment.
- Term 'Ecosystem' coined by **AG Tansley**
- Concept of ecosystem-Pioneered by **E.Odum**

NEET POWER TIPS

1. **Primary productivity** Amount of biomass or organic matter produced per unit area over time period by plants during of photosynthesis.
2. **Unit** - gm^{-2} (weight) or kcal m^{-2} (energy)
3. **Factors affecting Primary production**: Plant species inhabiting the area, environmental factors, availability of nutrients and photosynthetic capacity of plants.
4. Annual NPP of whole Biosphere = 170 billion tons (dry weight) of organic matter.
5. Annual NPP of ocean = 55 billion tons.
6. Net production efficiency = (NPP/ GPP) × 100.
7. Photosynthetic efficiency = GPP/Incident total solar radiation × 100.
8. **Detritus:** Raw material for decomposition, composed of dead plant and animal remains.
9. **Humus:** Dark coloured amorphous substance; highly resistant to microbial action; colloidal in nature.

Productivity and Decomposition

Productivity

- Productivity refers to Rate of biomass production.
- **Unit For productivity**- $gm^{-2}\ yr^{-1}$(weight) or kcal $m^{-1}\ yr^{-1}$ (energy).

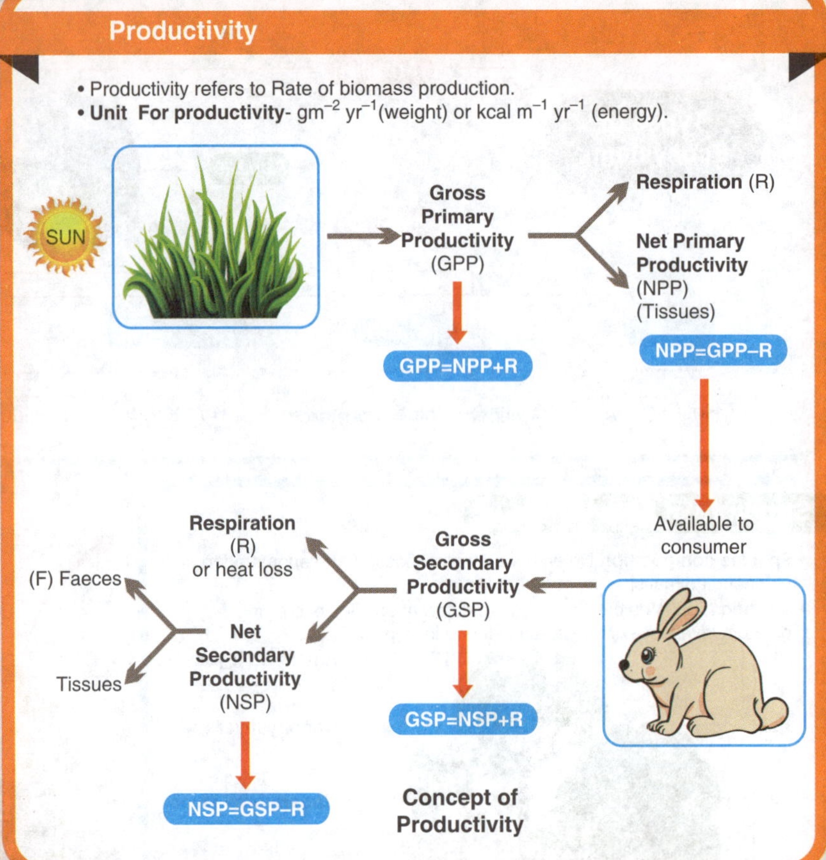

Concept of Productivity

Decomposition

- Decomposition is breakdown of complex organic matter into inorganic substances like CO_2, H_2O and nutrients.

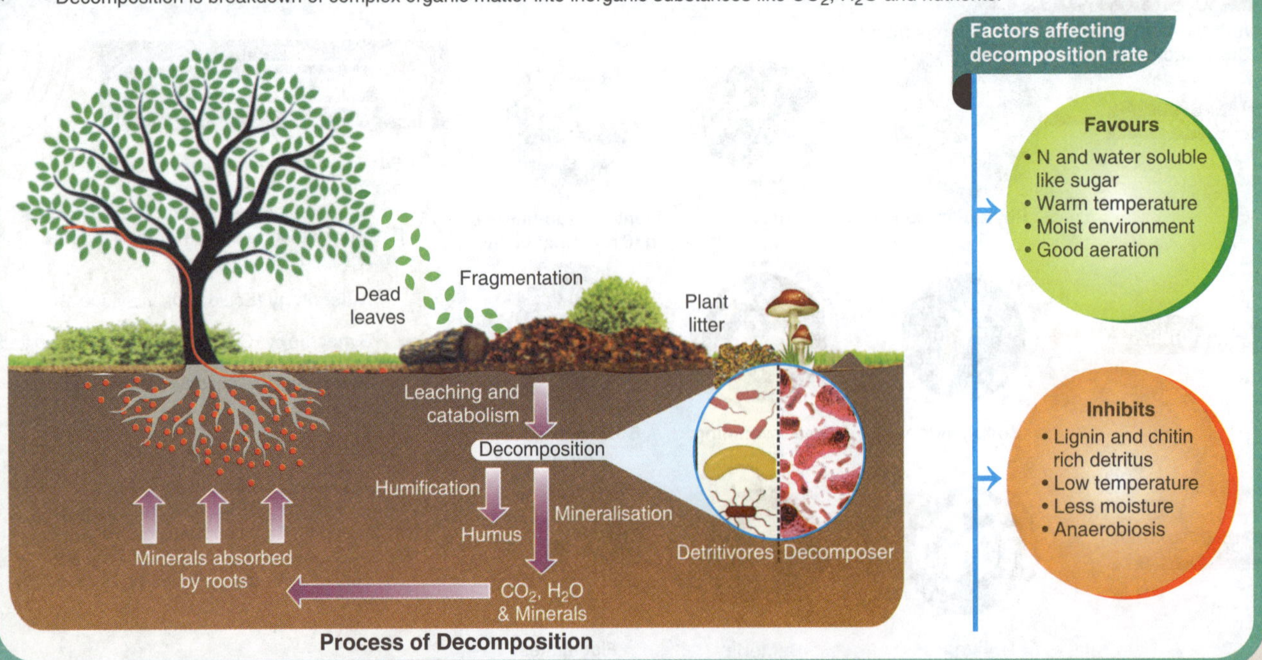

Process of Decomposition

Factors affecting decomposition rate

Favours
- N and water soluble like sugar
- Warm temperature
- Moist environment
- Good aeration

Inhibits
- Lignin and chitin rich detritus
- Low temperature
- Less moisture
- Anaerobiosis

NEET POWER TIPS

- Only 2-10% of **PAR** (Photosynthetically Active Radiation) is captured by plants and used to sustain the entire world.
- Unidirectional flow of energy: Sun → Producers → Consumers
- In 1942 **Lindemann** stated that only 10% energy is transferred to successive stages, rest 90% is released is the form of heat.
- 10% law of energy follows first and second law of thermodynamics.
- Pyramid of biomass shows a sharp decrease in biomass at higher trophic levels.
- Producers convert only 1% of the energy in the sunlight available to them into NPP.

Food Chain

- Sequence of transfer of nutrients and energy in the form of food from organism to organism.
- **Standing Crop:** Certain mass of living material at a particular time in each trophic level; measured in terms of biomass or number.

Types of Food Chains

Grazing Food Chain (GFC)
- Source of energy-Sun
- Lesser energy flow
- Major conduit of energy flow in aquatic ecosystem.

Grass → Goat → Man → Lion

Detritus Food Chain (DFC)
- Source of energy-Detritus
- More energy flow
- Major conduit of energy flow in terrestrial ecosystem.

Detritus → Earthworm → Sparrow → Falcon

- **Food Web:** Natural interconnection of food chains.
- **Trophic Level:** Specific place of an organism in a food chain characterised by their source of nutrition.

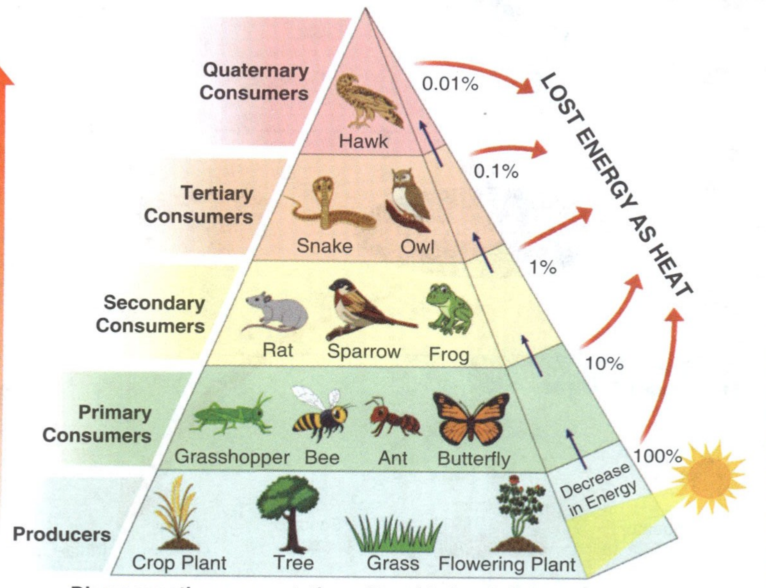

Diagrammatic representation of trophic levels in an ecosystem along with energy transfer

Ecological Pyramids

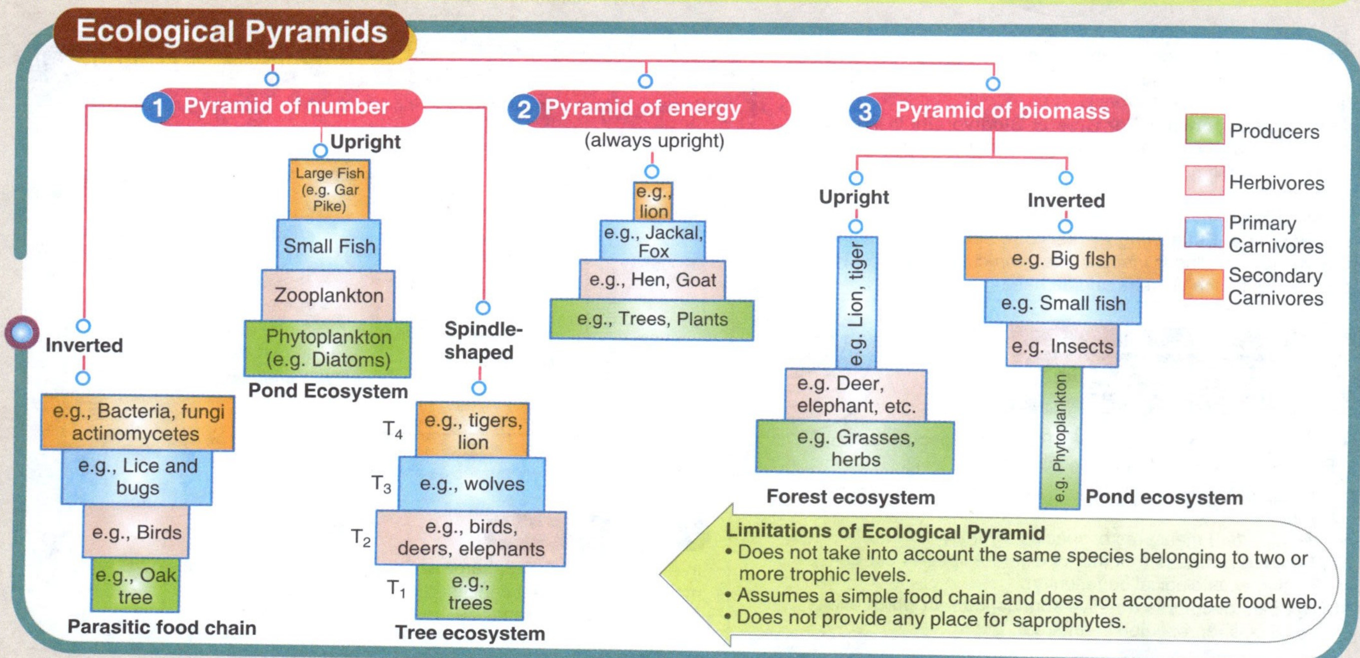

Limitations of Ecological Pyramid
- Does not take into account the same species belonging to two or more trophic levels.
- Assumes a simple food chain and does not accomodate food web.
- Does not provide any place for saprophytes.

Chapter 32 Biodiversity and Conservation

Biodiversity

Levels of Biodiversity

3 levels

Ecosystem diversity — Ecological diversity; e.g., India.

Species diversity — Species diversity; e.g., amphibian species (Western ghats >Eastern ghats).

Genetic diversity — Genetic diversity; e.g. *Rauwolfia vomitoria*, (reserpine concentration and potency) and variations in rice and mango.

Biodiversity Over Spatial Scale

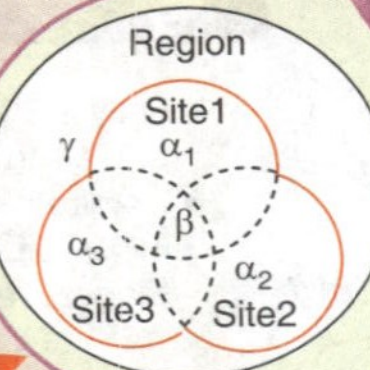

- α-**diversity**-Diversity within individual sites at a local scale.
- β-**diversity**-Diversity between habitats along environmental gradients.
- γ-**diversity**-Overall diversity in a region.

Global Biodiversity

- As per **IUCN** (2004) data-Over 1.5 million plant and animal species described so far.
- More complete species inventories are found in temperate countries than tropical countries.
- As per **Robert May**-About 7 million (only 22% of total species are recorded yet)
- Data from current available inventories
  - 70% of recorded species-Animals (70% of animals-Insects)
  - 22% of recorded species-Plants (including fungi)
  - Number of species of fungi > species of fishes + amphibians + reptiles + mammals

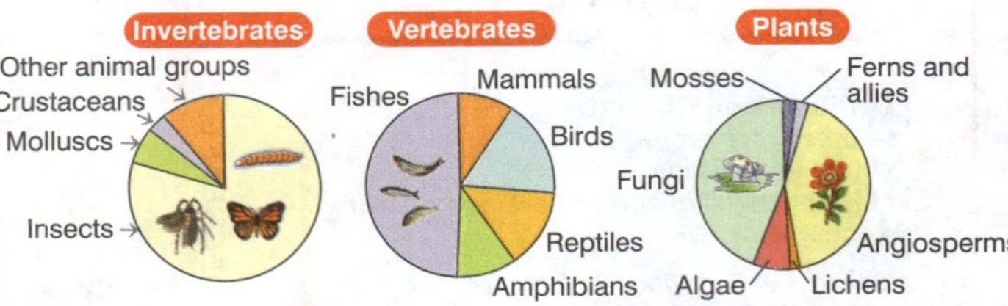

Patterns of Biodiversity

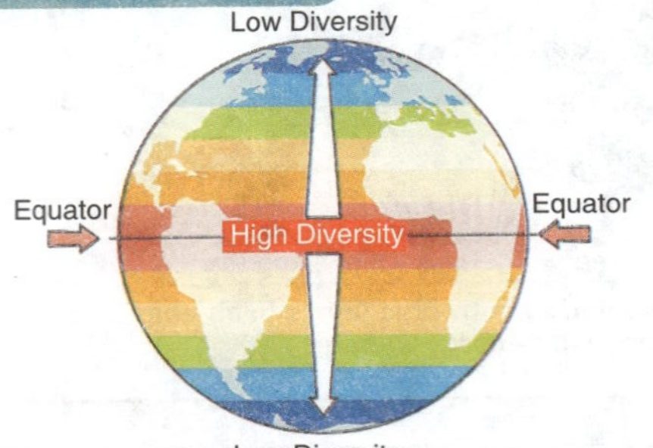

- Species diversity-Poles < Temperate < Tropic region.
- Tropical **Amazonian rainforest** (S. America)-'**Lungs of the planet**' with greatest biodiversity.

→ **Factors Responsible For Greater Biodiversity in Tropics**
- Less disturbance in tropics during the course of evolution.
- Less seasonality, relatively more constant and predictable environment.
- Availability of more solar energy (more productivity)

→ **Concerns in Estimating Prokaryotic Species**
- Conventional methods inapplicable; Non-cultural strains; Highly diverse species in bacteria and archaea

Biodiversity in India

- India-One of the 12 (as per WCHC, 2002) megadiversity countries of the world (2.4% of world's land area supporting 8.1% global biodiversity)
- Number of plants species-45,000 (1,00,000 yet to discovered and described as per May's estimate).
- Number of animals species-90,000 (3,00,000 as per May's estimate).

Species-Area Relationships (Alexander von Humboldt)

- Species richness increases with increasing explored area (upto a limit).

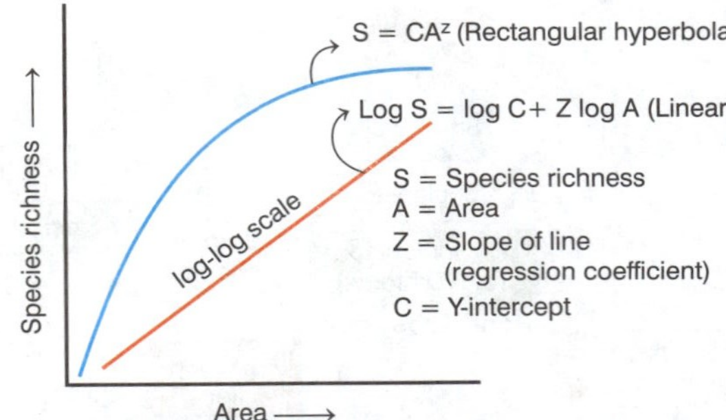

Showing species area relationship

Value of Z for species

- In a region → 0.1–0.2; Large areas → 0.6– 1.2; Frugivorous birds and mammals in different continent regions → around 1.15
- Graph becomes **steeper** as the explored area increases.

NEET POWER TIPS

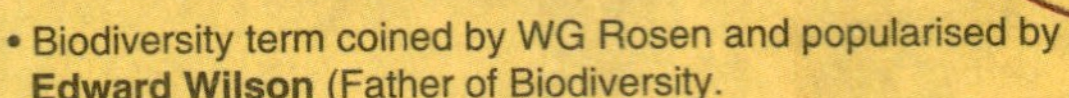

- Biodiversity term coined by WG Rosen and popularised by **Edward Wilson** (Father of Biodiversity.
- Concept of biodiversity hotspots was introduced by Norman Myers.
- Two important measures of species diversity
  - (a) **Species richness** (number of different species per unit area in an ecological community).
  - (b) **Species evenness** (relative abundance with which each species is represented in an area).

Importance of Species Diversity to the Ecosystem

- Communities with more species-more stable.
- **Attributes of Stable Community**
  - Does not show too much variation in productivity from years to years
  - Must be resilient/resistant to seasonal disturbances
  - Must be resilient to invasion by alien species.
- **David Tilman's Observation** -Plots with more species showed less year to year variation in total biomass; plots with increased diversity showed higher productivity.
- **Rivet's Popper Hypothesis** (Paul Ehrlich): Explained importance of species for proper functioning of ecosystem

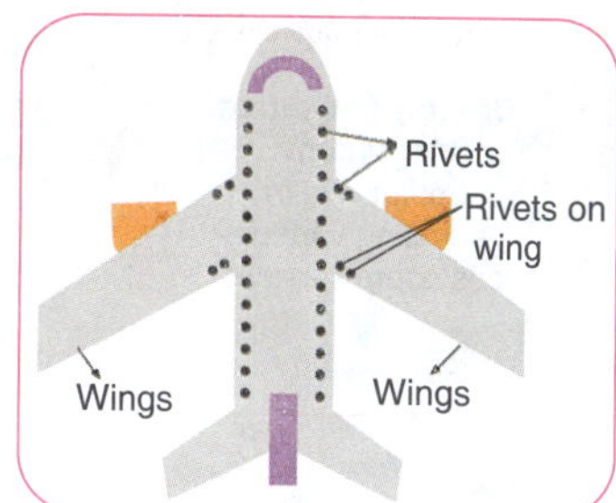

Airplane→Ecosystem

Popping a rivet -A species becomes **extinct** (eventually weakens the aeroplane)

Popping a rivet on wing- Key species becomes extinct (threatens the ecosystem)

Loss of Biodiversity

- Natural wealth getting lost rapidly due to human activities
- As per IUCN Red List (2004)-Extinction of 784 species in last 500 years, e.g.

Dodo (Mauritius)

Quagga (Africa)

Thylacine (Australia)

Stellar's sea cow (Russia)

- **Sixth extinction** in progress- **Anthropocene** mass extinction (100-1000 times faster), i.e., driven by human activity.
- **Effects of Biodiversity Losses**
  - (a) Decline in plant production
  - (b) Lowered resistance to environmental perturbations
  - (c) Increased variability in certain ecosystem processes

Causes of Biodiversity Losses

'Evil Quartet'

Over-exploitation
- E.g. passenger pigeon, Steller's sea Cow

Habitat loss and Fragmentation
- Most important cause
- E.g. degradation of tropical forests like Amazon for l and and farming.
- Fragmentation leads to decrease in population of some species.

Co-extinctions
E.g. Extinction of parasites upon extinction of host-passenger pigeon, plant-pollinator mutualism

Alien species Invasions
- E.g. Nile perch in lake Victoria (East Africa)- Extinction of 200 species of cichlid fish in lake
- Other examples are-Carrot grass (*Parthenium*), *Lantana* and *Eichhornia*.

IUCN Red List Categories

- **IUCN:** International Union for Conservation of Nature and Natural Resources
- Divides species into 9 categories

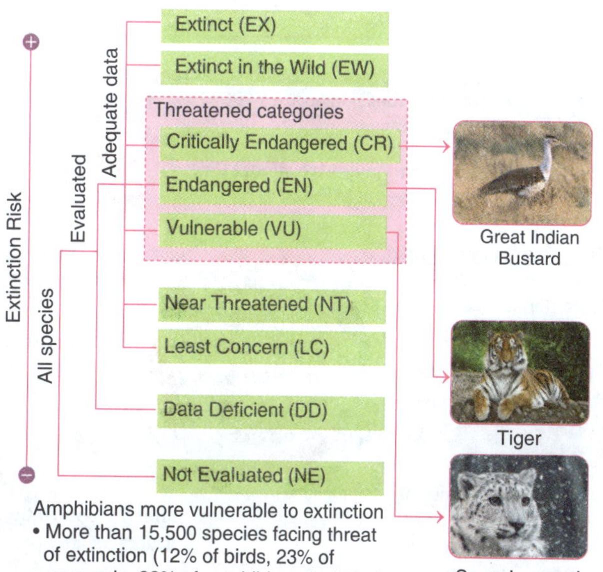

Amphibians more vulnerable to extinction
- More than 15,500 species facing threat of extinction (12% of birds, 23% of mammals, 32% of amphibians and 31% of gymnosperms).

Arguments for Biodiversity Conservation

Narrowly Utilitarian Argument (deriving a number of economic benefits)

Broadly Utilitarian Argument (major role in providing various ecosystem services)

- Maintaining food chains
- Maintaining the genetic diversity
- Maintaining ecosystem balance

Overall sustainability and growth

Ethical Argument (every species having an intrinsic value)

NEET POWER TIPS

- **Biodiversity Hotspots:** Areas extremely rich in species with high degree of endemism; 36 in world; 4 in India (Western ghats, Himalayas, Indo-Burma, Sundaland)
- **Endemism:** Presence of native species in a particular geographical area; e.g., Lion-tailed Macaque (Nilgiri hills)
- **Project tiger** launched in 1973.
- **Largest Tiger Reserve**-Nagarjun sagar-Srisailam Tiger Reserve

Approaches to Biodiversity Conservation

Ex situ Conservation
(species protected outside their natural habitat)

Botanical Gardens
Collection of living plants for purpose of scientific research, conservation, etc.

Zoo
Animals kept in enclosure for public exhibition and conservation purposes.

Seed Banks
- Store seeds to preserve genetic diversity
- A type of gene bank

Tissue Culture
In-vitro preservation and proliferation of isolated cells, tissues or organs in a comfortable condition

Cryopreservation
Preserving the biological samples in an extremely cold or sub-zero condition such as-196°C.

In situ Conservation
(species protected in their natural habitat)

Biosphere Reserves (18)
- Large protected area meant for conservation of plants and animals.
- Largest: Gulf of Kutch (Gujarat)
- **3 zones** : **Core** (No human activity), **Buffer** (Limited activity) and **Transition** (Allowed activity)

Wildlife Sanctuary (567)
- Designated by government to protect wildlife, flora and fauna
- Less restricted area
- Possess no specific boundary
- Largest-Rann of Kutch wildlife sanctuary, (Gujarat)

National Parks (106)
- Designated by national government for protection of natural environment
- Highly restricted area
- Possess definite boundary
- Largest-Hemis National Park (Ladakh)

Sacred Groves
- Forest patch protected by tribal communities, due to religious sanctity
- Possess large number of rare, endangered and endemic species
- E.g. Khasi and Jaintia Hills (Meghalaya), Western ghats, (Karnataka and Maharashtra), Aravalli Hills (Rajasthan), Sarguja, Chanda and Bastar (M.P.)

Important National Parks in India

- **Bandhavgarh National Park** — M.P-Tiger
- **Kanha National Park** — M.P-Tiger, Barasingha
- **Sunderban National Park** — West Bengal-Tiger
- **Jim Corbett National Park** — Uttarakhand-Tiger
- **Kaziranga National Park** — Assam-One-horned rhinoceros
- **Periyar National Park** — Kerala-Elephant, Tiger
- **Keoladeo National Park** — Rajasthan-Great Indian Bustard, Black buck

Conventions of Biodiversity

The Earth Summit
- Held in **Rio de Janeiro** (1992)
- Called upon nations to take appropriate measures for:
  - -Conservation of biodiversity
  - -Sustainable use of benefits from biodiversity

The World Summit on Sustainable Development
- Held in 2002, **Johannesburg,** South Africa
- Signed by 190 countries to achieve reduction in current rate of biodiversity loss at all levels by 2010.